# The Georgia F
# and Weapon Law
# Compendium

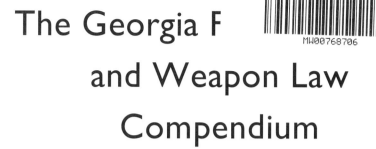

-

**GUNS**
**KNIVES**
**OTHER WEAPONS**

-

**USE**
**SAFETY**
**OWNERSHIP**
**LAW**

-

**FULL TEXT OF ALL OF THE GUN, KNIFE, AND WEAPONS LAWS FOUND IN THE OFFICIAL CODE OF GEORGIA**

-

*First Edition - Fall 2010*

Authored by: Robert Todd Bergin, Esq.
www.GeorgiaGunLaws.com

Copyright 2010 by Robert Todd Bergin, Esq.

**Pointed In!™ Press**
**Las Vegas, NV**
**www.PointedIn.com**

Proudly written, published, and printed in the United States of America
by Robert Todd Bergin, Esq.
www.GeorgiaGunLaws.com
Published by Pointed In!™ Press
www.PointedIn.com
ISBN 978-0-9827570-3-1 $19.95

First Publication: Fall 2010
Copyright 2010

# TABLE OF CONTENTS

# ABOUT THE AUTHOR

Todd Bergin is a California attorney located in Orange County, California. He earned his law degree from Whittier Law School, in Costa Mesa, California. Prior to law school, he first attended Marshall University in Huntington, West Virginia, but ultimately finished his undergraduate work at the University of Kentucky, in Lexington, Kentucky.

Prior to attending college, Mr. Bergin went to a small private high school in West Virginia. While he primarily grew up in Huntington, West Virginia, he had also lived in Chicago, Illinois; Atlanta, Georgia; Montgomery, Alabama; Lexington, Kentucky; and Charleston, South Carolina. He has also spent a great deal of time in the Washington, D.C., area, including Scientists' Cliffs in Calvert County, Maryland.

For nearly the past twelve years, Mr. Bergin has called Orange County, California, home. However, he and his wife consider moving from California almost daily, as the firearm laws and taxes are so oppressive so as to make any sane person seriously question the reasons for remaining in California.

In West Virginia, Mr. Bergin was raised by a conservative yet anti-gun mother. He was the one kid on the street who was not allowed to have toy guns as a child, forcing him to improvise with wooden sticks shaped like guns that fell from trees. While remaining indifferent to firearm-related issues most of his life, he began to get interested in firearms sometime around 2003 or 2004.

Prior to buying his first handgun, a GLOCK 23, Mr. Bergin sought out training to become proficient with firearms and has since become very proficient with them. However, he prefers Kimber 1911 handguns over any other handgun that he has yet to try, but is most fond of his Benelli M4 shotgun.

Mr. Bergin's training and interest did not stop there. He has since become a very active participant in the gun culture, having been extensively trained in the use of handguns, shotguns, and rifles, and continues to train to this day on a very regular basis. His handgun training has focused primarily on the use of the handgun from concealment, and he holds concealed permits in many states, and yes, including California. For years he would spend a great deal of free time studying the California Code, and primarily, the Penal Code, regarding firearms laws in the State of California. This went on for several years, with no consideration given to ultimately writing a book about California firearms laws.

As Mr. Bergin's interest in the firearm laws grew, he realized that to be completely content with his knowledge of the gun law, he had to learn everything he could about the gun law and organize it in a fashion that made sense. So he ultimately set out to outline the California gun law. This finally led to the creation of the first book, *The California Firearm, Knife, and Weapon Law Compendium*.

Of course, Mr. Bergin's writing did not end there. Due to the amount of time he spends in Nevada, he began outlining Nevada firearm laws, as well as the laws of other weapons, such as knives. This led to his second book, *The Nevada Firearm, Knife, and Weapon Law Compendium*, which was in print in Summer, 2010.

While researching the law, and while blogging on his gun law websites about current gun issues, Mr. Bergin became very interested in Colorado firearm law after reading about the dispute in Colorado regarding firearms on University of Colorado and Colorado State University college campuses, among other Colorado gun issues. Naturally, his interest in the college campus issue led him to begin reading Colorado gun law statutes on the General Assembly's website, which ultimately led to his outlining and study of Colorado gun law, and of course, the publication of a book on Colorado gun laws.

Now Mr. Bergin presents his fourth book, that on Georgia gun law, as well as Georgia knife laws, and the laws regarding other weapons. Georgia was very interesting because of Senate Bill 308, which became law in 2010, made sweeping changes to the gun law, and Mr. Bergin knew there would be questions. So, he sought out to answer them in this book you are holding.

Mr. Bergin is confident that more books will follow, as he enjoys reading about gun and knife laws across this nation, about how they can differ dramatically simply by crossing over a state line. He also believes that there should always be a thorough source of current information available at all times for those who desire it.

Mr. Bergin is not just an attorney writing about gun laws. Instead, he is a "gun guy," just like many of you, and he shows his supports by training extensively and by supporting pro-Second Amendment organizations. To be sure, Mr. Bergin is a life member at a nationally recognized firearm training institute in southern Nevada, and since joining, has averaged roughly one class per month. He is also a member of many organizations dedicated to protecting the Second Amendment, including a Life Member of the National Rifle Association, Life Member of the Gun Owners of America, Life Member of the California Pistol and Rifle Association, Life

Member of the Jews for the Preservation of Firearms Ownership, Life Member of the Second Amendment Foundation, a Life Member of the Rocky Mountain Gun Owners, Life Member of the Georgia Sports Shooting Association, a Life Member of GeorgiaCarry.org, and a Member of both the Gun Owners of California and Gun Owners of Nevada. He also is a donor to the Calguns Foundation, GeorgiaPacking.org, and the National Association for Gun Rights.

Mr. Bergin is available to discuss the contents of his books and is open to comments from the readers about anything excluded from the book, as well as different interpretations of the laws as represented in the books. He realizes that the law is ever-changing and also open to multiple interpretations, and is interested in hearing from others regarding their interpretations of the law.

Mr. Bergin's books may be purchased at www.PointedIn.com or www.GeorgiaGunLaws.com. Additionally, all of the books may be purchased on Amazon in the Kindle format.

Mr. Bergin invites you to visit his website at www.GeorgiaGunLaws.com and www.PointedIn.com for updates, ordering information, and to visit the regularly updated blogs. You may also contact Mr. Bergin at gunlawsnow@gmail.com. Please realize, however, that Mr. Bergin is unavailable to answer individual questions or provide legal advice of any kind about Georgia law, or the laws of any other state.

## ACKNOWLEDGMENTS

This book is the result of many factors, and a variety of people deserve my sincerest appreciation in completing this project.

I want to first thank my wife for believing in me. I greatly appreciate Jessica's patience during the long journey that led to my books being written. Thank you for standing by me all these years.

Second, thank you to my mother, Teri, who has always been instrumental to all of my successes in life.

Also, a thank you to other supporting family, including my children, Madison and Parker, as well as my brother and sister, Tyler and Taite.

I also appreciate the help I received in considering nuances in the gun law of the State of Georgia from a good friend of mine, Bill Carns. Bill is an accomplished firearms instructor and radio host of the show "2A Radio" on Republic Broadcasting, and he always made himself available to discuss and consider with me various gun laws during the development of his books.

Last but certainly not least, my sincerest appreciation to Linda Giles. Linda has been a close, personal friend of our family for more than thirty years. Without her assistance, I may have never made it past sentence diagrams in the seventh grade. She was the first person to review this book (and the other books) with a critical eye, and I am quite confident that never in her wildest dreams did she ever, ever think she would read so much about Georgia firearms law, or any firearms law in general for that matter, and she has now reviewed all four of Mr. Bergin's books. Thank you for always being there for me and my family, and for being a good friend.

# PURPOSE OF THIS BOOK

This book was written for anyone who will be handling, using, and/or owning some type of firearm, such as a rifle, shotgun, or handgun, or some type of knife or other weapon. Basically, this book is for everyone, even for those who do not plan to handle any of the above, as none of us has the privilege of looking into the future and knowing whether or not we would ever be in a situation where there exists a firearm or other type of deadly weapon. As such, it is all of our responsibility to be knowledgeable of the law, as well as have an understanding of basic safety issues, should we find ourselves in such a situation.

While the overall theme of this book is the lawful use and ownership of firearms, this book will also briefly touch upon the lawful ownership of other dangerous or deadly weapons, such as knives. Where the text of this book does not address certain dangerous or deadly weapons or explosives, portions of the law regarding these items as provided by the Georgia General Assembly can be found in the appendix of this book. However, almost everything that is relevant to most readers is included in the text of this book.

There are many reasons to read a book that discusses the law as it relates to firearms, knives, and other items and weapons that are considered dangerous and/or deadly weapons, and explosives. However, there is no need to speculate and discuss all the reasons to read this book, but in all probability, the reason to read a book such as this is because there is a desire to conduct our behavior in respect of the laws. Basically, most of us want to keep our butts out of trouble. In order to do this, it is important to know and understand the laws that relate to our activities.

Many readers of this book may be new to the self-defense and/or "gun culture,"[1] and may currently be considering firearm ownership, knife ownership, or both. People who are new to firearms and knives usually seek out information regarding the law of such items, and many wish to possess as much information as they can about the law as it pertains to the weapons they may be considering. Some readers may already be part of the culture and may already own many of the firearms and/or weapons discussed in this book and attach importance to being knowledgeable of the current law. Either way, you have selected the appropriate book in obtaining current information on the law of firearms and weapons as it

---

[1] The first time I heard the term "gun culture" was in a book by John Ross entitled *Unintended Consequences*. This may be one of the finest books I have ever read, and I highly recommend it to anyone who thinks he may be part of the "gun culture."

exists in Georgia.

However, if you currently find yourself in legal trouble regarding improper ownership, use, storage, transport, or some other issue, with any of the weapons this book addresses, please accept my best wishes and appreciation in choosing this text to assist you. But please, as soon as possible, seek and obtain competent legal counsel. <u>Do not depend on this book to assist you in your legal troubles</u>. Sure, this book may assist in guiding you regarding some basic considerations, but a talented attorney, well-versed in firearms, knife, or weapon law and with a strong criminal defense background will better assist you in your troubles. As explained at the beginning of the book, **THIS BOOK IS NOT LEGAL ADVICE**. Period.

Either way, you have chosen this book because you are interested in a decent understanding of the firearm laws, knife laws, and "other" weapon laws in the State of Georgia. You desire some sort of explanation of the laws in terms that are clear, concise, and in plain English. You wish to avoid trouble with the law yet enjoy to the fullest what rights you have left in regards to both firearms and knives. Further, you wish to have a single text that provides you with all of the above.

It is my desire that this book assists you with your goal of obtaining a better understanding of the law as it pertains to firearms, knives, and other weapons.

While this book is quite comprehensive, keep in mind that neither this book, and likely no other book, contains each and every federal, state, and local law and ordinances as they relate to knives and firearms. There are so many laws at all levels that creating one single book to cover it all and remain current would be an exercise in futility. Furthermore, the law changes often, and it is a difficult task for the author of a publication such as this to keep the book 100% current.

However, every effort has been made to keep this book current and accurate. Also, **this book will always be a "work in progress."** Laws change often, and in particular, firearm laws change often. Updated versions of this book will make every effort to keep up with the most recent changes. Furthermore, this book includes interpretations of the law. Every effort was made to discover each and every nuance, each and every source of information to accurately interpret each law addressed in this book. A worry when writing a book such as this is that something was missed. Despite checking each and every statute for cases that may impact the interpretation, and double-checking, and even triple-checking *everything*, is it possible something may not have been discovered, leading to a mistake being made? Certainly. Readers are encouraged to forward any discoveries they may have that impact the laws as presented in this book to the author for consideration.

In any event, this book covers most of the laws that the average person needs to know in order to lawfully handle, use, or own a knife or firearm, such as what requirements exist for one who desires to purchasing a firearm or a knife, or to carry or use the same. Additionally, a large portion of this book covers the concealed carry laws of Georgia with some basic, practical considerations for all those who are considering whether or not to carry a concealed weapon.

Aside from brief mention in various parts of this book, this text does not extensively cover laws as they pertain to law enforcement or military individuals, or hunters and the laws regulating hunting. This book was primarily written for, and assumes that the reader is, an average firearm, knife, and/or weapon owner who has not lost his ability to own and/or handle firearms under the law, and for those who are subject to exceptions in the law by virtue of serving our country, the state, any particular locality, or by operation of law.

However, there is an abundance of material in this book that is included that goes much further into the law than traditional firearm books. Instead of leaving out information that some may find valuable, this book was designed to be overly inclusive so that the readers may choose for themselves what is important and what may be ignored.

Included in the text of this book is an abundance of footnotes. This was a dilemma for the author, as using footnotes, especially as extensively as found in this book, can interfere with the flow of the text. However, a driving factor that led to this book being written was that most books of this nature lack any emphasis on the source for the assertions that are made, or an endnote is given and the endnote has five or six code sections and the reader has to try to figure it all out. Therefore, the author elected to leave the footnotes intact, no matter how trivial or repetitive. The reader will find a footnote attached to almost each and every assertion.

Please understand, that as tempting as it was to provide scathing commentary about the direction that this country's gun laws have moved over the last 100 years, this book is not intended to put forth a political agenda. There are simply too many bad laws, potential laws that are bad, and too many arguments to address, and quite often, these events move much too quickly for commentary in a book. Instead, there are numerous online chat forums and blogs dealing with such issues. At some point, the author of this book may have something along those lines at his website, www.GeorgiaGunLaws.com, but for now, the author is not involved in any political criticisms or commentary, aside from perhaps a slight indulgence here or there.

Instead, this book mainly discusses the laws regarding firearms, knives, and other weapons in a practical, informational sense. If it appears knife issues were slighted, they weren't. There simply are not many knife laws, and the knife laws rarely change. Knives, at least in Georgia, as is the case pretty much nationwide, are just not heavily regulated.

Additionally, and in all probability, people are more interested in firearm law than they are in laws regarding knives and other weapons. And while that consideration may be true, it seems logical to include a discussion regarding knives and other weapons in any book that addresses firearms, as most of the people that are into firearms tend to also be interested in knives and other weapons, at least to some degree. Certainly, if there are issues regarding weapons other than firearms, those readers will enjoy the convenience of owning a book that covers the current laws and common issues of all weapons.

In any event, the author hopes that the reader finds in this book a more comprehensive book regarding firearm, knife, and weapon law than has ever existed. It is the author's desire that this book serves to answer all of the reader's questions and concerns regarding the weapons laws addressed in this book.

# WARNING - READ THIS NOW!

This book regards and includes only Georgia law and some, but not all, federal laws as they regard issues addressed in this book, as well as commentary for each. This book does not make a point to include extensive discussions of federal law or local laws and ordinances. While there may be some reference to federal law and local ordinances, please be aware that these are selected references, and the author of this book by no means intended the book to be all-inclusive regarding federal and municipal law.

This book does not concern the laws of states other than Georgia. While there may be a reference to laws of another state, such reference would be only to compare or contrast a law in Georgia. Otherwise, this book strictly concerns Georgia law and mainly focuses on what may be found in the Official Code of Georgia, various Georgia administrative laws, and any Georgia case law that helps us understand and interpret the law. If you need information regarding the laws of another state or need more information on Federal Law, this book is not a resource to satisfy those needs. Yes, some Federal Law is included in this book; however, there is plenty more that this book does not discuss.

This book is not designed to provide specific legal advice. Instead, it is designed to provide the reader with a general overview of the law regarding firearms, knives, and other weapons. If you need legal advice, please do not rely on this book to provide the legal advice for your situation. Seek out adequate legal counsel to address your needs, as they likely go beyond the text and commentary as provided in this book.

As a prudent gun enthusiast, you are responsible to observe and obey all applicable federal, state, and local laws and regulations pertaining to the handling, use, and ownership of firearms, knives, and all other weapons.

A great deal of time and consideration has gone into this text to provide the reader with both the relevant laws pertaining to firearms, knife, and other weapons handling, use, and ownership under federal, state, and local laws, along with commentary designed to translate the laws from legalese to regular, everyday terms that most readers will find they can understand. But keep in mind, such efforts were strictly to provide this book as an educational text, and not as legal advice.

Despite the care and attention dedicated to this text, please realize that neither the author, the publisher, nor any distributor or retailer, provides any guarantees or warranties of any kind, either expressed or implied. The commentary of the relevant law is simply that - commentary. Such commentary should not be considered to be legal advice or a restatement of the law.

Please also understand that all the federal laws and state laws relevant to the use, handling, and the ownership of firearms, knives, and other weapons, are voluminous, and it would be a daunting task to provide each and every law, word for word, along with commentary. Therefore, it is important for you, the reader, to understand that this text is simply a summary of such laws, that no representations are made by either the author, publisher, any distributor or retailer, that this book includes all laws and regulations. The author, publisher, distributors and retailers expressly disclaim any and all potential liability that could ever exist from the reader's reliance upon information as provided in this text.

Furthermore, new bills are introduced every year to further restrict firearm use, ownership, and transfer. Many politicians and government figures have been quite frank regarding their interest to eliminate our rights under the Second Amendment. It is your responsibility as a citizen to pay attention to pending legislation and to observe and obey it if signed into law. It is also your responsibility, to you, your children, and future gun enthusiasts not yet born, to consider the right to bear arms when casting a ballot at the voting booth.

Additionally, laws addressed in this book, and in particular, the firearm laws, are subject to change at any moment, and by the time you read this book, changes have likely occurred. This book is also a "work in progress," and while every effort was made in researching each and every statute and applicable case to provide an interpretation of the law, the potential that something was overlooked always exists. Readers who question a particular interpretation of the law are encouraged to consult an attorney to answer their questions, compare the interpretation to other books on the subject, and to contact the author of this book to discuss.

Also included in this book is a fairly thorough discussion on basic firearm safety consideration and firearm competency. However, it is important to understand that despite the detailed discussion regarding firearms safety and the basic use of a firearm, this text is not a training manual, nor is this book an adequate substitute for such. This book is likely not complete as firearm safety is concerned. Basic firearm safety considerations are included in this text because the unfortunate reality is that for many individuals, safety is often overlooked. Will this book get through to such individuals? Perhaps not. But such considerations are here for them should they care to read it.

The author strongly suggests anyone who intends to purchase, own, use, or handle a firearm to seek out training from a professional in his or her local area prior to doing so. There is no reason at all that a firearm should ever be in the hands of someone who does not know even the most basic firearm safety considerations, such as to always treat the firearm as if it were loaded, knowing to keep the finger off the trigger, pointing the firearm in a safe direction, even if unloaded, and knowing how to safely check to see if a firearm is loaded and, if necessary, safely unload a firearm.

Finally, the author and publisher, or any reseller, retailer, or distributor assume no liability for any damages or negligence that may occur through the reader's use of firearms, knives, or other weapons, or any information included in this text. Regarding firearms, they should generally be handled only at a designated firing range under carefully controlled conditions. Readers of this text fully accept the responsibility for any and all accidents, damages and injuries that might occur from the handling and use of firearms or knives.

Thank you for your interest in this book. A great deal of time has gone into researching the material, sorting through and analyzing the law, and preparing it in a format that the reader can enjoy and understand. Hopefully it will answer most, if not all, of your questions.

# CHAPTER ONE

## Federal and State Government of the United States

The United States of America is a federal republic that consists of a federal district (Washington, D.C.), and fifty states. Our nation was established, or rather, was "constituted," by a document called the United States Constitution, which is the supreme law of the land. Each of the fifty states has its own individual constitution as well.

At the federal level, there are three branches of government: the Legislative branch, the Executive branch, and the Judicial branch. The State of Georgia also has the same three branches of government that operate at the state level; however, the legislature in the State of Georgia is called the Georgia General Assembly.

The Legislative branch consists of Congress at the federal level, and the Georgia General Assembly at the state level, as well as all agencies which were created and serve Congress and the general assembly. At the federal level, the Executive branch consists of the President of the United States, and, at the state level, the Governor. Finally, the Judicial branch consists of the Supreme Court and all federal courts at the federal level, and the State Supreme Court and the lower courts at the state level.

The Legislative branch passes laws which, at the federal level, are presented to the President, and at the state level, the state legislature presents laws to the Governor. Those laws are either signed by the President and the Governor, or they are vetoed (rejected), and either do not become laws or are enacted by meeting the voting requirements to override the veto. Various agencies created by Congress or the state legislature then administer the laws.

More often than not, these laws, which are usually in the form of statues, are incomplete. It would be impossible to write laws that cover every contingency; that is, for every type of situation that could arise from a given subject matter. Here we find the duties of the Judiciary, which considers the questions about whether laws were broken by interpreting the law and applying it to a set of facts of a given situation. Quite often, courts that make up the Judiciary also determine if the law is a violation of either the federal or state constitution. Decisions of the courts then become the law, often known as "case law" or "common law," and these decisions sort of "fill in the blanks" where the statute may have been incomplete, vague, or somehow inadequate to address a given set of facts.

The federal judiciary is broken up into circuits, and each circuit interprets the law for the states that make up its circuit. Georgia sits in the eleventh circuit, which also includes Alabama and Florida. Decisions rendered in one circuit apply only to the states that fall within that circuit, which can often lead to extremely different laws across the United States. The only federal court that creates law that applies to the entire United States as a whole is the Supreme Court.

## The United States Constitution

The United States Constitution is the supreme law of the land. It was created on September 17, 1787, and ratified June 21, 1788, and its purpose was to provide the structure and to organize the government of the United States and to define the relationship of the federal government to the individual states and the citizens (and even non-citizens) of the United States. Further, the Constitution was created to outline the powers and duties of each branch of the federal government as discussed above. The Constitution can be amended and has been numerous times. The first ten amendments are known as The Bill of Rights.

## The Bill of Rights

The Bill of Rights was introduced by James Madison and was ratified December 15, 1791. The ten amendments were designed to protect the citizens from persecutions of their freedoms and culture and to affirm their rights by virtue of being an American citizen. The protections and/or rights include the right to free speech under the First Amendment; protections from unreasonable search and seizure under the Fourth Amendment; the right to due process; the right against self-incrimination and other protections under the Fifth Amendment; various rights and protections that apply to criminal prosecutions, as provided under the Sixth Amendment; and of course, the right to keep and bear arms, as provided under the Second Amendment.

Of course, there are other protections and rights provided by the amendments in The Bill of Rights that are not mentioned, and they are also very important, and one should become familiar with those basic protections and rights. The Bill of Rights is included in the Appendices to this book.

## The Second Amendment

While the Second Amendment appears very simple, it could be argued that no other Amendment has created so many different interpretations and so much heated debate over its meaning. The Amendment is as follows:

> *"A well regulated Militia, being necessary to the*
> *security of a free State, the right of the people*
> *to keep and bear Arms, shall not be infringed."*

The terms "well regulated," "Militia," and "bear arms," have, over the last several years, been subject to extensive debate because issues that involve availability of firearms, self-defense, concealed carry, and the like, have become very hot button issues.

One of the most recent cases was *District of Columbia v. Heller.*[2] After hearing the merits of this case, the Supreme Court ruled that "the Second Amendment protects the individual right to possess a firearm unconnected with service in a militia, and to use that arm for traditionally lawful purposes, such as self-defense within the home." Basically, the Supreme Court declared as unconstitutional the District of Columbia's long time ban against fully assembled handguns to be lawfully kept in the home of its citizens.

As it stands, *Heller* did not answer many questions concerning firearm laws in this nation, and since Heller, the courts at all levels have seen an increase in lawsuits pertaining to firearm issues.

However, another case, *McDonald v. Chicago,*[3] furthered the rights of gun owners past the *Heller* case, wherein the Supreme Court held that the Second Amendment is indeed incorporated by the Due Process Clause of the Fourteenth Amendment and does in fact apply to the states. We'll soon see the potential rewards to such a long-awaited ruling.

The Second Amendment is undoubtedly the most hotly contested amendment included in the Bill of Rights. Politicians, mainly from the left, routinely

---

[2]*District of Columbia v. Heller*, 128 S Ct. 2783 (2008).

[3]*McDonald v. Chicago*, 561 U.S. ___ (2010).

distort the intentions of the Second Amendment for political gain, and, along with typical scare tactics, continue to push their agenda to limit or completely restrict firearms. There are currently many unconstitutional laws on the books regarding firearms that we must all live by, and it can take decades to reverse the damage caused by these bad laws.

How will these recent cases impact the firearm laws in the State of Georgia and elsewhere? Well, in the immediate future, very little. Changing laws takes time. Fortunately, many lawsuits have been filed in across this nation, in the wake of *Heller* and *McDonald*. Only time will tell, however, if the rights that have eroded away will ever be returned to us.

Fortunately, Georgia is a very "free" state when it comes to the laws regarding firearms, knives, and weapons.

## Legislative Law

Statutes are laws that have been codified. In Georgia, state statutes can be found in the Official Code of the State of Georgia, which is often referred to as the "Georgia State Code", or "GA ST §" for short. The Georgia General Assembly maintains a website where the code can be found in its entirety. The Georgia State Code is massive. In print, the code comprises a large series of books that is ever-growing.

For your reference, selected portions of the Official Code of the State of Georgia regarding firearm, knife, and weapons law is included in the appendices.

## Executive Law

Agencies of the United States or the State of Georgia have the power to pass laws if first authorized to do so by Congress or the general assembly. The regulations passed must fall within the scope of their powers and must be constitutional.

The series of regulations as enacted by the various federal agencies can be found on the general assembly's website, and the laws pertaining to issues addressed in this book may also be found in the back of this book for your convenience.

One must also be aware of executive orders, both by the President of the United States and by the Governor of Georgia. Presidential executive orders can be found online, as well as the executive orders enacted by the Governor.

## Judicial Law

Judicial law is often called "case law" or "common law." "Case law" consists of the rulings by the court when they have interpreted the statutory law and applied it to a set of facts. Case law has the same force and effect as the laws mentioned above and generally interprets statues, administrative law and regulations and applies such law to specific facts that arise from disputes and conflicts. Case law is the most volatile area of law, as it can change daily and vary from district to district, state to state, more than the other law. While statutes and regulations tend to be easier to find, read, and understand, case law tends to be harder to find, harder to read, and more difficult to understand. Case law is generally tailored very narrowly to address specific issues that pertain to a specific case, and therefore quite often appear incomplete, and many times leave open more questions than answers.

If you have questions in regards to case law, or any other law, it is best to consult an attorney for a translation of the meaning of the decision.

## Federal Law v. State Law

Federal laws are the laws of the United States and apply everywhere within the United States. Laws of the State of Georgia apply only to those individuals who are within the borders of Georgia. However, both sets of laws apply and both sets of laws must be observed. In situations where federal law and state law conflict, federal law governs.

Keep in mind that this book is about Georgia law. While this book at times touches briefly on various key federal laws, please remember that by no means is this book comprehensive regarding federal law, and in fact, it may even be grossly inadequate if you are looking for a study of federal law as it pertains to firearms, knives, and other weapons. However, very common federal law considerations that were selected for this book are included where applicable.

By reading this book, one will learn that, for the most part, Georgia law is specific about what it covers, and if the Georgia laws are silent as to a particular issue, then one may assume that under state law, there are no laws or prohibitions. However, there may be laws or prohibitions regarding the same issue under federal law. So always be mindful of the various laws that may be in place regarding an issue. While federal law tends to address broader issues, such as prohibited weapons, imported weapons, defining people who are prohibited from owning guns, and the like, you will look to Georgia law to determine issues such as buying and transporting firearms, concealed carry, self-defense issues, and even more prohibited places.

# CHAPTER TWO

# <u>Georgia Law</u>

### <u>The Georgia Constitution</u>

The current Constitution for the State of Georgia was drafted on September 25, 1981, and ratified on November 2, 1982. It became effective on July 1, 1983. It happens to be the newest state constitution, and it is Georgia's 10th Constitution, having replaced the previous Constitution effective in 1976.

The Constitution for the State of Georgia provides a protection for the right to keep and bear arms, and states the following:

> *"Arms, right to keep and bear. The right of the*
> *people to keep and bear arms shall not be infringed,*
> *but the General Assembly shall have the power to*
> *prescribe the manner in which arms may be borne."*
> - Article I, Section I, Paragraph VIII

The Constitution for the State of Georgia is silent regarding the citizens certain inalienable rights, which include the right to defend one's life and liberties.

The Georgia Code basically echos the Georgia Constitution, in that it states that the rights of Georgia citizens includes, without limitation, the right to keep and bear arms.[4]

Regarding state constitutions, most states explicitly provide for the right to keep and bear arms in each state constitution, and as demonstrated above, Georgia does as well. However, six states do not have constitutional protections for the right to bear arms, which include California, Iowa, Maryland, Minnesota, New Jersey, and New York.

### <u>Senate Bill 308 and Other Changes for 2011</u>

In 2010, Senate Bill 308 became law, and its purpose was to make sweeping changes to the Georgia State Code by clarifying where it is legal for license holders

---

[4]O.C.G.A. § 1-2-6 (a) and (a)(9).

to carry their firearms. This bill, known as the Georgia Common Sense Lawful Carry Act, protects citizens to make every effort to lawfully carry by making it much more clear than before exactly where these citizens are licensed to carry and where they are not. For instance, there is no more guessing about what is a "public gathering." Instead, prohibited places are specifically defined.

Of course, this bill, and other newly-enacted bills, made changes to other laws regarding the lawful carry of firearms and prohibited places. This book covers the laws that are **now** in effect after the effective date of SB 308. Additionally, the appendix includes relevant portions of the Georgia State Code, and all of the changes made by SB 308 and other new legislation are included.

### Georgia Firearm and Weapons Laws and Preemption

Many states have what is known as a "preemption law" on the books. Preemption laws generally operate to prevent governing bodies below the state level, in most cases, that being the state legislature, from enacting laws that are inconsistent with the laws enacted by the legislature. The result that is usually achieved with strong preemption laws is that the gun owner may look to one set of laws, which in most cases are the codified state laws, to determine how to conduct himself lawfully.

Without strong preemption laws, counties, cities, and other local municipalities may enact their own laws without regard to state law or the laws of other counties, cities, and local municipalities. This would lead to a confusing patchwork of laws where an innocent gun owner might cross an imaginary line and not realize that he just went from being a lawful gun owner to someone who is breaking the law.

Quite often, however, a preemption law was enacted long after a county, city, or municipal law had been in effect. This oftentimes means that the local law was "grandfathered in" and may remain on the books.

Also, just because a state has enacted a preemption law does not always mean that one should not be concerned about inconsistent local laws. For example, if it were state law that one may travel freely throughout the state with a loaded firearm in his car, and despite a preemption law, a local municipality forbids such a practice, to do so would violate the inconsistent local law and therefore subject the traveler to arrest. Sure, after a court fight the traveler might succeed in arguing against the local law. However, one must consider if he wants to be that person in a court battle, or if he prefers to abide by the local law and let someone else get arrested and test the law in court.

Regarding the State of Georgia, the General Assembly enacted a strong preemption law regarding firearms.[5] Basically, the General Assembly declared that the regulation of firearms is properly an issue of general, state-wide concern.[6] The General Assembly also declared that the lawful design, marketing, manufacture, and sale of firearms and ammunition to the public is not an unreasonably dangerous activity and does not constitute a nuisance.[7]

In the State of Georgia, no county or municipal corporation shall, by zoning or by ordinance, resolution, or other enactment, regulate in any manner gun shows; the possession, ownership, transport, carrying, transfer, sale, purchase, licensing, or registration of firearms or components of firearms; firearms dealers; or dealers in firearms components.[8]

Furthermore, the authority to bring suit and right to recover claims against any firearms or ammunition manufacturer, trade association, or dealer by or on behalf of any governmental entity for damages, abatement, or injunctive relief resulting from or relating to lawful design, manufacture, marketing, or the sale of firearms or ammunition to the public is reserved exclusively to the State of Georgia.[9] However, this reserved authority is not to prohibit a political subdivision or local government authority from brining an action against a firearms or ammunition manufacturer or dealer for breach of contract or breach of express warranty as to firearms or ammunition purchased by the political subdivision or local governmental entity.[10]

So, to summarize, the General Assembly has preempted the ability to regulate firearms. The General Assembly has preempted the ability to regulate the

---

[5]See O.C.G.A. § 16-11-173.

[6]O.C.G.A. § 16-11-173 (a)(1).

[7]O.C.G.A. § 16-11-173 (a)(2).

[8]O.C.G.A. § 16-11-173 (b)(1).

[9]O.C.G.A. § 16-11-173 (b)(2).

[10]O.C.G.A. § 16-11-173 (b)(2).

possession, ownership, transport, carrying, transfer, sale, purchase, licensing, or registration of firearms or components of firearms, firearms dealers, or dealers of firearms components. Local governments, such as counties, cities, municipalities, etc., may not regulate such affairs.

As discussed above, that is not to say that on occasion, local governmental entities do not attempt to regulate such affairs. So always be aware of local laws.

## Exceptions to the State of Georgia Preemption Law

A few narrow exceptions exist to the Georgia preemption law and are discussed below.

### Government Employees

Despite a strong preemption law, the General Assembly does allow counties or municipal corporations to regulate the transport, carrying, or possession of firearms by employees of the local unit of government in the course of their employment with such local unit.[11]

This means that local employees may be regulated in their transport, carry, or possession of firearms while they are working - not during their private time while they are "off the clock."

### Head of Household Requirements

The General Assembly does not prohibit municipalities or counties from enacting ordinances, resolutions, or other enactments from requiring the ownership of guns by heads of households within the political subdivision.[12] Interestingly enough, the town of Kennesaw, Georgia, actually has a law on the books that requires the head of each household to maintain a firearm in the house at all times.

### Discharge of Firearms Within Governmental Entity Boundaries

The General Assembly does not prohibit municipalities or county, by ordinance, resolution, or other enactment, from reasonably limiting or prohibiting

---

[11]O.C.G.A. § 16-11-173 (c).

[12]O.C.G.A. § 16-11-173 (d).

the discharge of firearms within the boundaries of the municipal corporation or county.[13]

It is common knowledge among those in the gun community that oftentimes a local government will use its power to shut down shooting ranges by arguing that the range is a nuisance. Because of the exception allowing localities the power to prohibit the discharge of weapons, localities may essentially ban shooting ranges from operating within their boundaries.

However, if the shooting range already exists, and an attempt is made by the locality to shut down the shooting range, they may not do so by deeming the shooting range as a nuisance for "changed circumstances," which generally means that as the town developed, the area around the range has become sensitive to the shooting range. Perhaps a developer built a residential neighborhood next to the shooting range. Such a situation will not provide a local entity the grounds to force the closure of a shooting range.

In any event, no sport shooting range shall be or shall become a nuisance, either public or private, solely as a result of changed conditions in or around the locality of such range if the range has been in operation for one year since the date on which it commenced operation as a sport shooting range.[14] This offers protections to the entrepreneur who works hard and uses his money to open a shooting range, only to have the town come in and try to shut him down years later.

Furthermore, subsequent physical expansion of the range or expansion of the types of firearms in use at the range shall not establish a new date of commencement of operations for purposes of the law.[15] This protects the business owner by allowing him to expand the business without fear that such expansion resets the start date of operation, thus allowing the town to come in and deem the business as a nuisance.

Also, no sport shooting range or unit of government or person owning, operating, or using a sport shooting range for the sport shooting of firearms shall be subject to any action for civil or criminal liability, damages, abatement, or

---

[13]O.C.G.A. § 16-11-173 (e).

[14]O.C.G.A. § 41-1-9 (b).

[15]O.C.G.A. § 41-1-9 (b).

injunctive relief resulting from or relating to noise generated by the operation of the range, if the range remains in compliance with noise control or nuisance abatement rules, regulations, statutes, or ordinances that apply to the range <u>on the date on which the range commenced operation</u>.[16] This protects the range owner from a change in laws that could be drafted to be so burdensome that it would be virtually impossible to comply with, thus allowing the town to come in and shut the range down.

Finally, any laws a town my enact regarding noise control, noise pollution, or noise abatement that may be adopted by a local governmental entity may not be applied retroactively to sport shooting ranges.[17]

So, while there exists an exception to the preemption statute regarding the discharge of firearms within a local government boundaries, there are protections afforded to established shooting ranges.

---

[16]O.C.G.A. § 41-1-9 (c).

[17]O.C.G.A. § 41-1-9 (d).

# CHAPTER THREE

## People Prohibited from Firearms and Other Weapons

Both the State of Georgia, as well as the federal government, have laws on the books that prohibit certain people from possessing, using, owning, handling, or otherwise being in control of firearms or other weapons. Read this section carefully, as violations of the prohibitions usually carry quite severe penalties upon conviction.

### People Prohibited From Possessing Firearms Under State Law - Felons

Generally, those who have been convicted of a felony may not have anything to do with firearms for the remainder of their lives, absent a pardon or some other very narrow exception that may exist.[18] Such prohibitions placed upon felons have been upheld by the Georgia courts.[19]

A "felony" is usually defined as any offense that is punishable by imprisonment for a term of one year or more, and may include civil (monetary) penalties as well. The State of Georgia defines a felony in this manner.[20]

A "forcible felony" is any felony which involves the use or threat of physical force or violence against any person and further includes crimes such as murder, felony murder, burglary, robbery, armed robbery, kidnapping, hijacking of an aircraft or motor vehicle, aggravated stalking, rape, aggravated child molestation, aggravated sexual battery, arson in the first degree, the manufacture, transport, distribution, or possession of explosives with the intent to kill, injure, intimidate, or destroy a public building, terroristic threats, or acts of treason or insurrection.[21]

Finally, a "firearm," for the purpose of these prohibitions, includes any handgun, rifle, shotgun, or other weapon which will or can be converted to expel

---

[18]See O.C.G.A. § 16-11-131.

[19]See *Landers v. State*, (1983) 250 Ga. 501, 299 S.E.2d 707.

[20]O.C.G.A. § 16-11-131 (a)(1).

[21]O.C.G.A. § 16-11-131 (e).

a projectile by the action of an explosive or electrical charge.[22]

Convicted Felons Who Receive, Possess, or Transport Firearm - In the State of Georgia, any person who is on probation as a felony first offender pursuant to Georgia law,[23] or who has been convicted of a felony by a court of the State of Georgia or of any other state, federal, or even by a court of any foreign nation, who receives, possesses, or transports any firearm, commits a felony and, upon conviction, shall be imprisoned for more than one year but not more than five years, unless the felony was a "forcible felony," in which case they will be imprisoned for five years.[24]

Convicted Felons Who Attempt to Purchase Firearm - Any person who is prohibited from possessing a firearm because of a conviction of a forcible felony or because of being on probation as a first offender for a forcible felony and who attempts to purchase or obtain transfer of a firearm is guilty of a felony and faces punishment of between one and five years.[25]

## Restoration of Rights for Felons Prohibited Under State Law

A few limited exceptions exist that allow one who was previously prohibited from any involvement with firearms to regain the right to bear arms.

Those Arrested for Felony But Not Convicted - Any person who was placed on probation as a first offender pursuant to Georgia Law[26] but who was subsequently discharged without court adjudication of guilt under the law[27] shall, upon such discharge, be relieved from the prohibition imposed upon them regarding firearms.[28]

---

[22]O.C.G.A. § 16-11-131 (a)(2).

[23]Specifically, Title 42, Chapter 8, Article 3.

[24]O.C.G.A. § 16-11-131 (h).

[25]O.C.G.A. § 16-11-131 (b.1).

[26]See Title 42, Chapter 8, Article 3.

[27]See O.C.G.A. § 42-8-62.

[28]O.C.G.A. § 16-11-131 (f).

Pardon - For those who have been convicted for a felony and have been pardoned by the President of the United States, by the State Board of Pardons and Paroles, or the person or agency empowered to grant pardons under the constitutions and laws of any other state or nation and, by the terms of the pardon, have expressly been authorized to receive, possess, or transport a firearm, then they may do so.[29]

Be aware that those who are convicted drug offenders who are later pardoned are ineligible to obtain a license to carry a concealed pistol or revolver, even if, subsequent to the pardon, they are permitted to possess a pistol or revolver inside their home, vehicle, or place of business without violating Georgia law.[30]

Applications for Relief - Felons may also be granted relief from the prohibitions imposed upon them should the secretary of the United States Department of the Treasury[31] present to the Board of Public Safety proof that the relief has been granted.[32] The proof of relief must present circumstances regarding the conviction, the individual's record and reputation, and that the acquisition, receipt, transfer, shipment, or possession of firearms by that person would not present a threat to the safety of the citizens of Georgia and that the relief sought would not be contrary to the public interest.[33]

Also, for those felons who were convicted under federal or state law of a felony pertaining to antitrust violations, unfair trade practices, or restraint of trade may, upon presenting to the Board of Public Safety proof, and it being established from said proof, that the circumstances regarding the conviction and the applicant's record and reputation are such that the acquisition, receipt, transfer, shipment, or possession of firearms by the person would not present a threat to the safety of the citizens of Georgia and that the granting of relief sought would not be contrary to

---

[29]O.C.G.A. § 16-11-131 (c).

[30]Op.Atty.Gen. No. U05-3, July 7, 2005; see also Op.Atty.Gen No. U97-29, October 1, 1997.

[31]See 18 U.S.C. § 925.

[32]O.C.G.A. § 16-11-131 (d).

[33]O.C.G.A. § 16-11-131 (d).

the public interest, shall be granted the relief from the prohibitions.[34]

When relief from the prohibitions has been granted, a record of such relief is to be entered upon the criminal history of the person that is maintained by the Georgia Crime Information Center.[35] The Board of Public Safety is also to maintain a list of the names of such persons, and that list is open for public inspection.[36]

## A Few State Law Considerations Regarding Felons and Firearms

For the purposes of the prohibition placed upon felons regarding firearms, toys or nonfunctional replicas do not constitute weapons for the purpose of establishing possession of a firearm by a convicted felon.[37] Despite this, Georgia courts have held that the operability of an instrument need not be shown where it is also shown that the convicted felon possessed any of the weapons listed in the statutory definition of "firearm."[38]

Also, for the convicted felon who attempts to acquire a concealed carry license, and somehow is issued the license by mistake, the use the mistake made by licensing authorities as a defense to a charge of being a convicted felon in possession of a firearm will be denied.[39]

## People Prohibited From Possessing Handguns Under State Law - Minors

Minors may possess handguns under certain circumstances as outlined in the chapter on "minors" and "juveniles." However, sometimes those exceptions do not apply because the minor would be considered "prohibited" from possessing or having within their custody or control a firearm. Minors who fall under a

---

[34]O.C.G.A. § 16-11-131 (d).

[35]O.C.G.A. § 16-11-131 (d).

[36]O.C.G.A. § 16-11-131 (d).

[37]See *Head v. State* (1984) 170 Ga.App. 324, 316 S.E.2d 791, *reversed* 253 Ga. 429, 322 S.E.2d 228, *on remand* 173 Ga.App. 247, 327 S.E.2d 239.

[38]See *Bryant v. State*, (1984) 169 Ga.App. 764, 315 S.E.2d 257.

[39]See *Daughtry v. State*, (1986) 180 Ga.App. 711, 350 S.E.d 53.

prohibition of handing a handgun are described below.

Minors Known to Have Violated Prohibitions - Minors who are known to have violated the prohibitions in place that forbid them to handle handguns without certain exceptions applying are not permitted to possess handguns.[40]

Substantial-Risk Minors - Additionally, minors who are a substantial risk to society may not be granted permission and may not possess, handguns of any kind.[41]

Convicted Minors - Finally, a minor who has been convicted of a forcible felony or forcible misdemeanor,[42] or who has been adjudicated delinquent under Georgia law[43] for an offense which would constitute a forcible felony or forcible misdemeanor if such minor were an adult, may not possess a handgun.[44]

## People Prohibited From Possessing Firearms and Ammunition Under Federal Law

Pursuant to federal law, it is unlawful for any of the following individuals to possess any firearm or ammunition:[45]

- one who has been convicted in any court of a crime by imprisonment for a term exceeding one year (a felony), even if time served was actually less[46]
- one who is a fugitive from justice[47]
- one who is an unlawful user of or addicted to any controlled substance as defined in the Controlled Substances Act (includes

---

[40]See O.C.G.A. §§ 16-11-132 (b) and 16-11-101.1.

[41]See O.C.G.A. §§ 16-11-132 (b) and 16-11-101.1.

[42]See O.C.G.A. § 16-1-3.

[43]See O.C.G.A. Title 15, Chapter 11, Article 1.

[44]See O.C.G.A. §§ 16-11-132 (b) and 16-11-101.1.

[45]18 U.S.C. § 922 (g).

[46]18 U.S.C. § 922 (g)(1).

[47]18 U.S.C. § 922 (g)(2).

marijuana)[48]

- one who has been adjudicated as a mental defective or who has been committed to a mental institution[49]
- one who is illegally or unlawfully in the United States or who has been admitted to the United States under a nonimmigrant visa, unless that nonimmigrant was admitted to the United States for lawful hunting or sporting purposes or is in possession of a hunting license or permit lawfully issued in the United States, is an official representative of a foreign government who is accredited to the United States Government or the Government's mission to an international organization having its headquarters in the United States, is *en route* to or from another country to which that alien is accredited, an official of a foreign government or a distinguished foreign visitor who has been so designated by the Department of State, or a foreign law enforcement officer of a friendly foreign government entering the United States on official law enforcement business[50]
- one who has been discharged from the Armed Forces under dishonorable conditions[51]
- one who, having been a citizen of the United States, has renounced his citizenship[52]
- one who is subject to a court order that was issued after a hearing of which such person received actual notice and which such person had an opportunity to participate, or was restrained from harassing, stalking, or threatening an intimate partner or person, or engaging in other conduct that would place an intimate partner in reasonable fear of bodily injury to the partner or child and includes a finding that such person represents a credible threat to the physical safety of such intimate partner or child or, by its terms, explicitly prohibits the use, attempted use, or

---

[48] 18 U.S.C. § 922 (g)(3) and 21 U.S.C. § 802.

[49] 18 U.S.C. § 922 (g)(4).

[50] 18 U.S.C. § 922 (g)(5), 8 U.S.C. § 1101 (a)(26), 18 U.S.C. § 922 (y)(2)(A) and (B).

[51] 18 U.S.C. § 922 (g)(6).

[52] 18 U.S.C. § 922 (g)(7).

threatened use of physical force against such intimate partner or child that would reasonably be expected to cause bodily injury[53]

- one who has been convicted in any court of a misdemeanor crime of domestic violence[54]

- employees of any of the persons above who are subject to federal firearms prohibitions if having a firearm is required for their employment[55]

Any of the above federal offenses may subject the offender to a fine and up to ten years in a federal prison.[56]

Under federal law, one who is under indictment for a crime punishable by imprisonment for a term exceeding one year may not ship or transport any firearm or ammunition or receive any firearm or ammunition which has been shipped or transported.[57]  Note that this prohibition does not prevent the person under indictment from maintaining possession of firearms or ammunition he has in his custody and control at the time of indictment.

### Users of Controlled Substances

Federal law prohibits anyone who is a user or is addicted to any controlled substance, including marijuana, from possessing, owning, purchasing, receiving, or having within his custody or control any firearms.[58]  Violating federal prohibition regarding drug users may subject the offender to a fine and up to ten years in a federal prison.[59]

---

[53] 18 U.S.C. § 922 (g)(8)(A), (B), and (C).

[54] 18 U.S.C. § 922 (g)(9).

[55] 18 U.S.C. § 922 (h).

[56] 18 U.S.C. § 924 (a)(2).

[57] 18 U.S.C. § 922 (n).

[58] 18 U.S.C. § 922 (g)(3) and 21 U.S.C. § 802.

[59] 18 U.S.C. § 924 (a)(2).

## Restoration of Rights for Those Prohibited Under Federal Law

A person who is prohibited from possessing, shipping, transporting, or receiving firearms or ammunition may make application to the Attorney General for relief from the disabilities imposed by Federal laws with respect to those acts regarding firearms.[60]

The Attorney General may grant such relief if it is established to his satisfaction that the circumstances regarding the disability, and the applicant's record and reputation, are such that the applicant will not likely act in a manner dangerous to public safety and that the granting of the relief would not be contrary to the public interest.[61]

Any person whose application for relief from disabilities is denied by the Attorney General may file a petition with the United States District Court for the district in which he resides for a judicial review of such denial.[62] The court may in its discretion admit additional evidence where failure to do so would result in a miscarriage of justice.[63]

A licensed importer, licensed manufacturer, licensed dealer, or licensed collector conducting lawful operations who applies for relief from the disabilities incurred by law, shall not be barred by such disability from further operations under his license pending final action on an application for relief filed pursuant to this section.[64]

When the Attorney General grants relief to any person, he shall promptly publish a notice regarding the relief given in the Federal Register notice of such action, together with the reasons stated therefor.[65]

---

[60] 18 U.S.C. § 925 (c).

[61] 18 U.S.C. § 925 (c).

[62] 18 U.S.C. § 925 (c).

[63] 18 U.S.C. § 925 (c).

[64] 18 U.S.C. § 925 (c).

[65] 18 U.S.C. § 925 (c).

# CHAPTER FOUR

## Minors / Juveniles

Most states have laws regarding "minor" or "juvenile" children and firearms or other weapons, and the State of Georgia is no different. The State of Georgia uses the term "minor," and federal law uses the term "juvenile." Both terms basically mean the same thing; that is, a minor and a juvenile is any person that has not yet achieved his or her 18th birthday.

Be certain to be aware of the federal laws in regard to juveniles and firearms or other weapons, and it is important to be aware of both state and federal laws because both apply to citizens of the State of Georgia and those who travel through or otherwise visit Georgia.

### Possession of Pistol or Revolver by Minor

Absent an exception, it is unlawful for any person under the age of 18 years to possess or have under his control a handgun.[66] A conviction based upon a first violation of this law is a misdemeanor with a fine not to exceed $1000 and potential imprisonment for up to 12 months.[67] A conviction based upon a second violation of this law is a felony and carries a punishment of imprisonment of up to three years along with a fine of up to $5000.[68]

Of course, exceptions exist. However, none of the following exceptions exist for the minor who has been convicted of a forcible felony or forcible misdemeanor,[69] or who has been adjudicated delinquent under Georgia law[70] for an offense that would constitute a forcible felony or forcible misdemeanor if such

---

[66]O.C.G.A. § 16-11-132 (b).

[67]O.C.G.A. § 16-11-132 (b).

[68]O.C.G.A. § 16-11-132 (b).

[69]As defined in O.C.G.A. § 16-1-3.

[70]See O.C.G.A. Title 15, Chapter 11, Article I.

person were an adult.[71]  Such a minor is still prohibited from handguns.

Attending Training Courses - Any person under the age of 18 years of age who is attending a hunter education course or a firearms safety course is not in violation of the law prohibiting minors from possessing or having in their control a handgun.[72]

Target Shooting - Any person under the age of 18 years of age who is engaging in practice in the use of a firearm or target shooting at an established range authorized by the governing body of the jurisdiction where the range is located is not in violation of the law prohibiting minors from possessing or having in their control a handgun.[73]

Competitive Shooting Events - Any person under the age of 18 years of age who is engaging in an organized competition involving the use of a firearm or participating in or practicing for a performance by an authorized organized group[74] which uses firearms in such a performance is not in violation of the law prohibiting minors from possessing or having in their control a handgun.[75]

Hunting and Fishing - Any person under the age of 18 years of age who is hunting or fishing pursuant to a valid license (if required), is engaged in legal hunting or fishing, or has permission of the owner of the land on which hunting or fishing is being conducted, and the handgun, whenever is loaded, is carried only in an open and fully exposed manner, is not in violation of the law prohibiting minors from possessing or having in their control a handgun.[76]  A handgun is deemed loaded if there is a cartridge in the chamber or cylinder of the handgun.[77]

---

[71]O.C.G.A. § 16-11-132 (d).

[72]O.C.G.A. § 16-11-132 (c)(1) and (c)(1)(A).

[73]O.C.G.A. § 16-11-132 (c)(1) and (c)(1)(B).

[74]See 26 U.S.C. § 501 (c)(3).

[75]O.C.G.A. § 16-11-132 (c)(1) and (c)(1)(C).

[76]O.C.G.A. § 16-11-132 (c)(1) and (c)(1)(D).

[77]O.C.G.A. § 16-11-132 (a).

Travel To and From Above Listed Events - Any person under the age of 18 years of age who is traveling to or from any of the above described activities is not in violation of the law prohibiting minors from possessing or having in their control a handgun, as long as they keep the firearm unloaded during the travel.[78] A handgun is deemed loaded if there is a cartridge in the chamber or cylinder of the handgun.[79]

Permission - Any person under the age of 18 years of age who is on real property under the control of such person's parent, legal guardian, or grandparent, and who has the permission of such person's parent or legal guardian to possess a handgun, is not in violation of the law prohibiting minors from possessing or having in their control a handgun.[80]

Self-Defense, Defense of Others, Defense of Property - Any person under the age of 18 years of age who is at such person's residence and who, with the permission of such person's parent or legal guardian, possesses the handgun for the purpose of exercising their rights to self-defense, defense of others, or defense of property, as is provided under Georgia law,[81] is not in violation of the law prohibiting minors from possessing or having in their control a handgun.[82]

Be sure to see below regarding instances where a parent or legal guardian may not give permission to a minor to possess a handgun.

## State Law Offenses Regarding Minors with Firearms and Other Weapons

Much of this material is repeated in the chapter involving weapons offenses, but because of the importance of being aware of these offenses, they are discussed in this chapter as well.

Furnishing or Allowing Minor to Possess Pistol or Revolver - It is unlawful for a person intentionally, knowingly, or recklessly to sell or furnish a pistol or

---

[78]O.C.G.A. § 16-11-132 (c)(1) and (c)(1)(E).

[79]O.C.G.A. § 16-11-132 (a).

[80]O.C.G.A. § 16-11-132 (c)(2).

[81]See O.C.G.A. §§ 16-3-21 and 16-3-23.

[82]O.C.G.A. § 16-11-132 (c)(3).

revolver to a minor.[83] Punishment for this offense which is considered a felony is a penalty of a fine of up to $5000 along with imprisonment from 3 to 5 years.[84]

Of course, the exceptions illustrated in this chapter as discussed above apply unless the person authorized to permit possession of a pistol or revolver by a minor knows of the minor's conduct that otherwise violates the laws prohibiting the minor from possessing or handling the firearm and that person fails to make reasonable efforts to prevent the minor from committing the offense.[85] At that point, the person authorized to give permission, which would be the parent or legal guardian, may not give permission or provide the handgun to the minor.

Additionally, it is unlawful for a parent or legal guardian intentionally, knowingly, or recklessly to furnish or to permit a minor to possess a pistol or revolver if such parent or legal guardian is aware of a substantial risk that the minor will use a pistol or revolver to commit a felony offense, or if the parent or legal guardian knows of such risk and fails to make reasonable efforts to prevent commission of the offense by the minor.[86]

Finally, a parent or legal guardian shall be deemed to have violated the above prohibitions if the parent or legal guardian furnishes to or permits possession of a pistol or revolver by any minor who has been convicted of a forcible felony or forcible misdemeanor,[87] or who has been adjudicated delinquent under Georgia law[88] for an offense which would constitute a forcible felony or forcible misdemeanor if such minor were an adult.[89]

Punishment for the offenses outlined in the previous three paragraphs, offenses which are considered felonies, carries a penalty of a fine of up to $5000

---

[83]O.C.G.A. § 16-11-101.1.

[84]O.C.G.A. § 16-11-101.1 (d).

[85]O.C.G.A. § 16-11-101.1 (c)(1).

[86]O.C.G.A. § 16-11-101.1 (c)(2).

[87]See O.C.G.A. § 16-1-3.

[88]See O.C.G.A. Title 15, Chapter 11, Article 1.

[89]O.C.G.A. § 16-11-101.1 (c)(3).

along with imprisonment from 3 to 5 years.[90]

A separate charge of contributing to the delinquency of a minor may also be brought against any individual that knowingly and wilfully provides to a minor access to a handgun, and/or assists the minor in violating laws regarding firearms on school property or at school functions.[91] However, in this case, minors are those who are under 17 years of age unless they are under the age of 18 years and also alleged to be a "deprived child" as defined by law.[92]

The purpose behind the statute that makes it unlawful for a person to intentionally, knowingly, or recklessly sell or furnish a handgun to a minor except for limited circumstances was intended to protect minors from their own inability to protect themselves from their dangerous conduct when handling handguns, including their own lack of judgment or inability to resist various peer pressures.[93]

Furnishing Knife or Metal Knuckles to Minor - A person is guilty of a misdemeanor of a high and aggravated nature when he or she knowingly sells or furnishes to a person under the age of 18 years any knuckles, whether made from metal, thermoplastic, wood, or other similar material, or a knife designed for the purpose of offense and defense.[94]

Toy Pistols and Mere Imitation Pistols Excluded - While it should appear obvious, it is not, which is why there is case law addressing it, but a toy pistol is not a pistol under the law, so toy pistols may be sold to minors.[95] Furthermore, the prohibition on the sale of a pistol to a minor contemplates the sale of an actual weapon and not a mere imitation of a weapon that is not reasonably capable of

---

[90]O.C.G.A. § 16-11-101.1 (d).

[91]See O.C.G.A. §§ 16-12-1 (b), (b)(5), 16-11-121, and 16-11-127.1.

[92]O.C.G.A. § 16-12-1 (a)(3); see also O.C.G.A. § 15-11-2 regarding "deprived children."

[93]See *McEachern v. Muldovan*, (1998) 234 Ga.App. 152, 505 S.E.2d 495.

[94]O.C.G.A. § 16-11-101.

[95]See *Mathews v. Caldwell*, (1908) 5 Ga.App. 336, 63 S.E. 250.

being put to the use for which the corresponding weapon is intended.[96] There is no liability for injuries received from a toy pistol sold to a minor.[97]

Minors Under 12 Prohibited From Hunting Alone - It is unlawful for any person who is under 12 years of age to hunt any wildlife in the State of Georgia unless that person is under the direct supervision of an adult during the period in which the person is hunting.[98] It is also unlawful for any person to cause or to knowingly permit such person's child or ward who is less than 12 years old to hunt any wildlife with a weapon in the State of Georgia unless that child or ward is under adult supervision.[99]

**Federal Law Regarding Juveniles**

Under federal law, a juvenile is someone who is under the age of 18. Of course, this corresponds with Georgia state law. There are three types of law that apply to minors and firearms, including Georgia law, federal law, and some local or municipal laws. Only Georgia law and some federal law are discussed in this book. There are just too many counties, cities, and other localities to keep up with. If you have a concern about a particular municipality and the laws governing that municipality, the laws are likely online, as just about every municipality has a web site. Google is your friend when looking for such laws and ordinances.

It shall be unlawful for any person who is a juvenile to knowingly possess a handgun or ammunition that is suitable for use only in a handgun.[100] However, there are exceptions.[101]

Farming and Ranching Activities - A juvenile may be in temporary possession of or may use a handgun and/or handgun ammunition in the course of employment, such as in the course of ranching or farming related to the activities

---

[96]See *Mathews v. Caldwell*, (1908) 5 Ga.App. 336, 63 S.E. 250.

[97]See *Mathews v. Caldwell*, (1908) 5 Ga.App. 336, 63 S.E. 250.

[98]O.C.G.A. § 27-3-41 (a).

[99]O.C.G.A. § 27-3-41 (b).

[100]18 U.S.C. § 922 (x)(2)(A) and (B).

[101]18 U.S.C. § 922 (x)(3).

at the residence of the juvenile, as long as the juvenile first has the permission of the land owner or lessee.[102]

Target Practice, Hunting, and Course of Instruction - A juvenile may be in temporary possession of or may use a handgun and/or handgun ammunition in the course and scope of activities where the juvenile is temporarily engaged in target practice, hunting, or a course of instruction in the safe and lawful use of a handgun.[103]

Prior Consent of Parent - A juvenile may temporarily possess and/or use a handgun and/or handgun ammunition if prior written consent of the juvenile's parent or guardian is given, provided that the parent or guardian himself is not prohibited by federal, state, or local law from possessing a firearm.[104] The written consent must remain on the juvenile's person at all times when the handgun is in the possession of the juvenile.[105]

Armed Forces - A juvenile may also possess a handgun and/or handgun ammunition if he is a member of the Armed Forces of the United States or the National Guard and who possesses or is armed with a handgun in the line of duty.[106]

Self-Defense Situations - Juveniles may also possess a handgun and/or handgun ammunition if used in self-defense of the juvenile or other persons against an intruder into the residence of the juvenile or a residence where the juvenile is an invited guest.[107]

Inheritance - A juvenile is subject to the exceptions if he takes a handgun or handgun ammunition subject to a transfer by inheritance of title; however, he may not take possession legally until he is of legal age unless one of the other

---

[102] 18 U.S.C. § 922 (x)(3)(A)(i).

[103] 18 U.S.C. § 922 (x)(3)(A)(i).

[104] 18 U.S.C. § 922 (x)(3)(A)(ii).

[105] 18 U.S.C. § 922 (x)(3)(A)(iii).

[106] 18 U.S.C. § 922 (x)(3)((B).

[107] 18 U.S.C. § 922 (x)(3)(D).

exceptions above exists.[108]

In any of the scenarios above, where a juvenile is in temporary custody of a handgun and/or handgun ammunition, he must transport the handgun unloaded and in a locked container when traveling to and from the activity and must also observe all state and local gun laws.[109]

A juvenile who violates federal law regarding possession of a handgun and/or handgun ammunition may be fined or imprisoned not more than one year, or both.[110] The good news for the juvenile is that if the offense he is charged with is possession of either a handgun or handgun ammunition, or both, and that juvenile has not been convicted in any court of an offense or adjudicated as a juvenile delinquent, the punishment will be probation.[111] However, a violation of probation for this offense may result in incarceration.[112]

### Juveniles, Weapons, and Schools

As we are all aware, there are extreme consequences for bringing firearms and other weapons onto school grounds, especially if the person who does this is a juvenile that attends the school. Many schools across the nation have a "zero tolerance" policy, and even children with pictures on their shirts, or toys, such as Lego men with little toy guns, can learn that these items may become a big deal for the family of the child who brought the item onto school grounds, such that these events are typically discussed on the evening news.

As a general rule of thumb, a juvenile on school grounds with anything resembling a weapon, firearm, explosive, or other object that could be construed as such, or portrays such, is bad. Very bad. Punishments can range from verbal reprimands to outright expulsion.

In Georgia, each student code of conduct will address conduct, such as

---

[108] 18 U.S.C. § 922 (x)(3)(C).

[109] 18 U.S.C. § 922 (x)(3)(A)(ii)(I).

[110] 18 U.S.C. § 924 (a)(6)(A)(i).

[111] 18 U.S.C. §§ 924 (a)(6)(A)(I), 924 (a)(6)(A)(ii)(I) and (II).

[112] 18 U.S.C. § 924 (a)(6)(A)(i).

possession of a weapon on school grounds, in school buildings, and at school activities.[113]  Any hint of a crime involving firearms or other dangerous weapons is to be reported to the principal.[114]  In fact, for any teacher, person employed at a public or private elementary or secondary school, dean or public safety officer employed by a college or university who has reasonable cause to believe there was a violation, not to report the potential violation has himself committed a crime.[115]

For more information about weapons in school zones and on school grounds, please refer to the chapters on concealed weapons licenses, weapons offenses, and traveling with firearms.

---

[113]O.C.G.A. § 20-2-751.5 (a) and (a)(12); see also O.C.G.A. § 16-11-127.1.

[114]O.C.G.A. § 20-2-1184.

[115]O.C.G.A. § 20-2-1184 (d).

# CHAPTER FIVE

## Buying Firearms in Georgia

Fortunately, the State of Georgia has very few laws on the books regulating the purchase or sale of firearms.  Georgia residents may almost freely buy any firearms they desire, subject to just a few Georgia state laws and the restrictions imposed by the federal government, some of which may be overcome by paying a tax to the federal government, as well as jumping through a few other hoops.

Georgia residents also need not be concerned about firearm registration, including handguns, as the preemption statutes (as discussed earlier in this book) prohibit any firearm registration by any local or municipal government.

### Purchasing Shotguns and Rifles in the State of Georgia

In Georgia, an individual need only be 18 years of age to purchase shotguns and rifles, so long as he is not a prohibited person under state or federal law.

There are some rifles and shotguns that are heavily controlled by the federal government which are known as Class III NFA weapons (National Firearms Act[116]), which may be bought in Georgia but only under certain exceptions and after certain requirements are satisfied.  Because the standards may vary from locality to locality, they are not discussed in this book, and it is recommended to those interested in Class III weapons to check with local authorities regarding the application process.

In any event, the age limit of 18 years of age is a purchasing requirement, and not an ownership requirement.  This means that one may be under the age of 18 and own a shotgun or rifle in the State of Georgia.

Purchase of Rifles and Shotguns in Other States by Georgia Residents - Residents of the State of Georgia may purchase rifles and shotguns in any state of the United States, provided such residents conform to applicable provisions of statutes and regulations of the United States, of the State of Georgia, and of the

---

[116]See 26 U.S.C. 53.

state in which the purchase is made.[117]

Purchase of Rifles and Shotguns Within the State of Georgia by Non-Residents - Residents of any state of the United States may purchase rifles and shotguns in the State of Georgia, provided such residents conform to applicable provisions of statutes and regulations of the United States, of the State of Georgia, and of the state in which the person resides.[118]

## Purchasing Handguns in the State of Georgia and the NICS

The laws for buying handguns and long guns in the State of Georgia are very common to most other states that respect the Second Amendment. Some requirements do exist, and some of which are state law, and some are federal law.

Age to Purchase a Handgun is 21 Years of Age - Under both state and federal law, to purchase a handgun, one must be 21 years of age.

National Instant Criminal Background Check System (NICS) - The Brady Handgun Violence Prevention Act[119] is responsible for the creation of the NICS. The Bureau will deny a transfer of a firearm to a prospective transferee if the transfer would violate federal law[120] or state law. All transfers or purchases of firearms conducted by a licensed importer, licensed manufacturer, or licensed dealer shall be subject to the NICS.[121]

Under federal law, a "licensed gun dealer" means any person who is a licensed importer, licensed manufacturer, or federally licensed firearms dealer.[122]

To the extent possible, the Georgia Crime Information Center, which is

---

[117]O.C.G.A. § 10-1-100.

[118]O.C.G.A. § 10-1-101.

[119]See 18 U.S.C. § 922 (t) and Public Law 103-159.

[120]See 18 U.S.C. § 922 (g) and (n), which is discussed in the chapter regarding "prohibited persons."

[121]O.C.G.A. § 16-11-172 (a).

[122]See 18 U.S.C. § 923.

within the Georgia Bureau of Investigation, shall provide to the NICS all necessary criminal history information and wanted person records in order to allow the NICS to function and enable the completion of background checks.[123]

Firearm purchases that are not subject to the NICS include any firearm, including any handgun with a matchlock, flintlock, percussion cap, or similar ignition system, manufactured in or before 1898,[124] any specific replicas of firearms,[125] and any firearm which is a "curio or relic" as defined by federal law.[126]

## Dealer Considerations Regarding Selling Firearms in Georgia

Dealers Must Be Licensed - The State of Georgia requires that all dealers of firearms be licensed prior to engaging in the sale of firearms. Any person, firm, retail dealer, pawnbroker, or corporation who shall sell, dispose of, or offer for sale, or cause or permit to be sold, disposed of, or offered for sale any pistol, revolver, or short-barreled firearm of less than 15 inches in length, whether the sale is on the property of the seller or on the property of another person or agent, shall obtain from the Department of Public Safety a license permitting the sale of such pistols, revolvers, and firearms.[127]

Private Party Transfers - The license requirement is not to apply to or otherwise prohibit the casual sales of such firearms between individuals or bona fide gun collectors.[128] So, no license is necessary for private party transfers.

Dealer Requirements - The applicant for a dealer license must provide a sworn affidavit that he or she is a citizen of the United States and has reached the

---

[123]O.C.G.A. § 16-11-127 (a); see also O.C.G.A. § 16-11-171 (1).

[124]O.C.G.A. § 16-11-172 (d)(1).

[125]O.C.G.A. § 16-11-172 (d)(2).

[126]O.C.G.A. § 16-11-172 (d)(3); see also 27 C.F.R. § 178.11 for definition of "curio or relic."

[127]O.C.G.A. § 43-16-2.

[128]O.C.G.A. § 43-16-2.

age of 21 years, and has not been convicted of a felony.[129] Also, each application for a Wholesale and Retail License must include a copy of a current Federal Firearms Dealer License issued by the Bureau of Alcohol, Tobacco, and Firearms.[130]

Annual Dealer and Employee of Dealer License Fee - An annual fee must be paid by the dealer to the Department of Public Safety in the amount of $25. [131] There is an annual fee for each employee of the dealer in the amount of $3, to also be paid to the Department of Public Safety. Fees may be paid by money order, company check, or certified check, but personal checks will not be accepted.[132]

Performance Bond Required - Upon approval of an application for a license, the dealer must execute a performance bond in the amount of $1000, which is to be executed by a surety company or by two individuals, but made payable to the State of Georgia.[133] Forms are furnished to the dealer by the Department of Public Safety.[134] The bond is to be in force for the period the license is to run, and must be renewed annually upon the renewal of the dealer's license to sell firearms.[135]

Display of Dealer License - Every recipient of a license to sell any firearms is to keep the license conspicuously displayed on this business premises.[136] In basic terms, the license must be easily seen by the general public.[137]

Revocation of Dealer License for Nonpayment of Fee - Any licensee who fails or neglects to pay the annual license fee prior to July 1 of each year will be

---

[129]O.C.G.A. § 43-16-3; see also Rules of Department of Public Safety Section 570-4-.06.

[130]Rules of Department of Public Safety Section 570-4-.06.

[131]O.C.G.A. § 43-16-5.

[132]Rules of Department of Public Safety Section 570-4-.06.

[133]Rules of Department of Public Safety Section 570-4-.07.

[134]Rules of Department of Public Safety Section 570-4-.07.

[135]Rules of Department of Public Safety Section 570-4-.07.

[136]O.C.G.A. § 43-16-5.

[137]Rules of the Department of Public Safety Section 570-4-.02.

notified by the Department of Public Safety of a pending revocation of the license, and the license will be revoked unless the fee is paid in full before August 1 of the same year.[138]

If the application has been revoked, the dealer may make an application for the license to be reinstated, and the application must include a fee of $10, in addition to the regular license fee required.[139] If the license was revoked for no other reason than the fee was not paid, the application shall be granted and the license shall be immediately reinstated.[140]

Revocation of Dealer License for Fraud, Violation of Ethics, or Crime - The Department of Public Safety has the power to revoke any license granted by it to any person, firm, retail dealer, wholesale dealer, pawnbroker, or corporation, or any agent or employee of any of those people or entities, if the Board of Public Safety finds that such has been guilty of fraud or willful misrepresentation, or guilty of any other crime of the State of Georgia that involves moral turpitude, or any crime wherein a knife or metal knuckles were sold or provided to a minor.[141]

Revocation Proceedings - All proceedings for the revocation of a dealer license as issued under Georgia law shall be governed by the Georgia Administrative Procedure Act.[142]

Surrender of License - After receiving notice that a license to sell firearms has been revoked, regardless of reasons for such revocation, the holder of the license must immediately surrender it to the Department of Public Safety or its authorized agent.[143] Failure to surrender the license will subject the holder to

---

[138]O.C.G.A. § 43-16-8.

[139]O.C.G.A. § 43-16-9.

[140]O.C.G.A. § 43-16-9.

[141]O.C.G.A. § 43-16-10; see also O.C.G.A. § 16-11-101.

[142]O.C.G.A. § 43-16-11 and Rules of Department of Public Safety Section 570-4-.04; see also Title 50 Chapter 13 of the O.C.G.A. regarding the proceedings for revocation.

[143]Rules of Department of Public Safety Section 570-4-.03.

penalties as provided by law.[144]

Keeping Firearm Records - As a condition of any license issued for the sale of firearms, each licensee is required to keep a record of the acquisition or disposition of firearms.[145] The record is to be identical in form and context to the firearms and disposition record as required under federal law.[146]

The record kept under the law is to be maintained on the licensed premises and shall be open to inspection of any duly authorized law enforcement officer during the ordinary hours of business, or at any other reasonable time, and shall be kept for a period of not less than 5 years.[147]

Of course, failure to maintain such records is grounds for a revocation of a dealer license.[148]

---

[144] Rules of Department of Public Safety Section 570-4-.03.

[145] O.C.G.A. § 43-16-10.1 (a).

[146] O.C.G.A. § 43-16-10.1 (b); see also Part 178 of Chapter I of Title 27 of the Code of Federal Regulations as it exists on July 1, 1988, regarding the format required under federal law.

[147] O.C.G.A. § 43-16-10.1 (c).

[148] O.C.G.A. § 43-16-10.1 (d).

# CHAPTER SIX

## Prohibited and Controlled Firearms and Weapons

Under the Georgia Firearms and Weapons Act, certain weapons and weapon devices are prohibited or controlled under Georgia state law.[149] Be mindful that weapons are prohibited and/or controlled under both state and federal law, and many of those federal law regulations are included at the end of this chapter.

### Possession of Sawed-Off Shotgun, Sawed-Off Rifle, Machine Gun, Dangerous Weapon, or Silencer Under State Law

No person shall have in his or her possession any sawed-off shotgun, sawed-off rifle, machine gun, dangerous weapon, or silencer, except as otherwise provided by law.[150]

Exceptions apply, naturally. This prohibition shall not apply to the following individuals:[151]

- a peace officer or other designated law enforcement professionals[152]
- a member of the National Guard, or the federal Armed Forces[153]
- those who have inoperative firearms[154]
- those who have registered the weapon under the National Firearms Act, 68A Stat. 725 (26 U.S.C. Sections 5841-5862)[155]
- security personnel of nuclear facilities[156]

---

[149]O.C.G.A. § 16-11-120.

[150]O.C.G.A. § 16-11-122; see also O.C.G.A. 16-11-124 for exceptions.

[151]O.C.G.A. § 16-11-124.

[152]O.C.G.A. § 16-11-124 (1).

[153]O.C.G.A. § 16-11-124 (2).

[154]O.C.G.A. § 16-11-124 (3).

[155]O.C.G.A. § 16-11-124 (4).

[156]O.C.G.A. § 16-11-124 (5).

Punishment for a violation of this prohibition is a five year prison sentence.[157]  The offense is committed when the offender <u>knowingly</u> has in his or her possession any of the prohibited items.[158]  Of course, the burden of proof, if charged with a violation of this prohibition, is on the defendant to show either he did not know he possessed the prohibited weapon, or an exception applies to allow him to possess the prohibited weapon.[159]

The following definitions apply to this prohibition.

"Dangerous weapon" means any weapon commonly known as a rocket launcher, bazooka, or recoilless rifle which fires explosive or nonexplosive rockets designed to injure or kill personnel or destroy heavy armor, or similar weapon used for such purpose.[160]  The term shall also mean a weapon commonly known as a "mortar" which fires high explosive from a metallic cylinder and which is commonly used by the armed forces as an antipersonnel weapon or similar weapon used for such purpose.[161]  The term also means a weapon commonly known as a "hand grenade" or other similar weapon which is designed to explode and injure personnel or similar weapon used for such purpose.[162]

"Machine gun" means any weapon which shoots or is designated to shoot, automatically, more than six shots, without manual reloading, by a single function of the trigger.[163]

"Person" means any individual, partnership, company, association, or corporation.[164]

---

[157]O.C.G.A. § 16-11-123.

[158]O.C.G.A. § 16-11-123.

[159]O.C.G.A. § 16-11-125.

[160]O.C.G.A. § 16-11-121 (1).

[161]O.C.G.A. § 16-11-121 (1).

[162]O.C.G.A. § 16-11-121 (1).

[163]O.C.G.A. § 16-11-121 (2).

[164]O.C.G.A. § 16-11-121 (3).

"Sawed-off rifle" means a weapon designed or redesigned, made or remade, and intended to be fired from the shoulder; and designed or redesigned, made or remade, to use the energy of the explosive in a fixed metallic cartridge to fire only a single projectile through a rifle bore for each single pull of the trigger; and which has a barrel or barrels of less than 16 inches in length or has an overall length of less than 26 inches.[165]

A "sawed-off shotgun" means a shotgun or any weapon made from a shotgun, whether by alteration, modification, or otherwise having one or more barrels less than 18 inches in length or if such weapon as modified has an overall length of 26 inches.[166]

"Shotgun" means a weapon designed or redesigned, made or remade, and intended to be fired from the shoulder; and designed or redesigned, and made or remade, to use the energy of the explosive in a fixed shotgun shell to fire through a small bore either a number of ball shot or a single projectile for each single pull of the trigger.[167]

Finally, a "silencer" means any device for silencing or diminishing the report of any portable weapon such as a rifle, carbine, pistol, revolver, machine gun, shotgun, fowling piece, or other device from which a shot, bullet, or projectile may be discharged by an explosive.[168]

<u>Considerations Regarding Measuring the Sawed-Off Weapon</u> - Where it is not a close question, great precision and scientific methodology in measurement of dimensions of weapons are not necessary to authorize a conviction for a sawed off weapon.[169] In fact, it may simply be measured by a yardstick, and such measurement is enough to uphold a conviction.[170]

---

[165]O.C.G.A. § 16-11-121 (4).

[166]O.C.G.A. § 16-11-121 (5).

[167]O.C.G.A. § 16-11-121 (6).

[168]O.C.G.A. § 16-11-121 (7).

[169]See *Thompson v. State*, (1994) 214 Ga.App. 889, 449 S.E.2d 364.

[170]See *Thompson v. State*, (1994) 214 Ga.App. 889, 449 S.E.2d 364.

### Possession of Sawed-Off Shotgun, Sawed-Off Rifle, Machine Gun, Dangerous Weapon, or Silencer Under Federal Law

Under federal law, what is known as a "sawed-off shotgun" under Georgia law is referred to as a "short-barreled shotgun," and federal law makes it unlawful for any person, other than one who is properly licensed, to transport in interstate commerce any short-barreled shotguns.[171]

Also under federal law, the measurement of a "short-barreled shotgun" is a shotgun having a barrel of less than 18 inches in length or an overall length of less than 26 inches in length.[172] Therefore, any shotgun under 18 inches in length is prohibited in Georgia, despite state law, without a license from the federal government.[173]

Under federal law, what is known as a "sawed-off rifle" under Georgia law, is referred to as a "short-barreled rifle," and federal law makes it unlawful for any person, other than one who is properly licensed, to transport in interstate commerce any short-barreled shotguns.[174]

A "short barreled rifle" under federal law is any rifle with a barrel of less than 18 inches and an overall length of less than 26 inches.[175]

### Zip Gun

A zip gun is a weapon or device that was not imported as a firearm by an importer licensed under federal law,[176] was not originally designed to be a firearm

---

[171] 18 U.S.C. § 922 (a)(4).

[172] 25 U.S.C. § 5845 (a)(1) and (2).

[173] Short-barreled shotguns are considered "Class 3" items under the National Firearms Act. While subject to certain restrictions under state and federal law, such may be legally possessed in Nevada under certain circumstances. For those interested in owning such items, please check with local authorities for requirements.

[174] 18 U.S.C. § 922 (a)(4).

[175] 25 U.S.C. § 5845 (a)(1) and (2).

[176] See 18 U.S.C. § 921 et seq.

by a manufacturer licensed under the same federal law, no tax was paid on the weapon or device, no exemption from the tax was granted,[177] and it is made or altered to expel a projectile by the force of an explosion or some other form of combustion.

### Class III Weapons

The State of Georgia does not impose any restrictions in addition to those imposed by federal law on "Class 3 Firearms."

---

[177]See Section 4181 and Subchapters F and G of 26 U.S.C. § 32.

# CHAPTER SEVEN

## Concealed Weapons License in Georgia

Of course, this is one of the most popular topics when discussing the gun laws of any state. Across this nation, concealed weapons license applications have skyrocketed, and that is likely to continue. As such, it is important to stay abreast of the most recent developments of any concealed carry laws in any state one might carry a weapon through.

This section includes the application process, as well as where one may lawfully carry with a concealed weapons license issued by the State of Georgia. This section is not exclusive, however, and one must read this entire book to be sure he has all the information he needs. And, it is always prudent to double-check any representations in this book or elsewhere regarding the latest information, as the laws may change without the license holder being aware.

### License to Carry Pistol or Revolver

Fortunately, the State of Georgia is a "shall issue" state. This means that if the applicant is able to satisfy certain criteria, he "shall" be issued a concealed weapons license. Unfortunately, the State of Georgia issues licenses only to Georgia residents.

Application for Weapons Carry License, Including Renewals - In Georgia, the judge of the probate court of each county, upon application under oath and upon a payment of a fee of $30, shall issue a weapons carry license or a renewal license.[178]

Applicant Must Be Georgia Resident - The applicant for a concealed weapons license must be a Georgia Resident.[179]

Armed Forces Exception to Georgia Residency Requirement - Licenses shall be issued to any person who is not a Georgia resident but who is on active duty with the United States Armed Forces but resides in a county within the State

---

[178]O.C.G.A. § 16-11-129 (a).

[179]O.C.G.A. § 16-11-129 (a).

of Georgia or on a military reservation within the State of Georgia at the time of application.[180]

Fee for Weapons Carry License - As stated above, the judge of the probate court charges a fee of $30.[181]

Term of Weapons Carry License - A Georgia weapons carry license is valid for a period of five years.[182]

Change of Residence - To move from one county to another county does not void or change the weapons carry license that has been granted.[183]

Application Forms For License or Renewal of License - Applicants shall submit the application for a weapons carry license or renewal license to the judge of the probate court in the county of residence on forms prescribed and furnished free of charge to persons wishing to apply for the license or renewal license.[184] Forms are designed to elicit information from the applicant that is relevant to his or her eligibility for a concealed weapons license, including citizenship.[185] Federal law prohibits a sheriff from requiring a Social Security Number as part of the information requested.

Forms are not to require data that is not pertinent or relevant, such as serial numbers, or other identification that is capable of being used as a *de facto* registration of firearms owned by the applicant.[186]

Application and license forms are to be furnished by the Department of Public Safety and are to be furnished to each judge of each probate court within the

---

[180]O.C.G.A. § 16-11-129 (a).

[181]O.C.G.A. § 16-11-129 (a).

[182]O.C.G.A. § 16-11-129 (a).

[183]O.C.G.A. § 16-11-129 (a).

[184]O.C.G.A. § 16-11-129 (a).

[185]O.C.G.A. § 16-11-129 (a).

[186]O.C.G.A. § 16-11-129 (a).

State of Georgia.[187]

Applicants Who Are Not United States Citizens - An applicant who is not a United States citizen shall provide sufficient personal identifying data, including, but without limitation, his or her place of birth, the United States issued alien or admission number as the Georgia Bureau of Investigation may prescribe by rule or regulation.[188] An applicant who is in nonimmigrant status is to provide proof of his or her qualifications for an exception to the federal firearm prohibition.[189]

## Licensing Exceptions - Applicants Who Will Be Denied A License

The State of Georgia has certain codified licensing exceptions to the "shall issue" licensing process. Any persons who are subject to these exceptions will be denied a Georgia issued concealed weapons license.

No weapons license will be issued to the following persons:[190]

- any person who is under 21 years of age[191]
- any person who is a convicted felon under the laws of the State of Georgia, any other state, federal law, or by laws of foreign nations, who has not been pardoned[192]
- any person against whom proceedings are pending for any felony[193]
- any person who is a fugitive from justice[194]
- any person who is prohibited from possessing or shipping a

---

[187]O.C.G.A. § 16-11-129 (a).

[188]O.C.G.A. § 16-11-129 (a).

[189]O.C.G.A. § 16-11-129 (a); see 18 U.S.C. § 922 (y) regarding the federal firearm prohibition.

[190]See O.C.G.A. § 16-11-129 (b) and (b)(2).

[191]O.C.G.A. § 16-11-129 (b)(2)(A).

[192]O.C.G.A. § 16-11-129 (b)(2)(B).

[193]O.C.G.A. § 16-11-129 (b)(2)(C).

[194]O.C.G.A. § 16-11-129 (b)(2)(D).

firearm in interstate commerce under federal law[195]

- any person who has been convicted of an offense arising out of
the unlawful manufacture or distribution of a controlled substance
or other drug;[196] although, if the first offender treatment without
adjudication of guilt for a conviction for this offense was entered,
and such sentence was successfully completed, and such person
has not had any other conviction since the completion of such
sentence for at least five years immediately preceding the date of
the application, he or she may be eligible for a weapons carry
license provided that no other licensing exception applies[197]
- any person who has had his or her weapons carry license revoked
under Georgia law[198]
- any person who has been convicted of pointing a gun or pistol at
another in violation of Georgia state law[199] who has not been free
of all restraint or supervision in connection to the crime and free
of any other conviction for at least five years immediately
preceding the date of application[200]
- any person who has been convicted of carrying a weapon without
a weapons carry license in violation of Georgia state law[201] who
has not been free of all restraint or supervision in connection to
the crime and free of any other conviction for at least five years
immediately preceding the date of application[202]
- any person who has been convicted of carrying a weapon or long

---

[195]O.C.G.A. § 16-11-129 (b)(2)(E); see also 18 U.S.C. § 922 (g) and (n).

[196]O.C.G.A. § 16-11-129 (b)(2)(F).

[197]O.C.G.A. § 16-11-129 (b)(3).

[198]O.C.G.A. § 16-11-129 (b)(2)(G).

[199]O.C.G.A. § 16-11-129 (b)(2)(H) and (b)(?)(H)(i); see also O.C.G.A. § 16-11-102.

[200]O.C.G.A. § 16-11-129 (b)(2)(H).

[201]O.C.G.A. § 16-11-129 (b)(2)(A) and (b)(2)(H)(ii); see also O.C.G.A. § 16-11-126.

[202]O.C.G.A. § 16-11-129 (b)(2)(H).

gun in an unauthorized location in violation of Georgia state law[203] who has not been free of all restraint or supervision in connection to the crime and free of any other conviction for at least five years immediately preceding the date of application[204]

-   any person who has been convicted of any misdemeanor involving the use or possession of a controlled substance who has not been free of all restraint or supervision in connection with the crime or free of a second conviction of any misdemeanor involving the use of a controlled substance[205]
-   any person who has been convicted of any misdemeanor involving the use or possession of a controlled substance who has not been free of all restraint or supervision in connection with the crime or free of any conviction under specific Georgia laws[206] for at least five years immediately preceding the date of application[207]
-   those who have been hospitalized as an inpatient in any mental hospital for at least five years preceding the date of application[208]
-   those who have been hospitalized as an inpatient in any alcohol or drug treatment center for at least five years preceding the date of application[209]

For the purposes of these exceptions, the following definitions apply.

"Controlled substance" means any drug, substance, or immediate precursor

---

[203]O.C.G.A. § 16-11-129 (b)(2)(A) and (b)(2)(H)(iii); see also O.C.G.A. § 16-11-127.

[204]O.C.G.A. § 16-11-129 (b)(2)(H).

[205]O.C.G.A. § 16-11-129 (b)(2)(I) and (b)(2)(I)(i); see also O.C.G.A. § 16-11-129 (b)(3).

[206]See O.C.G.A. § 16-11-129 (b)(2)(E) through (G).

[207]O.C.G.A. § 16-11-129 (b)(2)(I)(ii); see also O.C.G.A. § 16-11-129 (b)(3).

[208]O.C.G.A. § 16-11-129 (b)(2)(J).

[209]O.C.G.A. § 16-11-129 (b)(2)(J).

including in the definition of controlled substances under Georgia law.[210]

"Convicted" means a plea of guilty or a finding of guilt by a court of competent jurisdiction, or the acceptance of a plea of *nolo contendere*, irrespective of the pendency or availability of an appeal or an application for collateral relief.[211]

"Dangerous drug" means any drug defined under Georgia law as a dangerous drug.[212]

### Fingerprinting - Process and Fee

Following the completion of the application for a license or a renewal of a license, the judge of the probate court shall require the applicant to proceed to an appropriate law enforcement agency in the county with the completed application.[213] The law enforcement agency shall then capture the fingerprints of the applicant and will place the applicant's name on the blank license form.[214] The law enforcement agency shall place the fingerprint on a blank license form which has been furnished by the judge of the probate court.[215] The law enforcement agency may charge a fee of $5 from the applicant for its services in connection with the application.[216]

Fingerprints are to be in such form and of such quality as prescribed by the Georgia Crime Information Center and under standards adopted by the Federal Bureau of Investigation.[217] The Georgia Bureau of Investigation, which is authorized

---

[210]O.C.G.A. § 16-11-129 (b)(1) and (b)(1)(A); see also O.C.G.A. § 16-13-21 (4).

[211]O.C.G.A. § 16-11-129 (b)(1)(B).

[212]See O.C.G.A. § 16-12-71 regarding definition of "dangerous drug."

[213]O.C.G.A. § 16-11-129 (c).

[214]O.C.G.A. § 16-11-129 (c).

[215]O.C.G.A. § 16-11-129 (c).

[216]O.C.G.A. § 16-11-129 (c).

[217]O.C.G.A. § 16-11-129 (d)(1).

to process the fingerprints and provide a report,[218] may charge a fee as necessary to cover the costs of the records search.[219]

### Investigation of Applicant

For both the weapons carry license applications and the requests for license renewals, the judge of the probate court, within 5 days of receipt of the application or request, is to direct the law enforcement agency to request a fingerprint based criminal history records check from the Georgia Crime Information Center and Federal Bureau of Investigation for the purposes of determining the suitability of the applicant for a concealed weapons license.[220] The law enforcement agency is to turn the report over to the judge once received.[221]

Within the same time frame, that being 5 days, the probate judge is to direct the law enforcement agency to conduct a background check using the Federal Bureau's National Instant Criminal Background Check System (NICS) and return an appropriate report to the judge.[222]

Investigation of Alien or Non-Immigrant Status Individual - When a person who is not a United States citizen applies for a weapons carry license or a license renewal, the probate judge will also direct the law enforcement agency to conduct a search of the records maintained by the United States Bureau of Immigration and Customs Enforcement and to return an appropriate report to the judge.[223]

Duration of Investigation - The law enforcement agency has 30 days to notify the judge, by telephone and in writing, of any findings relating to the applicant which may bear on his or her eligibility for a weapons carry license or renewal of a

---

[218]See O.C.G.A. § 35-3-33.

[219]O.C.G.A. § 16-11-129 (d)(1).

[220]O.C.G.A. § 16-11-129 (d)(1).

[221]O.C.G.A. § 16-11-129 (d)(1).

[222]O.C.G.A. § 16-11-129 (d)(2).

[223]O.C.G.A. § 16-11-129 (d)(3).

license.[224]  However, if no derogatory information was found, a report is not required.[225]

### Issuance or Denial of License

No later than 10 days after the judge of the probate court receives the report from the law enforcement agency concerning the suitability of the applicant for a concealed weapons license, the judge shall issue the license, unless facts establishing ineligibility have been reported or unless the judge otherwise determines that the applicant has either not met all of the qualifications, is not of good moral character, or has failed to comply with any of the requirements under Georgia law.[226]

### Revocation of License and Possession of Revoked License

If, at any time during the time the license is valid, the probate judge in the county that issued the license learns or has found out that the licensee is not eligible to retain the license, the judge may, after notice and hearing, revoke the license of the person upon a finding that such person is no longer eligible to possess a carry license because of circumstances that exist that would have prevented that person from being issued a license, including falsification of the application, mental incompetency, or chronic alcohol or narcotic use.[227]

It is also unlawful for any person to possess a revoked license, and any person found in possession of such is guilty of a misdemeanor.[228]

### Concealed Weapons Holder Must Carry License

Any license holder must have in his or her possession the valid license whenever he or she is carrying a weapon under the authority granted under the law, and any failure to do so will be *prima facie* evidence of a violation of Georgia law

---

[224]O.C.G.A. § 16-11-129 (d)(4).

[225]O.C.G.A. § 16-11-129 (d)(4).

[226]O.C.G.A. § 16-11-129 (d)(4).

[227]O.C.G.A. § 16-11-129 (e).

[228]O.C.G.A. § 16-11-129 (e).

regarding unlawful carry of concealed weapons.[229]

## Loss of or Damage to License

Loss of any concealed weapons license issued under Georgia law, or damage to the same in any manner which shall render it illegible shall be reported to the probate judge in the county in which it was issued within 48 hours of the time loss or damage became known to the license holder.[230] The judge will issue another license and will take possession of and destroy the old license, or, if the license had been lost, the judge will issue a cancellation order and notify by telephone and writing each of the law enforcement agencies whose records were checked before the issuance of the original license.[231] Another fee of $30 will be charged by the judge for replacement.[232]

## Weapons Carry License Format and Specifications

Weapons carry licenses issued as prescribed by Georgia law shall be printed on durable but lightweight card stock which will be laminated in plastic to improve its wearing qualities and to inhibit alterations.[233] The card is to measure 3.25 inches long and 2.25 inches wide.[234]

Each card is to bear a serial number from within the county of issuance and shall bear the full name, residential address, birth date, weight, height, color of eyes, and sex of the licensee.[235] The license is also to show the date of issuance, the expiration date, and the probate court in which the license was issued, along with

---

[229]O.C.G.A. § 16-11-129 (e); see also O.C.G.A. § 16-11-126 regarding concealed carry offenses.

[230]O.C.G.A. § 16-11-129 (e).

[231]O.C.G.A. § 16-11-129 (e).

[232]O.C.G.A. § 16-12-129 (e).

[233]O.C.G.A. § 16-12-129 (f)(1).

[234]O.C.G.A. § 16-12-129 (f)(1).

[235]O.C.G.A. § 16-12-129 (f)(1).

the licensee's signature and either an original or facsimile signature by the judge.[236] There will also be on the license the seal of the court of issuance.[237] Finally, on all licenses issued prior to December 31, 2011, there will also be on the license a fingerprint of the licensee's right index finger.[238]

On or after January 1, 2012, all newly issued or renewal weapons carry licenses will incorporate overt and covert security features which shall be blended with the personal data printed on the license to form a significant barrier to imitation, replication, and duplication.[239] Also, at that time, the license shall be uniform as issued across the State of Georgia.[240]

### Licenses for Former Law Enforcement Officers

Except as otherwise provided by law,[241] any person who has served as a law enforcement officer for at least 10 of the 12 years immediately preceding the retirement of such person as a law enforcement officer shall be entitled to be issued a weapons carry license without the payment of any of the fees as required by anyone else.[242] Aside from the inapplicability of the fees, the rest of the provisions regarding licenses will apply to former law enforcement officers.[243]

"Law enforcement officer," as used regarding the concealed carry law, means any peace officer who is employed by the federal or State of Georgia government, or any political subdivision thereof and who is required by the terms of his or her employment, whether by election or by appointment, to give his or her

---

[236]O.C.G.A. § 16-12-129 (f)(1).

[237]O.C.G.A. § 16-12-129 (f)(1).

[238]O.C.G.A. § 16-12-129 (f)(1).

[239]O.C.G.A. § 16-12-129 (f)(2)(A); see the same code section for very a very detailed discussion regarding the new technology being used on future concealed weapons licenses.

[240]O.C.G.A. § 16-11-126 (f)(2)(B).

[241]See O.C.G.A. § 16-11-130.

[242]O.C.G.A. § 16-11-129 (h).

[243]O.C.G.A. § 16-11-129 (h).

full time to the preservation of public order or the protection of life and property, or the prevention of crime.[244] This includes conservation rangers.[245]

### Licenses for Employees of Private Detective and Private Security Businesses

Any person desiring to carry a firearm as a private detective or private security officer must apply for and obtain a license that is issued specifically for such employees, as a standard Georgia concealed weapons license may not be used for such endeavors.[246]

May Issue - The State of Georgia **"may"** issue (notice, this is not "shall" issue) grant a license to carry a pistol, revolver, or other firearm to any person who is at least 21 years of age and who is licensed or registered in accordance with Georgia law and who meets the qualifications and training requirements set forth under Georgia law as they pertain to private detective and private security guard businesses.[247]

Limitations on Type and Caliber of Firearm - There may be limits on type and caliber of such weapons, however, as imposed by the Department of Public Safety.[248]

Competency Certification - Also, no license will be issued or renewed until the applicant has presented proof that he is proficient in the use of firearms.[249] Periodic recertification may be required, and licenses may not be renewed if there is a failure to comply with the recertification.[250]

---

[244]O.C.G.A. § 16-11-129 (h).

[245]O.C.G.A. § 16-11-129 (h).

[246]O.C.G.A. § 43-38-10 (c).

[247]O.C.G.A. § 43-38-10 (a).

[248]O.C.G.A. § 43-38-10 (a).

[249]O.C.G.A. § 43-38-10 (b).

[250]O.C.G.A. § 43-38-10 (b).

Carry Openly and Fully Exposed, and Limits on Where Licensee May Carry Firearm - Those with a license issued for the purpose of working as a private detective or a security guard are authorized to carry the firearm in an open and fully exposed manner, but the carry of the firearm is specifically limited to the time the licensee is on duty or en route directly to and from his post or place of employment.[251] The licensee may not make any "stopover" while traveling to or from his post or place of employment.[252]

Carry Privileges - Where Licensee May Carry - A person who holds a specific private detective or private security guard license has certain carry privileges, and basically, he or she may carry anywhere a law enforcement officer may carry their duty weapon.[253]

Denial or Refusal to Issue License - A license may be denied to any applicant who fails to provide any required information or supporting documentation as required by law.[254] Also, the license may not be renewed upon a failure to comply with any weapons proficiency recertification requirements as prescribed under Georgia law.[255]

Summary Suspension of License - A license may be summarily suspended when revocation proceedings are pending, or upon any other sanction, upon a finding that the public health, safety, or welfare imperatively requires such emergency action.[256]

## Temporary Renewal Licenses

Any person who holds a weapons carry license under Georgia state law may, at the time he or she applies for a renewal of the license, also apply for a

---

[251] O.C.G.A. § 43-38-10 (d).

[252] O.C.G.A. § 43-38-10 (d).

[253] See O.C.G.A. § 43-38-10 (f); see also O.C.G.A. §§ 16-11-126, 16-11-127, and 16-11-129 regarding law enforcement exceptions.

[254] O.C.G.A. § 43-38-10 (g).

[255] O.C.G.A. § 43-38-10 (g).

[256] O.C.G.A. § 43-38-10 (h).

temporary renewal license if less than 90 days remain before the expiration of the current license or if the previous license has expired within the last 30 days.[257]  Of course, one is only eligible for the temporary renewal license if the probate judge has no facts or other information which would otherwise make the applicant ineligible for a five-year renewal license.[258]  This temporary renewal license is a "shall issue" license, just as the regular five-year license.[259]

The temporary renewal license shall be in the form of a paper receipt indicating the date on which the court received the renewal application and shall bear the name, address, sex, age, and race of the applicant, and shall be good for only 90 days from the date of issuance.[260]

During the period of validity of the temporary renewal license, if carried on or about the holder's person, together with the holder's previous license, it shall be valid in the same manner and for the same purposes as the five-year license.[261]

The fee for the renewal license is $1, paid to the probate court.[262]  Yes, that is correct - $1 - as in four quarters.

Temporary renewal licenses may be revoked the same as a regular license.[263]

### Failure to Receive License

If for any reason an eligible applicant fails to receive a license, temporary license, or renewal license within the time period required by Georgia law, and the application or request was properly filed, the applicant may bring an action in

---

[257] O.C.G.A. § 16-11-129 (i)(1).

[258] O.C.G.A. § 16-11-129 (i)(2).

[259] O.C.G.A. § 16-11-129 (i)(2).

[260] O.C.G.A. § 16-11-129 (i)(3).

[261] O.C.G.A. § 16-11-129 (i)(4).

[262] O.C.G.A. § 16-11-129 (i)(5).

[263] O.C.G.A. § 16-11-129 (i)(6).

mandamus or other legal proceeding in order to obtain the license, temporary license, or renewal license, and if successful in the matter, the applicant is entitled to recover his or her costs in such action, including any reasonable attorney's fees.[264]

## Visitors to Georgia Who Have Out-of-State Concealed Carry License

Any person licensed to carry a handgun or weapon in any other state whose laws recognize and give effect to a licensed issued pursuant to Georgia law is authorized to carry a weapon in the State of Georgia.[265] Visitors carrying within the State of Georgia must adhere to Georgia state law.[266]

However, for those of you who are Georgia residents, you may not carry within the State of Georgia based solely upon a concealed license from another state - you must have a Georgia concealed weapons license.[267] Georgia licensing authorities have no desire to see a Georgia resident who was denied a Georgia weapons license to acquire a license in another state that is recognized in Georgia, thereby going around the decision of Georgia authorities. Georgia residents must possess Georgia weapons license to lawfully carry within the State of Georgia.

## Concealed Carry While Hunting, Fishing, or Sport Shooting

A very nice exception exists to the requirement to have a concealed weapons license while carrying. Any person with a valid hunting or valid fishing license on his or her person, or any person who is not required to possess a hunting or fishing license while hunting or fishing, who is engaged in legal hunting, fishing, or sport shooting when the person has the permission of the owner of the land on which the activities are being conducted, may have or carry on his or her person a handgun or long gun without a valid weapons carry license.[268]

---

[264]O.C.G.A. § 16-11-129 (j).

[265]O.C.G.A. § 16-11-126 (e).

[266]O.C.G.A. § 16-11-126 (e).

[267]O.C.G.A. § 16-11-126 (e).

[268]O.C.G.A. § 16-11-126 (f).

The fee for a weapons carry license due to the probate court is $30.00.[269] Of course, this fee is exclusive of any fees charged by other agencies for the examination of criminal records and mental health records.[270]

## Concealed Carry for Licensees and Certain Specific Places

Those with concealed carry license must be well aware of where they may or may not carry. This section is of particular importance and must be understood. Also, please realize that just because Georgia permits concealed weapons license holders to enter certain state properties, other states may have different laws regarding the same places. This is not an area of the law that any concealed weapons license holder can ignore, as the consequences of a violation can be quite severe.

Schools - A person who is licensed in accordance with Georgia law may lawfully carry the weapon while dropping off or picking up a student at a school building, school function, or school property, or on a bus or transportation furnished by the school.[271] The license holder may also leave his firearm legally within a vehicle when such vehicle is parked at a school property or is in transit through a designated school zone.[272]

State. County, or Local Parks - A license holder may carry in state parks.[273] At one time, the County of Coweta had banned firearms within county parks. However, Georgia courts held that the Georgia firearm preemption law,[274] which prohibits local government entities from restricting in any fashion the carry or transport of firearms, preempts the county's ban on the carry of firearms within its

---

[269]O.C.G.A. § 15-9-60 (k)(12).

[270]O.C.G.A. § 15-9-60 (k)(12)

[271]O.C.G.A. § 116-11-127.1 (c)(7).

[272]O.C.G.A. § 116-11-127.1 (c)(7).

[273]O.C.G.A. § 16-11-126 (g).

[274]See O.C.G.A. § 16-11-173.

park property.[275]

State Historic Sites - A license holder may carry in state historic sites.[276]

State Forests - A license holder may carry in state forests.[277]

State Recreational Areas - A license holder may carry in state recreational areas.[278]

Rest Areas - A license holder may carry in a rest area.[279]

Public Transportation - A license holder may ride on public transportation and enter public transportation buildings and public transportation property.[280]

National Parks and National Wildlife Refuges - A license holder may carry in a National Park and a National Wildlife Refuge. On February 10, 2010, what is often referred to as "National Park Carry" went into effect. Basically, if a license holder carries a permit or license that is recognized in the state in which the National Park or wildlife refuge is located, that license holder may carry on that property.

Be careful, however. Most buildings in a National Forest, such as a ranger station or a visitor center, would be considered a federal building, and any open or concealed carry would be prohibited.

National Forests - While many states have laws on the books regarding lawful concealed carry in national forests, Georgia does not. If a license holder carries a permit or license that is recognized in the State of Georgia, he may lawfully

---

[275]See *GeorgiaCarry.Org, Inc., v. Coweta County*, (2007) 288 Ga.App. 748, 655 S.E.2d 346.

[276]O.C.G.A. § 16-11-126 (g).

[277]O.C.G.A. § 16-11-126 (g).

[278]O.C.G.A. § 16-11-126 (g).

[279]O.C.G.A. § 16-11-126 (g).

[280]O.C.G.A. § 16-11-126 (g).

carry concealed in a National Forest within the State of Georgia.

Be careful, however. Most buildings in a National Forest, such as a ranger station or a visitor center, would be considered a federal building, and any open or concealed carry would be prohibited.

Wildlife Management Area - A license holder may carry in a wildlife management area.[281] Be sure to read about prohibited acts in wildlife management areas, as discussed in the chapter relating to weapons related offenses.

Restaurants and Bars that Serve Alcohol - In Georgia, a license holder may carry concealed in a restaurant or bar that serves alcohol. The restaurant or bar owner must allow concealed carry, however, or the carry onto the property results in a criminal trespass.[282]

Airports - There are no Georgia laws on the books that prohibit a license holder from carrying a concealed handgun at an airport outside of the secure areas. However, under federal law, one may not carry concealed while on airport property. Oftentimes, there is a lot of confusion as to whether that means inside the sensitive areas only, or also outside the sensitive areas, such as the "loop" that we all take around and around until we see the passengers we are picking up. Some states allow concealed weapons to be possessed by license holders in any area that is not sensitive, meaning, an area where you must pass through a security checkpoint to get there. To take any firearm or weapon anywhere on airport property, inside or outside the secure area, always carries great risk of entanglements with law enforcement. Many airports have checkpoints on the road into the airport where random searches are conducted. Licensed or not, if you have a weapon, it is going to be a problem. Do yourself a favor - leave the firearms and weapons at home when you go to the airport.

Polling Places - A concealed weapons license holder may not carry his or her weapon within 150 feet of any polling place.[283] This prohibition does not apply to those concealed weapons license holder keeping their firearm in their locked

---

[281]O.C.G.A. § 16-11-126 (g).

[282]O.C.G.A. § 16-11-127 (b)(6).

[283]O.C.G.A. § 16-11-127 (b)(8).

motor vehicle in a parking lot or garage at or near the polling place.[284]

State Government Buildings - A concealed weapons license holder may not carry his or her weapon into state government buildings.[285]  However, the license holder may, where it is available, carry into the state government building if he notifies, upon arrival, any security personnel of the presence of the weapon and follows their direction regarding removal, securing, storing, or temporarily surrendering the weapon.  Also, this prohibition does not apply to those concealed weapons license holders keeping their firearms in their locked motor vehicle in a parking lot or garage at or near the state government building.[286]

Courthouse - A concealed weapons license holder may not carry his or her weapon into a state courthouse.[287]  However, the license holder may, where it is available, carry into the courthouse if he notifies, upon arrival, any security personnel of the presence of the weapon and follows their direction regarding removal, securing, storing, or temporarily surrendering the weapon.  Also, this prohibition does not apply to those concealed weapons license holders keeping their firearm in their locked motor vehicles in a parking lot or garage at or near the courthouse.[288]

State Capitol Building - It is unlawful for any person, other than specifically exempt individuals,[289] to enter, occupy, or remain within the state capitol building or any building that houses committee offices, committee rooms, or offices of members, officials, or employees of the General Assembly, or either house thereof, while in possession of any firearm, knife,[290] explosive or incendiary device or compound, bludgeon, knuckles, whether made from metal, thermoplastic, wood, or

---

[284]O.C.G.A. § 16-11-127 (d)(3).

[285]O.C.G.A. § 16-11-127 (b) and (b)(1).

[286]O.C.G.A. § 16-11-127 (d)(3).

[287]O.C.G.A. § 16-11-127 (b) and (b)(2).

[288]O.C.G.A. § 16-11-127 (d)(3).

[289]See O.C.G.A. §§ 16-11-126 through 16-11-127.2 for exempt individuals, which includes those with a concealed weapons license.

[290]As knives are defined in O.C.G.A. § 16-11-125.1.

other similar material, or any other dangerous or deadly weapon, instrument, or device.[291]

Jail or Prison - A concealed weapons license holder may not carry his or her weapon into a jail or prison.[292] However, the license holder may, where it is available, carry into the jail or prison if he notifies, upon arrival, any security personnel of the presence of the weapon and follows their direction regarding removal, securing, storing, or temporarily surrendering the weapon. Also, this prohibition does not apply to those concealed weapons license holders keeping their firearm in their locked motor vehicles in a parking lot or garage at or near the jail or prison.[293]

Churches, and Other Places of Worship - A concealed weapons license holder may not carry his or her weapon into a church or place of worship.[294] Also, this prohibition does not apply to those concealed weapons license holder keeping their firearms in their locked motor vehicles in a parking lot or garage at or near the church or other place of worship.[295]

Federal Buildings - Those with a concealed weapons license are still prohibited from carrying in federal buildings. This includes federal courthouses, as well as federal buildings such as the post office.

Place of Employment - Absent certain circumstances, those with a concealed weapons license may store their firearm in their locked motor vehicle on their employer's property, whether or not the employer and the property is public or private, and no conditions of employment may be based upon allowing the employer to search the employee's car.[296] However, very specific exceptions, circumstances, and other considerations, such as employer immunity, are also

---

[291]O.C.G.A. § 16-11-34.1 (b).

[292]O.C.G.A. § 16-11-127 (b) and (b)(3).

[293]O.C.G.A. § 16-11-127 (d)(3).

[294]O.C.G.A. § 16-11-127 (b) and (b)(4).

[295]O.C.G.A. § 16-11-127 (d)(3).

[296]O.C.G.A. § 16-11-135.

provided in the Georgia Code.[297]

Anywhere Else in the State - Except in regards to school safety zones and buildings in this zones, and at school functions,[298] a person who has a concealed weapons license[299] is authorized to carry a weapon in every location in this state that is not otherwise expressly prohibited under the law, provided that private property owners or persons in legal control of property through a lease, rental agreement, licensing agreement, contract, or any other agreement to control access to such property, shall have the right to forbid possession of a weapon or long gun on their property, except for employers as provided under Georgia law.[300]

## Alteration or Counterfeiting Concealed Weapons Licenses

A person who deliberately alters or counterfeits a weapons carry license or who possesses an altered or counterfeit weapons carry license with the intent to misrepresent any information contained on the license is guilty of a felony and is subject to prison time of one to five years.[301]

## Transport or Carry of a Pistol Without a License

This information is just too important. As such, it is found in multiple places within this book.

As stated above, one must have a license to carry a handgun (pistol or revolver), openly or concealed, anywhere except within your home, on private property within your control, your place of business if you own your own business, or within your motor vehicle.

Of course, there is an exception, as discussed elsewhere in this book, regarding those involved in lawful licensed fishing and hunting, so long as they have

---

[297]See O.C.G.A. § 16-11-135.

[298]See O.C.G.A. § 16-11-127.1.

[299]Pursuant to O.C.G.A. § 16-11-126.

[300]O.C.G.A. § 16-11-127 (c).

[301]O.C.G.A. § 16-11-129 (g); see also O.C.G.A. § 16-11-135 regarding employees rights to possess weapons.

the property owner's permission and the handgun, whenever loaded, is carried open and in a fully exposed manner.

## Transport or Carry of a Rifle or Shotgun Without a License

Again, this information is very important and therefore is repeated several times throughout this book.

The law regarding the lawful carry of a handgun <u>does not apply</u> to rifles and shotguns. A person may lawfully carry a rifle or shotgun openly in the State of Georgia, but not concealed.

## Reciprocity

In some instances, the Attorney General for the State of Georgia may enter into reciprocity agreements with other states regarding concealed carry licenses. When this happens, an agreement is made that some other state will recognize concealed weapons licenses issued by the State of Georgia, and the State of Georgia will recognize that other state's concealed weapons licenses.

As such, the following states recognize the Georgia concealed weapons license:

| | | | |
|---|---|---|---|
| Alabama | Alaska | Arizona | Arkansas |
| Colorado | Florida | Idaho | Indiana |
| Kentucky | Louisiana | Michigan | Mississippi |
| Montana | New Hampshire | North Carolina | North Dakota |
| Oklahoma | Pennsylvania | South Dakota | Tennessee |
| Texas | Utah | Vermont | Wyoming |

Also, he State of Georgia recognizes the following licenses issued by other states:

| | | | |
|---|---|---|---|
| Alabama | Alaska | Arizona* | Arkansas |

| | | | |
|---|---|---|---|
| Colorado | Florida* | Idaho* | Indiana* |
| Kentucky | Louisiana | Michigan | Mississippi |
| Missouri | Montana | New Hampshire* | North Carolina |
| North Dakota* | Oklahoma | Pennsylvania* | South Dakota |
| Tennessee | Texas* | Utah* | Wyoming |

A "*" next to the state name means that the State of Georgia recognizes both the resident issued, as well as the non-resident issued, concealed carry permit.

The State of Georgia does not recognize the following carry permits:

| | | | |
|---|---|---|---|
| California | Connecticut | District of Columbia | Delaware |
| Hawaii | Iowa | Kansas | Maine |
| Maryland | Minnesota | Massachusetts | Nebraska |
| Nevada | New Jersey | New Mexico | New York |
| Ohio | Oregon | Rhode Island | South Carolina |
| Vermont | Virginia | Washington | West Virginia |

Neither Illinois, nor Wisconsin, recognize any other state permit in the nation, as well as the District of Columbia permits. In fact, these two states refuse to allow their own citizens the ability to acquire a concealed weapons permit. Both states simply refuse to issue permits.

Be sure to observe the state law in whichever state you travel, as that state's laws govern. Of course, federal law applies nationwide.

# CHAPTER EIGHT

## Traveling with Firearms or Weapons in Georgia and Prohibited Places

In every state in the nation, for every gun owner, one of the most important considerations is how to travel about lawfully with a firearm or other controlled weapons. We all need to know exactly which places firearms and other weapons are prohibited or tightly controlled. Indeed, more people find themselves in trouble with the law from situations involving their travels with a weapon than any other firearm or weapon situation. A simple traffic accident can put a chain of events in place where the contents of an individual's car come under the scrutiny of law enforcement. Or simply strolling unwittingly onto a "school zone" can present problems.

Obviously, being aware of and observing state and federal law regarding travel with firearms and other weapons is of paramount concern to any reader of this book. Please read this information carefully and, if time has passed, be sure to double-check the author's website as well as other sources for information on the current laws, just to be sure.

### Transport or Carry of a Pistol Without a License

This information is just too important. As such, it is found in multiple places within this book.

As stated above, one must have a license to carry a handgun (pistol or revolver), openly or concealed, anywhere except within your home, on private property within your control, your place of business if you own your own business, or within your motor vehicle.

Of course, there is an exception, as discussed elsewhere in this book, regarding those involved in lawful licensed fishing and hunting, so long as they have the property owner's permission and the handgun, whenever loaded, is carried open and in a fully exposed manner.

### Transport or Carry of a Rifle or Shotgun Without a License

Again, this information is very important, and is repeated several times throughout this book.

The law regarding the lawful carry of a handgun <u>does not apply</u> to rifles and shotguns. A person may lawfully carry a rifle or shotgun openly in the State of Georgia, but not concealed.

### Offense of Carrying a Weapon Without a License

A person commits the offense of carrying a weapon without a license when he or she carries a weapon without a valid weapons carry license unless he or she meets one of the specific enumerated exceptions to having the license as provided by Georgia law.[302]

For a first offense conviction, the person is guilty of a misdemeanor, but for a second or any subsequent offense within five years, as measured from the dates of the previous arrests for which convictions were obtained to the date of the current arrest for which a conviction is obtained, the offender is guilty of a felony and is subject to imprisonment for not less than two years and not more than five years.[303]

For the purpose of these prohibitions, the following definitions apply.[304]

"Knife" means a cutting instrument designed for the purpose of offense and defense consisting of a blade that is greater than five inches in length which is fastened to a handle.[305]

"Weapon" means a knife or handgun.[306]

---

[302]O.C.G.A. § 16-11-126 (h)(1) and (h)(2); see also O.C.G.A. 16-11-126 in general regarding exceptions.

[303]O.C.G.A. § 16-11-126 (i)(1) and (i)(2).

[304]See O.C.G.A. § 16-11-125.1.

[305]O.C.G.A. § 16-11-125.1 (2).

[306]O.C.G.A. § 16-11-125.1 (5).

## Carrying a Handgun or Long Gun, Openly or Concealed, in Certain Places

The general rule regarding the carry of a handgun or a long gun is that any person who is not prohibited by law from possessing a handgun or long gun may have or carry on his or her person a handgun or long gun on his or her property or inside his or her home, motor vehicle, or place of business <u>without</u> a valid weapons carry license.[307] However, when traveling in a motor vehicle, the firearm must be completely in the open if it is loaded. Otherwise, the offense of carrying a concealed weapon has occurred.

## Travel with Long Gun

Also, regarding open carry of a long gun, any person who is not prohibited by law from possessing a handgun or long gun may have or carry on his or her person a long gun without a valid weapons carry license, provided that if the long gun is loaded, it shall be carried only in an open and fully exposed manner.[308] This means that if it is unloaded, it need not be carried in an open and fully exposed manner.

A "long gun" means a firearm with a barrel of at least 18 inches and an overall length of at least 26 inches designed or made and intended to be fired from the shoulder and designed or made to use the energy of the explosive in a fixed[309] shotgun shell to fire through a smooth bore either a number of ball shot or a single projectile for each single pull of the trigger or from which any shot, bullet, or other missile can be discharged;[310] or a metallic cartridge to fire only a single projectile through a rifle bore for each single pull of the trigger;[311] provided, however, that the term "long gun" shall not include a gun which discharges a single shot of .46 centimeters or less in diameter.[312]

---

[307]O.C.G.A. § 16-11-126 (a).

[308]O.C.G.A. § 16-11-126 (b).

[309]O.C.G.A. § 16-11-125.1 (4).

[310]O.C.G.A. § 16-11-125.1 (4)(A).

[311]O.C.G.A. § 16-11-125.1 (4)(B).

[312]O.C.G.A. § 16-11-125.1 (4).

## Travel with Handgun

Regarding handguns, any person who is not prohibited by law from possessing a handgun or long gun may have or carry any handgun provided that it is enclosed in a case and is unloaded.[313]

Any person who is not prohibited by law from possessing a handgun or long gun who is <u>eligible</u> for a weapons carry license may transport a handgun or long gun in any private passenger motor vehicle.[314]

Be cautious, however, because private property owners or persons in legal control of property through a lease, rental agreement, licensing agreement, contract, or any other agreement to control access to such property has the right to forbid possession of a weapon or long gun on their property, except as otherwise is provided by law.[315]

"Handgun" means a firearm of any description, loaded or unloaded, from which any shot, bullet, or other missile can be discharged by an action of an explosive where the length of barrel, not including any revolving, detachable, or magazine breech, does not exceed 12 inches, provided, however, that the term "handgun" shall not include a gun which discharges a single shot of .46 centimeters or less in diameter.[316]

## Rules and Regulations Regarding State Parks, Historic Sites, and Recreational Areas

In the State of Georgia, the Board of Natural Resources is the entity authorized to adopt and promulgate rules and regulations relating to the use or occupancy of state parks, historic sites, and recreational areas, as well as to regulate for the health, safety, and welfare of persons using these areas, so long as none of the Board's regulations repeal, diminish, or supersede the authority of the

---

[313]O.C.G.A. § 16-11-126 (c).

[314]O.C.G.A. § 16-11-126 (d).

[315]O.C.G.A. § 16-11-126 (d); see also O.C.G.A. § 16-11-135 regarding prohibitions on employers dictating carry policies to their employees.

[316]O.C.G.A. § 16-11-125.1 (1).

Department of Community Health regarding its rules and regulations for the protection of the public health.[317]

Despite this, the General Assembly has codified some laws regarding state parks, historic sites, and state recreational areas. Under Georgia law in regards to this area of law, a "park, historic site, or recreational area" is a park, historic site, or recreational area that is operated by or for and is under the custody and control of the Department of Natural Resources.[318]

## Unlawful Activities in State Parks, Historic Sites, and Recreational Areas

There are a few activities that are generally unlawful in state parks, historic sites, and recreational areas. These unlawful activities are not special to Georgia, as many other states have similar laws on the books.

Unlawful Hunting Activities - It is unlawful to hunt, trap, or otherwise pursue or catch any wildlife in any park, historic site, or recreational area, unless such activity involves the use of bows and arrows, primitive weapons, rifles, or shotguns, and has been approved by prior written permission of the commissioner of natural resources or the commissioner's authorized representative.[319] A violation of this prohibition is a criminal trespass and subjects the offender to a fine of up to $1000.[320]

Shooting Into Park from Outside Boundary - It is unlawful to shoot into a park, historic site, or recreational area from beyond the boundaries of such park, historic site, or recreational area.[321] A violation of this prohibition is a criminal trespass and subjects the offender to a fine of up to $1000.[322]

Possession of Weapons - It is unlawful for any person to use or possess in

---

[317]O.C.G.A. § 12-3-9 (a), (a)(1), and (a)(2).

[318]O.C.G.A. § 12-3-10 (a).

[319]O.C.G.A. § 12-3-10 (l).

[320]O.C.G.A. § 12-3-10 (r); see also O.C.G.A. § 12-3-11.

[321]O.C.G.A. § 12-3-10 (l).

[322]O.C.G.A. § 12-3-10 (r); see also O.C.G.A. § 12-3-11.

any park, historic site, or recreational area any handgun without a valid weapons carry license.[323] A violation of this prohibition is a criminal trespass and subjects the offender to a fine of up to $1000.[324]

Other Recreational Weapons - It is unlawful for any person to use or possess in any park, historic site, or recreational area bows and arrows, spring guns, air rifles, slingshots, or any other devices which discharge projectiles by any means, unless the device is unloaded and stored so as not to be readily accessible or unless such use had prior approval.[325] A violation of this prohibition is a criminal trespass and subjects the offender to a fine of up to $1000.[326]

### Weapons in School Safety Zones, School Buildings, Grounds, or at School Functions

Under Georgia law, a "school safety zone" means in or on any real property owned by or leased to any public or private elementary school, secondary school, or school board and used for elementary or secondary education and in or on any public or private technical school, vocation school, college, university, or institution of postsecondary education.[327] Some school zones may be clearly marked, but school boards are not required to post such signs.[328]

For the purposes of the laws regarding firearms and weapons on school safety zones, in school buildings, on school grounds, or at school functions, a "weapon" means and includes any pistol, revolver, or any weapon designed or intended to propel a missile of any kind, or any dirk, bowie knife, switchblade knife, ballistic knife, any other knife having a blade of two or more inches, straight-edge razor, razor blade, spring stick, knuckles, whether made from metal, thermoplastic, wood, or other similar material, blackjack, any bat, club, or other bludgeon-type weapon, or any flailing instrument consisting of two or more rigid parts connected

---

[323]O.C.G.A. § 12-3-10 (o)(3).

[324]O.C.G.A. § 12-3-10 (r); see also O.C.G.A. § 12-3-11.

[325]O.C.G.A. § 12-3-10 (o)(4).

[326]O.C.G.A. § 12-3-10 (r); see also O.C.G.A. § 12-3-11.

[327]O.C.G.A. § 16-11-127.1 (a) and (a)(1).

[328]O.C.G.A. § 16-11-127.1 (g).

in a manner as to allow them to swing freely, which may be known as a nun chahka, nunchaku, shuriken, or fighting chain, or any disc, of whatever configuration, having at least two points or pointed blades which is designed to be thrown or propelled and which may be known as a throwing star or oriental dart, or any weapon of the like kind, and any stun gun or taser as defined by Georgia law.[329]

The definition of "weapon" does not include baseball bats, hockey sticks, or other sports equipment commonly possessed by competitors for legitimate athletic purposes,[330] to firearms or other weapons used by participants in organized sport shooting events or firearms training courses,[331] to weapons possessed by persons participating in miliary training programs conducted by or on behalf of the United States Armed Forces or the Georgia Department of Defense,[332] weapons used by those engaged in law enforcement training,[333]

Considering those definitions, the general rule is that, absent exceptions, it shall be unlawful for any person to carry to or to possess, or have under his custody or control while within a school safety zone or at a school building, school function, or school property, or on a bus or other transportation furnished by the school, any weapon or explosive compound, other than fireworks[334] as defined under Georgia law.[335]

A license holder who violates this prohibition is guilty of a misdemeanor. Any person who is not a license holder who violates this prohibition is guilty of a felony and is subject to a fine of not more than $10,000 and a prison term of two to ten years.[336] Any person, license holder or not, who is convicted for a violation

---

[329]O.C.G.A. § 16-11-127.1 (a)(2); see also O.C.G.A. § 16-11-106 regarding a definition for stun gun or taser.

[330]O.C.G.A. § (c) and (c)(1).

[331]O.C.G.A. § (c) and (c)(2).

[332]O.C.G.A. § (c) and (c)(3).

[333]O.C.G.A. § (c) and (c)(4).

[334]See O.C.G.A. Title 25 Chapter 10 regarding definition of "fireworks."

[335]O.C.G.A. § 16-11-127.1 (b)(1).

[336]O.C.G.A. § 16-11-127.1 (b)(2).

of this prohibition and the violation involved a "dangerous weapon" or "machine gun" as defined by Georgia law[337] is to be punished by a fine of not more than $10,000 and/or a period of imprisonment ranging from five to ten years.[338]

It is no defense to a prosecution for a violation of this prohibition that school was not in session at the time of the offense,[339] the real property was being used for other purposes besides school purposes at the time of the offense,[340] or the offense took place on a school vehicle.[341]

Other Exceptions to the School Prohibition - There are many more exceptions to the school prohibition, in addition to those mentioned above, and include the following:

- peace officers, while acting in the performance of their official duties or when en route to or from their official duties[342]
- law enforcement officers of the United States government, while acting in the performance of their official duties or when en route to or from their official duties[343]
- a prosecuting attorney of the State of Georgia or of the United States, while acting in the performance of his official duties or when en route to or from his official duties[344]
- an employee of the Georgia Department of Corrections or a correctional facility operated by a political subdivision of the State of Georgia or of the United States and who is authorized by the head of such correctional agency or facility to carry a firearm, while acting in the performance of his official duties or when en

---

[337]See O.C.G.A. § 16-11-121 regarding definitions for "dangerous weapon" and "machine gun."

[338]O.C.G.A. § 16-11-127.1 (b)(3).

[339]O.C.G.A. § 16-11-127.1 (e) and (e)(1).

[340]O.C.G.A. § 16-11-127.1 (e) and (e)(2).

[341]O.C.G.A. § 16-11-127.1 (e) and (e)(3).

[342]O.C.G.A. § 16-11-127.1 (c)(5) and (c)(5)(A).

[343]O.C.G.A. § 16-11-127.1 (c)(5) and (c)(5)(B).

[344]O.C.G.A. § 16-11-127.1 (c)(5) and (c)(5)(C).

route to or from his official duties[345]

- a person employed as a campus police officer or school security officer who is authorized[346] to carry a weapon in accordance with Georgia law, while acting in the performance of his official duties or when en route to or from his official duties[347]

- medical examiners, coroners, and their investigators who are employed by the state or any political subdivision, while acting in the performance of their official duties or when en route to or from their official duties[348]

- those who are authorized in writing by a duly authorized official of the school to have in their possession or use as part of any activity being conducted at a school building, school property, or school function, the authorization of which shall specify the weapon or weapons which have been authorized and the time period for which the authorization is valid[349]

- a person, private investigator, or private security professional who is licensed to carry a pistol or revolver when such person carries or picks up a student at a school building, school function, or school property, or on a bus or other transportation furnished by the school when that person has any weapon legally kept within a vehicle when the vehicle is parked at the school property or is in transit through a designated school zone[350]

- a weapon possessed by a license holder which is under the possessor's control in a motor vehicle or which is in a locked compartment of a motor vehicle or one which is in a locked container in or a locked firearms rack which is on a motor vehicle which is being used by an adult over 21 years of age to bring to or

---

[345]O.C.G.A. § 16-11-127.1 (c)(5) and (c)(5)(D).

[346]See O.C.G.A. Title 20 Chapter 8.

[347]O.C.G.A. § 16-11-127.1 (c)(5) and (c)(5)(E).

[348]O.C.G.A. § 16-11-127.1 (c)(5) and (c)(5)(F).

[349]O.C.G.A. § 16-11-127.1 (c)(6).

[350]O.C.G.A. § 16-11-127.1 (c)(7); see also O.C.G.A. § 16-11-129 regarding concealed carry license holders, and O.C.G.A. § 43-38-10 regarding private security guards and private investigators who are licensed to carry a pistol or revolver.

pick up a student at a school building, school function, or school property, or on a bus or other transportation furnished by the school, or when such vehicle is used to transport someone to an activity being conducted on school property which has been authorized by a duly authorized official of the school, but does not include students attending the school[351]

- persons employed in fulfilling defense contracts with the government of the United States or agencies thereof when possession of the weapon is necessary for the manufacture, transport, installation, and testing under the requirements of such contract[352]

- employees of the State Board of Pardons and Paroles when specifically designated and authorized in writing by the members of the State Board of Pardons and Paroles to carry a weapon[353]

- the Attorney General and those members of his or her staff whom he or she specifically authorizes to carry a weapon[354]

- probation supervisors employed by and under the authority of the Department of Corrections pursuant to law[355] when specifically designated and authorized in writing by the director of the Division of Probation[356]

- public safety directors of municipal corporations[357]

- state and federal trial and appellate judges[358]

- United States attorneys and their assistants[359]

---

[351]O.C.G.A. § 16-11-127.1 (c)(8).

[352]O.C.G.A. § 16-11-127.1 (c)(9).

[353]O.C.G.A. § 16-11-127.1 (c)(10).

[354]O.C.G.A. § 16-11-127.1 (c)(11).

[355]See O.C.G.A. Title 42, Chapter 8, Article 2.

[356]O.C.G.A. § 16-11-127.1 (c)(12).

[357]O.C.G.A. § 16-11-127.1 (c)(13).

[358]O.C.G.A. § 16-11-127.1 (c)(14).

[359]O.C.G.A. § 16-11-127.1 (c)(15).

- clerks of the superior courts[360]
- teachers and other school personnel who are otherwise authorized to possess or carry weapons, provided that the weapon is in a locked compartment of a motor vehicle, or one which is in a locked container, or in a locked firearms rack which is on a motor vehicle[361]
- constables of any county of The State of Georgia[362]
- individuals who reside, work, or visit a private residence or business that happens to be located within a school safety zone[363]

## Firearms and Knives in Public and Private Places

A person is guilty of carrying a weapon or long gun in an unauthorized location and may be punished for a misdemeanor if he or she carries a weapon or long gun while[364] in a government building,[365] in a courthouse,[366] in a jail or prison,[367] in a place of worship,[368] in certain specific state mental health facilities,[369] in a bar,[370] on the premises of a nuclear power facility,[371] or within 150 feet of any polling

---

[360]O.C.G.A. § 16-11-127.1 (c)(16).

[361]O.C.G.A. § 16-11-127.1 (c)(17).

[362]O.C.G.A. § 16-11-127.1 (c)(18).

[363]O.C.G.A. § 16-11-127.1 (d)(1).

[364]O.C.G.A. § 16-11-127 (b).

[365]O.C.G.A. § 16-11-127 (b)(1).

[366]O.C.G.A. § 16-11-127 (b)(2).

[367]O.C.G.A. § 16-11-127 (b)(3).

[368]O.C.G.A. § 16-11-127 (b)(4).

[369]O.C.G.A. § 16-11-127 (b)(5); see also O.C.G.A. § 37-1-1.

[370]O.C.G.A. § 16-11-127 (b)(6).

[371]O.C.G.A. § 16-11-127 (b)(7); see also O.C.G.A. § 16-11-127.2.

place.[372]

Of course, exceptions apply and are discussed below.

Permission by Bar Owner - Bar owners may elect to allow those with a license to carry long guns or weapons on the bar premises. Patron-licensees who elect to do so will not be in violation of the prohibition.[373]

Polling Places - No person except for peace officers regularly employed by the federal, state, county, or municipal government or certified security guards shall be permitted to carry firearms within 150 feet of any polling place.[374]

Security Officer on Nuclear Facility - The prohibitions on firearms or weapons at a nuclear facility do not apply to a security officer authorized to carry the dangerous weapon under the law[375] who is acting in connection with his or her official duties on the premises of a federally licensed nuclear power facility.[376]

Firearms Used as Exhibits in Legal Proceedings - The prohibition does not apply to the use of weapons or long guns as exhibits in a legal proceeding, provided such weapons or long guns are secured and handled as directed by the personnel providing courtroom security or the judge hearing the case.[377]

Licensee Who Provides Notice - The prohibition does not apply to the license holder who approaches security or management personnel upon arrival at an ordinarily prohibited location and notifies such security or management personnel of the presence of a weapon or long gun and explicitly follows the security or management personnel's direction from removing, securing, storing, or

---

[372]O.C.G.A. § 16-11-127 (b); see also (b)(8) regarding polling places.

[373]O.C.G.A. § 16-11-127 (b)(6).

[374]O.C.G.A. §§ 16-11-127 (b)(8) and 21-2-413 (i).

[375]See O.C.G.A. § 16-11-124.

[376]O.C.G.A. § 16-11-127 (b)(7) and O.C.G.A. § 16-11-127.2 (c).

[377]O.C.G.A. § 16-11-127 (d)(1).

temporarily surrendering such weapon or long gun.[378]

In Vehicle Parked in Parking Facility on Otherwise Prohibited Property - The prohibition above does not apply to a weapon or long gun possessed by a license holder which is under the possessor's control in a motor vehicle, as long as the vehicle is locked, or the firearm is in a locked compartment of a motor vehicle, or is in a locked container or secured to a locked firearms rack which is within or on a motor vehicle and such vehicle is parked in a parking facility.

Definitions Under Firearm and Knife Prohibition - There are specific definitions that apply to the prohibition illustrated above.

A "bar" is an establishment that is devoted to the serving of alcoholic beverages for consumption by guests on the premises and in which the serving of food is only incidental to the consumption of those beverages, including, but not limited to, taverns, nightclubs, cocktail lounges, and cabarets.[379]

A "courthouse" is a building that is occupied by judicial courts and contains rooms in which judicial proceedings are held.[380]

A "government building" includes the following:[381]
-   A building in which a government entity is housed[382]
-   A building where a government entity meets in its official capacity; however, if the building is not publicly owned, such building shall only be considered a government building for the purposes of the prohibition during the time such government entity is meeting at such building[383]
-   the portion of any building that is not a publicly owned building

---

[378]O.C.G.A. § 16-11-127 (d)(2).

[379]O.C.G.A. § 16-11-127 (a)(1).

[380]O.C.G.A. § 16-11-127 (a)(2).

[381]O.C.G.A. § 16-11-127 (a)(3).

[382]O.C.G.A. § 16-11-127 (a)(3)(A).

[383]O.C.G.A. § 16-11-127 (a)(3)(B).

that is occupied by a government entity[384]

A "government entity" is an office, agency, authority, department, commission, board, body, division, instrumentality, or institution of the state or any county, municipal corporation, consolidated government, or local board of education within the State of Georgia.[385]

A "parking facility" is the real property owned or leased by one of the specific prohibited places that has been designated for the parking of motor vehicles at that prohibited place.[386]

State Capitol Building - It is unlawful for any person, other than specifically exempt individuals,[387] to enter, occupy, or remain within the state capitol building or any building that houses committee offices, committee rooms, or offices of members, officials, or employees of the General Assembly, or either house thereof, while in possession of any firearm, knife,[388] explosive or incendiary device or compound, bludgeon, knuckles, whether made from metal, thermoplastic, wood, or other similar material, or any other dangerous or deadly weapon, instrument, or device.[389]

## Federal Law "School Zone" - Public and Private Schools - Kindergarten Through 12th Grade

Federal law must also be considered regarding a school zone, and where state law conflicts with federal law, federal law controls. Despite the fact that federal law controls, Georgia may have a more expansive definition of what constitutes a "school zone," and indeed, the State of Georgia does have a broader definition; a "school zone" under Georgia law includes colleges and universities, and

---

[384]O.C.G.A. § 16-11-127 (a)(3)(C).

[385]O.C.G.A. § 16-11-127 (a)(4).

[386]O.C.G.A. § 16-11-127 (a)(5).

[387]See O.C.G.A. §§ 16-11-126 through 16-11-127.2 for exempt individuals, which includes those with a concealed weapons license.

[388]As knives are defined in O.C.G.A. § 16-11-125.1.

[389]O.C.G.A. § 16-11-34.1 (b).

other schools that the federal law does not cover. Be sure to understand and observe the Georgia law regarding designated school zones.

A "school zone" has been created under federal law[390] to define an area of 1000 feet around schools where firearms are prohibited. Violation of the federal law regarding school zones is generally a felony offense punishable by up to five years in prison and up to a $5000 fine, or both, but if prosecuted as a misdemeanor, then up to $5000 penalty only.[391]

It is important to note that the "school zone" applies only to public and private schools with students in kindergarten through 12th grade.

One will not be in violation of the prohibition on firearms in school zones if the firearm is within the school zone but is in a residence, place of business, or private property, or is otherwise unloaded, locked in a container, or locked in the trunk, or if the individual has permission.[392]

Those exempted from the prohibition include peace officers and persons in the military.[393]

### Prohibitions for Federal Buildings and Courthouses

Federal Buildings - Absent an exemption, any person who knowingly possesses or causes to be present a firearm or other dangerous weapon in a Federal facility (other than a Federal court facility), or attempts to do so, shall be fined or imprisoned not more than one year, or both.[394] If the possession or causation of a firearm to be present in a Federal facility or attempt to do such is coupled with the intent that the firearm or other dangerous weapon be used in the commission of a crime, the punishment is imprisonment for not more than 5 years and a fine, or

---

[390] 18 U.S.C. § 921 (a)(25).

[391] 18 U.S.C. § 924 (a)(4).

[392] 18 U.S.C. § 922 (q).

[393] 18 U.S.C. § 922 (q).

[394] 18 U.S.C. § 930 (a).

both.[395]

The exemption of the first prohibition discussed above includes the following persons:[396]

- the lawful performance of official duties by an officer, agent, or employee of the United States, a State, or a political subdivision thereof, who is authorized by law to engage in or supervise the prevention, detection, investigation, or prosecution of any violation of law[397]
- the possession of a firearm or other dangerous weapon by a Federal official or a member of the military if such possession is authorized by law[398]
- the lawful carrying of firearms or other dangerous weapons in a Federal facility incident to hunting or other lawful purposes[399]

This prohibition includes facilities such as airports and post offices, even with a valid state concealed handgun license.

Federal Courthouses - Absent an exemption, whoever knowingly possesses or causes to be present a firearm or other dangerous weapon in a Federal court facility, or attempts to do so, shall be fined and imprisoned not more than two years, or both.[400] Exemptions include:[401]

- the lawful performance of official duties by an officer, agent, or employee of the United States, a State, or a political subdivision thereof, who is authorized by law to engage in or supervise the prevention, detection, investigation, or prosecution of any

---

[395] 18 U.S.C. § 930 (b).

[396] 18 U.S.C. § 930 (d).

[397] 18 U.S.C. § 930 (d)(1).

[398] 18 U.S.C. § 930 (d)(2).

[399] 18 U.S.C. § 930 (d)(3).

[400] 18 U.S.C. § 930 (e)(1).

[401] 18 U.S.C. § 930 (e)(2).

violation of law[402]

- the possession of a firearm or other dangerous weapon by a Federal official or a member of the military if such possession is authorized by law

A "federal facility," for the purposes of these prohibitions, means a building or part thereof owned or leased by the Federal Government, where Federal employees are regularly present for the purpose of performing their official duties.[403]

A "dangerous weapon" means a weapon, device, instrument, material, or substance, animate or inanimate, that is used for, or is readily capable of, causing death or serious bodily injury, except that such term does not include a pocket knife with a blade of less than 2 ½ inches in length.[404]

The term "federal court facility" means the courtroom, judges' chambers, witness rooms, jury deliberation rooms, attorney conference rooms, prisoner holding cells, offices of the court clerks, the United States attorney, and the United States marshal, probation and parole offices, and adjoining corridors of any court of the United States.[405]

Notice concerning the prohibitions in Federal facility and courthouses shall be posted conspicuously at each public entrance to each facility or courthouse, and no person shall be convicted of an offense with respect to a federal facility if such notice is not posted at such facility, unless the person had actual notice prior to the offense.[406]

## Federal Protections for Interstate Travel with Firearms

It is very possible that the firearm laws in another state are much more restrictive than the firearm laws in your state. So, taking a family trip with firearms in the car could lead to problems.

---

[402] 18 U.S.C. § 930 (d)(1).

[403] 18 U.S.C. § 930 (g)(1).

[404] 18 U.S.C. § 930 (g)(2).

[405] 18 U.S.C. § 930 (g)(2).

[406] 18 U.S.C. § 930 (h).

Protections exist, however, for the traveler in what is known as the Firearms Owners' Protection Act ("FOPA").[407] This act revised many of the statutes in the famous 1968 Gun Control Act.[408]

Included in the FOPA is the "Safe Passage Provision"[409] which applies to any person not prohibited under federal law from possessing firearms. Persons who travel from one place to another for any lawful activity cannot be arrested for a firearm offense in a state that has strict gun control laws if the traveler is just passing through, with only short stops for food and gas, and the firearms and ammunition are not immediately accessible, are unloaded, and, in the case of a vehicle without a compartment separate from the driver's compartment, in a locked container.[410]

At this time, it is unclear if this provision applies to transportation of firearms through the District of Columbia. Also, the provision is silent regarding the definition of "unloaded," so the best bet is to have the firearm completely unloaded and even go as far as to store the ammunition completely separate and apart from the firearm to best avoid any potential trouble with law enforcement.

### Airline Travel with Firearms[411]

When traveling by air, a firearms owner must declare and check any firearms he wants to be stored and returned after the flight. Ammunition need not be declared.

All firearms must be unloaded and kept in a hard-sided container. The container must be locked. A locked container is defined as one that completely secures the firearms from access by anyone other than the owner. Cases that can be pulled open with very little effort are not considered locked containers.

Any key or combination must be provided to the security officer if he

---

[407]See 18 U.S.C. § 921 et seq.

[408]See 18 U.S.C. § 44.

[409]See 18 U.S.C. § 926A.

[410]18 U.S.C. § 926A.

[411]This entire section is as provided by the Transportation Security Administration.

chooses to inspect the container. The owner must remain present during the screening to take the key back. If the owner is not present at the time the officer chooses to inspect the container, the container will not be placed on the plane.

Ammunition must be securely packed in fiber (such as cardboard), wood, or metal boxes or other packaging that is specifically designed to carry small amounts of ammunition. Magazines or clips are not allowed to be used for packing ammunition unless they completely and securely enclose the ammunition, such as containers that securely cover the exposed portions of the magazine or by securely placing the magazine in a pouch, holder, holster, or lanyard.

Ammunition may be stored in the same hard-sided case as the firearm, so long as it is also packed as described above.

Black powder or percussion caps are not allowed on the plane whatsoever.

Violations of these provisions are dealt with through severe punishment and penalties of up to $10,000 per violation.

Airlines have their own additional requirements on the carrying of firearms and the amount of ammunition that one may transport in checked baggage. It is important to contact the carrier prior to traveling to inquire about their individual policies.

# CHAPTER NINE

## <u>Encounters with Law Enforcement</u>

For those who leave their private property at any time with a firearm, knife, or other weapon, there always exists the possibility that one will have an encounter with law enforcement. Therefore, it is important to have a plan on how to conduct one's behavior in the event of such encounter. Taking the wrong approach with a law enforcement professional can turn bad, even deadly, very quickly. The prudent course of action to take is to consider this issue at great length prior to any such encounter, because none of us knows when that encounter will ultimately occur.

In certain situations where a crime has occurred and law enforcement has become involved, weapons may be declared to be contraband and ultimately forfeited.[412] Such weapons may be sold,[413] destroyed,[414] or kept if they have a historical or instructional value.[415] Even if a crime has not occurred, an encounter with law enforcement could result in the forfeiture of a weapon, and it may be difficult to get the weapon back, if at all.

### <u>Basic Law Enforcement Encounter Considerations</u>

One should always minimize the amount of exposure he has to problems with law enforcement while carrying or transporting firearms. Most interactions with law enforcement for the average citizen deal with traffic stops, where the person has committed some offense and has been pulled over.

Knowing this, one should be careful to drive safely at all times with perhaps additional focus while armed and/or while transporting firearms. One should make sure he obeys all traffic laws and also make sure the car is operating properly before starting the journey, such as checking the headlights to ensure they are working properly, as well as the turn signals. Such malfunctions prompt many traffic stops.

---

[412]See O.C.G.A. § 17-5-51.

[413]See O.C.G.A. § 17-5-52.

[414]See O.C.G.A. § 17-5-52.

[415]See O.C.G.A. § 17-5-53.

Shotguns and rifles in general may be loaded but there must not be a round in the chamber of either a rifle or shotgun in order to transport it lawfully. Also consider the fact that for those who transport a rifle or shotgun in plain view, one can expect scrutiny from any law enforcement officer who notices the weapon during the traffic stop.

Finally, it is important to understand that during a traffic stop, officers may not know the Georgia Revised Statutes line by line. They are likely not well-versed in the concealed carry laws or gun law in general. Because they likely do not have a firm understanding of all of these laws, it is easy for someone who knows the laws to get frustrated with the officer rather quickly. Avoid allowing that frustration to create a truly adversarial situation. If any person in an encounter with law enforcement leaves the scene in handcuffs, there is a 100% guarantee it will not be the officer. Be cooperative and understanding.

## Traffic Stops by Law Enforcement

The prudent traveler will always travel with his firearms being stored and/or transported according to law. This will eliminate most problems with law enforcement.

For those who are concealed handgun license holders and armed at the time of an encounter with a law enforcement officer, you may or may not choose to inform the officer if you are carrying. Some states require this. Should you choose to notify the officer that you are armed, a great way to accomplish this during a traffic stop without any excitement or misunderstandings is to have your driver's license ready, along with the concealed carry license, and your hands on the steering wheel. There is no need to say anything; simply hand both licenses to the officer. He will choose how to proceed. Likely, he will inquire as to where the firearm is. Tell him. Also, ask permission before retrieving your registration and proof of insurance. Most officers know that those taking the time to acquire a concealed handgun license are likely not the sort of individual that they will have to be concerned with. However, that does not mean that you lower protocol. If anything, the fact that the officer now knows you are armed is argument enough to raise protocol, meaning, elevate the courtesy and respect you are giving to the officer. In the end, doing such will help more than hurt your situation.

Whether or not you are a license holder, you need not incriminate yourself, as you have a right to refuse any questioning. However, if you refuse to answer questions, there is a high probability of a major confrontation with the law enforcement officer. If you choose to answer the officer's questions, be sure to answer any questions you choose to answer truthfully. To lie is only going to make matters worse. If you believe you will be arrested, or you know you cannot truthfully answer a question without being arrested, simply say nothing or state that you will not answer any questions without first having an opportunity to consult your attorney.

### Law Enforcement Search of Vehicle

It is fairly common that at some point during a traffic stop, the law enforcement officer will ask to search the vehicle. The general rule of thumb is to refuse the search. Consent need not be given. If the officer chooses to search your vehicle anyway, do not get in the way. Allow him to do his job, and be respectful, so as to lower the odds of escalating the confrontation to an arrest.

# CHAPTER TEN

## Self-Defense, Defense of Property, and Defense of Others in Georgia

In the State of Georgia, there are laws on the books regarding self-defense, defense of real property, defense of personal property, and defense of others. There is also an abundance of case law that exists that helps in our interpretation of the codified law regarding defense situations.

For those who own firearms, knives, or other weapons for defense purposes, it is good to have a firm understanding on the laws regarding defense situations, because oftentimes situations that would otherwise be excused or justified under the law could actually become criminal acts for the person who believes he is defending himself, his property, or others under the law, simply by acting outside of the limits of the defense laws. Quite often, the line that one should not cross may not appeal to common sense, so it is important to know where the lines are.

It is important to note that the laws discussed below may not be narrowed down or impacted by local law, as there is a preemption law on the books to prevent different standards for the defense laws that depend on where the act occurred. Specifically, any rule, regulation, or policy of any agency of the state or any ordinance, resolution, rule, regulation, or policy of any county, municipality, or other political subdivision of the state which is in conflict with O.C.G.A. § 16-3-21 is null, void, and of no force and effect.[416]

Standing Ground - No Duty to Retreat - In Georgia, one may stand his ground and he has no duty to retreat, so long as the person using the defensive measures is not at fault for the victim's assault.[417] Also, any weapon used in a defensive measure must be legally possessed, or criminal charges are likely.

---

[416]O.C.G.A. § 16-3-21 (c).

[417]See O.C.G.A. § 16-3-21 (a); see also *Johnson v. State*, (1984) 253 Ga. 37, 315 S.E.2d 871 and Conklin v. State, (1985) 254 Ga. 558, 331 S.E.2d 532.

## Use of Physical Force in Self-Defense in Georgia

A person is justified in threatening or using force against another when and to the extent that he or she reasonably believes that such threat or force is necessary to defend himself or herself against another person's imminent use of unlawful force.[418] The "reasonable fear" required to justify the use of force must be based upon a danger that appears urgent and pressing at the time of the use of force.[419]

However, a person is not justified in using force under these circumstances if he[420] initially provokes the use of force against himself with the intent to use such force as an excuse to inflict bodily harm upon the assailant,[421] is attempting to commit, is committing, or is fleeing after the commission or attempted commission of a felony,[422] or was the aggressor or was engaged in a combat by agreement, unless he withdraws from the encounter and effectively communicates to the other person his intent to withdraw, and the other person, despite this communication, continues or threatens to continue the use of unlawful force.[423] Also, the use of force cannot be an act of revenge, after the circumstances leading to the reasonable fear have subsided.[424]

A person who uses threats or force described above, relating to the use of force in defense of habitation has no duty to retreat and has the right to stand his or her ground and use force as provided under the law, including deadly force.[425] Also, the person who used the justified force shall not be held liable to the person

---

[418]O.C.G.A. § 16-3-21 (a).

[419]See *Carter v. State*, (2009) 285 Ga. 565, 678 S.E.2d 909; see also *Andrews v. State*, (1997) 267 Ga. 473, 480 S.E.2d 29.

[420]O.C.G.A. § 16-3-21 (b).

[421]O.C.G.A. § 16-3-21 (b)(1).

[422]O.C.G.A. § 16-3-21 (b)(2).

[423]O.C.G.A. § 16-3-21 (b)(3).

[424]See *Hill v. State*, (2001) 250 Ga.App. 9, 550 S.E.2d 422; see also Lackey v. State, (1961) 217 Ga. 345, 122 S.E.2d 115.

[425]O.C.G.A. § 16-3-23.1.

against whom the use of force was justified, or to any person acting as an accomplice or assistant to such person in any civil action brought as a result of the threat or use of such force.[426]

In addition, a person who uses threats or force as described above shall be immune from criminal prosecution therefor unless in the use of deadly force, such person utilizes a weapon the carrying or possession of which is unlawful under the law regarding concealed carry or antiterroristic training.[427]

### Use of Physical Force in Defense of Another Person

A person is justified in threatening or using force against another when and to the extent that he or she reasonably believes that such threat or force is necessary to defend another person against another person's imminent use of unlawful force.[428]

As with self-defense, a person is not justified in using force under these circumstances if he[429] initially provokes the use of force against himself with the intent to use such force as an excuse to inflict bodily harm upon the assailant,[430] is attempting to commit, is committing, or is fleeing after the commission or attempted commission of a felony,[431] or was the aggressor or was engaged in a combat by agreement, unless he withdraws from the encounter and effectively communicates to the other person his intent to withdraw, and the other person, despite this communication, continues or threatens to continue the use of unlawful force.[432]

A person who uses threats or force described above, relating to the use of force in defense of habitation, has no duty to retreat and has the right to stand

---

[426]O.C.G.A. § 51-11-9.

[427]O.C.G.A. § 16-3-24.2.

[428]O.C.G.A. § 16-3-12 (a).

[429]O.C.G.A. § 16-3-21 (b).

[430]O.C.G.A. § 16-3-21 (b)(1).

[431]O.C.G.A. § 16-3-21 (b)(2).

[432]O.C.G.A. § 16-3-21 (b)(3).

his or her ground and use force as provided under the law, including deadly force.[433] Also, the person who used the justified force shall not be held liable to the person against whom the use of force was justified, or to any person acting as an accomplice or assistant to such person in any civil action brought as a result of the threat or use of such force.[434]

Finally, a person who uses threats or force as described above shall be immune from criminal prosecution therefor unless in the use of deadly force, such person utilizes a weapon the carrying or possession of which is unlawful under the law regarding concealed carry or antiterroristic training.[435]

## Use of Physical Force Against an Intruder in Defense of Habitation

A person is justified in threatening or using force against another when and to the extent that he or she reasonably believes that such threat or force is necessary to prevent or terminate such other's unlawful entry into or attack upon a habitation.[436]

However, such person is justified in the use of force which is intended or likely to cause death or great bodily harm in the following three situations:

- the entry is made or attempted in a violent and tumultuous manner and he or she reasonably believes that the entry is attempted or made for the purpose of assaulting or offering personal violence to any person in the dwelling or being therein and that such force is necessary to prevent the assault or offer of personal violence[437]
- that force is used against another person who is not a member of the family or household and who unlawfully and forcibly enters or has unlawfully and forcibly entered the residence and the person

---

[433]O.C.G.A. § 16-3-23.1.

[434]O.C.G.A. § 51-11-9.

[435]O.C.G.A. § 16-3-24.2.

[436]O.C.G.A. § 16-3-23.

[437]O.C.G.A. § 16-3-23 (1).

using the force knew or had reason to believe that an unlawful and forcible entry has occurred[438]

- the person using such force reasonably believes that the entry is made or attempted for the purpose of committing a felony therein and that such force is necessary to prevent the commission of the felony[439]

A person who uses threats or force described above, relating to the use of force in defense of habitation has no duty to retreat and has the right to stand his or her ground and use force as provided under the law, including deadly force.[440] Also, the person who used the justified force shall not be held liable to the person against whom the use of force was justified, or to any person acting as an accomplice or assistant to such person in any civil action brought as a result of the threat or use of such force.[441]

Also, a person who uses threats or force as described above shall be immune from criminal prosecution therefor unless in the use of deadly force, such person utilizes a weapon the carrying or possession of which is unlawful under the law regarding concealed carry or antiterroristic training.[442]

The term "habitation" means any dwelling, motor vehicle, or place of business.[443] The term "personal property" means the personal property other than a motor vehicle.[444] A person's "habitation" may also be a particular space in a jointly-occupied dwelling, provided that such person has obtained the right to occupy that space and exclude his co-inhabitants therefrom.[445] A trailer may also

---

[438]O.C.G.A. § 16-3-23 (2).

[439]O.C.G.A. § 16-3-23 (3).

[440]O.C.G.A. § 16-3-23.1.

[441]O.C.G.A. § 51-11-9.

[442]O.C.G.A. § 16-3-24.2.

[443]O.C.G.A. § 16-3-24.1.

[444]O.C.G.A. § 16-3-24.1.

[445]See Goerndt v. State, (1977) 144 Ga.App. 93, 240 E.S.2d 711.

be a person's habitation.[446]

## Use of Physical Force to Prevent a Forcible Felony

A person is justified in using force which is intended or likely to cause death or great bodily harm only if he or she reasonably believes that such force is necessary to prevent the commission of a forcible felony.[447]

As stated above, a person is not justified in using force under these circumstances if he[448]

-              initially provokes the use of force against himself with the intent to use such force as an excuse to inflict bodily harm upon the assailant,[449]
-              is attempting to commit, is committing, or is fleeing after the commission or attempted commission of a felony,[450]
-              or was the aggressor or was engaged in a combat by agreement, unless he withdraws from the encounter and effectively communicates to the other person his intent to withdraw, and the other person, despite this communication, continues or threatens to continue the use of unlawful force.[451]

A person who uses threats or force as described above shall be immune from criminal prosecution therefor unless in the use of deadly force, such person utilizes a weapon the carrying or possession of which is unlawful under the law regarding concealed carry or antiterroristic training.[452]

---

[446]See *Goerndt v. State*, (1977) 144 Ga.App. 93, 240 E.S.2d 711.

[447]O.C.G.A. § 16-3-21 (a).

[448]O.C.G.A. § 16-3-21 (h).

[449]O.C.G.A. § 16-3-21 (b)(1).

[450]O.C.G.A. § 16-3-21 (b)(2).

[451]O.C.G.A. § 16-3-21 (b)(3).

[452]O.C.G.A. § 16-3-24.2.

## Use of Force Allowed in Defense of (Real) Property

A person is justified in threatening or using force against another when and to the extent that he reasonably believes that such threat or force is necessary to prevent or terminate such other's trespass on or other tortious or criminal interference with any real property that is not habitation and that is not personal property.[453]  The real property must be:

- lawfully in the person's possession[454]
- lawfully in the possession of a member of his immediate family[455]
- belonging to a person whose property he has a legal duty to protect[456]

Regarding deadly force or force likely to produce great bodily harm in the defense of real property, it is generally not justified unless the person using such force reasonably believes that the force is necessary to prevent the commission of a forcible felony.[457]

A person who uses threats or force described above, relating to the use of force in defense of habitation, has no duty to retreat and has the right to stand his or her ground and use force as provided under the law, including deadly force.[458] Also, the person who used the justified force shall not be held liable to the person against whom the use of force was justified, or to any person acting as an accomplice or assistant to such person in any civil action brought as a result of the threat or use of such force.[459]

The term "habitation" means any dwelling, motor vehicle, or place of

---

[453]O.C.G.A. § 16-3-24 (a).

[454]O.C.G.A. § 16-3-24 (a)(1)

[455]O.C.G.A. § 16-3-24 (a)(2).

[456]O.C.G.A. § 16-3-24 (a)(3).

[457]O.C.G.A. § 16-3-24 (b).

[458]O.C.G.A. § 16-3-23.1.

[459]O.C.G.A. § 51-11-9.

business.[460] The term "personal property" means the personal property <u>other</u> than a motor vehicle.[461]

A person who uses threats or force as described above shall be immune from criminal prosecution therefor unless in the use of deadly force, such person utilizes a weapon the carrying or possession of which is unlawful under the law regarding concealed carry or antiterroristic training.[462]

### Defending a Murder or Manslaughter Prosecution in Family Situations

In defending a prosecution for murder or manslaughter arising from a potential self-defense, defense of others, defense of habitation, or a prevention of a forcible felony, and the defendant raises as a defense a justification, the defendant, in order to establish his or her reasonable belief that the use of force or deadly force was immediately necessary, may offer[463] relevant evidence that the defendant had been the victim of acts of family violence or child abuse committed by the deceased,[464] or relevant expert testimony regarding the condition of the mind of the defendant at the time of the offense, including relevant facts and circumstances relating to the family violence or child abuse that are the bases of the expert's opinion.[465]

---

[460]O.C.G.A. § 16-3-24.1.

[461]O.C.G.A. § 16-3-24.1.

[462]O.C.G.A. § 16-3-24.2.

[463]O.C.G.A. § 16-3-21 (d).

[464]O.C.G.A. § 16-3-21 (d)(1).

[465]O.C.G.A. § 16-3-21 (d)(2).

# CHAPTER ELEVEN

## Firearms and Weapons Offenses in Georgia

Most of the offenses discussed in this chapter would never be committed by individuals who read a book such as this, but they are included in an effort to inform each of you what offenses exist and how one might find himself in trouble with the law.

Also, many of these offenses are discussed elsewhere in this book where they are relevant, but in an effort to be sure the reader does not miss the material, the offenses are included here as well.

It is important to note that in the State of Georgia, a person cannot be considered or found guilty of a crime unless he has attained the age of 13 years of age at the time of the act, omission, or negligence constituting the crime.[466]

### Transport or Carry of a Pistol Without a License

This information is just too important. As such, it is found in multiple places within this book.

As stated above, one must have a license to carry a handgun (pistol or revolver), openly or concealed, anywhere except within his home, on private property within his control, his place of business if he owns his own business, or within your motor vehicle.

Of course, there is an exception, as discussed elsewhere in this book, regarding those involved in lawful licensed fishing and hunting, as long as they have the property owner's permission and the handgun, whenever loaded, is carried open and in a fully exposed manner.

### Transport or Carry of a Rifle or Shotgun Without a License

Again, this information is very important, and is repeated several times throughout this book.

---

[466]O.C.G.A. § 16-3-1.

The law regarding the lawful carry of a handgun <u>does not apply</u> to rifles and shotguns. A person may lawfully carry a rifle or shotgun openly in the State of Georgia, but not concealed.

## Offense of Carrying a Concealed Weapon Without a License

A person commits the offense of carrying a concealed weapon without a license when he or she carries a weapon concealed without a valid weapons carry license unless he or she meets one of the specific enumerated exceptions to having the license as provided by Georgia law.[467]

For a first offense conviction, the person is guilty of a misdemeanor, but for a second or any subsequent offense within five years, as measured from the dates of the previous arrests for which convictions were obtained to the date of the current arrest for which a conviction is obtained, the offender is guilty of a felony and is subject to imprisonment for not less than two years and not more than five years.[468]

A detailed explanation of the exceptions is discussed in the chapter regarding traveling with firearms.

Also, a detailed explanation of all of the exceptions to the "concealed carry laws"[469] may be found in the chapter addressing concealed weapons licenses.

<u>Interesting Weapons Carry Violation Considerations</u> - There exists an abundance of case law from the State of Georgia regarding situations where an individual was arrested for carrying a concealed weapon, and the court either agreed, or disagreed, that the weapon was concealed.

For instance, a person may not be convicted with a violation of this law if

---

[467]O.C.G.A. § 16-11-126 (h)(1) and (h)(2); see also O.C.G.A. 16-11-126 in general regarding exceptions.

[468]O.C.G.A. § 16-11-126 (i)(1) and (i)(2).

[469]Applicable "concealed carry laws" for the exceptions discussed are O.C.G.A. § 16-11-130 through O.C.G.A. § 16-11-127.2.

he was found with the butt end of the pistol sticking out of his pocket.[470] However, a pistol in the pocket is concealed, even if a police officer is able to immediately recognize the bulge in the person's pants is a pistol.[471] Additionally, a pistol that is carried in a manner so as to allow it to be exposed only one inch below the jacket and still be visible through an opening in the jacket has been ruled to be concealed, as it is neither "open" or "exposed."[472]

Within a motor vehicle, a gun that slightly protrudes from under the seat is considered concealed because it is not fully exposed.[473] The purpose of the law against concealed weapons without a license is to compel persons carrying weapons to display them so that others, knowing that they were armed and dangerous, could avoid them.[474] Handguns that are "half-hidden" within the passenger compartment of a car are not considered "fully exposed" and therefore constitute an illegal concealed weapon.[475]

The general rule is that, for a motorist without a firearms license, a gun must be either in the glove box, center console, or similar compartment, or the gun must be fully exposed for others to be able to view.[476] For the purposes of a "similar compartment," Georgia courts have held that a pocket in the inside of a car door was not a "similar compartment," because the pocket did not have a closing lid.[477]

---

[470]See *McCroy v. State*, (1980), 155 Ga.App. 777, 272 S.E.2d 747; see also *Goss v. State*, (1983) 165 Ga.App. 448, 301 S.E.2d 662.

[471]See *Gainer v. State*, (1985) 175 Ga.App. 759, 334 S.E.2d 385.

[472]See *Anderson v. State*, (1992) 203 Ga.App. 118, 416 S.E.2d 309.

[473]See *Moody v. State*, (1987) 184 Ga.App. 768, 362 S.E.2d 499.

[474]See *Parrish v. State*, (1997) 228 Ga.App. 177, 491 S.E.2d 433.

[475]See *Ross v. State*, (2002) 255 Ga.App. 462, 566 S.E.2d 47.

[476]See *Lindsey v. State*, (2004) 277 Ga. 772, 596 S.E.2d 140.

[477]See *Lindsey v. State*, (2004) 277 Ga. 772, 596 S.E.2d 140.

## Solicitation, Persuasion, Encouragement, or Enticement of Dealer to Transfer or Convey Firearm to Someone Other Than Buyer

Any person who attempts to solicit, persuade, encourage, or entice any dealer to transfer or otherwise convey a firearm other than to the actual buyer, as well as any other person who wilfully and intentionally aids or abets such person, is guilty of a felony.[478] The only exception is for federal law enforcement officers or peace officers[479] operating in the course and scope of their official duties or any other person who is under such officer's direct supervision.[480]

## Discharge of Gun or Pistol on or Near Highway

A person is guilty of a misdemeanor when, without legal justification, he discharges a gun or pistol on or within 50 yards of a public highway or street.[481] An example of a "legal justification" would be using the firearm in self-defense or defense of others near a road, such as at a gas station that sits near the corner of an intersection.

## Discharge of Firearm While Under the Influence

It is unlawful for any person to discharge a firearm while under the influence of alcohol or any drug, including marijuana, or any combination of both, to the extent that it is unsafe for the person to discharge the firearm.[482] An exception exists allowing a person so impaired to discharge a firearm in the event he is defending his life, health, or property.[483]

It is also unlawful for any person to discharge a firearm while the person's alcohol concentration is 0.08 grams or more at any time while discharging such firearm, or within three hours after such discharge of such firearm from alcohol

---

[478] O.C.G.A. § 16-11-113.

[479] "Peace officer" as defined in O.C.G.A. § 16-1-3.

[480] O.C.G.A. § 16-11-113.

[481] O.C.G.A. § 16-11-103.

[482] O.C.G.A. § 16-11-134 (a) and (a)(1).

[483] O.C.G.A. § 16-11-134 (a) and (a)(1).

consumed before such discharge ended.[484]

It is important to realize that the fact that any person charged for the offenses regarding discharge of a firearm while impaired may not rely on the fact that he was legally entitled to use the drug as a defense.[485] To violate this law is considered a misdemeanor of a high and aggravated nature.[486]

### Discharge of Firearm on Property of Another Person

It is unlawful for any person to fire or discharge a firearm on the property of another person, firm, or corporation without having first obtained permission from the owner or lessee of the property.[487] It should be noted that this prohibition does not apply to persons who fire or discharge a firearm in defense of person or property[488] or situations involving a shooting by a law enforcement officer.[489] A violation of this prohibition is considered a misdemeanor.[490]

### Pointing or Aiming Gun or Pistol at Another Person

A person is guilty of a misdemeanor when he intentionally and without legal justification points or aims a gun or pistol at another, whether the gun or pistol is loaded or unloaded.[491] However, the accidental or unintentional pointing of a weapon at another is not an offense.[492] Generally, the intent of the person who pointed or aimed the firearm is a question for a jury, and the jury may infer the

---

[484]O.C.G.A. § 16-11-134 (a)(2).

[485]O.C.G.A. § 16-11-134 (b).

[486]O.C.G.A. § 16-11-134 (c).

[487]O.C.G.A. § 16-11-104 (a).

[488]O.C.G.A. § 16-11-104 (a)(1).

[489]O.C.G.A. § 16-11-104 (a)(2).

[490]O.C.G.A. § 16-11-104 (b).

[491]O.C.G.A. § 16-11-102.

[492]See *Parsons v. State*, (1915) 16 Ga.App.212, 84 S.E. 974.

intention by looking to all of the facts and circumstances regarding the incident.[493]

If the pointing of a firearm places the victim in reasonable apprehension of immediate violent injury, then the felony of aggravated assault, rather than the misdemeanor of pointing a gun at another, has occurred.[494] In the event that the person who points the weapon at another happens to fire the weapon, and the weapon discharges and kills the other person, an involuntary manslaughter has occurred.[495]

Finally, one may not be charged with both the simple assault of pointing the gun at another, a misdemeanor, and the felony of aggravated assault, as the simple assault "merges" into the felony, and only the aggravated assault will be charged.[496]

**Aggravated Assault**

There are a variety of ways that one can commit the crime of "aggravated assault." They are discussed below.

Assault With a Deadly Weapon or Object - A person commits the offense of aggravated assault when he or she assaults with a deadly weapon or with any object, device, or instrument which, when used offensively against a person, is likely to or actually does result in serious bodily injury.[497]

Discharge of Firearm From Motor Vehicle - Aggravated assault also occurs when the person or persons, without legal justification, discharge a firearm from within a motor vehicle toward a person or persons.[498] This felony carries a prison

---

[493]See *Parsons v. State*, (1915) 16 Ga.App.212, 84 S.E. 974; see also *Hawkins v. State*, (1911) 8 Ga.App. 705, 70 S.E. 53.

[494]See *Savage v. State*, (2002) 274 Ga. 692, 558 S.E.2d 701.

[495]See *Leonard v. State*, (1909) 133 Ga. 435, 66 S.E. 251; see also *Irwin v. State*, (1911) 9 Ga.App. 865, 72 S.E. 440.

[496]See *Green v. State*, (1985) 175 Ga.App. 92, 332 S.E.2d 385; see also *Pace v. State*, (1999) 239 Ga.App. 506, 521 S.E.2d 444 and *Morrison v. State*, (1978) 147 Ga.App. 410, 249 S.E. 2d 131.

[497]O.C.G.A. § 16-5-21 (a)(2).

[498]O.C.G.A. § 16-5-21 (a)(3).

term of five to twenty years.[499]

      <u>Aggravated Assault In School Safety Zone</u> - Any person who commits the offense of aggravated assault involving the use of a firearm upon a student or teacher or other school personnel within a school safety zone[500] shall, upon conviction, be punished by imprisonment for not less than 5 years and not more than 20 years.[501]

## Theft of Firearm

      A person convicted of a "theft crime"[502] where the property which was the subject of the theft offense was a firearm will be guilty of a felony and subject to prison time ranging from 1 year to 10 years.[503]  For the purposes of theft crimes, a "firearm" is defined as any rifle, shotgun, pistol, or similar device which propels a projectile or projectiles through the energy of an explosive.[504]

## Criminal Activity with Use of Item with Altered Identification

      A person commits the offense of criminal use of an article with an altered identification mark when he or she buys, sells, receives, disposes of, conceals, or has in his or her possession, among other things, a firearm from which he or she knows the manufacturer's name plate, serial number, or any other distinguishing number or identification mark has been removed for the purpose of concealing or destroying the identity of the article.[505]  This is a felony offense and carries the punishment of one to five years in prison.[506]

---

[499]O.C.G.A. § 16-5-21 (h).

[500]See O.C.G.A. § 16-11-127.1 (a)(1) regarding the definition of "school safety zone."

[501]O.C.G.A. § 16-5-21 (i).

[502]See O.C.G.A. §§ 16-8-2 through 16-8-9 for specific theft crimes.

[503]O.C.G.A. § 16-8-12 (a) and (a)(6)(B).

[504]O.C.G.A. § 16-8-12 (a)(6)(A)(iii).

[505]O.C.G.A. § 16-9-70 (a).

[506]O.C.G.A. § 16-9-70 (b).

The one exception to this law occurs when any of the changes or alterations were customarily made or done as an established practice in the ordinary and regular conduct of business by the original manufacturer or by the manufacturer's duly appointed direct representative, or under specific authorization from the original manufacturer.[507]

## Alteration or Counterfeiting Concealed Weapons Licenses

A person who deliberately alters or counterfeits a weapons carry license or who possesses an altered or counterfeit weapons carry license with the intent to misrepresent any information contained on the license is guilty of a felony and is subject to prison time of one to five years.[508]

## Crimes Committed by Convicted Felson with Firearm

Any person who has been previously convicted of or who has previously entered a guilty plea to the offense of murder, armed robbery, kidnapping, rape, aggravated child molestation, aggravated sodomy, aggravated sexual battery, or any felony involving the use or possession of a firearm and who shall have on or within arm's reach of his or her person a firearm during the commission of, or attempt to commit, any of the following crimes, shall be punished by confinement for life:[509]

- any crime against or involving the person of another[510]
- the unlawful entry into a building or vehicle[511]
- a theft from a building or theft of a vehicle[512]
- specific drug crimes involving distribution and/or trafficking[513]

---

[507]O.C.G.A. § 16-9-70 (c).

[508]O.C.G.A. § 16-11-129 (g).

[509]O.C.G.A. § 16-11-133 (b) and (c).

[510]O.C.G.A. § 16-11-133 (b)(1).

[511]O.C.G.A. § 16-11-133 (b)(2).

[512]O.C.G.A. § 16-11-133 (b)(3).

[513]O.C.G.A. § 16-11-133 (b)(4) and (5).

## Disarming Peace Officers and Others In the Line of Duty

It is unlawful for any person knowingly to remove or attempt to remove a firearm, chemical spray, or baton from the possession of another person if[514] the other person is lawfully acting within the course and scope of employment[515] and the person has knowledge or reason to know that the other person is employed as[516] a peace officer,[517] probation officer with the power to arrest,[518] parole officer with the power to arrest,[519] jail officer or guard,[520] juvenile correctional officer.[521]

A violation of this law is a felony and subjects the offender to between one to five years in prison and potentially a fine of up to $10,000.[522]

## Possession of Firearm or Knife While Committing or Attempting to Commit Certain Specific Crimes

In Georgia, as with most other states, there are special circumstances which can make the punishment for crimes much more serious. In this case, if certain crimes are committed, they may carry a certain punishment, but if the same exact crime were committed while possessing a firearm or a knife, the punishment is much more severe. Such laws are usually considered to "enhance" the punishment of the crime if factors are present to trigger the enhancement.

For the purpose of the discussion in this section, the term "firearm" also

---

[514]O.C.G.A. § 16-10-33 (a).

[515]O.C.G.A. § 16-10-33 (a)(1).

[516]O.C.G.A. § 16-10-33 (a)(2).

[517]O.C.G.A. § 16-10-33 (a)(2)(A); see also § O.C.G.A. 35-8-2 (8) regarding definition of "peace officer."

[518]O.C.G.A. § 16-10-33 (a)(2)(B).

[519]O.C.G.A. § 16-10-33 (a)(2)(C).

[520]O.C.G.A. § 16-10-33 (a)(2)(D).

[521]O.C.G.A. § 16-10-33 (a)(2)(E).

[522]O.C.G.A. § 16-10-33 (b).

includes stun guns and tasers, which are defined as any device that is powered by electrical charging units, such as batteries, and emits an electrical charge in excess of 20,000 volts, or is otherwise capable of incapacitating a person by an electrical charge.[523] However, this does not include a "pellet gun."[524]

The general rule is that any person who has on or within arm's reach of his or her person a firearm or knife having a blade of three or more inches in length during the commission of, or attempt to commit,[525] any crime against or involving the person of another,[526] the unlawful entry into a building or vehicle,[527] a theft from a building or theft of a vehicle,[528] or any specific drug crimes,[529] commits a felony and, upon conviction of that felony, is to be punished by imprisonment for a period of five years.[530]

The element of possession of a firearm during the commission of a crime is satisfied if, during the commission of the crime, the firearm is only within arm's reach momentarily.[531] Also, to have a successful prosecution for this crime, it need not be demonstrated that the firearm is capable of being fired.[532] Also, the fact that the offender had a concealed weapons license is no defense to the crime.[533] Finally, the person could simply be an aider or abettor to the crime, and still be charged

---

[523]O.C.G.A. § 16 -11-106 (a).

[524]See *Fields v. State*, (1995) 216 Ga.App. 184, 453 S.E.2d 794.

[525]O.C.G.A. § 16-11-106 (b).

[526]O.C.G.A. § 16-11-106 (b)(1).

[527]O.C.G.A. § 16-11-106 (b)(2).

[528]O.C.G.A. § 16-11-106 (b)(3).

[529]See O.C.G.A. §§ 16-11-106 (b)(4) and (b)(5), 16-13-30, 16-13-21, 16-30-30.1, and 16-13-31 for complete information on specified drug crimes.

[530]See O.C.G.A. § 16-11-106.

[531]See *Humphreys v. State*, (2002) 253 Ga.App. 344, 559 S.E.2d 99.

[532]See *Herndon v. State*, (1997) 229 Ga.App. 457, 494 S.E.2d 262.

[533]See *Spence v. State*, (1975) 233 Ga. 527, 212 S.E.2d 357.

with this offense, even if the person did not actually possess the weapon.[534]

A second or any subsequent conviction carries the punishment of ten years in prison.[535] Notwithstanding any laws to the contrary, the sentencing for any second or subsequent conviction is not subject to be suspended by the court with probation in lieu of the prison time.[536] Also, any sentence enhancements under the law for this offense shall run consecutively to any other sentence that the person has received,[537] as this offense is considered a separate offense.[538] In certain circumstances under Georgia law, punishments for felonies may be reduced to a misdemeanor punishment,[539] but for this offense, that is not possible.[540]

### Possession of a Machine Gun, Sawed-Off Rifle, Sawed-Off Shotgun, or a Firearm Equipped with a Silencer While Committing or Attempting to Commit a Crime

It is unlawful for any person to possess or to use a machine gun, sawed-off rifle, sawed-off shotgun, or a firearm equipped with a silencer, as those items are defined under Georgia law,[541] during the commission or the attempted commission of any of the following offenses:[542]

- aggravated assault[543]

---

[534]See *Collins v. State*, (1997) 229 Ga.App. 210, 493 S.E.2d 592; see also *Williams v. State*, (1994) 214 Ga.App. 421, 447 S.E.2d 714.

[535]O.C.G.A. § 16-11-106 (c).

[536]O.C.G.A. § 16-11-106 (c).

[537]O.C.G.A. § 16-11-106 (b)(5).

[538]O.C.G.A. § 16-11-106 (e).

[539]See O.C.G.A. § 17-10-5.

[540]O.C.G.A. § 16-11-106 (d).

[541]See O.C.G.A. § 16-11-121.

[542]O.C.G.A. § 16-11-16- (a)(1).

[543]O.C.G.A. § 16-11-160 (a)(1)(A); see also O.C.G.A. § 16-5-21 for definition of "aggravated assault."

- aggravated battery[544]
- robbery[545]
- armed robbery[546]
- murder or felony murder[547]
- voluntary manslaughter[548]
- involuntary manslaughter[549]
- trafficking in drugs[550]
- making terroristic threats[551]
- arson[552]
- influencing witnesses[553]
- participating in criminal gang activity[554]

---

[544]O.C.G.A. § 16-11-160 (a)(1)(B); see also O.C.G.A. § 16-5-24 for definition of "aggravated battery."

[545]O.C.G.A. § 16-11-160 (a)(1)(C); see also O.C.G.A. § 16-8-40 for definition of "robbery."

[546]O.C.G.A. § 16-11-160 (a)(1)(D); see also O.C.G.A. § 16-8-41 for definition of "armed robbery."

[547]O.C.G.A. § 16-11-160 (a)(1)(E); see also O.C.G.A. § 16-5-1 for definition of "murder" or "felony murder."

[548]O.C.G.A. § 16-11-160 (a)(1)(F); see also O.C.G.A. § 16-5-2 for definition of "voluntary manslaughter."

[549]O.C.G.A. § 16-11-160 (a)(1)(G); see also O.C.G.A. § 16-5-3 for definition of "involuntary manslaughter."

[550]O.C.G.A. § 16-11-160 (a)(1)(H); see also O.C.G.A. Title 16, Chapter 13, Article 2 for specifics regarding drug offenses applicable to this prohibition.

[551]O.C.G.A. § 16-11-160 (a)(1)(I); see also O.C.G.A. § 16-11-37 for definition of "terroristic acts or threats."

[552]O.C.G.A. § 16-11-160 (a)(1)(J); see also O.C.G.A. §§ 16-7-60, 16-7-61, 16-7-62, and 16-7-63 for definitions of "arson."

[553]O.C.G.A. § 16-11-160 (a)(1)(K); see also O.C.G.A. § 16-10-93 for definition of "influencing witnesses."

[554]O.C.G.A. § 16-11-160 (a)(1)(L); see also O.C.G.A. § 16-15-4 for definition of "criminal gang activity."

A violation of this prohibition may result in a felony conviction that carries a punishment of imprisonment of ten years.[555] A life sentence will be given for any second conviction of this prohibition, and the life sentence may not be probated or suspended.[556]

### Wearing a Bulletproof Vest During Commission of Certain Crimes

It is unlawful for any person to wear a bulletproof vest during the commission or the attempted commission of any of the following offenses:[557]

- any crime against or involving the person of another in violation of any provisions of Title 16 for which a sentence of life imprisonment may be imposed[558]
- participating in specific drug crimes regarding distribution or trafficking[559]

A "bulletproof vest" means a bullet-resistant soft-body armor providing, as a minimum standard, the level of protection known as "threat level I," which means at least seven layers of bullet-resistant material providing protection from at least three shots of 158-grain lead ammunition fired from a .38 caliber handgun at a velocity of 850 feet per second.[560]

A violation of this prohibition may result in a felony conviction that carries a punishment of imprisonment of one to five years.[561] A life sentence will be given for any second conviction of this prohibition, and the life sentence may not be

---

[555]O.C.G.A. § 16-11-160 (b).

[556]O.C.G.A. § 16-11-160 (c) and (d).

[557]O.C.G.A. § 16-11-160 (a)(2)(B).

[558]O.C.G.A. § 16-11-160 (a)(2)(B)(i).

[559]O.C.G.A. § 16-11-160 (a)(2)(B)(ii) and (iii).

[560]O.C.G.A. § 16-11-160 (a)(2)(A).

[561]O.C.G.A. § 16-11-160 (b).

probated or suspended.[562]

## State Law Offenses Regarding Minors with Firearms and Other Weapons

Much of this material is repeated in the chapter involving weapons offenses, but because of the importance of being aware of these offenses, they are discussed in this chapter as well.

Furnishing or Allowing Minor to Possess Pistol or Revolver - It is unlawful for a person intentionally, knowingly, or recklessly to sell or furnish a pistol or revolver to a minor.[563] Punishment for this offense which is considered a felony is a penalty of a fine of up to $5000 along with imprisonment from 3 to 5 years.[564]

Of course, the exceptions illustrated in this chapter as discussed above apply unless the person authorized to permit possession of a pistol or revolver by a minor knows of the minor's conduct that otherwise violates the laws prohibiting the minor from possessing or handling the firearm and that person fails to make reasonable efforts to prevent the minor from committing the offense.[565] At that point, the person authorized to give permission, which would be the parent or legal guardian, may not give permission or provide the handgun to the minor.

Additionally, it is unlawful for a parent or legal guardian intentionally, knowingly, or recklessly to furnish or to permit a minor to possess a pistol or revolver if such parent or legal guardian is aware of a substantial risk that the minor will use a pistol or revolver to commit a felony offense, or if the parent or legal guardian knows of such risk and fails to make reasonable efforts to prevent commission of the offense by the minor.[566]

Finally, a parent or legal guardian shall be deemed to have violated the above prohibitions if the parent or legal guardian furnishes to or permits possession

---

[562]O.C.G.A. § 16-11-160 (c) and (d).

[563]O.C.G.A. § 16-11-101.1.

[564]O.C.G.A. § 16-11-101.1 (d).

[565]O.C.G.A. § 16-11-101.1 (c)(1).

[566]O.C.G.A. § 16-11-101.1 (c)(2).

of a pistol or revolver by any minor who has been convicted of a forcible felony or forcible misdemeanor,[567] or who has been adjudicated delinquent under Georgia law[568] for an offense which would constitute a forcible felony or forcible misdemeanor if such minor were an adult.[569]

Punishment for the offenses outlined in the previous three paragraphs, offenses which are considered felonies, carries a penalty of a fine of up to $5000 along with imprisonment from 3 to 5 years.[570]

A separate charge of contributing to the delinquency of a minor may also be brought against any individual that knowingly and willfully provides to a minor access to a handgun, and/or assists the minor in violating laws regarding firearms on school property or at school functions.[571] However, in this case, minors are those who are under 17 years of age unless they are under the age of 18 years and also alleged to be a "deprived child" as defined by law.[572]

The purpose behind the statute that makes it unlawful for a person to intentionally, knowingly, or recklessly sell or furnish a handgun to a minor except for limited circumstances was intended to protect minors from their own inability to protect themselves from their dangerous conduct when handling handguns, including their own lack of judgment or inability to resist various peer pressures.[573]

Furnishing Knife or Metal Knuckles to Minor - A person is guilty of a misdemeanor of a high and aggravated nature when he or she knowingly sells or furnishes to a person under the age of 18 years any knuckles, whether made from metal, thermoplastic, wood, or other similar material, or a knife designed for the

---

[567]See O.C.G.A. § 16-1-3.

[568]See O.C.G.A. Title 15, Chapter 11, Article 1.

[569]O.C.G.A. § 16-11-101.1 (c)(3).

[570]O.C.G.A. § 16-11-101.1 (d).

[571]See O.C.G.A. §§ 16-12-1 (b), (b)(5), 16-11-121, and 16-11-127.1.

[572]O.C.G.A. § 16-12-1 (a)(3); see also O.C.G.A. § 15-11-2 regarding "deprived children."

[573]See McEachern v. Muldovan, (1998) 234 Ga.App. 152, 505 S.E.2d 495.

purpose of offense and defense.[574]

Toy Pistols and Mere Imitation Pistols Excluded - While it should appear obvious, it is not, which is why there is case law addressing it, but a toy pistol is not a pistol under the law, so toy pistols may be sold to minors.[575] Furthermore, the prohibition on the sale of a pistol to a minor contemplates the sale of an actual weapon, and not a mere imitation of a weapon that is not reasonably capable of being put to the use for which the corresponding weapon is intended.[576] There is no liability for injuries received from a toy pistol sold to a minor.[577]

Minors Under 12 Prohibited From Hunting Alone - It is unlawful for any person who is under 12 years of age to hunt any wildlife in the State of Georgia unless that person is under the direct supervision of an adult during the period in which the person is hunting.[578] It is also unlawful for any person to cause or to knowingly permit such person's child or ward who is less than 12 years old to hunt any wildlife with a weapon in the State of Georgia unless that child or ward is under adult supervision.[579]

## Federal Law Regarding Juveniles and Handguns

Under federal law, a juvenile is someone who is under the age of 18. Of course, this corresponds with Georgia state law. There are three types of law that apply to minors and firearms, including Georgia law, federal law, and some local or municipal laws. Only Georgia law and some federal law are discussed in this book. There are just too many counties, cities, and other localities to keep up with. If you have a concern about a particular municipality and the laws governing that municipality, the laws are likely online, as just about every municipality has a web site. Google is your friend when looking for such laws and ordinances.

---

[574]O.C.G.A. § 16-11-101.

[575]See *Mathews v. Caldwell*, (1908) 5 Ga.App. 336, 63 S.E. 250.

[576]See *Mathews v. Caldwell*, (1908) 5 Ga.App. 336, 63 S.E. 250.

[577]See *Mathews v. Caldwell*, (1908) 5 Ga.App. 336, 63 S.E. 250.

[578]O.C.G.A. § 27-3-41 (a).

[579]O.C.G.A. § 27-3-41 (b).

It shall be unlawful for any person who is a juvenile to knowingly possess a handgun or ammunition that is suitable for use only in a handgun.[580] However, there are exceptions.[581]

Farming and Ranching Activities - A juvenile may be in temporary possession of or may use a handgun and/or handgun ammunition in the course of employment, such as in the course of ranching or farming related to the activities at the residence of the juvenile, as long as the juvenile first has the permission of the land owner or lessee.[582]

Target Practice, Hunting, and Course of Instruction - A juvenile may be in temporary possession of or may use a handgun and/or handgun ammunition in the course and scope of activities where the juvenile is temporarily engaged in target practice, hunting, or a course of instruction in the safe and lawful use of a handgun.[583]

Prior Consent of Parent - A juvenile may temporarily possess and/or use a handgun and/or handgun ammunition if prior written consent of the juvenile's parent or guardian is given, provided that the parent or guardian himself is not prohibited by federal, state, or local law from possessing a firearm.[584] The written consent must remain on the juvenile's person at all times when the handgun is in the possession of the juvenile.[585]

Armed Forces - A juvenile may also possess a handgun and/or handgun ammunition if he is a member of the Armed Forces of the United States or the National Guard and who possesses or is armed with a handgun in the line of duty.[586]

---

[580] 18 U.S.C. § 922 (x)(2)(A) and (B).

[581] 18 U.S.C. § 922 (x)(3).

[582] 18 U.S.C. § 922 (x)(3)(A)(i).

[583] 18 U.S.C. § 922 (x)(3)(A)(i).

[584] 18 U.S.C. § 922 (x)(3)(A)(ii).

[585] 18 U.S.C. § 922 (x)(3)(A)(iii).

[586] 18 U.S.C. § 922 (x)(3)((B).

Self-Defense Situations - Juveniles may also possess a handgun and/or handgun ammunition if used in self-defense of the juvenile or other persons against an intruder into the residence of the juvenile or a residence where the juvenile is an invited guest.[587]

Inheritance - A juvenile is subject to the exceptions if he takes a handgun or handgun ammunition subject to a transfer by inheritance of title; however, he may not take possession legally until he is of legal age unless one of the other exceptions above exists.[588]

In any of the scenarios above, where a juvenile is in temporary custody of a handgun and/or handgun ammunition, he must transport the handgun unloaded and in a locked container when traveling to and from the activity and must also observe all state and local gun laws.[589]

A juvenile who violates federal law regarding possession of a handgun and/or handgun ammunition may be fined or imprisoned not more than one year, or both.[590] The good news for the juvenile is that if the offense he is charged with is possession of either a handgun or handgun ammunition, or both, and that juvenile has not been convicted in any court of an offense or adjudicated as a juvenile delinquent, the punishment will be probation.[591] However, a violation of probation for this offense may result in incarceration.[592]

## Unlawful Possession of Device on Person or to Place in Possession of Passenger

It is unlawful for any person, with the intention of avoiding or interfering with a security measure or of introducing into any terminal any explosive, destructive device, firearm, knife, or other device designed or modified for the

---

[587] 18 U.S.C. § 922 (x)(3)(D).

[588] 18 U.S.C. § 922 (x)(3)(C).

[589] 18 U.S.C. § 922 (x)(3)(A)(ii)(I).

[590] 18 U.S.C. § 924 (a)(6)(A)(i).

[591] 18 U.S.C. §§ 924 (a)(6)(A)(I) and 924 (a)(6)(A)(ii)(I) and (II).

[592] 18 U.S.C. § 924 (a)(6)(A)(i).

purpose of offense and defense to[593] have any such item on his or her person,[594] or to place, or cause to be placed, or attempt to place or cause to be placed any such item[595] in a container or freight of a transportation company,[596] in the baggage or possessions of any person or any transportation company without the knowledge of the passenger or transportation company,[597] or aboard any aircraft, bus, or rail vehicle.[598]

Any person violating these prohibitions is guilty of a felony and shall, upon conviction, be sentenced to imprisonment for not less than one year and not more than 20 years, with a fine not to exceed $15,000, or both.[599]

Of course, one does not violate these prohibitions if he first notifies a law enforcement official or other person employed to provide security for a transportation company of the presence of such item as soon as possible after learning of its presence, and surrenders the item as directed by the authorities he reported the item to.[600] Also, those who have a valid weapons carry license observed under Georgia State law,[601] unless the possession of the weapon would somehow violate federal law,[602] would not be in violation of state law.

See the glossary in the back of this book for important definitions under

---

[593] O.C.G.A. § 16-12-127 (a).

[594] O.C.G.A. § 16-12-127 (a)(1).

[595] O.C.G.A. § 16-12-127 (a)(2).

[596] O.C.G.A. § 16-12-127 (a)(2)(A).

[597] O.C.G.A. § 16-12-127 (a)(2)(B)

[598] O.C.G.A. § 16-12-127 (a)(2)(C).

[599] O.C.G.A. § 16-12-127 (b).

[600] O.C.G.A. § 16-12-127 (c).

[601] O.C.G.A. § 16-12-127 (a).

[602] O.C.G.A. § 16-12-127 (a).

these prohibitions, all of which may also be found in the code.[603]

### Hunting Offenses Involving Firearms and Other Weapons

While this book has no focus on the hunting laws in general, there are quite a few offenses in the laws regarding hunting and fishing activities, and they should be considered here.

Hunting On or Discharging Weapon From or Across Public Road Prohibited - It is unlawful for any person while hunting to discharge any weapon from or across any public road in the State of Georgia.[604] A violation of this prohibition, if convicted, results in a fine of not less than $50 and not more than $1000, and/or imprisonment for up to twelve months.[605]

Possession of Centerfire or Rimfire Firearm While Bow Hunting or Hunting with Muzzleloading Firearm - It is unlawful for any person to possess any centerfire or rimfire firearm other than a handgun[606] while hunting with a bow and arrow during archery or primitive weapons season for deer, or to possess a loaded handgun while hunting with a bow and arrow during archery or primitive weapons season for deer, or while hunting with a muzzleloading firearm during primitive weapons season for deer, unless such person possesses a valid weapons carry license.[607]

Hunting While Under the Influence - A person shall not hunt under any of the following circumstances:[608]

- while he is under the influence of alcohol to the extent that it is less safe for the person to hunt[609]

---

[603]See O.C.G.A. § 16-12-122.

[604]O.C.G.A. § 27-3-10 (a).

[605]O.C.G.A. § 27-3-10 (b).

[606]"Handgun" as defined in O.C.G.A. § 16-11-125.1.

[607]O.C.G.A. § 27-3-6; see also O.C.G.A. § 16-11-129.

[608]O.C.G.A. § 27-3-7 (a).

[609]O.C.G.A. § 27-3-7 (b)(1).

- under the influence of any drug to the extent that it is less safe for the person to hunt[610]
- under the combined influence of alcohol and any drug to the extent that it is less safe for the person to hunt[611]
- the person's alcohol concentration is 0.10 grams or more at any time within three hours after hunting from alcohol consumed before such hunting ended[612]
- there is any amount of marijuana or a controlled substance present in the person's blood or urine, or both, including the metabolites and derivatives of each or both without regard to whether or not any alcohol is present in the person's breath or blood[613]

One who is legally entitled to drink alcohol or use a particular drug may not use that entitlement as a defense to a charge for violating the law.[614] Also, any person who exercises the privilege of hunting in the State of Georgia is deemed to have given consent to a chemical test or tests of his or her blood, breath, urine, or other bodily substances for the purpose of determining the presence of any alcohol or drug if arrested.[615]

Using Firearm or Archery Tackle in a Manner to Endanger the Bodily Safety of Another Person While Hunting - Any person who, while hunting wildlife, uses a firearm or archery tackle in a manner to endanger the bodily safety of another person by consciously disregarding a substantial and unjustifiable risk that his act or omission will cause harm to or endanger the safety of another person, and such disregard is a gross deviation from the standard of care that a reasonable person would exercise in the same situation, is guilty of a misdemeanor.[616]

---

[610]O.C.G.A. § 27-3-7 (b)(2).

[611]O.C.G.A. § 27-3-7 (b)(3).

[612]O.C.G.A. § 27-3-7 (b)(4).

[613]O.C.G.A. § 27-3-7 (b)(5).

[614]O.C.G.A. § 27-3-7 (c).

[615]O.C.G.A. § 27-3-7 (g)(1).

[616]O.C.G.A. § 16-11-108 (a).

If the activity illustrated above results in serious bodily harm to another person, the person who engaged in the reckless conduct is guilty of a felony, subjecting them to a fine of not more than $5000 and by a prison sentence of one to ten years.[617]

The arresting officer, when dealing with this situation, is to take the hunting license of the person charged.[618] The license is to be attached to the court's copy of the citation, warrant, accusation, or indictment, and is to be forwarded to the court having jurisdiction for the offense.[619] A copy of such is to be forwarded, within 15 days of its issuance, to the Game and Fish Division of the Department of Natural Resources.[620] Despite this, one charged may apply for a temporary hunting license during the pendency of charges.[621]

If the person is ultimately convicted of committing this offense, the court is to forward the person's hunting license and copy of the disposition of the case to the director of the Game and Fish Division of the Department of Natural Resources within 15 days of such conviction.[622] Also at this time, the court shall also require the person to surrender any temporary hunting licenses issued during the time leading up to trial.[623] Of course, if the person is not convicted, the court shall return the hunting license to the person.[624]

### Prohibited Acts in Wildlife Management Areas

Possession of Firearms in Wildlife Management Area During Off-Season - It shall be unlawful for any person on any wildlife management area owned or

---

[617]O.C.G.A. § 16-11-108 (a).

[618]O.C.G.A. § 16-11-108 (b).

[619]O.C.G.A. § 16-11-108 (b).

[620]O.C.G.A. § 16-11-108 (b).

[621]See O.C.G.A. § 16-11-108 (c) for details.

[622]O.C.G.A. § 16-11-108 (d)(1).

[623]O.C.G.A. § 16-11-108 (d)(1).

[624]O.C.G.A. § 16-11-108 (d)(2).

operated by the state to possess a firearm, <u>other than a handgun</u>, during a closed hunting season for that area, unless the firearm is unloaded and stored in a motor vehicle so as not to be readily accessible, or to possess a handgun during a closed hunting season for that area, unless the person is a concealed weapons license holder.[625]

It is also unlawful to possess a loaded firearm <u>other than a handgun</u> in a motor vehicle during a legal open hunting season for that area or to possess a loaded handgun in a motor vehicle unless that person is a concealed weapons license holder.[626]

<u>Prohibition on Hunting Near Road</u> - It is unlawful to hunt within a wildlife management area within 50 yards of any road which receives regular maintenance for the purpose of public vehicular access.[627]

<u>Target Practice</u> - It is unlawful to take part in target practice within a wildlife management area, unless the practice is at an authorized shooting range that is made available by the state, and even then, only in a manner consistent with the rules for shooting ranges.[628]

### Prohibited Acts in Public Fishing Areas

It is unlawful for any person on any public fishing area owned or operated by the state to possess a firearm, other than a handgun, during closed hunting season for that area, unless the firearm is unloaded and stored in a motor vehicle so as not to be readily accessible, or unless that person possesses a valid concealed weapons license.[629] It is also unlawful to do so in the same area during legal open hunting season absent a concealed weapons license.[630]

---

[625]O.C.G.A. §§ 27-3-1.1 and 27-3-1.1 (1).

[626]O.C.G.A. § 27-3-1.1 (2).

[627]O.C.G.A. § 27-3-1.1 (4).

[628]O.C.G.A. § 27-3-1.1 (5).

[629]O.C.G.A. § 27-4-11.1 (a) and (a)(1).

[630]O.C.G.A. § 27-4-11.1 (a) and (a)(2).

## Antiterroristic Training

The Georgia Assembly has a set of laws dealing with the prohibition on antiterroristic training that is known as the "Georgia Antiterroristic Training Act."[631] This sort of state law is common.

Basically, it is unlawful to teach, train, or demonstrate to any other person the use, application, or making of any illegal firearm, dangerous weapon, explosive, or incendiary device capable of causing injury or death to persons, if the person who is teaching has reason to know, or intends that such teaching will be unlawfully employed for use in or in furtherance of a civil disorder, riot, or insurrection.[632] To communicate such instruction either directly, in writing, or over a computer or computer network is considered a violation of this prohibition.[633] This violation occurs whether the person doing the teaching is teaching one person or a group of people.[634]

A violation of this prohibition results in a felony act and carries a penalty of up to $5000 and between one and five years imprisonment.[635]

Exceptions exist for a peace officer acting within the course and scope of his duties,[636] any training for law enforcement officers,[637] any activities of the National Guard or the United States Armed Forces,[638] any hunter education classes that are taught under the auspices of the Department of Natural Resources,[639] or any other classes intended to teach the safe handling of firearms for hunting,

---

[631]O.C.G.A. § 16-11-150.

[632]O.C.G.A. § 16-11-151 (b) and (b)(1).

[633]O.C.G.A. § 16-11-151 (b)(1).

[634]O.C.G.A. § 16-11-151.

[635]O.C.G.A. § 16-11-151 (c).

[636]O.C.G.A. § 16-11-152 (1).

[637]O.C.G.A. § 16-11-152 (2).

[638]O.C.G.A. § 16-11-152 (3).

[639]O.C.G.A. § 16-11-152 (4).

recreation, competition, or self-defense.[640]

## Unauthorized Military Bodies

No body of men, other than the organized militia, components of the United States Armed Forces, and bodies of the police and state constabulary and other organizations that might be formed by the government, shall associate themselves as a military unit or parade, and no such group shall demonstrate in public with firearms.[641]

Any person who actively participates in an unauthorized military organization or who parades with any unauthorized body of men is guilty of a misdemeanor.[642]

## Exemptions of Concealed Carry Laws

Specifically defined concealed carry violations[643] shall not apply to or affect any of the following persons, so long as such persons are employed in the designated offices or when authorized by federal or state law, regulations, or order:[644]

- peace officers[645] and retired peace officers so long as they remain certified whether employed by the state or a political subdivision of the state, or of another state or political subdivision of that other state, but only if such other state provides a similar privilege for the peace officers of that state[646]
- wardens, superintendents, and keepers of correctional institutions, jails, or other institutions for the detention of

---

[640]O.C.G.A. § 16-11-152 (4).

[641]O.C.G.A. § 38-2-277 (a).

[642]O.C.G.A. § 38-2-277 (d).

[643]See O.C.G.A. § 16-11-126 through O.C.G.A. § 16-11-127.2.

[644]O.C.G.A. § 16-11-130 (a).

[645]See O.C.G.A. § 16-1-3 (11) for specifically defined peace officers.

[646]O.C.G.A. § 16-11-130 (a)(1).

persons accused or convicted of an offense[647]

- persons in the military service of the state or of the United States[648]
- persons employed in fulfilling defense contracts with the federal government or federal agencies when possession of the weapon is necessary for manufacture, transport, installation, and testing under the requirements of the contract[649]
- specific government attorneys and their investigatory agents[650]
- state court solicitors-generals' and their investigatory agents[651]
- specific employees of the State Board of Pardons and Paroles[652]
- the Attorney General and specific members of his or her staff upon authorization[653]
- specific probation officers and specific agents of the probation officers[654]
- public safety directors of municipal corporations[655]
- explosive ordinance technicians[656] and persons certified to handle animals for the purpose of detecting explosives, while in the performance of their duties[657]
- specific state and federal judges, full time or part time, retired or

---

[647]O.C.G.A. § 16-11-130 (a)(2).

[648]O.C.G.A. § 16-11-130 (a)(3).

[649]O.C.G.A. § 16-11-130 (a)(4).

[650]O.C.G.A. § 16-11-130 (a)(5).

[651]O.C.G.A. § 16-11-130 (a)(6).

[652]O.C.G.A. § 16-11-130 (a)(7).

[653]O.C.G.A. § 16-11-130 (a)(8).

[654]O.C.G.A. § 16-11-130 (a)(9).

[655]O.C.G.A. § 16-11-130 (a)(10).

[656]As defined in O.C.G.A. § 16-7-80.

[657]O.C.G.A. § 16-11-130 (a)(11); see also O.C.G.A. § 35-8-13.

currently active[658]
- United States Attorneys and Assistant United States Attorneys[659]
- county medical examiners, coroners, and their sworn officers[660]
- clerks of the superior courts[661]
- certain other specific government professionals and retirees[662]

## An Important Note Regarding Knives in Georgia

The general rule of thumb regarding knives in the State of Georgia is that knives may have a blade up to 5 inches in length and be carried lawfully. However, in school zones, the blade may only be 2 inches in length. Open carry of a knife is allowed so long as the knife was not specifically designed for the purpose of offense and defense.[663] Knives allowed to be carried in a lawful fashion include fixed blade knives, folding knives, dirks, daggers, automatic knives, balisongs, and stilettos. However, there is no preemption law regarding knives, so any government within the State of Georgia that is below the state level may apply local restrictions.

---

[658]O.C.G.A. § 16-11-130 (a)(12).

[659]O.C.G.A. § 16-11-130 (a)(13).

[660]O.C.G.A. § 16-11-130 (a)(14).

[661]O.C.G.A. § 16-11-130 (a)(15).

[662]See O.C.G.A. § 16-11-130 (b) and (c).

[663]O.C.G.A. § 16-11-126.

# CHAPTER TWELVE

## <u>Miscellaneous Provisions of Law</u>

Of course, there are always random laws on the books in regards to firearms, knives, and other weapons, which are discussed here.

### <u>Employees' Rights Regarding Firearms and Weapons</u>

Unless otherwise provided by law, no private or public employer, including the state and its political subdivisions, shall establish, maintain, or enforce any policy or rule that has the effect of allowing such employer or its agents to search the locked, privately owned vehicles of employees, or invited guests, on the employer's parking lot or access thereto.[664]

That being said, none of the aforementioned employers may condition employment upon any agreement by a prospective employee that prohibits the employee from entering the parking lot and access thereto when the employee's privately owned motor vehicle contains a firearm that is locked and out of sight within the trunk, glove box, or other enclosed compartment or area within such privately owned motor vehicle, provided that the employee possesses a Georgia weapons carry license.[665]

Exceptions apply, and are as follows:[666]

- searches by law enforcement pursuant to valid search warrants or valid warrantless searches based upon probable cause under exigent circumstances[667]
- searches of vehicles owned or leased by an employer[668]
- situations where a reasonable person would believe that accessing

---

[664]O.C.G.A. § 16-11-135 (a).

[665]O.C.G.A. § 16-11-135 (b).

[666]O.C.G.A. § 16-11-135 (c).

[667]O.C.G.A. § 16-11-135 (c)(1).

[668]O.C.G.A. § 16-11-135 (c)(2).

a locked vehicle of an employee is necessary to prevent an immediate threat to human health, life, or safety[669]

- upon employee consent under specific circumstances[670]

Further restrictions and considerations that are very specific in nature regarding employer-employee rights and immunities regarding searches and parking on workplace lots may be found in the Georgia Code, all of which are included in the back of this book.[671]

## Protections Afforded to Sport Shooting Ranges

This issue is discussed above with State of Georgia preemption issues, but it is an important consideration and to ensure that it is not overlooked, is discussed here as well.

Basically, the General Assembly does not prohibit municipalities or county, by ordinance, resolution, or other enactment, from reasonably limiting or prohibiting the discharge of firearms within the boundaries of the municipal corporation or county.[672]

However, it is common knowledge among those in the gun community that oftentimes a local government will use its power to shut down shooting ranges by arguing that the range is a nuisance. Because of the exception allowing localities the power to prohibit the discharge of weapons, localities may essentially ban shooting ranges from operating within their boundaries.

So, if the shooting range already exists and is established, and an attempt later is made by the locality to shut down the shooting range, the locality may not do so by deeming the shooting range as a nuisance for "changed circumstances," which generally means that as the town developed, the area around the range has become sensitive to the shooting range. Perhaps a developer built a residential neighborhood next to the shooting range.

---

[669]O.C.G.A. § 16-11-135 (c)(3).

[670]O.C.G.A. § 16-11-135 (c)(4).

[671]O.C.G.A. § 16-11-135 (d)

[672]O.C.G.A. § 16-11-173 (e).

In any event, no sport shooting range shall be or shall become a nuisance, either public or private, solely as a result of changed conditions in or around the locality of such range if the range has been in operation for one year since the date on which it commenced operation as a sport shooting range.[673] This offers protections to the entrepreneur who works hard and uses his money to open a shooting range, only to have the town come in and try to shut him down years later.

Furthermore, subsequent physical expansion of the range or expansion of the types of firearms in use at the range shall not establish a new date of commencement of operations for purposes of the law.[674] This protects the business owner by allowing him to expand the business without fear that such expansion resets the start date of operation, thus allowing the town to come in and deem the business as a nuisance.

Also, no sport shooting range or unit of government or person owning, operating, or using a sport shooting range for the sport shooting of firearms shall be subject to any action for civil or criminal liability, damages, abatement, or injunctive relief resulting from or relating to noise generated by the operation of the range, if the range remains in compliance with noise control or nuisance abatement rules, regulations, statutes, or ordinances that apply to the range on the date on which the range commenced operation.[675] This protects the range owner from a change in laws that could be drafted to be so burdensome that it would be virtually impossible to comply with, thus allowing the town to come in and shut the range down.

Finally, any laws a town my enact regarding noise control, noise pollution, or noise abatement that may be adopted by a local governmental entity may not be applied retroactively to sport shooting ranges.[676]

So, while there exists an exception to the preemption statute regarding the discharge of firearms within local government boundaries, there are protections afforded to established shooting ranges.

---

[673]O.C.G.A. § 41-1-9 (b).

[674]O.C.G.A. § 41-1-9 (b).

[675]O.C.G.A. § 41-1-9 (c).

[676]O.C.G.A. § 41-1-9 (d).

## Prohibition of Denial of Insurance Coverage Based on Firearms on Property

No policy of insurance issued or delivered in the State of Georgia covering any loss, damages, expense, or liability may exclude or deny coverage because the insured, members of the insured's family, or employees of the insured will keep or carry in a lawful manner firearms on the property or premises of the insured.[677]

## Powers of Government in Times of Emergency

Closing Places Where Firearms and Ammunition are Sold - When any force of the organized militia is or has been called out for the performance of any duty under Georgia law,[678] it shall be lawful for the commanding officer of the force, if in his judgment that for the purposes of law and order in the area the places where arms and ammunition are sold must be closed, he may do so, if in his judgment disorder is likely to occur.[679]

For any person who sells or disperses arms or ammunition in violation of such an order from a commanding officer, that person is guilty of a felony and is subject to two to five years in prison.[680]

Emergency Powers of the Governor - As we all know, in certain situations, the Governor may declare a state of emergency or that a disaster exists.[681] When declaring a state of emergency or that a disaster exists, the Governor has additional powers and may elect to take certain actions, all which fall under what are known as "emergency powers."

Included in the emergency powers are the ability to seize, take for temporary use, or condemn property for the protection of the public in accordance

---

[677] O.C.G.A. § 33-24-30.1.

[678] See O.C.G.A. § 38-2-6.

[679] O.C.G.A. § 38-2-301 (a).

[680] O.C.G.A. § 38-2-301 (b).

[681] See O.C.G.A. § 38-3-51.

with condemnation proceedings as provided by law,[682] and to perform and exercise such other functions, powers, and duties as may be deemed necessary to promote and secure the safety and protection of the civilian population.[683]

The Governor may also commandeer or utilize any private property if he finds this necessary to cope with the emergency or disaster[684] and suspend or limit the sale, dispensing, or transportation of firearms, explosives, and combustibles.[685] However, any limitation on firearms under these powers is not to include an individual firearm owned by a private citizen which was legal and owned by that citizen prior to the declaration of the state of emergency or disaster, or was subsequently acquired in compliance with all of the applicable laws of the State of Georgia and of the United States.[686]

So, while there are protections for gun owners, or anyone else wanting to protect themselves, their family, and their property, during a state of emergency or disaster, there is some question about how the individual's rights would shake out. It is better to consider the above and be prepared for such a scenario than not to know what the state can and cannot do in the event of a state of emergency or disaster.

---

[682]O.C.G.A. § 38-3-51 (c) and (c)(2).

[683]O.C.G.A. § 38-3-51 (c) and (c)(4).

[684]O.C.G.A. § 38-3-51 (d) and (d)(4).

[685]O.C.G.A. § 38-3-51 (d) and (d)(8).

[686]O.C.G.A. § 38-3-51 (d) and (d)(8).

# CHAPTER THIRTEEN

## <u>Firearms Safety Considerations</u>

Whether you are pro-gun or anti-gun, one point every citizen can likely agree on is that gun safety is of paramount concern. No firearms related book would be complete without a few words on firearms safety and the safe handling of firearms.

### Basic Firearms Safety Considerations

**1. Treat each and every firearm as if it were loaded.** When you first handle any firearm, be sure to inspect it to determine if it is loaded or unloaded. If you do not know how to check a particular gun as to whether it is loaded or not, you should leave it alone and seek assistance from someone who is more knowledgeable about that gun. To insure your safety and the safety of those around you, it is always best to assume that a gun is loaded, even if you think it is unloaded, and even if you have already checked it. By doing this, you will create a habit of handling a gun safely. It will be second-nature to handle a gun as if it were loaded. It is important always to respect the firearm, and to understand the dangers presented by someone who improperly handles a firearm.

**2. Never point the muzzle of the firearm towards any object that you are unwilling to destroy.** Always keep the muzzle of the gun pointed in a safe direction. The best place to point a firearm is a direction where an accidental discharge (commonly called a negligent discharge, or "ND") of the firearm will not cause injury or damage to yourself or others. Never quit paying attention to where you or others are pointing a firearm. It is never amusing, and is instead very dangerous, and in very poor taste, to point a firearm at yourself, another person, or an animal that you do not intend to shoot. Again, it is important always to respect the firearm and to understand the dangers presented by someone who improperly handles a firearm.

**3. Keep your finger off the trigger at all times while handling a firearm up until the point in time that you are pointed in at your target and ready to fire.** Keep your trigger finger outside the trigger guard that surrounds the trigger until you are ready to fire. The best place for the finger is along the frame of the weapon, with the tip of the finger resting gently on top of the reference point, which is usually a slide stop, a screw, or some other physical feature along the side of the frame, which is actually simply holding the finger down the side of the frame or receiver. That way, if you were to drop the gun for any reason, or suddenly grip the firearm for any reason, you do not advertently apply pressure to the trigger.

If you choose to handle a firearm in the fashion described above, it will actually become uncomfortable to hold a firearm with your finger on the trigger. You will create a level of consciousness of where your finger is that you will not have to give much thought. For some, this is very similar to wearing a seat belt when in an automobile. Some people are so aware of the safety risks of not wearing a seat belt that they cannot even sit in a car comfortably without the seat belt on, even if the car is not moving and is not going to move. If they are in a car, the seat belt will be on. They will do this without even giving it any thought.

The proper handling of a firearm is the same. If you handle a firearm properly, after some time of doing so, you will ultimately develop a level of consciousness that allows you to respect a firearm without having to give it any thought; it will be natural.

**4. Be aware of your target and everything around and behind it.** A prudent shooter will check the areas around, behind, and in front of a target to ensure that the area is safe before shooting.

When you fire a gun, rarely does the bullet stop at the target. Instead, the bullet travels downrange somewhere before coming to a rest. If there is someone or something downrange that you do not want to shoot at, you should not be shooting at that target. If you are ever in doubt of what is downrange, it is prudent not to shoot the firearm at all. Most importantly, before shooting any firearm, get a good sense of where all the people are around you. Check behind you, in front of you, and to your sides. Check this area regularly so as to raise the safety level for yourself and others around you.

**5. Penetration and Zone of Danger Information**. In general, a residential home is built with walls that are constructed with two layers of 5/8 inch sheet rock. It is safe to assume that just about any type of bullet, no matter how small and powerless or how big and powerful, will penetrate the sheet rock and continue to travel out the other side. Consider this when handling a firearm at your home and you are either unsure of what is on the other side of the structure or you know what is on the other side and know it is something you would prefer not to point a gun at or shoot at.

Further, the range of typical rifle bullets can be as short as 4500 feet to as high as 17,000 feet. This is nearly a mile to over three miles! Pistol rounds do not travel as far, generally with a range of about 4500 feet to as high as 7500 feet. The range of a shotgun is much shorter, with ranges from about 700 feet to 2,500 feet. So, in considering what is behind your target, a safe rule of thumb is to assume that at a minimum, the typical downrange zone of danger if you fire a gun is one mile.

### Additional Firearms Safety Considerations

Consider your attitude on any day that you might be handling a firearm. If you have had a bad day, are angry, troubled, or even if you simply did not get a good night's rest the night before, perhaps you should not be handling a firearm, as your judgment and ability to focus on safety may be impaired.

Transport guns and ammunition in a safe, secure, and legal fashion. Store guns and ammunition safely, securely, and legally. Just because you are off doing other things and are not currently dealing with your firearm, safety considerations still exist. The responsible firearms owner will spend good time considering just how to store his firearms and ammunition. Ideally, firearms and ammunition are never stored together.

Consider using a firearms safety device on your firearms that will prevent the weapon from being fired until unlocked. Common devices are trigger locks and cable locks. All firearms and ammunition should be stored in some sort of locked container, or, better yet, in a gun safe. The more you lock up your firearm, the less chance there is that the firearm will be involved in some sort of unfortunate situation.

Shoot only where it is safe and legal.

Learn how your firearm functions and how to operate properly the firearm. It is amazing how many people do not know how their firearm functions. For instance, it is shocking how many people do not know what a "trigger reset" is. A gun owner who has no clue what a trigger reset is does not fully understand how his firearm works. If you do not know what the trigger reset is, what other things do you not know? As a firearms owner, it is your responsibility to know.

As a gun owner, you have a great responsibility to yourself and others to become thoroughly familiar with your firearm and how to handle it in a safe fashion. You should be able to identify the various parts of your firearm and how to maintain them in safe, working condition. You should know how to load the firearm, unload the firearm, and clear the inevitable malfunction from your gun. Various firearms operate differently, so you should become inherently familiar with each and every firearm you own.

When shooting with friends, never assume their firearm functions the same as firearms you are already familiar with. There are many resources to answer any questions you may have regarding a particular firearm. If you bought the firearm, included with it should have been an owner's manual and field strip guide. A field strip guide provides detail regarding taking the gun apart for routine cleaning and maintenance, as well as problem solving. Furthermore, such information is on the manufacturer's website, or you could contact either the manufacturer directly or locate a local gunsmith. A responsible firearms enthusiast who plans on handling firearms in any regards will insist on taking a class prior to handling the particular firearm. Find a local gun club or organization that either has classes for novices or can recommend local classes for novices. People who are part of the gun culture are usually very friendly and eager to help newcomers participate in the sport.

Learn how to confirm that the firearm is safe to shoot and confirm each and every time you pick up your firearm.

Learn how to check to be sure the barrel is clear of obstructions.

Never handle firearms while under the influence of drugs or alcohol. Any chemical impairments coupled with the handling and/or use of a firearm greatly increase the odds of a bad situation. Drugs, even some over-the-counter drugs and prescription drugs, as well as alcohol, can dramatically impair your judgment as well as mental functions and physical coordination.

Further, no celebration exists that justifies shooting a firearm in happiness and celebration. It is common in other countries to fire a gun into the air in celebration of New Year's Eve or other national holidays. Any responsible firearms owner will refuse to participate and even strongly discourage such activity. Whatever goes up, must come down. And a bullet fired into the air will ultimately return to earth and could seriously injure or kill someone.

At all times while handling firearms, you and others around you should wear ear and eye protection and should dress appropriately for a day of shooting.

The loud noise, often called the report, can cause permanent hearing damage. Further, the debris, including the shell casing of a bullet, unfired powder, and hot gas, all of which are emitted each time most types of firearms are fired, can result in injuries to your eyes.

If you are shooting with others, consider wearing fitted clothing. Open-collared shirts and blouses will allow a discharged shell casing to travel down into the garment, and ultimately trapping that shell, often referred to as "hot brass," to be pinned up against your body where it will burn your skin. Hot brass cools very quickly, but some people tend to dance around in an attempt to create space between the skin and the hot brass. This can be very dangerous to everyone involved, as such excitement could cause someone involved to be distracted at the same moment as pulling the trigger. Wear appropriate clothing when you plan to shoot a firearm in the presence of others who are also shooting firearms.

### Safety Considerations and Children

These considerations are important even if you do not keep a firearm in the house. Many people do, and accidents tend to happen in someone else's house.

Always lock up firearms and/or render them inoperable with a firearms safety device of your choosing. Do so even if you do not have children, but make sure to do so if you have children. Small children are able to work firearms.

Test yourself. Pick up an unloaded firearm with your opposite hand; that is, if you are left-handed, pick it up right-handed, and vice versa. Unless you have been trained otherwise, your trigger finger will automatically rest on the trigger. A child will pick up a firearm in the same fashion, no matter which hand he uses. This is a very scary thought.

Talk to your children about firearms at an age they can begin to appreciate what you are telling them. A four-year-old will understand basic considerations about "staying away" from things, such as ovens and irons. Therefore, he can learn to stay away from firearms.

Some considerations for you to discuss with children so they know how to handle a situation when they happen upon a firearm include:
1. Stopping everything.
2. Do not touch the gun.
3. Leave the area immediately.
4. Tell a parent about the gun right away.

If you intend to teach your children how to handle firearms safely, do so with toy firearms, such as those made by popular brands as "Nerf," that make little rubber and foam projectiles. Teach your child with toys such as this about safe handling of firearms, how and where to point them, and when not to point them, etc.

The bottom line is, educate your children. Do not scare them. Educate them. Help them appreciate and respect the dangers but not fear the tool.

**Final Safety Considerations**

Are some of these considerations repetitive of the above comments? Most likely. But when dealing with safety considerations, one cannot over-emphasize enough.

When you pick up or are handed a gun, make sure it is unloaded. If you are being handed a gun, ask that it be unloaded and the action open before being handed to you.

Do not ever leave firearms unattended, unloaded or not, unless locked up safely in a secure container.

Never load a gun until you are ready to use it and unload it when you are finished using it.

Use only ammunition intended for your gun. Usually the caliber is marked on the barrel, and it must match the markings on the ammo box and ammo cartridge.

Wear adequate eye protection when shooting.

Wear adequate hearing protection when shooting.

Wear adequate clothing when shooting.

Never shoot while drinking or taking drugs, even prescription medications if they have adverse effects on your perception or judgment.

# CHAPTER FOURTEEN

## Firearms Competency

### All Firearms Owners and Their Families Should Seek Training

As the heading above states, everyone who handles or is around firearms should seek training and at least obtain minimal skills in safely handling firearms. As a person handling firearms, one should ask himself if he is truly competent in the handling of firearms. A simple self-assessment is a great idea when considering competence.

Many industries, including the military, consider the "four levels of competence," which is a very common training evaluation model first published in 1959. This model includes the four levels of confidence, including:

- **Unconscious Incompetence**: The person is unaware that he cannot perform a task.
- **Conscious Incompetence**: The person is aware of the task, but cannot do it.
- **Conscious Competence**: The person is able to think through something step by step and can perform the task.
- **Unconscious Competence**: The person can do the task without thinking about the intermediate steps.

Complete an assessment of yourself, considering each and every firearm or weapon you own. Consider: what level of training have you attained with the various firearms that you own?

A prudent firearms owner will receive enough training to bring himself into a consciously competent or unconsciously competent firearms user, for both his safety and the safety of those around him.

But do not just stop there. Do what you can to educate those around you, including your children, once they are old enough to learn and appreciate the rewards, but also the dangers, of handling firearms.

The bottom line is: **seek adequate training. <u>Today</u>.**

# Appendix One

## Glossary

Bar: means an establishment that is devoted to the serving of alcoholic beverages for consumption by guests on the premises and in which the serving of food is only incidental to the consumption of those beverages, including, but not limited to, taverns, nightclubs, cocktail lounges, and cabarets

Center: means the Georgia Crime Information Center within the Georgia Bureau of Investigation

Conviction: includes a final judgment of conviction entered upon a verdict or finding of guilty of a crime or upon a plea of guilty

Courthouse: means a building occupied by judicial courts and containing rooms in which judicial proceedings are held

Dangerous weapon: means any weapon commonly known as a "rocket launcher," "bazooka," or "recoilless rifle," which fires explosive or non-explosive rockets designed to injure or kill personnel or destroy heavy armor, or similar weapon used for such purpose; the term also includes a weapon commonly known as a "mortar," which fires high explosive from a metallic cylinder and which is commonly used by the armed forces as an antipersonnel weapon or similar weapon used for such purpose; the term also means a weapon commonly known as a "hand grenade" or other similar weapon which is designed to explode and injure personnel or similar weapon used for such purpose

Dealer: means any person licensed as a dealer under federal law (18 U.S.C. § 921, et seq.), or under state law (O.C.G.A. Title 43 Chapter 16)

| | |
|---|---|
| Felony: | means a crime punishable by death, by imprisonment for life, or by imprisonment for more than 12 months; also includes a conviction by a court-martial under the Uniform Code of Military Justice for an offense that would constitute a felony under the laws of the United States |
| Firearm: | any rifle, shotgun, pistol, or similar device which propels a projectile or projectiles through the energy of an explosive; in some instances within Georgia law, the term "firearm" includes stun guns and tasers; in some cases it may also mean the frame or receiver of a firearm, any firearm muffler, firearm silencer, or any destructive device as defined under federal law (18 U.S.C. § 921 (a)(3)). |
| Forcible felony: | means any felony which involves the use or threat of physical force or violence against any person |
| Forcible misdemeanor: | means any misdemeanor which involves the use or threat of physical force or violence against any person |
| Government building: | means the following: 1) the building in which a government entity is housed, 2) the building where a government entity meets in its official capacity, provided, however, that such building is not a publicly owned building, such building shall be considered a government building for the purposes of Georgia law only during the time such government entity is meeting in the building, and 3) the portion of any building that is not publicly owned that is being occupied by a government entity |
| Habitation: | any dwelling, motor vehicle, or place of business |

| | |
|---|---|
| Handgun: | means a firearm of any description, loaded or unloaded, from which any shot, bullet, or other missile can be discharged by an action of an explosive where the length of the barrel, not including any revolving, detachable, or magazine breech, does not exceed 12 inches; provided, however, that the term "handgun" shall not include a gun which discharges a single shot of .46 centimeters or less in diameter |
| Knife: | means a cutting instrument designed for the purpose of offense and defense and consisting of a blade that is greater than 5 inches in length and which is fastened to a handle |
| License holder: | means a person who holds a valid weapons carry license |
| Loaded: | a firearm is considered loaded if there is a cartridge in the chamber of cylinder of the handgun |
| Long gun: | means a firearm with a barrel length of at least 18 inches and an overall length of at least 26 inches, designed or made and intended to be fired from the shoulder, and designed or made to use the energy of the explosive in either 1) a fixed shotgun shell to fire through a smooth bore, either a number of ball shot or a single projectile for each single pull of the trigger from which any shot, bullet, or other missile can be discharged, or 2) metallic cartridge to fire only a single projectile through a rifle bore for each single pull of the trigger, provided for both, however, that the term "long gun" shall not include a gun which discharges a single shot of .46 centimeters or less in diameter |
| Machine gun: | means a weapon which shoots or is designed to shoot, automatically, more than six shots, without manual reloading, by a single function of the trigger |
| Minor: | any person under the age of 18 years; under some Georgia laws, a "minor" may be someone under the age of 17 |

| | |
|---|---|
| Misdemeanor: | any crime other than a felony |
| Parking facility: | means real property owned or leased by a government entity, courthouse, jail, prison, place of worship, or bar that has been designated by such government entity, courthouse, jail, prison, place of worship, or bar for the parking of motor vehicles at such place |
| Person: | means any individual, partnership, company, association, or corporation |
| Personal property: | any personal property other than a motor vehicle |
| Pistol: | same as a "handgun," means a firearm of any description, loaded or unloaded, from which any shot, bullet, or other missile can be discharged by an action of an explosive where the length of the barrel, not including any revolving, detachable, or magazine breech, does not exceed 12 inches; provided, however, that the term "handgun" shall not include a gun which discharges a single shot of .46 centimeters or less in diameter |
| Reasonable belief: | means that the person concerned, acting as a reasonable person, believes that the described facts exist |
| Revolver: | same as a "handgun," means a firearm of any description, loaded or unloaded, from which any shot, bullet, or other missile can be discharged by an action of an explosive where the length of the barrel, not including any revolving, detachable, or magazine breech, does not exceed 12 inches; provided, however, that the term "handgun" shall not include a gun which discharges a single shot of .46 centimeters or less in diameter |

| | |
|---|---|
| Sawed-off rifle: | means a weapon designed or redesigned, made or remade, and intended to be fired from the shoulder; and designed or redesigned, made or remade, to use the energy of the explosive in a fixed metallic cartridge to fire only a single projectile through a rifle bore for each single pull of the trigger; and which has a barrel or barrels of less than 16 inches in length, or has an overall length of less than 26 inches |
| Sawed-off shotgun: | means a shotgun or any weapon made from a shotgun, whether by alteration, modification, or otherwise having one or more barrels less than 18 inches in length, or if such weapon as modified has an overall length of less than 26 inches |
| School safety zone: | means in or on any real property owned by or leased to any public or private elementary school, secondary school, or school board, and used for elementary or secondary education, and in or on any public or private technical school, vocational school, college, university, or institution of postsecondary education |
| Shotgun: | means a weapon designed or redesigned, made or remade, and intended to be fired from the shoulder; and designed or redesigned, and made or remade, to use the energy of the explosive in a fixed shotgun shell to fire through a smooth bore either a number of ball shot or single projectile for each single pull of the trigger |
| Silencer: | means any device for silencing or diminishing the report of any portable weapon such as a rifle, carbine, pistol, revolver, machine gun, shotgun, fowling piece, or other device from which a shot, bullet, or projectile may be discharged by an explosive |

| | |
|---|---|
| Sport shooting range: | means an area designated and operated by a person for the sport shooting of firearms and not available for such use by the general public without payment of a fee, membership contribution, or dues, or by invitation of an authorized person, or any area so designated and operated by a unit of government, regardless of the terms of admission thereto |
| Stun gun: | any device that is powered by electrical charging units such as batteries, and emits an electrical charge in excess of 20,000 volts, or is otherwise capable of incapacitating a person by an electrical charge |
| Taser: | any device that is powered by electrical charging units such as batteries, and emits an electrical charge in excess of 20,000 volts, or is otherwise capable of incapacitating a person by an electrical charge |
| Weapon: | means a knife or a handgun; may also mean any pistol, revolver, or any weapon designed or intended to propel a missile of any kind, or any dirk, bowie knife, switchblade knife, ballistic knife, or other knife having a blade of 2 or more inches, straight-edge razor, razor blade, spring stick, knuckles, whether made from metal, thermoplastic, wood, or other similar material, blackjack, any bat, club, or other bludgeon-type weapon, or any flailing instrument consisting of two or more rigid parts connected in such a manner as to allow them to swing freely, which may be known as nun chahka, nun chuck, nunchaku, shuriken, or fighting chain, or any disc, of whatever configuration, having at least two points or pointed blades which is designed to be thrown or propelled and which may be known as a throwing star or oriental dart, or any weapon of like kind, and any stun gun or taser |
| Weapons carry license: | same as "license," means a license issued pursuant to O.C.G.A. § 16-11-129; a "weapons carry license" |

# Appendix Two

# Official Code of Georgia Annotated
# Quick Index

## Chapter 10. Offenses Against Public Administration
## Article 2. Obstruction of Public Administration and Related Offenses

O.C.G.A. § 16-10-33. Disarming Peace Officers and Others in Line of Duty.

## Article 3. Escape and Other Offenses Related to Confinement

O.C.G.A. § 16-10-51. Jumping Bail.

## Chapter 11. Offenses Against Public Order and Safety
## Article 2. Offenses Against Public Order

O.C.G.A. § 16-11-34.1. Disruption of State Senate or House of Representatives.

## Article 4. Dangerous Instrumentalities and Practices
## Part 1. General Provisions

O.C.G.A. § 16-11-101. Furnishing Metal Knuckles or Knife to Minor.
O.C.G.A. § 16-11-101.1. Furnishing or Allowing Minor to Possess Pistol or Revolver.
O.C.G.A. § 16-11-102. Pointing or Aiming Gun or Pistol at Another Person.
O.C.G.A. § 16-11-103. Discharge of Gun or Pistol on or Near Highway.
O.C.G.A. § 16-11-104. Discharge of Firearm on Property of Another Person.
O.C.G.A. § 16-11-105. Repealed.
O.C.G.A. § 16-11-106. Possession of Firearm or Knife While Committing or Attempting to Commit Certain Specific Crimes.
O.C.G.A. § 16-11-108. Using Firearm or Archery Tackle in a Manner to Endanger the Bodily Safety of Another Person While Hunting.
O.C.G.A. § 16-11-113. Solicitation, Persuasion, Encouragement, or Enticement of Dealer to Transfer or Convey Firearm to Someone Other Than Buyer.

## Part 2. Possession of Dangerous Weapons

O.C.G.A. § 16-11-120. The Georgia Firearms and Weapons Act.
O.C.G.A. § 16-11-121. Definitions.
O.C.G.A. § 16-11-122. Possession of Sawed-Off Shotgun, Sawed-Off Rifle, Machine Gun, Dangerous Weapon, or Silencer.
O.C.G.A. § 16-11-123. Punishment for Possession of Sawed-Off Shotgun, Sawed-Off Rifle, Machine Gun, Dangerous Weapon, or Silencer.
O.C.G.A. § 16-11-124. Exceptions.
O.C.G.A. § 16-11-125. Burden of Proof for Defense of Exception.
O.C.G.A. § 16.11.125.1. Definitions.

## Part 3. Carrying and Possession of Firearms

O.C.G.A. § 16-11-126. Carrying a Concealed Weapon.
O.C.G.A. § 16-11-127. Firearms and Knives in Public and Private Places; Licensees.
O.C.G.A. § 16-11-127.1. Weapons in School Safety Zones, School Buildings, Grounds, or at School Functions.
O.C.G.A. § 16-11-127.2. Weapons Possession on Nuclear Power Facility Premises.

## Chapter 4. Fish
## Article 1. General Provisions

O.C.G.A. § 27-4-8. Unlawful to Use Firearms and Other Devices to Take Fish.
O.C.G.A. § 27-4-11.1. Public Fishing Areas.

## Article 2. Noncommercial Fishing
## Part 1. General Provisions

O.C.G.A. § 27-4-33. Spearing of Fish.

## Title 28. General Assembly
## Chapter 5. Financial Affairs
## Article 4. Claims Advisory Board
## Part 3. Compensation of Persons for Injuries Sustained While Preventing Crime or While Aiding Officers of the Law

O.C.G.A. § 28-5-104. Applicability of Law; Compensation Limits.

## Title 33. Insurance
## Chapter 24. Insurance Generally
## Article 1. General Provisions

O.C.G.A. § 33-24-30.1. Prohibition of Denial of Coverage Based on Firearms on Property.

## Title 35. Law Enforcement Officers and Agencies
## Chapter 2. Department of Public Safety
## Article 2. Georgia State Patrol

O.C.G.A. § 35-2-49.1. Disability from Injuries Incurred in the Line of Duty.

## Chapter 3. Georgia Bureau of Investigation
## Article 1. General Provisions

O.C.G.A. § 35-3-4. Duties, Fingerprinting, and Photographs.
O.C.G.A. § 35-3-11. Agents Under Merit System.

## Article 2. Georgia Crime Information Center

O.C.G.A. § 35-3-33. Functions.

## Article 6. Division of Forensic Services

O.C.G.A. § 35-3-151. Duties and Responsibilities.

## Chapter 8. Employment and Training of Peace Officers.

O.C.G.A. § 35-8-26. Tasers and Electronic Control Weapons.

## Chapter 9. Special Policemen

O.C.G.A. § 35-9-9. Powers and Duties.


## Title 37. Mental Health
## Chapter 1. Governing and Regulation of Mental Health
## Article 2. Powers and Duties of the Department of Behavioral Health and Developmental Disabilities

O.C.G.A. § 37-1-27. Suicide Prevention Program.

## Title 38. Military, Emergency Management, and Veterans' Affairs
## Chapter 2. Military Affairs
## Article 2. Military Administration
## Part 5. Armories and Other Facilities

O.C.G.A. § 38-2-194. Control of Armories and Other Facilities.

## Article 3. Personnel
## Part 4. Rights, Privileges, and Prohibitions

O.C.G.A. § 38-2-277. Unauthorized Military Bodies.

## Article 4. Active Duty Powers

O.C.G.A. § 38-2-301. Closing Places Where Firearms and Ammunition is Sold.

## Chapter 3. Emergency Management
## Article 3. Emergency Powers
## Part 1. Governor

O.C.G.A. § 38-3-51. Emergency Powers of Governor.

## Chapter 5. Drivers' Licenses
## Article 2. Issuance, Expiration, and Renewal of License

O.C.G.A. § 40-5-22. Persons Not to be Issued License.

## Title 41. Nuisances
## Chapter 1. General Provisions

O.C.G.A. § 41-1-9. Shooting Ranges Not to be Deemed Nuisances Due to Changed Circumstances.

# Appendix Three

# Georgia State Code
# (Includes Changes to the Law Pursuant to SB 308)

**Title 1. General Provisions**
**Chapter 2. Persons and Their Rights**

**O.C.G.A. § 1-2-6. Rights of the Citizens.**
(a) The rights of citizens include, without limitation, the following:
(1) The right of personal security;
(2) The right of personal liberty;
(3) The right of private property and the disposition thereof;
(4) The right of the elective franchise;
(5) The right to hold office, unless disqualified by the Constitution and laws of this state;
(6) The right to appeal to the courts;
(7) The right to testify as a witness;
(8) The right to perform any civil function; and
(9) The right to keep and bear arms.
(b) All citizens are entitled to exercise all their rights as citizens, unless specially prohibited by law.

**Title 10. Commerce and Trade**
**Chapter 1. Selling and Other Trade Practices**
**Article 6. Interstate Purchase of Rifles and Shotguns**

**O.C.G.A. § 10-1-100. Purchase of Rifles and Shotguns in Other States by Georgia Residents.**
    Residents of the State of Georgia may purchase rifles and shotguns in any state of the United States, provided such residents conform to applicable provisions of statutes and regulations of the United States, of the State of Georgia, and of the state in which the purchase is made.

**O.C.G.A. § 10-1-101. Purchase by Non-Residents in the State of Georgia.**
    Residents of any state of the United States may purchase rifles and shotguns in the State of Georgia, provided such residents conform to applicable provisions of statutes and regulations of the United States, of the State of Georgia, and of the state in which such persons reside.

**Chapter 11. Business Records**

**O.C.G.A. § 10-11-2. Preservation and/or Destruction of Records.**
    Unless a specific period is designated by law for their preservation, business records which persons pursuant to the laws of this state are required to keep or preserve may be destroyed after the expiration of three years from the making of such records without constituting an offense under such laws. This Code section does not apply to minute books of corporations or to records of sales or other transactions involving weapons or poisons capable of use in the commission of crimes.

**O.C.G.A. § 12-3-9. Rules and Regulations Regarding State Parks, Historic Sites, and Recreational Areas.**

(a) The Board of Natural Resources is authorized to adopt and promulgate rules and regulations relating to:

(1) The use or occupancy of state parks, historic sites, and recreational areas; and

(2) The protection of the health, safety, and welfare of persons using state parks, historic sites, and recreational areas, and the protection of state property thereon, provided that nothing in this Code section shall be construed to repeal, diminish, or supersede the authority of the Department of Community Health to promulgate rules and regulations for the protection of the public health.

(b) Nothing in this Code section shall be construed to give additional authority to the Board of Natural Resources to adopt and promulgate rules and regulations relating to the game and fish laws of this state.

**O.C.G.A. § 12-3-10. Unlawful Activities.**

(a) As used in this Code section, the term "park, historic site, or recreational area" means a park, historic site, or recreational area which is operated by or for and is under the custody and control of the department.

(b) It shall be unlawful for any person to enter upon any park, historic site, or lands managed by the Department of Natural Resources except when in compliance with all applicable laws and all rules, regulations, and permits adopted pursuant to paragraph (1) of subsection (a) of Code Section 12-3-9.

(c) It shall be unlawful for any person, in any manner, to mark on, deface, injure, displace, dig, excavate, remove, or construct on any real or personal property on any park, historic site, or recreational area, except when done with special written permission granted by the commissioner of natural resources or his authorized representative.

(d) It shall be unlawful for any person to drive a vehicle on any roads in a park, historic site, or recreational area in excess of 35 miles per hour. It shall also be unlawful for any person to drive a vehicle in excess of 15 miles per hour within 200 feet of an intensive-use area in a park, historic site, or recreational area. As used in this subsection, the term "vehicle" means any wheeled conveyance for the transportation of persons or materials. As used in this subsection, the term "intensive-use area" means a picnic area, a beach or pool area, a check-in station, or a camping or cabin area.

(e) It shall be unlawful for any person to have or use a privately owned boat on any of the following state park lakes:

(1) A. H. Stephens Federal Lake and Lake Liberty; or

(2) John D. Tanner Lake (the 24 acre lake), provided that this prohibition shall apply only from May 1 through Labor Day of each year.

(f) Reserved.

(g) It shall be unlawful for any person to have or use a boat, other than one on official business, with other than paddles or a portable bow or stern mounted electric trolling motor on any of the following state park lakes:

(1) Black Rock Mountain Lake;

(2) James H. "Sloppy" Floyd Lake;

(3) A. H. Stephens-Lake Buncombe;

(4) Franklin D. Roosevelt-Lake Franklin or Lake Delano;

(5) John D. Tanner Lake (the 12 acre lake);

(5.1) John D. Tanner Lake (the 24 acre lake), provided that this prohibition shall apply only from the day after Labor Day each year through April 30 of the following year;

(6) Sweetwater Creek Lake;

(7) Hard Labor Creek Lake (the 37 acre lake);

(8) Fort Mountain Lake;

(9) Vogel Lake; or

(10) Unicoi Lake.

(h) It shall be unlawful for any person to use a boat, other than one on official business, with a motor which is neither an electric trolling motor nor ten horsepower or less on the following state park lakes:

(1) Fort Yargo Lake;

(2) Hamburg Lake;

(3) Hard Labor Creek Lake (the 275 acre lake);

(4) High Falls Lake;

(5) Indian Springs Lake;

(6) Kolomoki Mounds Lake;

(7) Stephen C. Foster Lake;

(8) Laura S. Walker Lake (between 7:00 A.M. eastern standard time or eastern daylight time, whichever is applicable, and 11:00 A.M. eastern standard time or eastern daylight time, whichever is applicable, and between 6:00 P.M. eastern standard time or 7:00 P.M. eastern daylight time, whichever is applicable, and sunset);

(9) Little Ocmulgee Lake (between 7:00 A.M. eastern standard time or eastern daylight time, whichever is applicable, and 11:00 A.M. eastern standard time or eastern daylight time, whichever is applicable, and between 6:00 P.M. eastern standard time or 7:00 P.M. eastern daylight time, whichever is applicable, and sunset); and

(10) Magnolia Springs Lake (between 7:00 A.M. eastern standard time or eastern daylight time, whichever is applicable, and 11:00 A.M. eastern standard time or eastern daylight time, whichever is applicable, and between 6:00 P.M. eastern standard time or 7:00 P.M. eastern daylight time, whichever is applicable, and sunset).

(i) It shall be unlawful for any person to fish in waters of any park, historic site, or recreational area, except for boat fishing between the hours of 7:00 A.M. and sunset and bank fishing between the hours of 7:00 A.M. and 10:00 P.M. It shall also be unlawful to fish in waters of any park, historic site, or recreational area which have been closed and posted by the department for fisheries management purposes.

(j) It shall be unlawful to fish commercially or to buy or sell fish caught in the waters of any park, historic site, or recreational area.

(k) It shall be unlawful to fish with any device other than a pole and line or rod and reel in the waters of any park, historic site, or recreational area, except with the written permission of the commissioner of natural resources or his authorized representative.

(l) It shall be unlawful to hunt, trap, or otherwise pursue or catch any wildlife in any park, historic site, or recreational area, unless such activity involves the use of bows and arrows, primitive weapons, rifles, or shotguns and has been approved by prior written permission of the commissioner of natural resources or the commissioner's authorized representative. It shall also be unlawful to shoot into a park, historic site, or recreational area from beyond the boundaries of such park, historic site, or recreational area.

(m) It shall be unlawful for any intoxicated person to enter or remain on any park, historic site, or recreational area. It shall also be unlawful for any person to consume or use alcoholic beverages or intoxicants in any public use area of a park, historic site, or recreational area. As used in this subsection, the term "public use area" shall not include cabins, rooms, trailers, tents, and conference facilities which facilities are rented for exclusive use by one individual or group.

(n) It shall be unlawful for any person to use in any park, historic site, or recreational area any electronic device for the detection of metals, minerals, artifacts, or lost articles or for treasure hunting.

(o)(1) It shall be unlawful for any person to use or possess in any park, historic site, or recreational area any fireworks, explosives, or firecrackers, unless stored so as not to be readily accessible or unless such use has been approved by prior written permission of the commissioner of natural resources or his or her authorized representative.

(2) It shall be unlawful for any person to use or possess in any park, historic site, or recreational area any firearms other than a handgun, as such term is defined in Code Section 16-11-125.1.

(3) It shall be unlawful for any person to use or possess in any park, historic site, or recreational area any handgun without a valid weapons carry license issued pursuant to Code Section 16-11-129.

(4) It shall be unlawful for any person to use or possess in any park, historic site, or recreational area bows and arrows, spring guns, air rifles, slingshots, or any other device which discharges projectiles by any means, unless the device is unloaded and stored so as not to be readily accessible or unless such use has been approved within restricted areas by prior written permission of the commissioner of natural resources or his or her authorized representative.

(p) It shall be unlawful to refuse to leave a park, historic site, or recreational area after violating any law or regulation of the Board of Natural Resources promulgated pursuant to Code Section 12-3-9 and after being directed to leave by an authorized representative of the department.

(q) It shall be unlawful for any person to park a vehicle at any place within any park, historic site, or recreational area, including upon the right of way of any county, state, or federal highway which traverses the park, historic site, or recreational area, where signs placed at the direction of the commissioner of natural resources or his official designee prohibit parking or condition the privilege of parking upon the purchase and display of a parking permit. The posting of signs at the entrances of a park, historic site, or recreational area designating the places for which a parking permit is required shall constitute sufficient notice for the entire park, historic site, or recreational area.

(r) Any person who violates any of the provisions of this Code section commits the offense of criminal trespass.

(s)(1) The jurisdiction of the probate courts of the several counties of this state is enlarged and extended so that probate courts, acting by and through the judge or presiding officer, shall have the right and power to receive pleas of guilty and impose sentence upon defendants violating the provisions of this Code section.

(2) When a person is arrested for any violation of the provisions of this Code section, the arresting officer may, at his discretion, choose to issue to the offender a summons to appear before a court of jurisdiction. Every such summons shall show:

(A) That it is issued by authority of the department;

(B) The name of the person summoned or, if the person to be summoned refuses to give his name or the officer serving the summons believes the name given is false or if the officer is for other cause unable to ascertain the correct name of the person to be summoned, a fictitious name plainly identified as such;

(C) The offense with which the person being summoned is charged and the date and location of the alleged offense;

(D) The location of the court and the day and hour at which he is summoned to appear;

(E) That failure to so appear is a violation of Georgia laws and subject to prosecution;

(F) The date the summons is served; and

(G) The name and official designation of the officer serving it.

(3) Personal delivery of the summons to the person charged or, if the violation is for a vehicle parking violation and the vehicle illegally parked is unattended, the placement of the summons on the windshield of the driver's side of the illegally parked vehicle shall constitute due and proper service of the summons.

(4) Every person so summoned shall appear at the place and on the date ordered except in cases where a bond has been posted in lieu of the summons or where the court has granted a continuance.

(5) The officer serving a summons pursuant to this subsection shall, on or before the return date of the summons, deliver a copy thereof to the court before which it is returnable, or to the clerk of such court, and shall file any information and such affidavits as may be required with respect to the alleged offense.

(6) If the person charged shall fail to appear as specified in the summons, the judge having jurisdiction of the offense may issue a warrant ordering the apprehension of the person commanding that he be brought before the court to answer the charge contained within the summons and the charge of his failure to appear as required. The person shall then be allowed to make a reasonable bond to appear on a given date before the court.

## O.C.G.A. § 12-3-10.1. Violations of Regulations.

(a) Any person who violates any rules and regulations adopted pursuant to paragraph (1) of subsection (a) of Code Section 12-3-9 and who refuses to cease such violation after notice may be directed to leave the park, historic site, or recreational area on which the violation occurs. A person shall have no legal authority, right, or privilege to remain upon a state park, historic site, or recreational area after receiving such a direction.

(b) Any person violating the provisions of this Code section shall be guilty of a misdemeanor.

## O.C.G.A. § 12-3-11. Civil Penalties.

Any person who violates any provision of Code Section 12-3-9 or 12-3-10 or the provisions of any law administered by the department concerning parks, historic sites, and recreational areas, or any regulations or orders promulgated and administered thereunder, shall be liable civilly for a penalty in a maximum amount of $1,000.00 for each and every violation thereof, such civil penalty to be recoverable by a civil action brought in the name of the commissioner of natural resources by the prosecuting attorney of the county in which the alleged violator resides. The commissioner on his motion may, or, upon complaint of any interested party charging a violation, shall refer the matter directly to the prosecuting attorney of the county in which the violator resides. The proceeds from all civil penalties arising from enforcement of such laws, regulations, and orders shall, except as otherwise provided in this Code section, be applied initially toward payment of the proper officers of the trial court as prescribed by law. The money remaining after such officers have been compensated shall be remitted promptly by the clerk of the court in which the case is disposed of to the treasurer of the county in which the civil penalty is assessed, or other officer having charge of the fiscal affairs of the county, who shall deposit the funds in the general fund of the county, such funds to be allocated to the county board of education for school purposes. The clerk of the court in which each case is disposed shall promptly make a written report to the department showing the disposition of each case. For making each report, he shall be entitled to an additional fee of $1.00 in each case, unless otherwise prohibited by law, to be added to the costs allowed by law against the defendant, to be retained by the clerk as his special compensation for making the report. The civil penalty prescribed in this Code section shall be concurrent with, alternative to, and cumulative of any and all other civil, criminal, or alternative rights, remedies, forfeitures, or penalties provided, allowed, or available to the department with respect to any violation of the laws administered by the department and any regulations or orders promulgated and administered thereunder.

## Title 15. Courts
## Chapter 9. Probate Courts
## Article 3. Costs and Compensation

**O.C.G.A. § 15-9-60. Costs of Probate Court.**

    (a) The judges or clerks of the probate courts of this state shall be entitled to charge and collect the sums enumerated in this Code section.

    (b) All sums that the probate courts may be required to collect pursuant to Code Sections 15-23-7, 15-9-60.1, and 36-15-9 and all other sums as may be required by law shall be in addition to the sums provided in this Code section. The sums provided for in this Code section are exclusive of costs for service of process, fees for publication of citation or notice, or any additional sums as may be provided by law.

    (c) The fees provided for in this Code section shall be paid into the county treasury less and except only such sums as are otherwise directed to be paid by law, which sums shall be remitted as provided by law by either the probate court or the county.

    (d) Subject to the provisions of Code Section 15-9-61, and except for the filing of a proceeding in which the filing party also files with the court a sworn affidavit that the party is unable because of indigence to pay the cost of court, all sums specified in this Code section shall be paid to the court at the time of filing or as thereafter incurred for services rendered. In accordance with Code Section 15-9-61, the judges of the probate courts are entitled to an advance cost of $ 30.00 for deposit to be made before filing any proceeding.

    (e) Cost in decedent's estates:

    (1) Except as otherwise provided, the cost in an initial proceeding regarding the estate of a decedent or of a missing individual believed to be dead shall be $130.00 for all services rendered by the judge or clerk of the probate court through the entry of the final order on such initial proceedings, exclusive of recording charges;

    (2) As used in this subsection, the term "initial proceeding" shall mean the first proceeding filed in the probate court in connection with or regarding the estate of a decedent or of a missing individual believed to be dead, including, but not necessarily limited to, the following proceedings: petition for temporary letters of administration; petition for letters of administration; petition to probate will in common form; petition to probate will in solemn form; petition to probate will in solemn form and for letters of administration with will annexed; petition for order declaring no administration necessary; petition for year's support; petition for presumption of death of missing individual believed to be dead; any proceeding for ancillary administration by a foreign personal representative; or any other proceeding by which the jurisdiction of the probate court is first invoked with regard to the estate of a decedent or of a missing individual believed to be dead;

    (3) As used in this subsection, the term "initial proceeding" shall not include a petition to establish custodial account for missing heir, a petition to enter a safe-deposit box, or any other petition or proceeding for which a specific cost is otherwise set forth in this Code section;

    (4) Except as otherwise provided, the cost shall be $ 75.00 for all services rendered by the judge or clerk of the probate court through the entry of the final order, exclusive of recording charges, in any of the proceedings listed in paragraph (2) of this subsection filed subsequent to the filing of an initial proceeding regarding the estate of the same decedent or missing individual believed to be dead;

    (5) Except as otherwise provided, the cost shall be $ 50.00 for all services rendered by the judge or clerk of the probate court through the entry of the final order, exclusive of recording charges, for the filing of the following proceedings or pleadings regarding the estate of a decedent or of a missing individual believed to be dead: petition for letters of administration with will annexed (will previously

probated); petition of personal representative for leave to sell property; petition for leave to sell perishable property; petition for leave to sell or encumber property previously set aside as year's support; petition by administrator for waiver of bond, grant of certain powers, or both; petition for discharge; petition by personal representative for approval of a division in kind; petition to determine heirs; petition by personal representative for direction under will; petition by personal representative to compromise a disputed claim or debt; petition by or against personal representative for an accounting or final settlement; petition to resign as personal representative and for the appointment of a successor; petition to remove a personal representative and for the appointment of a successor; citation against a personal representative for failure to make returns or for alleged mismanagement of estate; a caveat, objection, or other responsive pleading by which the proceeding becomes contested filed by any person to whom notice or citation has been issued; petition or motion to intervene as an interested party; and any other petition application, motion, or other pleading for which no specific cost is set forth in this Code section filed regarding the estate of a decedent or of a missing individual believed to be dead;

(6) Except as otherwise provided, the cost shall be $ 25.00 for all services rendered by the judge or clerk of the probate court through the entry of the final order, exclusive of recording charges, for the filing of the following proceedings, pleadings, or documents regarding the estate of a decedent or of a missing individual believed to be dead: petition to change accounting period; petition to enter a safe-deposit box; petition or motion for attorneys' fees; petition or motion of personal representative for extra compensation; or inventory, appraisement, or annual, intermediate, or final returns of personal representatives; and

(7) Except as otherwise provided, the cost shall be $ 10.00 for all services rendered by the judge or clerk of the probate court, exclusive of recording charges, for the filing of the following proceedings, pleadings, or documents regarding the estate of a decedent or of a missing person believed to be dead: notice of claim or claim of a creditor, if such notice or claim is filed with and accepted by the court; declination to serve of nominated personal representative; or renunciation of right of succession.

(f) Costs in minor guardianship matters:

(1) Except as otherwise provided, the cost in a proceeding regarding the person, property, or person and property of a minor shall be $75.00 for all services rendered by the judge or clerk of the probate court through the entry of the final order on such proceeding, exclusive of recording charges, including, but not necessarily limited to, the following proceedings: petition for temporary letters of guardianship of the person of a minor; petition for letters of guardianship of person, property, or person and property of a minor by person other than natural guardian; petition for letters of guardianship of property of a minor, by natural guardian, with bond --personal property over $5,000.00; petition for order that natural guardian not be required to become legally qualified guardian of the property; application of guardian for letters of dismission; or any other proceeding by which the jurisdiction of the probate court is first invoked with regard to the person, property, or person and property of a minor; and

(2) Except as otherwise provided, the costs for all services rendered by the judge or clerk of the probate court shall be as set forth below for the following proceedings, pleadings, or documents regarding the person, property, or person and property of a minor, exclusive of recording charges:

(A) Petition of guardian for leave to sell $70.00

(B) Petition to compromise doubtful claim of minor 70.00

(C) Petition for leave to encroach on corpus 30.00

(D) Petition to change accounting period 25.00

(E) Inventory or annual, intermediate, or final return (each) 30.00

(F) Petition or motion for attorneys' fees 70.00

(G) Petition to terminate temporary guardianship of minor 30.00

(H) Any other petition, application, motion, or other pleading for which no specific cost is set forth in this Code section filed regarding an existing guardianship of a minor 30.00

(g) Costs in adult guardianship matters:

(1) Except as otherwise provided, the cost in a proceeding regarding the person, property, or person and property of an adult alleged to be incapacitated shall be $150.00 for all services rendered by the judge or clerk of the probate court through the entry of the final order on such proceeding, exclusive of recording charges, including, but not necessarily limited to, the following proceedings: petition for the appointment of an emergency guardian for an alleged gravely incapacitated adult; petition for the appointment of an emergency and permanent guardian for an alleged gravely incapacitated adult; petition for the appointment of a guardian for an alleged incapacitated adult; or any other proceeding by which the jurisdiction of the probate court is first invoked with regard to an adult alleged to be incapacitated; and

(2) Except as otherwise provided, the cost for all services rendered by the judge or clerk of the probate court shall be as set forth below for the following proceedings, pleadings, or documents regarding the person, property, or person and property of an incapacitated adult, exclusive of recording charges:

(A) Petition of guardian for leave to sell $70.00

(B) Petition to compromise doubtful claim 70.00

(C) Petition for leave to encroach on corpus 30.00

(D) Petition to change accounting period 25.00

(E) Inventory or annual, intermediate, or final return (each) 30.00

(F) Petition or motion for attorneys' fees 70.00

(G) Petition to terminate or modify guardianship of incapacitated 70.00

(H) Application of guardian for letters of dismission 75.00

(I) Any other petition, application, motion, or other pleading for which no specific cost is set forth in this Code section filed regarding an existing guardianship of an adult 70.00

(h) Costs in matters involving sterilization, involuntary treatment, habilitation, or temporary placement:

(1) Except as otherwise provided, the cost in a proceeding filed under Chapter 20 of Title 31, Chapter 36A of Title 31, or Chapter 3, 4, or 7 of Title 37 shall be $130.00 for all services rendered by the judge or clerk of the probate court through the entry of the final order on such proceeding, exclusive of recording charges;

(2) There shall be no cost assessed for the receipt and consideration of affidavits in support of an order to apprehend under Part 1 of Article 3 of Chapter 3 of Title 37 or Part 1 of Article 3 of Chapter 7 of Title 37 or for the issuance of the order to apprehend; and

(3) There shall be no cost assessed for the receipt and consideration of a petition in support of an order to apprehend under Part 3 of Article 3 of Chapter 3 of Title 37 or Part 3 of Article 3 of Chapter 7 of Title 37 or for the issuance of the order to apprehend a patient alleged to be in noncompliance with an involuntary outpatient treatment order.

(i) Costs for hearings in contested matters:

(1) For conducting trials of contested matters or for formal hearing on the denial of an application for a weapons carry license before the probate court, the cost shall be $25.00 per one-half day or portion thereof;

(2) There shall be no additional cost for the initial hearing in adult guardianship matters or in matters involving sterilization, involuntary treatment, habilitation, or involuntary placement; and

(3) There shall be no cost for any hearing in an uncontested matter.

(j) Custodial accounts. For each account accepted by the judge of the probate court as custodian for a minor, incapacitated adult, or missing or unknown heir or beneficiary, there shall be a one-time fee of 8 percent of the fund deducted from the fund when first accepted.

(k) Miscellaneous costs. Except as otherwise provided, the judge or clerk of the probate court shall be entitled to the following costs for the proceedings, pleading, documents, or services itemized:

(1) Application for writ of habeas corpus $ 75.00

(2) Petition to establish lost papers, exclusive of recording charges 50.00

(3) Petition for or declaration of exemptions 25.00

(4) Petition to change birth certificate 75.00

(5) For all services rendered by the judge or clerk of the probate court through the entry of the final order, exclusive of recording charges, for any application or petition by which the jurisdiction of the probate court is first invoked for which no cost is set forth in this Code section or other applicable law 70.00

(6) Issuance of any order, including a rule nisi, in any matter for which the costs set forth in this Code section do not include all services to be rendered by the judge or clerk of the probate court, exclusive of recording charges 30.00

(7) Motions, amendments, or other pleadings filed in any matter for which the cost set forth in this Code section does not include all services to be rendered by the judge or clerk of the probate court, exclusive of recording charges, and no other cost is set forth in this Code section 15.00

(8) For processing appeals to superior court, exclusive of recording 30.00

(9) For issuance of writ of fieri facias (fi.fa.) 10.00

(10) Reserved.

(11) For issuance of permit to discharge fireworks 30.00

(12) Application for weapons carry license (exclusive of fees charged by other agencies for the examination of criminal records and mental health records) $30.00

(13) For issuance of a replacement weapons carry license  5.00

(14) Application for marriage license if the applicants have completed premarital education pursuant to Code Section 19-3-30.1 No fee

(14.1) Application for a marriage license if the applicants have not completed premarital education pursuant to Code Section 19-3-30.1 40.00

(15) For the safekeeping of a will 15.00

(16) For issuance of a veteran's license No fee

(17) For issuance of a peddler's license 15.00

(18) For issuance of a certificate of residency 10.00

(19) Registration of junk dealer 10.00

(20) Certification of publication of application for insurance company charter 10.00

(21) Recording of marks and brands, each 15.00

(22) Exemplification 15.00

(23) Certification under seal of copies (plus copy cost) 10.00

(24) Certified copies of letters of personal representative, temporary administrator, or guardian, each, including copy cost 10.00

(25) For issuance of a subpoena, each 10.00

(26) For filing and recording of oath or bond of any official, officer, or employee of any municipality or authority within the county, each 10.00

(27) For filing and recording of oath or bond of county official or officer No fee

(28) For examination of records or files by employee of the probate court to provide abstract of information contained therein or to provide copies therefrom, per estate or name 10.00

(29) Recording, per page 2.00

(30) Copies, per page 1.00

**O.C.G.A. § 15-11-28. Court Jurisdiction Over Juveniles.**

(a) Exclusive original jurisdiction. Except as provided in subsection (b) of this Code section, the court shall have exclusive original jurisdiction over juvenile matters and shall be the sole court for initiating action:

(1) Concerning any child:

(A) Who is alleged to be delinquent;

(B) Who is alleged to be unruly;

(C) Who is alleged to be deprived;

(D) Who is alleged to be in need of treatment or commitment as a mentally ill or mentally retarded child;

(E) Who is alleged to have committed a juvenile traffic offense as defined in Code Section 15-11-73; or

(F) Who has been placed under the supervision of the court or on probation to the court; provided, however, that such jurisdiction shall be for the sole purpose of completing, effectuating, and enforcing such supervision or a probation begun prior to the child's seventeenth birthday; or

(2) Involving any proceedings:

(A) For obtaining judicial consent to the marriage, employment, or enlistment in the armed services of any child if such consent is required by law;

(B) Under the Interstate Compact on Juveniles, or any comparable law, if enacted or adopted in this state;

(C) For the termination of the legal parent-child relationship and the rights of the biological father who is not the legal father of the child, other than that in connection with adoption proceedings under Article 1 of Chapter 8 of Title 19, in which the superior courts shall have concurrent jurisdiction to terminate the legal parent-child relationship and the rights of the biological father who is not the legal father of the child;

(D) Under Article 3 of this chapter, relating to prior notice to a parent or guardian relative to an unemancipated minor's decision to seek an abortion; or

(E) Brought by a local board of education pursuant to Code Section 20-2-766.1.

(b) Criminal jurisdiction.

(1) Except as provided in paragraph (2) of this subsection, the court shall have concurrent jurisdiction with the superior court over a child who is alleged to have committed a delinquent act which would be considered a crime if tried in a superior court and for which the child may be punished by loss of life, imprisonment for life without possibility of parole, or confinement for life in a penal institution.

(2)(A) The superior court shall have exclusive jurisdiction over the trial of any child 13 to 17 years of age who is alleged to have committed any of the following offenses:

(i) Murder;

(ii) Voluntary manslaughter;

(iii) Rape;

(iv) Aggravated sodomy;

(v) Aggravated child molestation;

(vi) Aggravated sexual battery; or

(vii) Armed robbery if committed with a firearm.

(A.1) The granting of bail or pretrial release of a child charged with an offense enumerated in subparagraph (A) of this paragraph shall be governed by the provisions of Code Section 17-6-1.

(B) After indictment, the superior court may after investigation and for extraordinary cause transfer any case involving a child 13 to 17 years of age alleged to have committed any offense enumerated in subparagraph (A) of this paragraph which is not punishable by loss of life, imprisonment for life without possibility of parole, or confinement for life in a penal institution. Any such transfer shall be appealable by the State of Georgia pursuant to Code Section 5-7-1. Upon such a transfer by the superior court, jurisdiction shall vest in the juvenile court and jurisdiction of the superior court shall terminate. Any case transferred by the superior court to the juvenile court pursuant to this subparagraph shall be subject to the designated felony provisions of Code Section 15-11-63 and the transfer of the case from superior court to juvenile court shall constitute notice to the child that such case is subject to the designated felony provisions of Code Section 15-11-63.

(C) Before indictment, the district attorney may, after investigation and for extraordinary cause, decline prosecution in the superior court of a child 13 to 17 years of age alleged to have committed an offense specified in subparagraph (A) of this paragraph. Upon declining such prosecution in the superior court, the district attorney shall immediately cause a petition to be filed in the appropriate juvenile court for adjudication. Any case transferred by the district attorney to the juvenile court pursuant to this subparagraph shall be subject to the designated felony provisions of Code Section 15-11-63 and the transfer of the case from superior court to juvenile court shall constitute notice to the child that such case is subject to the designated felony provisions of Code Section 15-11-63.

(D) The superior court may transfer any case involving a child 13 to 17 years of age alleged to have committed any offense enumerated in subparagraph (A) of this paragraph and convicted of a lesser included offense not included in subparagraph (A) of this paragraph to the juvenile court of the county of the child's residence for disposition. Upon such a transfer by the superior court, jurisdiction shall vest in the juvenile court and jurisdiction of the superior court shall terminate.

(E) Within 30 days of any proceeding in which a child 13 to 17 years of age is convicted of certain offenses over which the superior court has exclusive jurisdiction as provided in subparagraph (A) of this paragraph or adjudicated delinquent on the basis of conduct which if committed by an adult would constitute such offenses, the superior court shall provide written notice to the school superintendent or his or her designee of the school in which such child is enrolled or, if the information is known, of the school in which such child plans to be enrolled at a future date. Such notice shall include the specific criminal offense that such child committed. A local school system to which the child is assigned may request further information from the court's file.

(c) Custody and support jurisdiction.

(1) Where custody is the subject of controversy, except in those cases where the law gives the superior courts exclusive jurisdiction, in the consideration of these cases the juvenile court shall have concurrent jurisdiction to hear and determine the issue of custody and support when the issue is transferred by proper order of the superior court.

(2)(A) In any case where a child is alleged to be a deprived child as defined in paragraph (8) of Code Section 15-11-2, the juvenile court upon a finding of deprivation shall have jurisdiction to order temporary child support for such child to be paid by that person or those persons determined to be legally obligated to support such child. In determining such temporary child support, the juvenile court shall apply the child support guidelines provided in Code Section 19-6-15. Where there is an existing order of a superior court or other court of competent jurisdiction setting child support for the child, the juvenile court may order the child support obligor in the existing order to make such payments instead to the caretaker of the child on a temporary basis but shall not otherwise modify the terms of the existing order. A copy of the juvenile court's order shall be filed in the clerk's office of the court that entered the existing order. The juvenile court shall have jurisdiction to order temporary child support for the child to be paid by any other person determined to be legally obligated to support such child.

(B) Temporary child support orders entered pursuant to subparagraph (A) of this paragraph shall be enforceable by the juvenile court through the contempt powers of the juvenile court as provided in Code Section 15-11-5 so long as the juvenile court is entitled to exercise jurisdiction over the deprivation case.

(d) Age limit for new actions. The juvenile court shall not have jurisdiction to initiate any new action against an individual for acts committed after he or she has reached the age of 17 years. This subsection does not affect the court's jurisdiction to enter extension orders pursuant to Code Section 15-11-58.

(e) Concurrent jurisdiction as to legitimation petitions.

(1) The juvenile court shall have concurrent jurisdiction to hear any legitimation petition transferred to the juvenile court by proper order of the superior court.

(2) The juvenile court shall have jurisdiction to hear any legitimation petition filed pursuant to Code Section 19-7-22 as to a child with respect to whom a deprivation proceeding is pending in the juvenile court at the time the legitimation petition is filed.

(3) Notwithstanding the provisions of paragraphs (1) and (2) of this subsection, after a petition for legitimation is granted, if a demand for a jury trial as to support has been properly filed by either parent, then the case shall be transferred to superior court for such jury trial.

### Part 7. Delinquent and Unruly Children

### O.C.G.A. § 15-11-63. Designated Felony Acts and Restrictive Custody.

(a) As used in this Code section, the term:

(1) "A carefully arranged and monitored home visit" means a home visit during which a child is monitored by appropriate personnel of the Department of Juvenile Justice designated pursuant to regulations of the commissioner of juvenile justice.

(2) "Designated felony act" means an act which:

(A) Constitutes a second or subsequent offense under subsection (b) of Code Section 16-11-132 if committed by a child 13 to 17 years of age;

(B) If done by an adult, would be one or more of the following crimes:

(i) Kidnapping or arson in the first degree, if done by a child 13 or more years of age;

(ii) Aggravated assault, arson in the second degree, aggravated battery, robbery, armed robbery not involving a firearm, or battery in violation of Code Section 16-5-23.1 if the victim is a teacher or other school personnel, if done by a child 13 or more years of age;

(iii) Attempted murder or attempted kidnapping, if done by a child 13 or more years of age;

(iv) Reserved.

(v) Hijacking a motor vehicle, if done by a child 13 or more years of age;

(vi) Any violation of Code Section 16-7-82, 16-7-84, or 16-7-86 if done by a child 13 or more years of age;

(vii) Any other act which, if done by an adult, would be a felony, if the child committing the act has three times previously been adjudicated delinquent for acts which, if done by an adult, would have been felonies;

(viii) Any violation of Code Section 16-13-31, relating to trafficking in cocaine, illegal drugs, marijuana, or methamphetamine;

(ix) Any criminal violation of Code Section 16-14-4, relating to racketeering; or

(x) Any violation of Code Section 16-10-52, relating to escape, if the child involved in the commission of such act has been previously adjudicated to have committed a designated felony;

(C) Constitutes a second or subsequent adjudication of delinquency based upon a violation of Code Section 16-7-85 or 16-7-87;

(C.1) Constitutes any violation of Code Section 16-15-4, relating to criminal street gangs;

(C.2) Constitutes a second or subsequent adjudication of delinquency based on a violation of Code Section 16-11-127.1 or is a first violation of Code Section 16-11-127.1 involving:

(i) Any weapon, as such term is defined in Code Section 16-11-127.1, together with an assault;

(ii) A firearm as defined in paragraph (2) of subsection (a) of Code Section 16-11-131; or

(iii) A dangerous weapon or machine gun as defined in Code Section 16-11-121;

(D) Constitutes an offense within the exclusive jurisdiction of the superior court pursuant to subparagraph (b)(2)(A) of Code Section 15-11-28 which is transferred by the superior court to the juvenile court for adjudication pursuant to subparagraph (b)(2)(B) of Code Section 15-11-28 or which is transferred by the district attorney to the juvenile court for adjudication pursuant to subparagraph (b)(2)(C) of Code Section 15-11-28; or

(E) Constitutes a second or subsequent violation of Code Sections 16-8-2 through 16-8-9, relating to theft, if the property which was the subject of the theft was a motor vehicle.

(3) "Intensive supervision" means the monitoring of a child's activities on a more frequent basis than regular aftercare supervision, pursuant to regulations of the commissioner of juvenile justice.

(b) Where a child is found to have committed a designated felony act, the order of disposition shall be made within 20 days of the conclusion of the dispositional hearing and shall include a finding based on a preponderance of the evidence as to whether, for the purposes of this Code section, the child does or does not require restrictive custody under this Code section, in connection with which the court shall make specific written findings of fact as to each of the elements set forth in paragraphs (1) through (5) of subsection (c) of this Code section as related to the particular child. If the court finds that restrictive custody under this Code section is not required, the order of disposition shall be as otherwise provided in this article. If the court finds that restrictive custody is required, it shall continue the proceeding and enter an order of disposition for restrictive custody. Every order under this Code section shall be a dispositional order, shall be made after a dispositional hearing, and shall state the grounds for the order.

(c) In determining whether restrictive custody is required, the court shall consider:

(1) The needs and best interests of the child;

(2) The record and background of the child;

(3) The nature and circumstances of the offense, including whether any injury involved was inflicted by the child or another participant;

(4) The need for protection of the community; and

(5) The age and physical condition of the victim.

(d) Notwithstanding subsection (c) of this Code section, the court shall order restrictive custody in any case where the child is found to have committed a designated felony act in which the child inflicted serious physical injury upon another person who is 62 years of age or more.

(e) When the order is for restrictive custody in the case of a child found to have committed a designated felony act:

(1) The order shall provide that:

(A) The child shall be placed in the custody of the Department of Juvenile Justice for an initial period of five years;

(B) The child shall initially be confined in a youth development center for a period set by the order, to be not less than 12 nor more than 60 months; provided, however, that time spent in secure detention prior to placement in a youth development center shall be counted toward the period set by the order; and, provided, further, that, where the order of the court is made in compliance with subsection (f) of this Code section, the child shall initially be confined in a youth development center for 18 months;

(C) After the period set under subparagraph (B) of this paragraph, the child shall be placed under intensive supervision for a period of 12 months; and

(D) The child may not be released from a youth development center or transferred to a nonsecure facility during the period provided in subparagraph (B) of this paragraph nor may the child be released from intensive supervision during the period provided in subparagraph (C) of this paragraph, unless by court order. No home visits shall be permitted during the first six-month period of confinement in a youth development center unless authorized by the court except for emergency visits for medical treatment or severe illness or death in the family. All home visits must be carefully arranged and monitored while a child is confined in a youth development center, whether such confinement is pursuant to a court order or otherwise;

(2) During the placement or any extension thereof:

(A) After the expiration of the period provided in subparagraph (C) of paragraph (1) of this subsection, the child shall not be released from intensive supervision without the written approval of the commissioner of juvenile justice or such commissioner's designated deputy;

(B) While in a youth development center, the child may be permitted to participate in all youth development center services and programs and shall be eligible to receive special medical and treatment services, regardless of the time of confinement in the youth development center. After the first six months of confinement in a youth development center, a child may be eligible to participate in youth development center sponsored programs including community work programs and sheltered workshops under the general supervision of a youth development center staff outside of the youth development center; and, in cooperation and coordination with the Department of Human Services, the child may be allowed to participate in state sponsored programs for evaluation and services under the Division of Rehabilitation Services of the Department of Labor and the Department of Behavioral Health and Developmental Disabilities;

(C) The child shall not be discharged from the custody of the Department of Juvenile Justice unless a motion therefor is granted by the court, which motion shall not be made prior to the expiration of one year of custody; and

(D) Unless otherwise specified in the order, the Department of Juvenile Justice shall report in writing to the court not less than once every six months during the placement on the status, adjustment, and progress of the child; and

(3) Upon the expiration of the initial period of placement in a youth development center, or any extension thereof, the placement may be extended on motion by the Department of Juvenile Justice, after a dispositional hearing, for an additional period of 12 months, provided that no initial placement or extension of custody under this Code section may continue beyond the individual's twenty-first birthday.

(f) When the order is for restrictive custody in the case of a child found to have committed any designated felony act and such child has been found by a court to have committed a designated felony act on a prior occasion, regardless of the age of the child at the time of commission of such prior act, the order of the court shall be made pursuant to subparagraph (e)(1)(B) of this Code section.

(g) The Department of Juvenile Justice shall retain the power to continue the confinement of the child in a youth development center or other program beyond the periods specified by the court within the term of the order.

(h) Any court making a finding or adjudication that a child has committed a designated felony act shall identify the school last attended by such child and the school which such child intends to attend and shall transmit a copy of such adjudication or finding to the principals of the school which the child last attended and the school which the child intends to attend within 15 days of the adjudication or finding. Such information shall be subject to notification, distribution, and requirements as provided in Code Section 20-2-671.

## Title 16. Crimes and Offenses
## Chapter 1. General Provisions

**O.C.G.A. § 16-1-3. Definitions.**

As used in this title, the term:

(1) "Affirmative defense" means, with respect to any affirmative defense authorized in this title, unless the state's evidence raises the issue invoking the alleged defense, the defendant must present evidence thereon to raise the issue. The enumeration in this title of some affirmative defenses shall not be construed as excluding the existence of others.

(2) "Agency" means:

(A) When used with respect to the state government, any department, commission, committee, authority, board, or bureau thereof; and

(B) When used with respect to any political subdivision of the state government, any department, commission, committee, authority, board, or bureau thereof.

(3) "Another" means a person or persons other than the accused.

(4) "Conviction" includes a final judgment of conviction entered upon a verdict or finding of guilty of a crime or upon a plea of guilty.

(5) "Felony" means a crime punishable by death, by imprisonment for life, or by imprisonment for more than 12 months.

(6) "Forcible felony" means any felony which involves the use or threat of physical force or violence against any person.

(7) "Forcible misdemeanor" means any misdemeanor which involves the use or threat of physical force or violence against any person.

(8) "Government" means the United States, the state, any political subdivision thereof, or any agency of the foregoing.

(9) "Misdemeanor" and "misdemeanor of a high and aggravated nature" mean any crime other than a felony.

(10) "Owner" means a person who has a right to possession of property which is superior to that of a person who takes, uses, obtains, or withholds it from him and which the person taking, using, obtaining, or withholding is not privileged to infringe.

(11) "Peace officer" means any person who by virtue of his office or public employment is vested by law with a duty to maintain public order or to make arrests for offenses, whether that duty extends to all crimes or is limited to specific offenses.

(12) "Person" means an individual, a public or private corporation, an incorporated association, government, government agency, partnership, or unincorporated association.

(13) "Property" means anything of value, including but not limited to real estate, tangible and intangible personal property, contract rights, services, choses in action, and other interests in or claims to wealth, admission or transportation tickets, captured or domestic animals, food and drink, and electric or other power.

(14) "Prosecution" means all legal proceedings by which a person's liability for a crime is determined, commencing with the return of the indictment or the filing of the accusation, and including the final disposition of the case upon appeal.

(15) "Public place" means any place where the conduct involved may reasonably be expected to be viewed by people other than members of the actor's family or household.

(16) "Reasonable belief" means that the person concerned, acting as a reasonable man, believes that the described facts exist.

(17) "State" means the State of Georgia, all land and water in respect to which this state has either exclusive or concurrent jurisdiction, and the airspace above such land and water.

(18) "Without authority" means without legal right or privilege or without permission of a

person legally entitled to withhold the right.

(19) "Without his consent" means that a person whose concurrence is required has not, with knowledge of the essential facts, voluntarily yielded to the proposal of the accused or of another.

## O.C.G.A. § 16-1-10. Punishments for Other Crimes.

Any conduct that is made criminal by this title or by another statute of this state and for which punishment is not otherwise provided, shall be punished as for a misdemeanor.

## Chapter 3. Defenses to Criminal Prosecutions
## Article 1. Responsibility

## O.C.G.A. § 16-3-1. Minimum Age: 13 Years.

A person shall not be considered or found guilty of a crime unless he has attained the age of 13 years at the time of the act, omission, or negligence constituting the crime.

## Article 2. Justification and Excuse

## O.C.G.A. § 16-3-21. Use of Force in Self-Defense or Defense of Others; Justifiable Homicide Effect of Conflicting Rules.

(a) A person is justified in threatening or using force against another when and to the extent that he or she reasonably believes that such threat or force is necessary to defend himself or herself or a third person against such other's imminent use of unlawful force; however, except as provided in Code Section 16-3-23, a person is justified in using force which is intended or likely to cause death or great bodily harm only if he or she reasonably believes that such force is necessary to prevent death or great bodily injury to himself or herself or a third person or to prevent the commission of a forcible felony.

(b) A person is not justified in using force under the circumstances specified in subsection (a) of this Code section if he:

(1) Initially provokes the use of force against himself with the intent to use such force as an excuse to inflict bodily harm upon the assailant;

(2) Is attempting to commit, committing, or fleeing after the commission or attempted commission of a felony; or

(3) Was the aggressor or was engaged in a combat by agreement unless he withdraws from the encounter and effectively communicates to such other person his intent to do so and the other, notwithstanding, continues or threatens to continue the use of unlawful force.

(c) Any rule, regulation, or policy of any agency of the state or any ordinance, resolution, rule, regulation, or policy of any county, municipality, or other political subdivision of the state which is in conflict with this Code section shall be null, void, and of no force and effect.

(d) In a prosecution for murder or manslaughter, if a defendant raises as a defense a justification provided by subsection (a) of this Code section, the defendant, in order to establish the defendant's reasonable belief that the use of force or deadly force was immediately necessary, may be permitted to offer:

(1) Relevant evidence that the defendant had been the victim of acts of family violence or child abuse committed by the deceased, as such acts are described in Code Sections 19-13-1 and 19-15-1, respectively; and

(2) Relevant expert testimony regarding the condition of the mind of the defendant at the time of the offense, including those relevant facts and circumstances relating to the family violence or child abuse that are the bases of the expert's opinion.

## O.C.G.A. § 16-3-23. Use of Force Allowed in Defense of Habitation.

A person is justified in threatening or using force against another when and to the extent that he or she reasonably believes that such threat or force is necessary to prevent or terminate such other's unlawful entry into or attack upon a habitation; however, such person is justified in the use of force which is intended or likely to cause death or great bodily harm only if:

(1) The entry is made or attempted in a violent and tumultuous manner and he or she reasonably believes that the entry is attempted or made for the purpose of assaulting or offering personal violence to any person dwelling or being therein and that such force is necessary to prevent the assault or offer of personal violence;

(2) That force is used against another person who is not a member of the family or household and who unlawfully and forcibly enters or has unlawfully and forcibly entered the residence and the person using such force knew or had reason to believe that an unlawful and forcible entry occurred; or

(3) The person using such force reasonably believes that the entry is made or attempted for the purpose of committing a felony therein and that such force is necessary to prevent the commission of the felony.

## O.C.G.A. § 16-3-23.1. No Duty to Retreat; Use of Force in Defending Home, Property, Self, and Others.

A person who uses threats or force in accordance with Code Section 16-3-21, relating to the use of force in defense of self or others, Code Section 16-3-23, relating to the use of force in defense of a habitation, or Code Section 16-3-24, relating to the use of force in defense of property other than a habitation, has no duty to retreat and has the right to stand his or her ground and use force as provided in said Code sections, including deadly force.

## O.C.G.A. § 16-3-24. Use of Force Allowed in Defense of Property.

(a) A person is justified in threatening or using force against another when and to the extent that he reasonably believes that such threat or force is necessary to prevent or terminate such other's trespass on or other tortious or criminal interference with real property other than a habitation or personal property:

(1) Lawfully in his possession;

(2) Lawfully in the possession of a member of his immediate family; or

(3) Belonging to a person whose property he has a legal duty to protect.

(b) The use of force which is intended or likely to cause death or great bodily harm to prevent trespass on or other tortious or criminal interference with real property other than a habitation or personal property is not justified unless the person using such force reasonably believes that it is necessary to prevent the commission of a forcible felony.

## O.C.G.A. § 16-3-24.1. Definition of "Habitation" and "Personal Property."

As used in Code Sections 16-3-23 and 16-3-24, the term "habitation" means any dwelling, motor vehicle, or place of business, and "personal property" means personal property other than a motor vehicle.

## O.C.G.A. § 16-3-24.2. Immunity from Criminal Prosecution Where Use of Force is Justified.

A person who uses threats or force in accordance with Code Section 16-3-21, 16-3-23, 16-3-23.1, or 16-3-24 shall be immune from criminal prosecution therefor unless in the use of deadly force, such person utilizes a weapon the carrying or possession of which is unlawful by such person under Part 2 or 3 of Article 4 of Chapter 11 of this title.

# Chapter 5. Crimes Against the Person
## Article 2. Assault and Battery

**O.C.G.A. § 16-5-21. Offense of Aggravated Assault.**

(a) A person commits the offense of aggravated assault when he or she assaults:

(1) With intent to murder, to rape, or to rob;

(2) With a deadly weapon or with any object, device, or instrument which, when used offensively against a person, is likely to or actually does result in serious bodily injury; or

(3) A person or persons without legal justification by discharging a firearm from within a motor vehicle toward a person or persons.

(b) Except as provided in subsections (c) through (k) of this Code section, a person convicted of the offense of aggravated assault shall be punished by imprisonment for not less than one nor more than 20 years.

(c) A person who knowingly commits the offense of aggravated assault upon a peace officer while the peace officer is engaged in, or on account of the performance of, his or her official duties shall, upon conviction thereof, be punished by imprisonment for not less than five nor more than 20 years.

(d) Any person who commits the offense of aggravated assault against a person who is 65 years of age or older shall, upon conviction thereof, be punished by imprisonment for not less than three nor more than 20 years.

(e)(1) As used in this subsection, the term "correctional officer" shall include superintendents, wardens, deputy wardens, guards, and correctional officers of state, county, and municipal penal institutions who are certified by the Georgia Peace Officer Standards and Training Council pursuant to Chapter 8 of Title 35 and employees of the Department of Juvenile Justice who are known to be employees of the department or who have given reasonable identification of their employment. The term "correctional officer" shall also include county jail officers who are certified or registered by the Georgia Peace Officer Standards and Training Council pursuant to Chapter 8 of Title 35.

(2) A person who knowingly commits the offense of aggravated assault upon a correctional officer while the correctional officer is engaged in, or on account of the performance of, his or her official duties shall, upon conviction thereof, be punished by imprisonment for not less than five nor more than 20 years.

(f) Any person who commits the offense of aggravated assault in a public transit vehicle or station shall, upon conviction thereof, be punished by imprisonment for not less than three nor more than 20 years. For purposes of this Code section, "public transit vehicle" has the same meaning as in subsection (c) of Code Section 16-5-20.

(g) Any person who commits the offense of aggravated assault upon a person in the course of violating Code Section 16-8-2 where the property that was the subject of the theft was a vehicle engaged in commercial transportation of cargo or any appurtenance thereto, including without limitation any such trailer, semitrailer, container, or other associated equipment, or the cargo being transported therein or thereon, shall upon conviction be punished by imprisonment for not less than five years nor more than 20 years, a fine not less than $50,000.00 nor more than $200,000.00, or both such fine and imprisonment. For purposes of this subsection, the term "vehicle" includes without limitation any railcar.

(h) A person convicted of an offense described in paragraph (3) of subsection (a) of this Code section shall be punished by imprisonment for not less than five nor more than 20 years.

(i) Any person who commits the offense of aggravated assault involving the use of a firearm upon a student or teacher or other school personnel within a school safety zone as defined in paragraph (1) of subsection (a) of Code Section 16-11-127.1 shall, upon conviction thereof, be punished by imprisonment for not less than five nor more than 20 years.

(j) If the offense of aggravated assault is committed between past or present spouses, persons who are parents of the same child, parents and children, stepparents and stepchildren, foster parents and foster children, or other persons excluding siblings living or formerly living in the same household, the defendant shall be punished by imprisonment for not less than three nor more than 20 years.

(k) Any person who commits the offense of aggravated assault with intent to rape against a child under the age of 14 years shall be punished by imprisonment for not less than 25 nor more than 50 years. Any person convicted under this subsection shall, in addition, be subject to the sentencing and punishment provisions of Code Section 17-10-6.2.

(l) A person who knowingly commits the offense of aggravated assault upon an officer of the court while such officer is engaged in, or on account of the performance of, his or her official duties shall, upon conviction thereof, be punished by imprisonment for not less than five nor more than 20 years. As used in this subsection, the term 'officer of the court' means a judge, attorney, clerk of court, deputy clerk of court, court reporter, court interpreter or probation officer.

## Article 3. Kidnapping, False Imprisonment, and Related Offenses

**O.C.G.A. § 16-5-44.1. Carjacking and Motor Vehicle Hijacking in General.**

(a) As used in this Code section:

(1) "Firearm" means any handgun, rifle, shotgun, or similar device or weapon which will or can be converted to expel a projectile by the action of an explosive or electrical charge and includes stun guns and tasers as defined by subsection (a) of Code Section 16-11-106, as amended, and any replica, article, or device having the appearance of a firearm.

(2) "Motor vehicle" means any vehicle which is self-propelled.

(3) "Weapon" means an object, device, or instrument which when used against a person is likely to or actually does result in serious bodily injury or death or any replica, article, or device having the appearance of such a weapon including, but not limited to, any object defined as a weapon by Code Section 16-11-127.1 or as a dangerous weapon by Code Section 16-11-121.

(b) A person commits the offense of hijacking a motor vehicle when such person while in possession of a firearm or weapon obtains a motor vehicle from the person or presence of another by force and violence or intimidation or attempts or conspires to do so.

(c) A person convicted of the offense of hijacking a motor vehicle shall be punished by imprisonment for not less than ten nor more than 20 years and a fine of not less than $10,000.00 nor more than $100,000.00, provided that any person who has previously committed an offense under the laws of the United States or of Georgia or of any of the several states or of any foreign nation recognized by the United States which if committed in Georgia would have constituted the offense of hijacking a motor vehicle shall be punished by imprisonment for life and a fine of not less than $100,000.00 nor more than $500,000.00. For purposes of this subsection, "state" shall include the District of Columbia and any territory, possession, or dominion of the United States.

(d) The offense of hijacking a motor vehicle shall be considered a separate offense and shall not merge with any other offense; and the punishment prescribed by subsection (c) of this Code section shall not be deferred, suspended, or probated.

(e) Any property which is used, intended for use, derived, or realized, directly or indirectly, from a violation of this Code section is forfeited to the state and no property interest shall exist therein. Any action declaring such forfeiture shall be governed by the provisions of Code Section 16-13-49.

## Chapter 8. Offenses Involving Theft
## Article 1. Theft

**O.C.G.A. § 16-8-12. Punishment.**

(a) A person convicted of a violation of Code Sections 16-8-2 through 16-8-9 shall be punished as for a misdemeanor except:

(1) If the property which was the subject of the theft exceeded $500.00 in value, by imprisonment for not less than one nor more than ten years or, in the discretion of the trial judge, as for a misdemeanor;

(2) If the property was any amount of anhydrous ammonia, as defined in Code Section 16-11-111, by imprisonment for not less than one nor more than ten years, a fine not to exceed the amount provided by Code Section 17-10-8, or both;

(3) If the property was taken by a fiduciary in breach of a fiduciary obligation or by an officer or employee of a government or a financial institution in breach of his or her duties as such officer or employee, by imprisonment for not less than one nor more than 15 years, a fine not to exceed the amount provided by Code Section 17-10-8, or both;

(4) If the crime committed was a violation of Code Section 16-8-2 and if the property which was the subject of the theft was a memorial to the dead or any ornamentation, flower, tree, or shrub placed on, adjacent to, or within any enclosure of a memorial to the dead, by imprisonment for not less than one nor more than three years. Nothing in this paragraph shall be construed as to cause action taken by a cemetery, cemetery owner, lessee, trustee, church, religious or fraternal organization, corporation, civic organization, or club legitimately attempting to clean, maintain, care for, upgrade, or beautify a grave, gravesite, tomb, monument, gravestone, or other structure or thing placed or designed for a memorial of the dead to be a criminal act;

(5)(A) The provisions of paragraph (1) of this subsection notwithstanding, if the property which was the subject of the theft was a motor vehicle or was a motor vehicle part or component which exceeded $100.00 in value or if the theft or unlawful activity was committed in violation of subsection (b) of Code Section 10-1-393.5 or in violation of subsection (b) of Code Section 10-1-393.6 or while engaged in telemarketing conduct in violation of Chapter 5B of Title 10, by imprisonment for not less than one nor more than ten years or, in the discretion of the trial judge, as for a misdemeanor; provided, however, that any person who is convicted of a second or subsequent offense under this paragraph shall be punished by imprisonment for not less than one year nor more than 20 years.

(B) Subsequent offenses committed under this paragraph, including those which may have been committed after prior felony convictions unrelated to this paragraph, shall be punished as provided in Code Section 17-10-7;

(6)(A) As used in this paragraph, the term:

(i) "Destructive device" means a destructive device as such term is defined by Code Section 16-7-80.

(ii) "Explosive" means an explosive as such term is defined by Code Section 16-7-80.

(iii) "Firearm" means any rifle, shotgun, pistol, or similar device which propels a projectile or projectiles through the energy of an explosive.

(B) If the property which was the subject of the theft offense was a destructive device, explosive, or firearm, by imprisonment for not less than one nor more than ten years;

(7) If the property which was the subject of the theft is a grave marker, monument, or memorial to one or more deceased persons who served in the military service of this state, the United States of America or any of the states thereof, or the Confederate States of America or any of the states thereof, or a monument, plaque, marker, or memorial which is dedicated to, honors, or recounts the military service of any past or present military personnel of this state, the United States of America or any of the states thereof, or the Confederate States of America or any of the states thereof, and if

such grave marker, monument, memorial, plaque, or marker is privately owned or located on privately owned land, by imprisonment for not less than one nor more than three years if the value of the property which was the subject of the theft is $300.00 or less, and by imprisonment for not less than three years and not more than five years if the value of the property which was the subject of the theft is more than $300.00;

(8) If the property that was the subject of the theft was a vehicle engaged in commercial transportation of cargo or any appurtenance thereto, including without limitation any such trailer, semitrailer, container, or other associated equipment, or the cargo being transported therein or thereon, by imprisonment for not less than three years nor more than ten years, a fine not less than $5,000.00 nor more than $50,000.00, and, if applicable, the revocation of the defendant's commercial driver's license in accordance with Code Section 40-5-151, or any combination of such penalties. For purposes of this paragraph, the term "vehicle" includes without limitation any railcar; or

(9) Notwithstanding the provisions of paragraph (1) of this subsection, if the property of the theft was ferrous metals or regulated metal property, as such terms are defined in Code Section 10-1-350, and the sum of the aggregate amount of such property, in its original and undamaged condition, plus any reasonable costs which are or would be incurred in the repair or the attempt to recover any property damaged in the theft or removal of such regulated metal property, exceeds $500.00, by imprisonment for not less than one nor more than five years, a fine of not more than $5,000.00, or both.

(b) Except as otherwise provided in paragraph (5) of subsection (a) of this Code section, any person who commits the offense of theft by deception when the property which was the subject of the theft exceeded $500.00 in value and the offense was committed against a person who is 65 years of age or older shall, upon conviction thereof, be punished by imprisonment for not less than five nor more than ten years.

(c) Where a violation of Code Sections 16-8-2 through 16-8-9 involves the theft of a growing or otherwise unharvested commercial agricultural product which is being grown or produced as a crop, such offense shall be punished by a fine of not less than $500.00 and not more than the maximum fine otherwise authorized by law. This minimum fine shall not in any such case be subject to suspension, stay, or probation. This minimum fine shall not be required in any case in which a sentence of confinement is imposed and such sentence of confinement is not suspended, stayed, or probated; but this subsection shall not prohibit imposition of any otherwise authorized fine in such a case.

### Article 2. Robbery

### O.C.G.A. § 16-8-41. Armed Robbery; Robberies Committed Through Intimidation.

(a) A person commits the offense of armed robbery when, with intent to commit theft, he or she takes property of another from the person or the immediate presence of another by use of an offensive weapon, or any replica, article, or device having the appearance of such weapon. The offense of robbery by intimidation shall be a lesser included offense in the offense of armed robbery.

(b) A person convicted of the offense of armed robbery shall be punished by death or imprisonment for life or by imprisonment for not less than ten nor more than 20 years.

(c)(1) The preceding provisions of this Code section notwithstanding, in any case in which the defendant commits armed robbery and in the course of the commission of the offense such person unlawfully takes a controlled substance from a pharmacy or a wholesale druggist and intentionally inflicts bodily injury upon any person, such facts shall be charged in the indictment or accusation and, if found to be true by the court or if admitted by the defendant, the defendant shall be punished by imprisonment for not less than 15 years.

(2) As used in this subsection, the term:

(A) "Controlled substance" means a drug, substance, or immediate precursor in Schedules

I through V of Code Sections 16-13-25 through 16-13-29.

(B) "Pharmacy" means any place licensed in accordance with Chapter 4 of Title 26 wherein the possessing, displaying, compounding, dispensing, or retailing of drugs may be conducted, including any and all portions of any building or structure leased, used, or controlled by the licensee in the conduct of the business licensed by the State Board of Pharmacy at the address for which the license was issued. The term pharmacy shall also include any building, warehouse, physician's office, or hospital used in whole or in part for the sale, storage, or dispensing of any controlled substance.

(C) "Wholesale druggist" means an individual, partnership, corporation, or association registered with the State Board of Pharmacy under Chapter 4 of Title 26.

(d) Any person convicted under this Code section shall, in addition, be subject to the sentencing and punishment provisions of Code Sections 17-10-6.1 and 17-10-7.

## Chapter 9.  Forgery and Fraudulent Practices
## Article 5.  Removal or Alteration of Identification from Property

### O.C.G.A. § 16-9-70.  Criminal Activity with Use of Item with Altered Identification Mark.

(a) A person commits the offense of criminal use of an article with an altered identification mark when he or she buys, sells, receives, disposes of, conceals, or has in his or her possession a radio, piano, phonograph, sewing machine, washing machine, typewriter, adding machine, comptometer, bicycle, firearm, safe, vacuum cleaner, dictaphone, watch, watch movement, watch case, or any other mechanical or electrical device, appliance, contrivance, material, vessel as defined in Code Section 52-7-3, or other piece of apparatus or equipment, other than a motor vehicle as defined in Code Section 40-1-1, from which he or she knows the manufacturer's name plate, serial number, or any other distinguishing number or identification mark has been removed for the purpose of concealing or destroying the identity of such article.

(b) A person convicted of the offense of criminal use of an article with an altered identification mark shall be punished by imprisonment for not less than one nor more than five years.

(c) This Code section does not apply to those cases or instances where any of the changes or alterations enumerated in subsection (a) of this Code section have been customarily made or done as an established practice in the ordinary and regular conduct of business by the original manufacturer or by his duly appointed direct representative or under specific authorization from the original manufacturer.

## Chapter 10.  Offenses Against Public Administration
## Article 2.  Obstruction of Public Administration and Related Offenses

### O.C.G.A. § 16-10-33.  Disarming Peace Officers and Others in Line of Duty.

(a) It shall be unlawful for any person knowingly to remove or attempt to remove a firearm, chemical spray, or baton from the possession of another person if:

(1) The other person is lawfully acting within the course and scope of employment; and

(2) The person has knowledge or reason to know that the other person is employed as:

(A) A peace officer as defined in paragraph (8) of Code Section 35-8-2;

(B) A probation officer, or other employee with the power of arrest, by the Department of Corrections;

(C) A parole supervisor, or other employee with the power of arrest, by the State Board of Pardons and Paroles;

(D) A jail officer or guard by a county or municipality and has the responsibility of supervising inmates who are confined in a county or municipal jail or other detention facility; or

(E) A juvenile correctional officer by the Department of Juvenile Justice and has the primary responsibility for the supervision and control of youth confined in such department's programs and facilities.

(b) Any person who violates subsection (a) of this Code section shall, upon conviction thereof, be punished by imprisonment for not less than one nor more than five years or a fine of not more than $ 10,000.00, or both.

(c) A violation of this Code section shall constitute a separate offense. A sentence imposed under this Code section may be imposed separately from and consecutive to or concurrent with a sentence for any other offense related to the act or acts establishing the offense under this Code section.

## Article 3. Escape and Other Offenses Related to Confinement

### O.C.G.A. § 16-10-51. Jumping Bail.

(a) Any person who has been charged with or convicted of the commission of a felony under the laws of this state and has been set at liberty on bail or on his own recognizance upon the condition that he will subsequently appear at a specified time and place commits the offense of felony-bail jumping if, after actual notice to the defendant in open court or notice to the person by mailing to his last known address or otherwise being notified personally in writing by a court official or officer of the court, he fails without sufficient excuse to appear at that time and place. A person convicted of the offense of felony-bail jumping shall be punished by imprisonment for not less than one nor more than five years or by a fine of not more than $5,000.00, or both.

(b) Any person who has been charged with or convicted of the commission of a misdemeanor and has been set at liberty on bail or on his own recognizance upon the condition that he will subsequently appear at a specified time and place commits the offense of misdemeanor-bail jumping if, after actual notice to the defendant in open court or notice to the person by mailing to his last known address or otherwise being notified personally in writing by a court official or officer of the court, he fails without sufficient excuse to appear at that time and place. A person convicted of the offense of misdemeanor-bail jumping shall be guilty of a misdemeanor.

(c)(1) Any person who has been charged with or convicted of the commission of any of the misdemeanors listed in paragraph (2) of this subsection and has been set at liberty on bail or on his or her own recognizance upon the condition that he or she will subsequently appear at a specified time and place and who, after actual notice to the defendant in open court or notice to the defendant by mailing to the defendant's last known address or otherwise being notified personally in writing by a court official or officer of the court, leaves the state to avoid appearing in court at such time commits the offense of out-of-state-bail jumping. A person convicted of the offense of out-of-state-bail jumping shall be guilty of a felony and shall be punished by imprisonment for not less than one year nor more than five years or by a fine of not less than $1,000.00 nor more than $5,000.00, or both.

(2) Paragraph (1) of this subsection shall apply only to the following misdemeanors:

(A) Abandonment, as provided in Code Sections 19-10-1 and 19-10-2;

(B) Simple assault, as provided in Code Section 16-5-20;

(C) Carrying a weapon or long gun in an unauthorized location, as provided in Code Section 16-11-127;

(D) Bad checks, as provided in Code Section 16-9-20;

(E) Simple battery, as provided in Code Section 16-5-23;

(F) Bribery, as provided in Code Section 16-10-3;

(G) Failure to report child abuse, as provided in Code Section 19-7-5;

(H) Criminal trespass, as provided in Code Section 16-7-21;

(I) Contributing to the delinquency of a minor, as provided in Code Section 16-12-1;

(J) Escape, as provided in Code Sections 16-10-52 and 16-10-53;

(K) Tampering with evidence, as provided in Code Section 16-10-94;

(L) Family violence, as provided in Code Section 19-13-6;

(M) Deceptive business practices, as provided in Code Section 16-9-50;

(N) Reserved;

(O) Fraud in obtaining public assistance, food stamps, or Medicaid, as provided in Code Section 49-4-15;

(P) Reckless conduct, as provided in Code Section 16-5-60;

(Q) Any offense under Chapter 8 of this title which is a misdemeanor;

(R) Any offense under Chapter 13 of this title which is a misdemeanor;

(S) Driving under the influence of alcohol or drugs, as provided in Code Section 40-6-391;

(T) Driving without a license in violation of Code Section 40-5-20 or driving while a license is suspended or revoked as provided in Code Section 40-5-121; and

(U) Any offense under Code Section 40-6-10, relating to requirement of the operator or owner of a motor vehicle to have proof of insurance.

(d) Subsections (b) and (c) of this Code section shall not apply to any person who has been charged or convicted of the commission of a misdemeanor under the laws of this state and has been set at liberty after posting a cash bond and fails to appear in court at the specified time and place where such failure to appear, in accordance with the rules of the court having jurisdiction over such misdemeanor, is construed as an admission of guilt and the cash bond is forfeited without the need for any further statutory procedures and the proceeds of the cash bond are applied and distributed as any fine imposed by the court would be.

## Chapter 11. Offenses Against Public Order and Safety
## Article 2. Offenses Against Public Order

**O.C.G.A. § 16-11-34.1. Disruption of State Senate or House of Representatives.**

(a) It shall be unlawful for any person recklessly or knowingly to commit any act which may reasonably be expected to prevent or disrupt a session or meeting of the Senate or House of Representatives, a joint session thereof, or any meeting of any standing or interim committee, commission, or caucus of members thereof.

(b) It shall be unlawful for any person, other than those persons who are exempt from the provisions of Code Sections 16-11-126 through 16-11-127.2, to enter, occupy, or remain within the state capitol building or any building housing committee offices, committee rooms, or offices of members, officials, or employees of the General Assembly or either house thereof while in the possession of any firearm; knife as such term is defined in Code Section 16-11-125.1; explosive or incendiary device or compound; bludgeon; knuckles, whether made from metal, thermoplastic, wood, or other similar material; or any other dangerous or deadly weapon, instrument, or device.

(c) It shall be unlawful for any person purposely or recklessly and without authority of law to obstruct any street, sidewalk, hallway, office, or other passageway in that area designated as Capitol Square by Code Section 50-2-28 in such a manner as to render it impassable without unreasonable inconvenience or hazard or to fail or refuse to remove such obstruction after receiving a reasonable official request or the order of a peace officer to do so.

(d) It shall be unlawful for any person willfully and knowingly to enter or to remain upon the floor of the Senate or the floor of the House of Representatives or within any cloakroom, lobby, or anteroom adjacent to such floor unless such person is authorized, pursuant to the rules of the Senate or House of Representatives or pursuant to authorization given by the Senate or House of Representatives, to enter or remain upon the floor or within such area.

(e) It shall be unlawful for any person willfully and knowingly to enter or to remain in the gallery of the Senate or the gallery of the House of Representatives in violation of rules governing admission to such gallery adopted by the Senate or the House of Representatives or pursuant to authorization given by such body.

(f) It shall be unlawful for any person willfully and knowingly to enter or to remain in any room, chamber, office, or hallway within the state capitol building or any building housing committee offices, committee rooms, or offices of members, officials, or employees of the General Assembly or either house thereof with intent to disrupt the orderly conduct of official business or to utter loud, threatening, or abusive language or engage in any disorderly or disruptive conduct in such buildings or areas.

(g) It shall be unlawful for any person to parade, demonstrate, or picket within the state capitol building or any building housing committee offices, committee rooms, or offices of members, officials, or employees of the General Assembly or either house thereof with intent to disrupt the orderly conduct of official business or to utter loud, threatening, or abusive language or engage in any disorderly or disruptive conduct in such buildings or areas.

(h)(1) Any person violating this Code section for the first time shall be guilty of a misdemeanor.

(2) Any person violating this Code section for the second time shall be guilty of a misdemeanor of a high and aggravated nature.

(3) Any person violating this Code section for the third or any subsequent time shall be guilty of a felony and, upon conviction thereof, shall be punished by imprisonment for not less than one nor more than three years.

(i) The enactment of this Code section shall not repeal any other provision of law proscribing or regulating any conduct otherwise prohibited by this Code section.

### Article 4. Dangerous Instrumentalities and Practices
### Part 1. General Provisions

**O.C.G.A. § 16-11-101. Furnishing Metal Knuckles or Knife to Minor.**

A person is guilty of a misdemeanor of a high and aggravated nature when he or she knowingly sells to or furnishes to a person under the age of 18 years knuckles, whether made from metal, thermoplastic, wood, or other similar material, or a knife designed for the purpose of offense and defense.

**O.C.G.A. § 16-11-101.1. Furnishing or Allowing Minor to Possess Pistol or Revolver.**

(a) For the purposes of this Code section, the term:

(1) "Minor" means any person under the age of 18 years.

(2) 'Pistol or revolver' means a handgun as defined in subsection (a) of Code Section 16-11-125.1.

(b) It shall be unlawful for a person intentionally, knowingly, or recklessly to sell or furnish a pistol or revolver to a minor, except that it shall be lawful for a parent or legal guardian to permit possession of a pistol or revolver by a minor for the purposes specified in subsection (c) of Code Section 16-11-132 unless otherwise expressly limited by subsection (c) of this Code section.

(c)(1) It shall be unlawful for a parent or legal guardian to permit possession of a pistol or revolver by a minor if the parent or legal guardian knows of a minor's conduct which violates the provisions of Code Section 16-11-132 and fails to make reasonable efforts to prevent any such violation of Code Section 16-11-132.

(2) Notwithstanding any provisions of subsection (c) of Code Section 16-11-132 or any other law to the contrary, it shall be unlawful for any parent or legal guardian intentionally, knowingly, or recklessly to furnish to or permit a minor to possess a pistol or revolver if such parent or legal guardian is aware of a substantial risk that such minor will use a pistol or revolver to commit a felony offense or

if such parent or legal guardian who is aware of such substantial risk fails to make reasonable efforts to prevent commission of the offense by the minor.

(3) In addition to any other act which violates this subsection, a parent or legal guardian shall be deemed to have violated this subsection if such parent or legal guardian furnishes to or permits possession of a pistol or revolver by any minor who has been convicted of a forcible felony or forcible misdemeanor, as defined in Code Section 16-1-3, or who has been adjudicated delinquent under the provisions of Article 1 of Chapter 11 of Title 15 for an offense which would constitute a forcible felony or forcible misdemeanor, as defined in Code Section 16-1-3, if such minor were an adult.

(d) Upon conviction of a violation of subsection (b) or (c) of this Code section, a person shall be guilty of a felony and punished by a fine not to exceed $ 5,000.00 or by imprisonment for not less than three nor more than five years, or both.

### O.C.G.A. § 16-11-102.  Pointing or Aiming Gun or Pistol at Another Person.

A person is guilty of a misdemeanor when he intentionally and without legal justification points or aims a gun or pistol at another, whether the gun or pistol is loaded or unloaded.

### O.C.G.A. § 16-11-103.  Discharge of Gun or Pistol on or Near Highway.

A person is guilty of a misdemeanor when, without legal justification, he discharges a gun or pistol on or within 50 yards of a public highway or street.

### O.C.G.A. § 16-11-104.  Discharge of Firearm on Property of Another Person.

(a) It shall be unlawful for any person to fire or discharge a firearm on the property of another person, firm, or corporation without having first obtained permission from the owner or lessee of the property. This Code section shall not apply to:

(1) Persons who fire or discharge a firearm in defense of person or property; and

(2) Law enforcement officers.

(b) Any person who violates subsection (a) of this Code section is guilty of a misdemeanor.

### O.C.G.A. § 16-11-105.

Reserved. Repealed (Discharge of firearm on Sunday)

### O.C.G.A. § 16-11-106.  Possession of Firearm or Knife While Committing or Attempting to Commit Certain Specific Crimes.

(a) For the purposes of this Code section, the term "firearm" shall include stun guns and tasers. A stun gun or taser is any device that is powered by electrical charging units such as batteries and emits an electrical charge in excess of 20,000 volts or is otherwise capable of incapacitating a person by an electrical charge.

(b) Any person who shall have on or within arm's reach of his or her person a firearm or a knife having a blade of three or more inches in length during the commission of, or the attempt to commit:

(1) Any crime against or involving the person of another;

(2) The unlawful entry into a building or vehicle;

(3) A theft from a building or theft of a vehicle;

(4) Any crime involving the possession, manufacture, delivery, distribution, dispensing, administering, selling, or possession with intent to distribute any controlled substance or marijuana as provided in Code Section 16-13-30, any counterfeit substance as defined in Code Section 16-13-21, or any noncontrolled substance as provided in Code Section 16-13-30.1; or

(5) Any crime involving the trafficking of cocaine, marijuana, or illegal drugs as provided in Code Section 16-13-31, and which crime is a felony, commits a felony and, upon conviction thereof,

shall be punished by confinement for a period of five years, such sentence to run consecutively to any other sentence which the person has received.

(c) Upon the second or subsequent conviction of a person under this Code section, the person shall be punished by confinement for a period of ten years. Notwithstanding any other law to the contrary, the sentence of any person which is imposed for violating this Code section a second or subsequent time shall not be suspended by the court and probationary sentence imposed in lieu thereof.

(d) The punishment prescribed for the violation of subsections (b) and (c) of this Code section shall not be reducible to misdemeanor punishment as is provided by Code Section 17-10-5.

(e) Any crime committed in violation of subsections (b) and (c) of this Code section shall be considered a separate offense.

## O.C.G.A. § 16-11-108. Using Firearm or Archery Tackle in a Manner to Endanger the Bodily Safety of Another Person While Hunting.

(a) Any person who while hunting wildlife uses a firearm or archery tackle in a manner to endanger the bodily safety of another person by consciously disregarding a substantial and unjustifiable risk that his act or omission will cause harm to or endanger the safety of another person and the disregard constitutes a gross deviation from the standard of care which a reasonable person would exercise in the situation is guilty of a misdemeanor; provided, however, if such conduct results in serious bodily harm to another person, the person engaging in such conduct shall be guilty of a felony and, upon conviction thereof, shall be punished by a fine of not more than $5,000.00 or by imprisonment for not less than one nor more than ten years, or both.

(b) Whenever a person is charged with violating subsection (a) of this Code section, the arresting law enforcement officer shall take the hunting license of the person so charged. The hunting license shall be attached to the court's copy of the citation, warrant, accusation, or indictment and shall be forwarded to the court having jurisdiction of the offense. A copy of the citation, warrant, accusation, or indictment shall be forwarded, within 15 days of its issuance, to the Game and Fish Division of the Department of Natural Resources.

(c) In order to obtain a temporary hunting license, a person charged with violating subsection (a) of this Code section must present to the director of the Game and Fish Division of the Department of Natural Resources a certificate of satisfactory completion, after the date of the incident for which the person was charged and regardless of the person's age or date of birth, of a hunter education course prescribed by the Board of Natural Resources. A temporary hunting license issued under such circumstances shall be valid until the next March 31 or until suspended or revoked under any provision of this title or of Title 27. The director of the Game and Fish Division of the Department of Natural Resources may renew the temporary hunting license during the pendency of charges.

(d)(1) If the person is convicted of violating subsection (a) of this Code section, the court shall, within 15 days of such conviction, forward the person's hunting license and a copy of the record of the disposition of the case to the Game and Fish Division of the Department of Natural Resources. At this time, the court shall also require the person to surrender any temporary hunting licenses issued pursuant to the provisions of subsection (c) of this Code section.

(2) If the person is not convicted of violating subsection (a) of this Code section, the court shall return the hunting license to the person.

## O.C.G.A. § 16-11-113. Solicitation, Persuasion, Encouragement, or Enticement of Dealer to Transfer or Convey Firearm to Someone Other Than Buyer.

Any person who attempts to solicit, persuade, encourage, or entice any dealer to transfer or otherwise convey a firearm other than to the actual buyer, as well as any other person who willfully and intentionally aids or abets such person, shall be guilty of a felony. This Code section shall not apply to a federal law enforcement officer or a peace officer, as defined in Code Section 16-1-3, in the performance of his or her official duties or other person under such officer's direct supervision.

## Part 2. Possession of Dangerous Weapons

### O.C.G.A. § 16-11-120.  The Georgia Firearms and Weapons Act.
This part shall be known and may be cited as the 'Georgia Firearms and Weapons Act.'

### O.C.G.A. § 16-11-121.  Definitions.
As used in this part, the term:

(1) "Dangerous weapon" means any weapon commonly known as a "rocket launcher," "bazooka," or "recoilless rifle" which fires explosive or nonexplosive rockets designed to injure or kill personnel or destroy heavy armor, or similar weapon used for such purpose. The term shall also mean a weapon commonly known as a "mortar" which fires high explosive from a metallic cylinder and which is commonly used by the armed forces as an antipersonnel weapon or similar weapon used for such purpose. The term shall also mean a weapon commonly known as a "hand grenade" or other similar weapon which is designed to explode and injure personnel or similar weapon used for such purpose.

(2) "Machine gun" means any weapon which shoots or is designed to shoot, automatically, more than six shots, without manual reloading, by a single function of the trigger.

(3) "Person" means any individual, partnership, company, association, or corporation.

(4) "Sawed-off rifle" means a weapon designed or redesigned, made or remade, and intended to be fired from the shoulder; and designed or redesigned, made or remade, to use the energy of the explosive in a fixed metallic cartridge to fire only a single projectile through a rifle bore for each single pull of the trigger; and which has a barrel or barrels of less than 16 inches in length or has an overall length of less than 26 inches.

(5) "Sawed-off shotgun" means a shotgun or any weapon made from a shotgun whether by alteration, modification, or otherwise having one or more barrels less than 18 inches in length or if such weapon as modified has an overall length of less than 26 inches.

(6) "Shotgun" means a weapon designed or redesigned, made or remade, and intended to be fired from the shoulder; and designed or redesigned, and made or remade, to use the energy of the explosive in a fixed shotgun shell to fire through a smooth bore either a number of ball shot or a single projectile for each single pull of the trigger.

(7) "Silencer" means any device for silencing or diminishing the report of any portable weapon such as a rifle, carbine, pistol, revolver, machine gun, shotgun, fowling piece, or other device from which a shot, bullet, or projectile may be discharged by an explosive.

### O.C.G.A. § 16-11-122.  Possession of Sawed-Off Shotgun, Sawed-Off Rifle, Machine Gun, Dangerous Weapon, or Silencer.
No person shall have in his possession any sawed-off shotgun, sawed-off rifle, machine gun, dangerous weapon, or silencer except as provided in Code Section 16-11-124.

### O.C.G.A. § 16-11-123.  Punishment for Possession of Sawed-Off Shotgun, Sawed-Off Rifle, Machine Gun, Dangerous Weapon, or Silencer.
A person commits the offense of unlawful possession of firearms or weapons when he or she knowingly has in his or her possession any sawed-off shotgun, sawed-off rifle, machine gun, dangerous weapon, or silencer, and, upon conviction thereof, he or she shall be punished by imprisonment for a period of five years.

### O.C.G.A. § 16-11-124.  Exceptions.
This part shall not apply to:

(1) A peace officer of any duly authorized police agency of this state or of any political subdivision thereof, or a law enforcement officer of any department or agency of the United States who is regularly employed and paid by the United States, this state, or any such political subdivision, or an employee of the Department of Corrections of this state who is authorized in writing by the commissioner of corrections to transfer or possess such firearms while in the official performance of his duties;

(2) A member of the National Guard or of the armed forces of the United States to wit: the army, navy, marine corps, air force, or coast guard who, while serving therein, possesses such firearm in the line of duty;

(3) Any sawed-off shotgun, sawed-off rifle, machine gun, dangerous weapon, or silencer which has been modified or changed to the extent that it is inoperative. Examples of the requisite modification include weapons with their barrel or barrels filled with lead, hand grenades filled with sand, or other nonexplosive materials;

(4) Possession of a sawed-off shotgun, sawed-off rifle, machine gun, dangerous weapon, or silencer by a person who is authorized to possess the same because he has registered the sawed-off shotgun, sawed-off rifle, machine gun, dangerous weapon, or silencer in accordance with the dictates of the National Firearms Act, 68A Stat. 725 (26 U.S.C. Sections 5841-5862); and

(5) A security officer employed by a federally licensed nuclear power facility or a licensee of such facility, including a contract security officer, who is trained and qualified under a security plan approved by the United States Nuclear Regulatory Commission or other federal agency authorized to regulate nuclear facility security; provided, however, that this exemption shall apply only while such security officer is acting in connection with his or her official duties on the premises of such nuclear power facility or on properties outside the facility property pursuant to a written agreement entered into with the local law enforcement agency having jurisdiction over the facility. The exemption under this paragraph does not include the possession of silencers.

## O.C.G.A. § 16-11-125.  Burden of Proof for Defense of Exception.

In any complaint, accusation, or indictment and in any action or proceeding brought for the enforcement of this part it shall not be necessary to negative any exception, excuse, proviso, or exemption contained in this part, and the burden of proof of any such exception, excuse, proviso, or exemption shall be upon the defendant.

## O.C.G.A. § 16.11.125.1.  Definitions.

As used in this part, the term:

(1) 'Handgun' means a firearm of any description, loaded or unloaded, from which any shot, bullet, or other missile can be discharged by an action of an explosive where the length of the barrel, not including any revolving, detachable, or magazine breech, does not exceed 12 inches; provided, however, that the term 'handgun' shall not include a gun which discharges a single shot of .46 centimeters or less in diameter.

(2) 'Knife' means a cutting instrument designed for the purpose of offense and defense consisting of a blade that is greater than five inches in length which is fastened to a handle.

(3) 'License holder' means a person who holds a valid weapons carry license.

(4) 'Long gun' means a firearm with a barrel length of at least 18 inches and overall length of at least 26 inches designed or made and intended to be fired from the shoulder and designed or made to use the energy of the explosive in a fixed:

(A) Shotgun shell to fire through a smooth bore either a number of ball shot or a single projectile for each single pull of the trigger or from which any shot, bullet, or other missile can be discharged; or

(B) Metallic cartridge to fire only a single projectile through a rifle bore for each single pull of the trigger;

provided, however, that the term 'long gun' shall not include a gun which discharges a single shot of .46 centimeters or less in diameter.

(5) 'Weapon' means a knife or handgun.

(6) 'Weapons carry license' or 'license' means a license issued pursuant to Code Section 16-11-129.

## Part 3.  Carrying and Possession of Firearms

### O.C.G.A. § 16-11-126.  Carrying a Concealed Weapon.

(a) Any person who is not prohibited by law from possessing a handgun or long gun may have or carry on his or her person a weapon or long gun on his or her property or inside his or her home, motor vehicle, or place of business without a valid weapons carry license.

(b) Any person who is not prohibited by law from possessing a handgun or long gun may have or carry on his or her person a long gun without a valid weapons carry license, provided that if the long gun is loaded, it shall only be carried in an open and fully exposed manner.

(c) Any person who is not prohibited by law from possessing a handgun or long gun may have or carry any handgun provided that it is enclosed in a case and unloaded.

(d) Any person who is not prohibited by law from possessing a handgun or long gun who is eligible for a weapons carry license may transport a handgun or long gun in any private passenger motor vehicle; provided, however, that private property owners or persons in legal control of the property through a lease, rental agreement, licensing agreement, contract, or any other agreement to control access to such property shall have the right to forbid possession of a weapon or long gun on their property, except as provided in Code Section 16-11-135.

(e) Any person licensed to carry a handgun or weapon in any state whose laws recognize and give effect to a license issued pursuant to this part shall be authorized to carry a weapon in this state, but only while the licensee is not a resident of this state; provided, however, that such licensee shall carry the weapon in compliance with the laws of this state.

(f) Any person with a valid hunting or fishing license on his or her person, or any person not required by law to have a hunting or fishing license, who is engaged in legal hunting, fishing, or sport shooting when the person has the permission of the owner of the land on which the activities are being conducted may have or carry on his or her person a handgun or long gun without a valid weapons carry license while hunting, fishing, or engaging in sport shooting.

(g) Notwithstanding Code Sections 12-3-10, 27-3-1.1, 27-3-6, and 16-12-122 through 16-12-127, any person with a valid weapons carry license may carry a weapon in all parks, historic sites, or recreational areas, as such term is defined in Code Section 12-3-10, including all publicly owned buildings located in such parks, historic sites, and recreational areas, in wildlife management areas, and on public transportation; provided, however, that a person shall not carry a handgun into a place where it is prohibited by federal law.

(h)(1) No person shall carry a weapon without a valid weapons carry license unless he or she meets one of the exceptions of having such license as provided in subsections (a) through (g) of this Code section.

(2) A person commits the offense of carrying a weapon without a license when he or she violates the provisions of paragraph (1) of this subsection.

(i) Upon conviction of the offense of carrying weapon without a valid weapons carry license, a person shall be punished as follows:

(1) For the first offense, he or she shall be guilty of a misdemeanor; and

(2) For the second offense within five years, as measured from the dates of the previous arrests for which convictions were obtained to the date of the current arrest for which a conviction

is obtained, and for any subsequent offense, he or she shall be guilty of a felony and, upon conviction thereof, shall be imprisoned for not less than two years and not more than five years.

## O.C.G.A. § 16-11-127. Firearms and Knives in Public and Private Places; Licensees.

(a) As used in this Code section, the term:

(1) 'Bar' means an establishment that is devoted to the serving of alcoholic beverages for consumption by guests on the premises and in which the serving of food is only incidental to the consumption of those beverages, including, but not limited to, taverns, nightclubs, cocktail lounges, and cabarets.

(2) 'Courthouse' means a building occupied by judicial courts and containing rooms in which judicial proceedings are held.

(3) 'Government building' means:

(A) The building in which a government entity is housed;

(B) The building where a government entity meets in its official capacity; provided, however, that is such building is not a publicly owned building, such building shall be considered a government building for the purposes of this Code section only during the time such government entity is meeting at such building; or

(C) The portion of any building that is not a publicly owned building that is occupied by a government entity.

(4) 'Government entity' means an office, agency, authority, department, commission, board, body, division, instrumentality, or institution of the state or any county, municipal corporation, consolidated government, or local board of education within this state.

(5) 'Parking facility' means real property owned or leased by a government entity, courthouse, jail, prison, place of worship, or bar that has been designated by such government entity, courthouse, jail, prison, place of worship, or bar for the parking of motor vehicles at a government building or at such courthouse, jail, prison, place of worship, or bar.

(b) A person shall be guilty of carrying a weapon or long gun in an unauthorized location and punished as for a misdemeanor when he or she carries a weapon or long gun while:

(1) In a government building;

(2) In a courthouse;

(3) In a jail or prison;

(4) In a place of worship;

(5) In a state mental health facility as defined in Code Section 37-1-1 which admits individuals on an involuntary basis for treatment of mental illness, developmental disability, or addictive disease; provided, however, that carrying a weapon or long gun in such location in a manner in compliance with paragraph (3) of subsection (d) of this Code section shall not constitute a violation of this subsection;

(6) In a bar, unless the owner of the bar permits the carrying of weapons or long guns by license holders;

(7) On the premises of a nuclear power facility, except as provided in Code Section 16-11-127.2, and the punishment provisions of the Code Section 16-11-127.2 shall supersede the punishment provisions of this Code section; or

(8) Within 150 feet of any polling place, except as provided in subsection (i) of Code Section 21-2-413.

(c) Except as provided in Code Section 16-11-127.1, a license holder or person recognized under subsection (e) of Code Section 16-11-126 shall be authorized to carry a weapon as provided in Code Section 16-11-135 and in every location in this state not listed in subsection (b) of this Code section; provided, however, that private property owners or persons in legal control of property though a lease, rental agreement, licensing agreement, contract, or any other agreement to control access to such property shall have the right to forbid possession of a weapon or long gun on their property, except as provided in Code Section 16-11-135. A violation of subsection (b) of this Code section shall not create or give rise to a civil action for damages.

(d) Subsection (b) of this Code section shall not apply:

(1) To the use of weapons or long guns as exhibits in a legal proceeding, provided such weapons or long guns are secured and handled as directed by the personnel providing courtroom security or the judge hearing the case;

(2) To a license holder who approaches security or management personnel upon arrival at a location described in subsection (b) of this Code section and notifies such security or management personnel of the presence of the weapon or long gun and explicitly follows the security or management personnel's direction from removing, securing, storing, or temporarily surrendering such weapon or long gun; and

(3) To a weapon or long gun possessed by a license holder which is under the possessor's control in a motor vehicle or is in a locked compartment of a motor vehicle or one which is in a locked container in or a locked firearms rack which is on a motor vehicle and such vehicle is parked in a parking facility.

## O.C.G.A. § 16-11-127.1. Weapons in School Safety Zones, School Buildings, Grounds, or at School Functions.

(a) As used in this Code section, the term:

(1) 'School safety zone' means in or on any real property owned by or leased to any public or private elementary school, secondary school, or school board and used for elementary or secondary education and in or on any public or private technical school, vocational school, college, university, or institution of postsecondary education.

(2) 'Weapon' means and includes any pistol, revolver, or any weapon designed or intended to propel a missile of any kind, or any dirk, bowie knife, switchblade knife, ballistic knife, any other knife having a blade of two or more inches, straight-edge razor, razor blade, spring stick, knuckles, whether made from metal, thermoplastic, wood, or other similar material, blackjack, any bat, club, or other bludgeon-type weapon, or any flailing instrument consisting of two or more rigid parts connected in such a manner as to allow them to swing freely, which may be known as a nun chahka, nun chuck, nunchaku, shuriken, or fighting chain, or any disc, of whatever configuration, having at least two points or pointed blades which is designed to be thrown or propelled and which may be known as a throwing star or oriental dart, or any weapon of like kind, and any stun gun or taser as defined in subsection (a) of Code Section 16-11-106. This paragraph excludes any of these instruments used for classroom work authorized by the teacher.

(b)(1) Except as otherwise provided in subsection (c) of this Code section, it shall be unlawful for any person to carry to or to possess or have under such person's control while within a school safety zone or at a school building, school function, or school property or on a bus or other transportation furnished by the school any weapon or explosive compound, other than fireworks the possession of which is regulated by Chapter 10 of Title 25.

(2) Any license holder who violates this subdivision shall be guilty of a misdemeanor. Any person who is not a license holder who violates this subsection shall be guilty of a felony and, upon conviction thereof, be punished by a fine of not more than $10,000.00, by imprisonment for not less than two nor more than ten years, or both.

(3) Any person convicted of a violation of this subsection involving a dangerous weapon or machine gun, as such terms are defined in Code Section 16-11-121, shall be punished by a fine of not more than $10,000.00 or by imprisonment for a period of not less than five nor more than ten years, or both.

(4) A child who violates this subsection shall be subject to the provisions of Code Section 15-11-63.

(c) The provisions of this Code section shall not apply to:

(1) Baseball bats, hockey sticks, or other sports equipment possessed by competitors for legitimate athletic purposes;

(2) Participants in organized sport shooting events or firearm training courses;

(3) Persons participating in military training programs conducted by or on behalf of the armed forces of the United States or the Georgia Department of Defense;

(4) Persons participating in law enforcement training conducted by a police academy certified by the Georgia Peace Officer Standards and Training Council or by a law enforcement agency of the state or the United States or any political subdivision thereof;

(5) The following persons, when acting in the performance of their official duties or when en route to or from their official duties:

(A) A peace officer as defined by Code Section 35-8-2;

(B) A law enforcement officer of the United States government;

(C) A prosecuting attorney of this state or of the United States;

(D) An employee of the Georgia Department of Corrections or a correctional facility operated by a political subdivision of this state or the United States who is authorized by the head of such correctional agency or facility to carry a firearm;

(E) A person employed as a campus police officer or school security officer who is authorized to carry a weapon in accordance with Chapter 8 of Title 20; and

(F) Medical examiners, coroners, and their investigators who are employed by the state or any political subdivision thereof;

(6) A person who has been authorized in writing by a duly authorized official of the school to have in such person's possession or use as part of any activity being conducted at a school building, school property, or school function a weapon which would otherwise be prohibited by this Code section. Such authorization shall specify the weapon or weapons which have been authorized and the time period during which the authorization is valid;

(7) A person who is licensed in accordance with Code Section 16-11-129 or issued a permit pursuant to Code Section 43-38-10, when such person carries or picks up a student at a school building, school function, or school property or on a bus or other transportation furnished by the school or a person who is licensed in accordance with Code Section 16-11-129 or issued a permit pursuant to Code Section 43-38-10 when he or she has any weapon legally kept within a vehicle when such vehicle is parked at such school property or is in transit through a designated school zone.

(8) A weapon possessed by a license holder which is under the possessor's control in a motor vehicle or which is in a locked compartment of a motor vehicle or one which is in a locked container in or a locked firearms rack which is on a motor vehicle which is being used by an adult over 21 years of age to bring to or pick up a student at a school building, school function, or school property or on a bus or other transportation furnished by the school, or when such vehicle is used to transport someone to an activity being conducted on school property which has been authorized by a duly authorized official of the school; provided, however, that this exception shall not apply to a student attending such school;

(9) Persons employed in fulfilling defense contracts with the government of the United States or agencies thereof when possession of the weapon is necessary for manufacture, transport, installation, and testing under the requirements of such contract;

(10) Those employees of the State Board of Pardons and Paroles when specifically designated and authorized in writing by the members of the State Board of Pardons and Paroles to carry a weapon;

(11) The Attorney General and those members of his or her staff whom he or she specifically authorizes in writing to carry a weapon;

(12) Probation supervisors employed by and under the authority of the Department of Corrections pursuant to Article 2 of Chapter 8 of Title 42, known as the "State-wide Probation Act,"

when specifically designated and authorized in writing by the director of the Division of Probation;

(13) Public safety directors of municipal corporations;

(14) State and federal trial and appellate judges;

(15) United States attorneys and assistant United States attorneys;

(16) Clerks of the superior courts;

(17) Teachers and other school personnel who are otherwise authorized to possess or carry weapons, provided that any such weapon is in a locked compartment of a motor vehicle or one which is in a locked container in or a locked firearms rack which is on a motor vehicle; or

(18) Constables of any county of this state.

(d)(1) This Code section shall not prohibit any person who resides or works in a business or is in the ordinary course transacting lawful business or any person who is a visitor of such resident located within a school safety zone from carrying, possessing, or having under such person's control a weapon within a school safety zone; provided, however, it shall be unlawful for any such person to carry, possess, or have under such person's control while at a school building or school function or on school property, a school bus, or other transportation furnished by the school any weapon or explosive compound, other than fireworks the possession of which is regulated by Chapter 10 of Title 25.

(2) Any person who violates this subsection shall be subject to the penalties specified in subsection (b) of this Code section.

(3) This subsection shall not be construed to waive or alter any legal requirement for possession of weapons or firearms otherwise required by law.

(e) It shall be no defense to a prosecution for a violation of this Code section that:

(1) School was or was not in session at the time of the offense;

(2) The real property was being used for other purposes besides school purposes at the time of the offense; or

(3) The offense took place on a school vehicle.

(f) In a prosecution under this Code section, a map produced or reproduced by any municipal or county agency or department for the purpose of depicting the location and boundaries of the area of the real property of a school board or a private or public elementary or secondary school that is used for school purposes or the area of any campus of any public or private technical school, vocational school, college, university, or institution of postsecondary education, or a true copy of the map, shall, if certified as a true copy by the custodian of the record, be admissible and shall constitute prima-facie evidence of the location and boundaries of the area, if the governing body of the municipality or county has approved the map as an official record of the location and boundaries of the area. A map approved under this Code section may be revised from time to time by the governing body of the municipality or county. The original of every map approved or revised under this subsection or a true copy of such original map shall be filed with the municipality or county and shall be maintained as an official record of the municipality or county. This subsection shall not preclude the prosecution from introducing or relying upon any other evidence or testimony to establish any element of this offense. This subsection shall not preclude the use or admissibility of a map or diagram other than the one which has been approved by the municipality or county.

(g) A county school board may adopt regulations requiring the posting of signs designating the areas of school boards and private or public elementary and secondary schools as 'Weapon-free and Violence-free School Safety Zones.'

## O.C.G.A. § 16-11-127.2. Weapons Possession on Nuclear Power Facility Premises.

(a) Except as provided in subsection (c) of this Code section, it shall be unlawful for any person to carry, possess, or have under such person's control while on the premises of a nuclear power facility a weapon or long gun. Any person who violates this subsection shall be guilty of a misdemeanor.

(b) Any person who violates subsection (a) of this Code section with the intent to do bodily harm on the premises of a nuclear power facility shall be guilty of a felony and, upon conviction thereof, shall be punished by a fine of not more than $10,000.00, by imprisonment for not less than two nor more than 20 years, or both.

(c) This Code section shall not apply to a security officer authorized to carry dangerous weapons pursuant to Code Section 16-11-124 who is acting in connection with his or her official duties on the premises of a federally licensed nuclear power facility; nor shall this Code section apply to persons designated in paragraph (3), (4), (5), or (9) of subsection (c) of Code Section 16-11-127.1.

## GA ST § 16-11-128. Reserved.

## O.C.G.A. § 16-11-129. License to Carry Pistol or Revolver.

(a) *Application for weapons carry license or renewal license; term.*

The judge of the probate court of each county may, on application under oath and on payment of a fee of $30.00, issue a weapons carry license or renewal license valid for a period of five years to any person whose domicile is in that county or who is on active duty with the United States armed forces and who is not a domiciliary of this state but who either resides in that county or on a military reservation located in whole or in part in that county at the time of such application. Such license or renewal license shall authorize that person to carry any weapon in any county of this state notwithstanding any change in that person's county of residence or state of domicile. Applicants shall submit the application for a weapons carry license or renewal license to the judge of the probate court on forms prescribed and furnished free of charge to persons wishing to apply for the license or renewal license. An applicant who is not a United States citizen shall provide sufficient personal identifying data, including without limitation his or her place of birth and United States issued alien or admission number, as the Georgia Bureau of Investigation may prescribe by rule or regulation. An applicant who is in nonimmigrant status shall provide proof of his or her qualifications for an exception to the federal firearm prohibition pursuant to 18 U.S.C. Section 922(y). Forms shall be designed to elicit information from the applicant pertinent to his or her eligibility under this Code section, including citizenship, but shall not require data which is nonpertinent or irrelevant such as serial numbers or other identification capable of being used as a de facto registration of firearms owned by the applicant. The Department of Public Safety shall furnish application forms and license forms required by this Code section. The forms shall be furnished to each judge of each probate court within the state at no cost.

(b) *Licensing exceptions.*

(1) As used in this subsection, the term:

(A) 'Controlled substance' means any drug, substance, or immediate precursor included in the definition of controlled substances in paragraph (4) of Code Section 16-13-21.

(B) 'Convicted' means a plea of guilty or a finding of guilt by a court of competent jurisdiction or the acceptance of a plea of nolo contendere, irrespective of the pendency or availability of an appeal or an application for collateral relief.

(C) 'Dangerous drug' means any drug defined as such in Code Section 16-13-71.

(2) No weapons carry license shall be issued to:

(A) Any person under 21 years of age;

(B) Any person who has been convicted of a felony by a court of this state or any other state; by a court of the United States including its territories, possessions, and dominions; or by a court of any foreign nation and has not been pardoned for such felony by the President of the United States, the State Board of Pardons and Paroles, or the person or agency empowered to grant pardons under the constitution or laws of such state or nation;

(C) Any person against whom proceedings are pending for any felony;

(D) Any person who is a fugitive from justice;

(E) Any person who is prohibited from possessing or shipping a firearm in interstate commerce pursuant to subsections (g) and (n) of 18 U.S.C. Section 922;

(F) Any person who has been convicted of an offense arising out of the unlawful manufacture or distribution of a controlled substance or other dangerous drug;

(G) Any person who has had his or her weapons carry licensed revoked pursuant to subsection (e) of this Code section;

(H) Any person who has been convicted of any of the following:

(i) Pointing a gun or a pistol at another in violation of Code Section 16-11-102;

(ii) Carrying a weapon without a weapons carry license in violation of Code Section 16-11-126; or

(iii) Carrying a weapon or long gun in an unauthorized location in violation of Code Section 16-11-127

and has not been free of all restraint or supervision in connection therewith and free of any other conviction for at least five years immediately preceding the date of the application;

(I) Any person who has been convicted of any misdemeanor involving the use or possession of a controlled substance and has not been free of all restraint or supervision in connection therewith or free of:

(i) A second conviction of any misdemeanor involving the use or possession of a controlled substance; or

(ii) Any conviction under subparagraphs (E) through (G) of this paragraph for at least five years immediately preceding the date of the application; or

(J) Any person who has been hospitalized as an inpatient in any mental hospital or alcohol or drug treatment center within the five years immediately preceding the application. The judge of the probate court may require any applicant to sign a waiver authorizing any mental hospital or treatment center to inform the judge whether or not the applicant has been an inpatient in any such facility in the last five years and authorizing the superintendent of such facility to make to the judge a recommendation regarding whether the applicant is a threat to the safety of others and whether a license to carry a weapon should be issued. When such a waiver is required by the judge, the applicant shall pay a fee of $3.00 for reimbursement of the cost of making such a report by the mental health hospital, alcohol or drug treatment center, or the Department of Behavioral Health and Developmental Disabilities, which the judge shall remit to the hospital, center, or department. The judge shall keep any such hospitalization or treatment information confidential. It shall be at the discretion of the judge, considering the circumstances surrounding the hospitalization and the recommendation of the superintendent of the hospital or treatment center where the individual was a patient, to issue the weapons carry license or renewal license.

(3) If the first offender treatment without adjudication of guilt for a conviction contained in subparagraph (F) or (I) of paragraph (2) of this subsection was entered and such sentence was successfully completed and such person has not had any other conviction since the completion of such sentence and for at least five years immediately preceding the date of the application, he or she shall be eligible for a weapons carry license provided that no other license exception applies.

(c) *Fingerprinting.*

Following completion of the application for a license or the renewal of a license, the judge of the probate court shall require the applicant to proceed to an appropriate law enforcement agency in the county with the completed application. The appropriate local law enforcement agency in each county shall then capture the fingerprints of the applicant for a weapons carry license or renewal license and place the name of the applicant on the blank license form. The appropriate local law enforcement agency shall place the fingerprint on a blank license form which has been furnished to the law enforcement agency by the judge of the probate court if a fingerprint is required to be furnished by subsection (f) of this Code section. The law enforcement agency shall be entitled to a fee of $5.00 from the applicant for its services in connection with the application.

(d) *Investigation of applicant; issuance of license; renewal.*

(1) For both weapons carry license applications and requests for license renewals, the judge of the probate court shall within five days following the receipt of the application or request direct the law enforcement agency to request a fingerprint based criminal history records check from the Georgia Crime Information Center and Federal Bureau of Investigation for purposes of determining the suitability of the applicant and return an appropriate report to the judge of the probate court. Fingerprints shall be in such form and of such quality as prescribed by the Georgia Crime Information Center and under standards adopted by the Federal Bureau of Investigation. The Georgia Bureau of Investigation may charge such fee as is necessary to cover the cost of the records search.

(2) For both weapons carry license applications and requests for license renewals, the judge of the probate court shall within five days following the receipt of the application or request also direct the law enforcement agency to conduct a background check using the Federal Bureau of Investigation´s National Instant Criminal Background Check System and return an appropriate report to the probate judge.

(3) When a person who is not a United States citizen applies for a weapons carry license or renewal of a license under this Code section, the judge of the probate court shall direct the law enforcement agency to conduct a search of the records maintained by the United States Bureau of Immigration and Customs Enforcement and return an appropriate report to the probate judge. As a condition to the issuance of a license or the renewal of a license, an applicant who is in nonimmigrant status shall provide proof of his or her qualifications for an exception to the federal firearm prohibition pursuant to 18 U.S.C. Section 922(y).

(4) The law enforcement agency shall notify the judge of the probate court within 30 days, by telephone and in writing, of any findings relating to the applicant which may bear on his or her eligibility for a weapons carry license or renewal license under the terms of this Code section. When no derogatory information is found on the applicant bearing on his or her eligibility to obtain a license or renewal license, a report shall not be required. The law enforcement agency shall return the application and the blank license form with the fingerprint thereon directly to the judge of the probate court within such time period. Not later than ten days after the judge of the probate court receives the report from the law enforcement agency concerning the suitability of the applicant for a license, the judge of the probate court shall issue such applicant a license or renewal license to carry any weapon unless facts establishing ineligibility have been reported or unless the judge determines such applicant has not met all the qualifications, is not of good moreal character, or has failed to comply with any of the requirements contained in this Code section.  The judge of the probate court shall date stamp the report from the law enforcement agency to show the date on which the report was received by the judge of the probate court.

(e) *Revocation, loss, or damage to license.*

If, at any time during the period for which the weapons carry license was issued, the judge of the probate court of the county in which the license was issued shall learn or have brought to his or her attention in any manner any reasonable ground to believe the licensee is not eligible to retain the license, the judge may, after notice and hearing, revoke the license of the person upon a finding that such person is not eligible for a weapons carry license pursuant to subsection (b) of this Code section or an adjudication of falsification of application, mental incompetency, or chronic alcohol or narcotic usage. It shall be unlawful for any person to possess a license which has been revoked, and any person found in possession of any such revoked license, except in the performance of his or her official duties, shall be guilty of a misdemeanor. It shall be required that any license holder under this Code section have in his or her possession his or her valid license whenever he or she is carrying a weapon under the authority granted by this Code section, and his or her failure to do so shall be prima-facie evidence of a violation of Code Section 16-11-126. Loss of any license issued in accordance with this Code section or damage to the license in any manner which shall render it illegible shall be reported to the judge of the probate court of the county in which it was issued within 48 hours of the time the loss or damage becomes known to the license holder. The judge of the probate court shall thereupon issue a replacement for and shall take custody of and destroy a damaged license; and in any case in which a license has been lost, he or she shall issue a cancellation order and notify by telephone and in writing each of the law enforcement agencies whose records were checked before issuance of the original license. The judge shall charge the fee specified in subsection (k) of Code Section 15-9-60 for such services.

(f)(1) *Weapons carry license specifications.*

Weapons carry licenses issued as prescribed in this Code section shall be printed on durable but lightweight card stock, and the completed card shall be laminated in plastic to improve its wearing qualities and to inhibit alterations. Measurements shall be 3 1/4 inches long, and 2 1/4 inches wide. Each shall be serially numbered within the county of issuance and shall bear the full name, residential address, birth date, weight, height, color of eyes, and sex of the licensee. The license shall show the date of issuance, the expiration date, and the probate court in which issued and shall be signed by the licensee and bear the signature or facsimile thereof of the judge. The seal of the court shall be placed on the face before the license is laminated. Licenses issued on and before December 31, 2011, shall bear a clear print of the licensee's right index finger; however, if the right index fingerprint cannot be secured for any reason, the print of another finger may be used but such print shall be marked to identify the finger from which the print is taken.

(2)(A) On and after January 1, 2012, newly issued or renewal weapons carry licenses shall incorporate overt and covert security features which shall be blended with the personal data printed on the license to form a significant barrier to imitation, replication, and duplication. There shall be a minimum of three different ultraviolet colors used to enhance the security of the license incorporating variable data, color shifting characteristics, and front edge only perimeter visibility. The weapons carry license shall have a color photograph viewable under ambient light on both the front and back of the license. The license shall incorporate custom optical variable devices featuring the great seal of the State of Georgia as well as matching demetalized optical variable devices viewable under ambient light from the front and back of the license incorporating microtext and unique alphanumeric serialization specific to the license holder. The license shall be of similar material, size, and thickness of a credit card and have a holographic laminate to secure and protect the license for the duration of the license period.

(B) Using the physical characteristics of the license set forth in subparagraph (A) of this paragraph, The Council of Probate Court Judges of Georgia shall create specifications for the probate courts so that all weapons carry licenses in this state shall be uniform and so that probate courts can petition the Department of Administrative Services to purchase the equipment and supplies necessary for producing such licenses. The department shall follow the competitive bidding procedure set forth in Code Section 50-5-102.

(g) *Alteration or counterfeiting of license; penalty.*

A person who deliberately alters or counterfeits a weapons carry license or who possesses an altered or counterfeit weapons carry license with the intent to misrepresent any information contained in such license shall be guilty of a felony and, upon conviction thereof, shall be punished by imprisonment for a period of not less than one nor more than five years.

(h) *Licenses for former law enforcement officers.*

Except as otherwise provided in Code Section 16-11-130, any person who has served as a law enforcement officer for at least ten of the 12 years immediately preceding the retirement of such person as a law enforcement officer shall be entitled to be issued a weapons carry license as provided for in this Code section without the payment of any of the fees provided for in this Code section. Such person shall comply with all the other provisions of this Code section relative to the issuance of such licenses. As used in this subsection, the term 'law enforcement officer' means any peace officer who is employed by the United States government or by the State of Georgia or any political subdivision thereof and who is required by the terms of his or her employment, whether by election or appointment, to give his or her full time to the preservation of public order or the protection of life and property or the prevention of crime. Such term shall include conservation rangers.

(i) *Temporary renewal licenses.*

(1) Any person who holds a weapons carry license under this Code section may, at the time he or she applies for a renewal of the license, also apply for a temporary renewal license if less than 90 days remain before expiration of the license he or she then holds or if the previous license has expired within the last 30 days.

(2) Unless the judge of the probate court knows or is made aware of any fact which would make the applicant ineligible for a five-year renewal license, the judge shall at the time of application issue a temporary renewal license to the applicant.

(3) Such a temporary renewal license shall be in the form of a paper receipt indicating the date on which the court received the renewal application and shall show the name, address, sex, age, and race of the applicant and that the temporary renewal license expires 90 days from the date of issue.

(4) During its period of validity the temporary renewal permit, if carried on or about the holder's person together with the holder's previous license, shall be valid in the same manner and for the same purposes as a five-year license.

(5) A $1.00 fee shall be charged by the probate court for issuance of a temporary renewal license.

(6) A temporary renewal license may be revoked in the same manner as a five-year license.

(j) When an eligible applicant fails to receive a license, temporary permit, or renewal license within the time period required by this Code section and the application or request has been properly filed, the applicant may bring an action in mandamus or other legal proceeding in order to obtain a license, temporary license, or renewal license. If such applicant is the prevailing party, he or she shall be entitled to recover his or her costs in such action, including any reasonable attorney's fees.

## O.C.G.A. § 16-11-130. Exemptions of Concealed Carry Laws.

(a) Code Sections 16-11-126 through 16-11-127.2 shall not apply to or affect any of the following persons if such persons are employed in the offices listed below or when authorized by federal or state law, regulations, or order:

(1) Peace officers, as such term is defined in paragraph (11) of Code Section 16-1-3, and retired peace officers so long as they remain certified whether employed by the state or a political subdivision of the state or another state or a political subdivision of another state but only if such other state provides a similar privilege for the peace officers of this state;

(2) Wardens, superintendents, and keepers of correctional institutions, jails, or other institutions for the detention of persons accused or convicted of an offense;

(3) Persons in the military service of the state or of the United States;

(4) Persons employed in fulfilling defense contracts with the government of the United States or agencies thereof when possession of the weapon is necessary for manufacture, transport, installation, and testing under the requirements of such contract;

(5) District attorneys, investigators employed by and assigned to a district attorney's office, assistant district attorneys, attorneys employed by the Prosecuting Attorneys' Council of Georgia, and any retired district attorney, assistant district attorney, or district attorney's investigator if such retired employee is receiving benefits under Title 47 or is retired in good standing and receiving benefits from a county or municipal retirement system;

(6) State court solicitors-general; investigators employed by and assigned to a state court solicitor-general's office; assistant state court solicitors-general; the corresponding personnel of any city court expressly continued in existence as a city court pursuant to Article VI, Section X, Paragraph

I, subparagraph (5) of the Constitution; and the corresponding personnel of any civil court expressly continued as a civil court pursuant to said provision of the Constitution;

(7) Those employees of the State Board of Pardons and Paroles when specifically designated and authorized in writing by the members of the State Board of Pardons and Paroles to carry a weapon or long gun;

(8) The Attorney General and those members of his or her staff whom he or she specifically authorizes in writing to carry a weapon or long gun;

(9) Chief probation officers, probation officers, intensive probation officers, and surveillance officers employed by and under the authority of the Department of Corrections pursuant to Article 2 of Chapter 8 of Title 42, known as the 'State-wide Probation Act,' when specifically designated and authorized in writing by the director of Division of Probation;

(10) Public safety directors of municipal corporations;

(11) Explosive ordnance disposal technicians, as such term is defined by Code Section 16-7-80, and persons certified as provided in Code Section 35-8-13 to handle animals trained to detect explosives, while in the performance of their duties;

(12) State and federal trial and appellate judges, full-time and permanent part-time judges of municipal and city courts, and former state trial and appellate judges retired from their respective offices under state retirement;

(13) United States Attorneys and Assistant United States Attorneys;

(14) County medical examiners and coroners and their sworn officers employed by county government; and

(15) Clerks of the superior courts.

(b) Code Sections 16-11-126 through 16-11-127.2 shall not apply to or affect persons who at the time of their retirement from service with the Department of Corrections were chief probation officers, probation officers, intensive probation officers, or surveillance officers, when specifically designated and authorized in writing by the director of the Division of Probation.

(c) Code Sections 16-11-126 through 16-11-127.2 shall not apply to or affect any:

(1) Sheriff, retired sheriff, deputy sheriff, or retired sheriff or deputy sheriff if such retired deputy sheriff is eligible to receive or is receiving benefits under the Peace Officers´ Annuity and Benefit Fund provided under Chapter 17 of Title 47, the Sheriffs' Retirement Fund of Georgia provided under Chapter 16 of Title 47, or any other public retirement system established under the laws of this state for service as a law enforcement officer;

(2) Member of the Georgia State Patrol or agent of the Georgia Bureau of Investigation or retired member of the Georgia State Patrol or agent of the Georgia Bureau of Investigation if such retired member or agent is receiving benefits under the Employees´ Retirement System;

(3) Full-time law enforcement chief executive engaging in the management of a county, municipal, state, state authority, or federal law enforcement agency in the State of Georgia, including any college or university law enforcement chief executive that is registered or certified by the Georgia Peace Officer Standards and Training Council; or retired law enforcement chief executive that formerly managed a county, municipal, state, state authority, or federal law enforcement agency in the State of Georgia, including any college or university law enforcement chief executive that was registered or certified at the time of his or her retirement by the Georgia Peace Officer Standards and Training Council, if such retired law enforcement chief executive is receiving benefits under the Peace Officers´ Annuity and Benefit Fund provided under Chapter 17 of Title 47 or is retired in good standing and receiving benefits from a county, municipal, State of Georgia, state authority, or federal retirement system; or

(4) Police officer of any county, municipal, state, state authority, or federal law enforcement agency in the State of Georgia, including any college or university police officer that is registered or certified by the Georgia Peace Officer Standards and Training Council, or retired police officer of any

county, municipal, state, state authority, or federal law enforcement agency in the State of Georgia, including any college or university police officer that was registered or certified at the time of his or her retirement by the Georgia Peace Officer Standards and Training Council, if such retired employee is receiving benefits under the Peace Officers´ Annuity and Benefit Fund provided under Chapter 17 of Title 47 or is retired in good standing and receiving benefits from a county, municipal, State of Georgia, state authority, or federal retirement system.

In addition, any such sheriff, retired sheriff, deputy sheriff, retired deputy sheriff, active or retired law enforcement chief executive, or other law enforcement officer referred to in this subsection shall be authorized to carry a handgun on or off duty anywhere within the state and the provisions of Code Sections 16-11-126 through 16-11-127.2 shall not apply to the carrying of such firearms.

    (d) A prosecution based upon a violation of Code Section 16-11-126, 16-11-127 need not negative any exemptions.

### O.C.G.A. § 16-11-131. Convicted Felons Prohibited From Possession of Firearms.

    (a) As used in this Code section, the term:

    (1) "Felony" means any offense punishable by imprisonment for a term of one year or more and includes conviction by a court-martial under the Uniform Code of Military Justice for an offense which would constitute a felony under the laws of the United States.

    (2) "Firearm" includes any handgun, rifle, shotgun, or other weapon which will or can be converted to expel a projectile by the action of an explosive or electrical charge.

    (b) Any person who is on probation as a felony first offender pursuant to Article 3 of Chapter 8 of Title 42 or who has been convicted of a felony by a court of this state or any other state; by a court of the United States including its territories, possessions, and dominions; or by a court of any foreign nation and who receives, possesses, or transports any firearm commits a felony and, upon conviction thereof, shall be imprisoned for not less than one nor more than five years; provided, however, that if the felony as to which the person is on probation or has been previously convicted is a forcible felony, then upon conviction of receiving, possessing, or transporting a firearm, such person shall be imprisoned for a period of five years.

    (b.1) Any person who is prohibited by this Code section from possessing a firearm because of conviction of a forcible felony or because of being on probation as a first offender for a forcible felony pursuant to this Code section and who attempts to purchase or obtain transfer of a firearm shall be guilty of a felony and shall be punished by imprisonment for not less than one nor more than five years.

    (c) This Code section shall not apply to any person who has been pardoned for the felony by the President of the United States, the State Board of Pardons and Paroles, or the person or agency empowered to grant pardons under the constitutions or laws of the several states or of a foreign nation and, by the terms of the pardon, has expressly been authorized to receive, possess, or transport a firearm.

    (d) A person who has been convicted of a felony, but who has been granted relief from the disabilities imposed by the laws of the United States with respect to the acquisition, receipt, transfer, shipment, or possession of firearms by the secretary of the United States Department of the Treasury pursuant to 18 U.S.C. Section 925, shall, upon presenting to the Board of Public Safety proof that the relief has been granted and it being established from proof submitted by the applicant to the satisfaction of the Board of Public Safety that the circumstances regarding the conviction and the applicant's record and reputation are such that the acquisition, receipt, transfer, shipment, or possession of firearms by the person would not present a threat to the safety of the citizens of Georgia and that the granting of the relief sought would not be contrary to the public interest, be granted relief from the disabilities imposed by this Code section. A person who has been convicted under federal or state law of a felony pertaining to antitrust violations, unfair trade practices, or restraint of trade shall, upon presenting to the Board of Public Safety proof, and it being established from said proof, submitted by the applicant to the satisfaction of the Board of Public Safety that the circumstances regarding the conviction and the applicant's record and reputation are such that the acquisition, receipt, transfer, shipment, or possession of firearms by the person would not present a threat to the safety of the citizens of Georgia and that the granting of the relief sought would not be contrary to the public interest, be granted relief from the disabilities imposed by this Code section. A record that the relief has been granted by the board shall be entered upon the criminal history of the person maintained by the Georgia Crime Information Center and the board shall maintain a list of the names of such persons which shall be open for public inspection.

(e) As used in this Code section, the term "forcible felony" means any felony which involves the use or threat of physical force or violence against any person and further includes, without limitation, murder; felony murder; burglary; robbery; armed robbery; kidnapping; hijacking of an aircraft or motor vehicle; aggravated stalking; rape; aggravated child molestation; aggravated sexual battery; arson in the first degree; the manufacturing, transporting, distribution, or possession of explosives with intent to kill, injure, or intimidate individuals or destroy a public building; terroristic threats; or acts of treason or insurrection.

(f) Any person placed on probation as a first offender pursuant to Article 3 of Chapter 8 of Title 42 and subsequently discharged without court adjudication of guilt pursuant to Code Section 42-8-62 shall, upon such discharge, be relieved from the disabilities imposed by this Code section.

### O.C.G.A. § 16-11-132. Possession of Pistol or Revolver by Minor.

(a) For the purposes of this Code section, a handgun is considered loaded if there is a cartridge in the chamber or cylinder of the handgun.

(b) Notwithstanding any other provisions of this part and except as otherwise provided in this Code section, it shall be unlawful for any person under the age of 18 years to possess or have under such person's control a handgun. A person convicted of a first violation of this subsection shall be guilty of a misdemeanor and shall be punished by a fine not to exceed $1,000.00 or by imprisonment for not more than 12 months, or both. A person convicted of a second or subsequent violation of this subsection shall be guilty of a felony and shall be punished by a fine of $5,000.00 or by imprisonment for a period of three years, or both.

(c) Except as otherwise provided in subsection (d) of this Code section, the provisions of subsection (b) of this Code section shall not apply to:

(1) Any person under the age of 18 years who is:

(A) Attending a hunter education course or a firearms safety course;

(B) Engaging in practice in the use of a firearm or target shooting at an established range authorized by the governing body of the jurisdiction where such range is located;

(C) Engaging in an organized competition involving the use of a firearm or participating in or practicing for a performance by an organized group under 26 U.S.C. Section 501(c)(3) which uses firearms as a part of such performance;

(D) Hunting or fishing pursuant to a valid license if such person has in his or her possession such a valid hunting or fishing license if required; is engaged in legal hunting or fishing; has permission of the owner of the land on which the activities are being conducted; and the handgun, whenever loaded, is carried only in an open and fully exposed manner; or

(E) Traveling to or from any activity described in subparagraphs (A) through (D) of this paragraph if the pistol or revolver in such person's possession is not loaded;

(2) Any person under the age of 18 years who is on real property under the control of such person's parent, legal guardian, or grandparent and who has the permission of such person's parent or legal guardian to possess a handgun; or

(3) Any person under the age of 18 years who is at such person's residence and who, with

the permission of such person's parent or legal guardian, possesses a handgun for the purpose of exercising the rights authorized in Code Section 16-3-21 or 16-3-23.

(d) Subsection (c) of this Code section shall not apply to any person under the age of 18 years who has been convicted of a forcible felony or forcible misdemeanor, as defined in Code Section 16-1-3, or who has been adjudicated delinquent under the provisions of Article 1 of Chapter 11 of Title 15 for an offense which would constitute a forcible felony or forcible misdemeanor, as defined in Code Section 16-1-3, if such person were an adult.

## O.C.G.A. § 16-11-133. Crimes Committed with Firearm by Convicted Felon.

(a) As used in this Code section, the term:

(1) "Felony" means any offense punishable by imprisonment for a term of one year or more and includes conviction by a court-martial under the Uniform Code of Military Justice for an offense which would constitute a felony under the laws of the United States.

(2) "Firearm" includes any handgun, rifle, shotgun, stun gun, taser, or other weapon which will or can be converted to expel a projectile by the action of an explosive or electrical charge.

(b) Any person who has previously been convicted of or who has previously entered a guilty plea to the offense of murder, armed robbery, kidnapping, rape, aggravated child molestation, aggravated sodomy, aggravated sexual battery, or any felony involving the use or possession of a firearm and who shall have on or within arm's reach of his or her person a firearm during the commission of, or the attempt to commit:

(1) Any crime against or involving the person of another;

(2) The unlawful entry into a building or vehicle;

(3) A theft from a building or theft of a vehicle;

(4) Any crime involving the possession, manufacture, delivery, distribution, dispensing, administering, selling, or possession with intent to distribute any controlled substance as provided in Code Section 16-13-30; or

(5) Any crime involving the trafficking of cocaine, marijuana, or illegal drugs as provided in Code Section 16-13-31, and which crime is a felony, commits a felony and, upon conviction thereof, shall be punished by confinement for a period of 15 years, such sentence to run consecutively to any other sentence which the person has received.

(c) Upon the second or subsequent conviction of a convicted felon under this Code section, such convicted felon shall be punished by confinement for life. Notwithstanding any other law to the contrary, the sentence of any convicted felon which is imposed for violating this Code section a second or subsequent time shall not be suspended by the court and probationary sentence imposed in lieu thereof.

(d) Any crime committed in violation of subsections (b) and (c) of this Code section shall be considered a separate offense.

## O.C.G.A. § 16-11-134. Discharge of Firearm While Under Influence of Alcohol and Controlled Substances, Including Marijuana.

(a) It shall be unlawful for any person to discharge a firearm while:

(1) Under the influence of alcohol or any drug or any combination of alcohol and any drug to the extent that it is unsafe for the person to discharge such firearm except in the defense of life, health, and property;

(2) The person's alcohol concentration is 0.08 grams or more at any time while discharging such firearm or within three hours after such discharge of such firearm from alcohol consumed before such discharge ended; or

(3) Subject to the provisions of subsection (b) of this Code section, there is any amount of marijuana or a controlled substance, as defined in Code Section 16-13-21, present in the person's blood

or urine, or both, including the metabolites and derivatives of each or both without regard to whether or not any alcohol is present in the person's breath or blood.

(b) The fact that any person charged with violating this Code section is or has been legally entitled to use a drug shall not constitute a defense against any charge of violating this Code section; provided, however, that such person shall not be in violation of this Code section unless such person is rendered incapable of possessing or discharging a firearm safely as a result of using a drug other than alcohol which such person is legally entitled to use.

(c) Any person convicted of violating subsection (a) of this Code section shall be guilty of a misdemeanor of a high and aggravated nature.

## O.C.G.A. § 16-11-135. Employer May Not Search Locked, Privately Owned Vehicles, and May Not Condition Employment Upon Abiding Employer-Mandated Firearm Storing Requirements.

(a) Except as provided in this Code section, no private or public employer, including the state and its political subdivisions, shall establish, maintain, or enforce any policy or rule that has the effect of allowing such employer or its agents to search the locked privately owned vehicles of employees or invited guests on the employer's parking lot and access thereto.

(b) Except as provided in this Code section, no private or public employer, including the state and its political subdivisions, shall condition employment upon any agreement by a prospective employee that prohibits an employee from entering the parking lot and access thereto when the employee's privately owned motor vehicle contains a firearm that is locked out of sight within the trunk, glove box, or other enclosed compartment or area within such privately owned motor vehicle, provided that any applicable employees possess a Georgia weapons carry license.

(c) Subsection (a) of this Code section shall not apply:

(1) To searches by certified law enforcement officers pursuant to valid search warrants or valid warrantless searches based upon probable cause under exigent circumstances;

(2) To vehicles owned or leased by an employer;

(3) To any situation in which a reasonable person would believe that accessing a locked vehicle of an employee is necessary to prevent an immediate threat to human health, life, or safety; or

(4) When an employee consents to a search of his or her locked privately owned vehicle by licensed private security officers for loss prevention purposes based on probable cause that the employee unlawfully possesses employer property.

(d) Subsections (a) and (b) of this Code section shall not apply:

(1) To an employer providing applicable employees with a secure parking area which restricts general public access through the use of a gate, security station, security officers, or other similar means which limit public access into the parking area, provided that any employer policy allowing vehicle searches upon entry shall be applicable to all vehicles entering the property and applied on a uniform and frequent basis;

(2) To any penal institution, correctional institution, detention facility, diversion center, jail, or similar place of confinement or confinement alternative;

(3) To facilities associated with electric generation owned or operated by a public utility;

(4) To any United States Department of Defense contractor, if such contractor operates any facility on or contiguous with a United States military base or installation or within one mile of an airport;

(5) To an employee who is restricted from carrying or possessing a firearm on the employer's premises due to a completed or pending disciplinary action;

(6) Where transport of a firearm on the premises of the employer is prohibited by state or federal law or regulation;

(7) To parking lots contiguous to facilities providing natural gas transmission, liquid

petroleum transmission, water storage and supply, and law enforcement services determined to be so vital to the State of Georgia, by a written determination of the Georgia Department of Homeland Security, that the incapacity or destruction of such systems and assets would have a debilitating impact on public health or safety; or

(8) To any area used for parking on a temporary basis.

(e) No employer, property owner, or property owner's agent shall be held liable in any criminal or civil action for damages resulting from or arising out of an occurrence involving the transportation, storage, possession, or use of a firearm, including, but not limited to, the theft of a firearm from an employee's automobile, pursuant to this Code section unless such employer commits a criminal act involving the use of a firearm or unless the employer knew that the person using such firearm would commit such criminal act on the employer's premises. Nothing contained in this Code section shall create a new duty on the part of the employer, property owner, or property owner's agent. An employee at will shall have no greater interest in employment created by this Code section and shall remain an employee at will.

(f) In any action relating to the enforcement of any right or obligation under this Code section, an employer, property owner, or property owner's agent's efforts to comply with other applicable federal, state, or local safety laws, regulations, guidelines, or ordinances shall be a complete defense to any employer, property owner, or property owner's agent's liability.

(g) In any action brought against an employer, employer's agent, property owner, or property owner's agent relating to the criminal use of firearms in the workplace, the plaintiff shall be liable for all legal costs of such employer, employer's agent, property owner, or property owner's agent if such action is concluded in such employer, employer's agent, property owner, or property owner's agent's favor.

(h) This Code section shall not be construed so as to require an employer, property owner, or property owner's agent to implement any additional security measures for the protection of employees, customers, or other persons. Implementation of remedial security measures to provide protection to employees, customers, or other persons shall not be admissible in evidence to show prior negligence or breach of duty of an employer, property owner, or property owner's agent in any action against such employer, its officers or shareholders, or property owners.

(i) All actions brought based upon a violation of subsection (a) of this Code section shall be brought exclusively by the Attorney General.

(j) In the event that subsection (e) of this Code section is declared or adjudged by any court to be invalid or unconstitutional for any reason, the remaining portions of this Code section shall be invalid and of no further force or effect. The General Assembly declares that it would not have enacted the remaining provisions of this Code section if it had known that such portion hereof would be declared or adjudged invalid or unconstitutional.

(k) Nothing in this Code section shall restrict the rights of private property owners or persons in legal control of property through a lease, a rental agreement, a contract, or any other agreement to control access to such property. When a private property owner or person in legal control of property through a lease, a rental agreement, a contract, or any other agreement is also an employer, his or her rights as a private property owner or person in legal control of property shall govern.

## Part 4.  Antiterroristic Training

## O.C.G.A. § 16-11-150.  The Georgia Antiterroristic Training Act.

This part shall be known and may be cited as the 'Georgia Antiterroristic Training Act.'

**O.C.G.A. § 16-11-151. Illegal Activity Relating to Illegal Firearms, Dangerous Weapons, and Explosives.**

(a) As used in this Code section, the term "dangerous weapon" has the same meaning as found in paragraph (1) of Code Section 16-11-121.

(b) It shall be unlawful for any person to:

(1) Teach, train, or demonstrate to any other person the use, application, or making of any illegal firearm, dangerous weapon, explosive, or incendiary device capable of causing injury or death to persons either directly or through a writing or over or through a computer or computer network if the person teaching, training, or demonstrating knows, has reason to know, or intends that such teaching, training, or demonstrating will be unlawfully employed for use in or in furtherance of a civil disorder, riot, or insurrection; or

(2) Assemble with one or more persons for the purpose of being taught, trained, or instructed in the use of any illegal firearm, dangerous weapon, explosive, or incendiary device capable of causing injury or death to persons if such person so assembling knows, has reason to know, or intends that such teaching, training, or instruction will be unlawfully employed for use in or in furtherance of a civil disorder, riot, or insurrection.

(c) Any person who violates any provision of subsection (b) of this Code section shall be guilty of a felony and, upon conviction thereof, shall be punished by a fine of not more than $5,000.00 or by imprisonment for not less than one nor more than five years, or both.

**O.C.G.A. § 16-11-152. Exceptions.**

This part shall not apply to:

(1) Any act of any peace officer which is performed in the lawful performance of official duties;

(2) Any training for law enforcement officers conducted by or for any police agency of the state or any political subdivision thereof or any agency of the United States;

(3) Any activities of the National Guard or of the armed forces of the United States; or

(4) Any hunter education classes taught under the auspices of the Department of Natural Resources, or other classes intended to teach the safe handling of firearms for hunting, recreation, competition, or self-defense.

### Part 4A. Enhanced Criminal Penalties.

**O.C.G.A. § 16-11-160. Commission or Attempted Commission of Certain Offenses While Possessing a Machine Gun, Sawed-Off Rifle, Sawed-Off Shotgun, or a Firearm Equipped with a Silencer.**

(a)(1) It shall be unlawful for any person to possess or to use a machine gun, sawed-off rifle, sawed-off shotgun, or a firearm equipped with a silencer, as those terms are defined in Code Section 16-11-121, during the commission or the attempted commission of any of the following offenses:

(A) Aggravated assault as defined in Code Section 16-5-21;

(B) Aggravated battery as defined in Code Section 16-5-24;

(C) Robbery as defined in Code Section 16-8-40;

(D) Armed robbery as defined in Code Section 16-8-41;

(E) Murder or felony murder as defined in Code Section 16-5-1;

(F) Voluntary manslaughter as defined in Code Section 16-5-2;

(G) Involuntary manslaughter as defined in Code Section 16-5-3;

(H) Sale, possession for sale, transportation, manufacture, offer for sale, or offer to manufacture controlled substances in violation of any provision of Article 2 of Chapter 13 of this title, the "Georgia Controlled Substances Act";

(I) Terroristic threats or acts as defined in Code Section 16-11-37;

(J) Arson as defined in Code Section 16-7-60, 16-7-61, or 16-7-62 or arson of lands as defined in Code Section 16-7-63;

(K) Influencing witnesses as defined in Code Section 16-10-93; and

(L) Participation in criminal gang activity as defined in Code Section 16-15-4.

(2)(A) As used in this paragraph, the term "bulletproof vest" means a bullet-resistant soft body armor providing, as a minimum standard, the level of protection known as "threat level I," which means at least seven layers of bullet-resistant material providing protection from at least three shots of 158-grain lead ammunition fired from a .38 caliber handgun at a velocity of 850 feet per second.

(B) It shall be unlawful for any person to wear a bulletproof vest during the commission or the attempted commission of any of the following offenses:

(i) Any crime against or involving the person of another in violation of any of the provisions of this title for which a sentence of life imprisonment may be imposed;

(ii) Any felony involving the manufacture, delivery, distribution, administering, or selling of controlled substances or marijuana as provided in Code Section 16-13-30; or

(iii) Trafficking in cocaine, illegal drugs, marijuana, or methamphetamine as provided in Code Section 16-13-31.

(b) Any person who violates paragraph (1) of subsection (a) of this Code section shall be guilty of a felony, and, upon conviction thereof, shall be punished by confinement for a period of ten years, such sentence to run consecutively to any other sentence which the person has received. Any person who violates paragraph (2) of subsection (a) of this Code section shall be guilty of a felony, and, upon conviction thereof, shall be punished by confinement for a period of one to five years, such sentence to run consecutively to any other sentence which the person has received.

(c) Upon the second or subsequent conviction of a person under this Code section, the person shall be punished by life imprisonment. Notwithstanding any other law to the contrary, the sentence of any person which is imposed for violating this Code section a second or subsequent time shall not be suspended by a court or a probationary sentence imposed in lieu thereof.

(d) The punishment prescribed for the violation of subsections (a) and (c) of this Code section shall not be probated or suspended as is provided by Code Section 17-10-7.

(e) Any crime committed in violation of this Code section shall be considered a separate offense.

**O.C.G.A. § 16-11-161. Adoption and Enforcement of Consistent Local and Municipal Laws.**

Nothing in this part shall be construed to prohibit a local governing authority from adopting and enforcing laws consistent with this part relating to gangs and gang violence. Where local laws or ordinances duplicate or supplement this part, this part shall be construed as providing alternative remedies and not as preempting the field.

**O.C.G.A. § 16-11-162. Applicability of Part 4A.**

This part shall not apply to persons who use force in defense of others as provided by Code Section 16-3-21. This part is intended to supplement not to supplant Code Section 16-11-106.

**O.C.G.A. § 16-11-171. Definitions.**

As used in this part, the term:

(1) "Center" means the Georgia Crime Information Center within the Georgia Bureau of Investigation.

(2) "Dealer" means any person licensed as a dealer pursuant to 18 U.S.C. Section 921, et seq., or Chapter 16 of Title 43.

(3) "Firearm" means any weapon that is designed to or may readily be converted to expel

a projectile by the action of an explosive or the frame or receiver of any such weapon, any firearm muffler or firearm silencer, or any destructive device as defined in 18 U.S.C. Section 921(a)(3).

(4) "Involuntarily hospitalized" means hospitalized as an inpatient in any mental health facility pursuant to Code Section 37-3-81 or hospitalized as an inpatient in any mental health facility as a result of being adjudicated mentally incompetent to stand trial or being adjudicated not guilty by reason of insanity at the time of the crime pursuant to Part 2 of Article 6 of Title 17.

(5) "NICS" means the National Instant Criminal Background Check System created by the federal "Brady Handgun Violence Prevention Act" (P. L. No. 103-159).

## O.C.G.A. § 16-11-172. Transfers and Purchases of Firearms Conducted Through Licensed Entity; NICS.

(a) All transfers or purchases of firearms conducted by a licensed importer, licensed manufacturer, or licensed dealer shall be subject to the NICS. To the extent possible, the center shall provide to the NICS all necessary criminal history information and wanted person records in order to complete an NICS check.

(b) The center shall forward to the Federal Bureau of Investigation information concerning persons who have been involuntarily hospitalized as defined in this part for the purpose of completing an NICS check.

(c) Any government official who willfully or intentionally compromises the identity, confidentiality, and security of any records and data pursuant to this part shall be guilty of a felony and fined no less than $5,000.00 and shall be subject to automatic dismissal from his or her employment.

(d) The provisions of this part shall not apply to:

(1) Any firearm, including any handgun with a matchlock, flintlock, percussion cap, or similar type of ignition system, manufactured in or before 1898;

(2) Any replica of any firearm described in paragraph (1) of this subsection if such replica is not designed or redesigned to use rimfire or conventional center-fire fixed ammunition or uses rimfire or conventional center-fire fixed ammunition which is no longer manufactured in the United States and which is not readily available in the ordinary channels of commercial trade; and

(3) Any firearm which is a curio or relic as defined by 27 C.F.R. 178.11.

## O.C.G.A. § 16-11-173. Legislative Intent and Declaration; Suits Against Firearm Dealers.

(a)(1) It is declared by the General Assembly that the regulation of firearms is properly an issue of general, state-wide concern.

(2) The General Assembly further declares that the lawful design, marketing, manufacture, and sale of firearms and ammunition to the public is not unreasonably dangerous activity and does not constitute a nuisance per se.

(b)(1) No county or municipal corporation, by zoning or by ordinance, resolution, or other enactment, shall regulate in any manner gun shows; the possession, ownership, transport, carrying, transfer, sale, purchase, licensing, or registration of firearms or components of firearms; firearms dealers; or dealers in firearms components.

(2) The authority to bring suit and right to recover against any firearms or ammunition manufacturer, trade association, or dealer by or on behalf of any governmental unit created by or pursuant to an Act of the General Assembly or the Constitution, or any department, agency, or authority thereof, for damages, abatement, or injunctive relief resulting from or relating to the lawful design, manufacture, marketing, or sale of firearms or ammunition to the public shall be reserved exclusively to the state. This paragraph shall not prohibit a political subdivision or local government authority from bringing an action against a firearms or ammunition manufacturer or dealer for breach of contract or express warranty as to firearms or ammunition purchased by the political subdivision or local government authority.

(c) A county or municipal corporation may regulate the transport, carrying, or possession of firearms by employees of the local unit of government in the course of their employment with such local unit of government.

(d) Nothing contained in this Code section shall prohibit municipalities or counties by ordinance, resolution, or other enactment, from requiring the ownership of guns by heads of households within the political subdivision.

(e) Nothing contained in this Code section shall prohibit municipalities or counties, by ordinance, resolution, or other enactment, from reasonably limiting or prohibiting the discharge of firearms within the boundaries of the municipal corporation or county.

## Chapter 12. Offenses Against Public Health and Morals
## Article 1. General Provisions

**O.C.G.A. § 16-12-1. Contributing to the Delinquency of a Minor.**

(a) As used in this Code section, the term:

(1) "Delinquent act" means a delinquent act as defined in Code Section 15-11-2.

(2) "Felony" means any act which constitutes a felony under the laws of this state, the laws of any other state of the United States, or the laws of the United States.

(3) "Minor" means any individual who is under the age of 17 years or any individual under the age of 18 years who is alleged to be a deprived child as such is defined in Code Section 15-11-2, relating to juvenile proceedings.

(4) "Serious injury" means an injury involving a broken bone, the loss of a member of the body, the loss of use of a member of the body, the substantial disfigurement of the body or of a member of the body, an injury which is life threatening, or any sexual abuse of a child under 16 years of age by means of an act described in subparagraph (a)(4)(A), (a)(4)(G), or (a)(4)(I) of Code Section 16-12-100.

(b) A person commits the offense of contributing to the delinquency, unruliness, or deprivation of a minor when such person:

(1) Knowingly and willfully encourages, causes, abets, connives, or aids a minor in committing a delinquent act as such is defined in Code Section 15-11-2, relating to juvenile proceedings;

(2) Knowingly and willfully encourages, causes, abets, connives, or aids a minor in committing an act which would cause such minor to be found to be an unruly child as such is defined in Code Section 15-11-2, relating to juvenile proceedings;

(3) Willfully commits an act or acts or willfully fails to act when such act or omission would cause a minor to be found to be a deprived child as such is defined in Code Section 15-11-2, relating to juvenile proceedings;

(4) Knowingly and willfully hires, solicits, engages, contracts with, conspires with, encourages, abets, or directs any minor to commit any felony which encompasses force or violence as an element of the offense or delinquent act which would constitute a felony which encompasses force or violence as an element of the offense if committed by an adult; or

(5) Knowingly and willfully provides to a minor any weapon as defined in paragraph (2) of subsection (a) of Code Section 16-11-127.1 or any weapon as defined in Code Section 16-11-121 to commit any felony which encompasses force or violence as an element of the offense or delinquent act which would constitute a felony which encompasses force or violence as an element of the offense if committed by an adult.

(6) Knowingly and willfully hires, solicits, engages, contracts with, conspires with, encourages, abets, or directs any minor to commit any smash and grab burglary which would constitute a felony if committed by an adult.

(c) It shall not be a defense to the offense provided for in this Code section that the minor has not been formally adjudged to have committed a delinquent act or has not been found to be unruly or deprived.

(d) A person convicted pursuant to paragraph (1) or (2) of subsection (b) of this Code section shall be punished as follows:

(1) Upon conviction of the first or second offense, the defendant shall be guilty of a misdemeanor and shall be fined not more than $1,000.00 or shall be imprisoned for not more than 12 months, or both fined and imprisoned; and

(2) Upon the conviction of the third or subsequent offense, the defendant shall be guilty of a felony and shall be fined not less than $1,000.00 nor more than $5,000.00 or shall be imprisoned for not less than one year nor more than three years, or both fined and imprisoned.

(d.1) A person convicted pursuant to paragraph (3) of subsection (b) of this Code section shall be punished as follows:

(1) Upon conviction of an offense which resulted in the serious injury or death of a child, without regard to whether such offense was a first, second, third, or subsequent offense, the defendant shall be guilty of a felony and shall be punished as provided in subsection (e) of this Code section;

(2) Upon conviction of an offense which does not result in the serious injury or death of a child and which is the first conviction, the defendant shall be guilty of a misdemeanor and shall be fined not more than $1,000.00 or shall be imprisoned for not more than 12 months, or both fined and imprisoned;

(3) Upon conviction of an offense which does not result in the serious injury or death of a child and which is the second conviction, the defendant shall be guilty of a high and aggravated misdemeanor and shall be fined not less than $1,000.00 nor more than $5,000.00 or shall be imprisoned for not less than one year, or both fined and imprisoned; and

(4) Upon the conviction of an offense which does not result in the serious injury or death of a child and which is the third or subsequent conviction, the defendant shall be guilty of a felony and shall be fined not less than $10,000.00 or shall be imprisoned for not less than one year nor more than five years, or both fined and imprisoned.

(e) A person convicted pursuant to paragraph (4) or (6) of subsection (b) or paragraph (1) of subsection (d.1) of this Code section shall be guilty of a felony and punished as follows:

(1) Upon conviction of the first offense, the defendant shall be imprisoned for not less than one nor more than ten years; and

(2) Upon conviction of the second or subsequent offense, the defendant shall be imprisoned for not less than three years nor more than 20 years.

## O.C.G.A. § 16-12-1.1. Those with Convictions Residing, Domiciled With, or Employed at Child Care Facilities.

(a) As used in this Code section the term:

(1) "Facility" means any day-care center, family day-care home, group-care facility, group day-care home, or similar facility at which any child who is not a member of an operator's family is received for pay for supervision and care, without transfer of legal custody, for fewer than 24 hours per day.

(2) "Operator" means any person who applies for or holds a permit or license to operate a facility.

(b) It shall be unlawful for any operator of a facility to knowingly have any person reside at, be domiciled at, or be employed at any such facility if such person has been convicted of or has entered a plea of guilty or nolo contendere to or has been adjudicated a delinquent for:

(1) A violation of Code Section 16-4-1, relating to criminal attempt, when the crime attempted is any of the crimes specified in paragraphs (2) through (10) of this subsection;

(2) A violation of Code Section 16-5-23.1, relating to battery, when the victim at the time of such offense was a minor;

(3) A violation of any provision of Chapter 6 of this title, relating to sexual offenses, when the victim at the time of such offense was a minor;

(4) A violation of Code Section 16-12-1, relating to contributing to the delinquency of a minor;

(5) A violation of Code Section 16-5-1, relating to murder;

(6) A violation of Code Section 16-5-2, relating to voluntary manslaughter;

(7) A violation of Code Section 16-6-2, relating to aggravated sodomy;

(8) A violation of Code Section 16-6-3, relating to rape;

(9) A violation of Code Section 16-6-22.2, relating to aggravated sexual battery; or

(10) A violation of Code Section 16-8-41, relating to armed robbery, if committed with a firearm.

(c) Any person violating subsection (b) of this Code section shall be guilty of a misdemeanor.

## Article 4.  Offenses Against Public Transportation
## Part 2.  Transportation Passenger Safety

### O.C.G.A. § 16-12-122.  Definitions.

As used in this part, the term:

(1) "Aircraft" means any machine, whether heavier or lighter than air, used or designed for navigation of or flight in the air.

(2) "Avoid a security measure" means to take any action that is intended to result in any person, baggage, container, or item of any type being allowed into a secure area without being subjected to security measures or the assembly of items into an object or substance that is prohibited under the laws of this state or of the United States or any of their agencies, political subdivisions, or authorities after such items have passed through a security measure into a secure area.

(3) "Bus" means any passenger bus or coach or other motor vehicle having a seating capacity of not less than 15 passengers operated by a transportation company for the purpose of carrying passengers or freight for hire.

(4) "Charter" means a group of persons, pursuant to a common purpose and under a single contract and at a fixed charge for the vehicle in accordance with a transportation company's tariff, who have acquired the exclusive use of an aircraft, bus, or rail vehicle to travel together as a group to a specified destination.

(5) "Interfere with a security measure" means to take any action that is intended to defeat, disable, or prevent the full operation of equipment or procedures designed or intended to detect any object or substance, including, but not limited to, disabling of any device so that it cannot fully function, creation of any diversion intended to defeat a security measure, or packaging of any item or substance so as to avoid detection by a security measure.

(6) "Passenger" means any person served by the transportation company; and, in addition to the ordinary meaning of passenger, the term shall include any person accompanying or meeting another person who is transported by such company, any person shipping or receiving freight, and any person purchasing a ticket or receiving a pass.

(7) "Rail vehicle" means any railroad or rail transit car, carriage, coach, or other vehicle, whether self-propelled or not and designed to be operated upon a rail or rails or other fixed right of way by a transportation company for the purpose of carrying passengers or freight or both for hire.

(8) "Secure area" means any enclosed or unenclosed area within a terminal whereby access is restricted in any manner or the possession of items subject to security measures is prohibited. Access to a secure area may be restricted to persons specifically authorized by law, regulation, or policy of the governing authority or transportation company operating said terminal, and such access into a secure area may be conditioned on passing through security measures, and possession of items may be

restricted to designated persons who are acting in the course of their official duties.

(9) "Security measure" means any process or procedure by which employees, agents, passengers, persons accompanying passengers, containers, baggage, freight, or possessions of passengers or persons accompanying passengers are screened, inspected, or examined by any means for the purpose of ensuring the safety and welfare of aircraft, bus, or rail vehicles and the employees, agents, passengers, and freight of any transportation company. The security measures may be operated by or under the authority of any governmental entity, transportation company, or any entity contracting therewith.

(10) "Terminal" means an aircraft, bus, or rail vehicle station, depot, any such transportation facility, or infrastructure relating thereto operated by a transportation company or governmental entity or authority. This term includes a reasonable area immediately adjacent to any designated stop along the route traveled by any coach or rail vehicle operated by a transportation company or governmental entity operating aircraft, bus, or rail vehicle transportation facility and parking lots or parking areas adjacent to a terminal.

(11) "Transportation company" or "company" means any person, group of persons, or corporation providing for-hire transportation to passengers or freight by aircraft, by bus upon the highways in this state, by rail vehicle upon any public or private right of way in this state, or by all, including passengers and freight in interstate or intrastate travel. This term shall also include transportation facilities owned or operated by local public bodies; by municipalities; and by public corporations, authorities, boards, and commissions established under the laws of this state, any of the several states, the United States, or any foreign nation.

## O.C.G.A. § 16-12-123. Hijack of Bus or Rail Vehicle, or Boarding Plane, Bus, or Rail with Certain Items.

(a)(1) A person commits the offense of bus or rail vehicle hijacking when he or she:

(A) Seizes or exercises control by force or violence or threat of force or violence of any bus or rail vehicle within the jurisdiction of this state;

(B) By force or violence or by threat of force or violence seizes or exercises control of any transportation company or all or any part of the transportation facilities owned or operated by any such company; or

(C) By force or violence or by threat of force or violence substantially obstructs, hinders, interferes with, or otherwise disrupts or disturbs the operation of any transportation company or all or any part of a transportation facility.

(2) Any person convicted of the offense of bus or rail hijacking shall be guilty of a felony and, upon conviction thereof, shall be punished by imprisonment for life or by imprisonment for not less than one nor more than 20 years.

(b) Any person who boards or attempts to board an aircraft, bus, or rail vehicle with any explosive, destructive device, or hoax device as such term is defined in Code Section 16-7-80; firearm for which such person does not have on his or her person a valid weapons carry license issued pursuant to Code Section 16-11-129 unless possessing such firearm is prohibited by federal law; hazardous substance as defined by Code Section 12-8-92; or knife or other device designed or modified for the purpose of offense and defense concealed on or about his or her person or property which is or would be accessible to such person while on the aircraft, bus, or rail vehicle shall be guilty of a felony and, upon conviction thereof, shall be sentenced to imprisonment for not less than one nor more than ten years. The prohibition of this subsection shall not apply to any law enforcement officer, peace officer retired from a state or federal law enforcement agency, person in the military service of the state or of the United States, or commercial security personnel employed by the transportation company who is in possession of weapons used within the course and scope of employment; nor shall the prohibition apply to persons transporting weapons contained in baggage which is not accessible to passengers if the presence of such weapons has been declared to the transportation company and such weapons have been secured in a manner prescribed by state or federal law or regulation for the purpose of transportation or shipment. The provisions of this subsection shall not apply to any privately owned aircraft, bus, or rail vehicle if the owner of such aircraft or vehicle has given his or her express permission to board the aircraft or vehicle with the item.

(c) The company may employ reasonable security measures, including any method or device, to detect concealed weapons, explosives, or hazardous material in baggage or freight or upon the person of the passenger. Upon the discovery of any such item or material in the possession of a person, unless the item is a weapon in the possession of a person exempted under subsection (b) of this Code section from the prohibition of that subsection (b), the company shall obtain possession and retain custody of such item or materials until they are transferred to the custody of law enforcement officers.

**O.C.G.A. § 16-12-127. Unlawful Possession of Device on Person or To Place in Possession of Passenger.**

(a) It shall be unlawful for any person, with the intention of avoiding or interfering with a security measure or of introducing into a terminal any explosive, destructive device, or hoax device as defined in Code Section 16-7-80; firearm for which such person does not have on his or her person a valid weapons carry license issued pursuant to Code Section 16-11-129 unless possessing such firearm is prohibited by federal law; hazardous substance as defined by Code Section 12-8-92; or knife or other device designed or modified for the purpose of offense and defense, to:

(1) Have any such item on or about his or her person, or

(2) Place or cause to be placed or attempt to place or cause to be placed any such item:

(A) In a container or freight of a transportation company;

(B) In the baggage or possessions of any person or any transportation company without the knowledge of the passenger or transportation company; or

(C) Aboard such aircraft, bus, or rail vehicle.

(b) A person violating the provisions of this Code section shall be guilty of a felony and shall, upon conviction, be sentenced to imprisonment for not less than one year nor more than 20 years, a fine not to exceed $15,000.00, or both. A prosecution under this Code section shall not be barred by the imposition of a civil penalty imposed by any governmental entity.

(c) It is an affirmative defense to a violation of this Code section if a person notifies a law enforcement officer or other person employed to provide security for a transportation company of the presence of such item as soon as possible after learning of its presence and surrenders or secures such item as directed by the law enforcement officer or other person employed to provide security for a transportation company.

**O.C.G.A. § 16-12-128. Nature of Part is Cumulative and Supplemental.**

(a) This part shall be cumulative and supplemental to any other law of this state. A conviction or acquittal under any of the criminal provisions of Code Section 16-12-123, 16-12-124, 16-12-125, or 16-12-126 shall not be a bar to any other civil or criminal proceeding.

(b) In addition to any other penalty imposed by law for a violation of this part, the court may require the defendant to make restitution to any affected public or private entity for the reasonable costs or damages associated with the offense. Restitution made pursuant to this subsection shall not preclude any party from obtaining any other civil or criminal remedy available under any other provision of law. The restitution authorized by this subsection is supplemental and not exclusive.

**O.C.G.A. § 16-13-21. Definitions.**

As used in this article, the term:

(1) "Administer" means the direct application of a controlled substance, whether by injection,

inhalation, ingestion, or by any other means, to the body of a patient or research subject by:

(A) A practitioner or, in his presence, by his authorized agent; or

(B) The patient or research subject at the direction and in the presence of the practitioner.

(2) "Agent" of a manufacturer, distributor, or dispenser means an authorized person who acts on behalf of or at the direction of a manufacturer, distributor, or dispenser. It does not include a common or contract carrier, public warehouseman, or employee of the carrier or warehouseman.

(3) "Bureau" means the Drug Enforcement Administration, United States Department of Justice, or its successor agency.

(4) "Controlled substance" means a drug, substance, or immediate precursor in Schedules I through V of Code Sections 16-13-25 through 16-13-29 and Schedules I through V of 21 C.F.R. Part 1308.

(5) "Conveyance" means any object, including aircraft, vehicle, or vessel, but not including a person, which may be used to carry or transport a substance or object.

(6) "Counterfeit substance" means:

(A) A controlled substance which, or the container or labeling of which, without authorization, bears the trademark, trade name, or other identifying mark, imprint, number, or device, or any likeness thereof, of a manufacturer, distributor, or dispenser other than the person who in fact manufactured, distributed, or dispensed the controlled substance;

(B) A controlled substance or noncontrolled substance, which is held out to be a controlled substance or marijuana, whether in a container or not which does not bear a label which accurately or truthfully identifies the substance contained therein; or

(C) Any substance, whether in a container or not, which bears a label falsely identifying the contents as a controlled substance.

(6.1) "Dangerous drug" means any drug, other than a controlled substance, which cannot be dispensed except upon the issuance of a prescription drug order by a practitioner authorized under this chapter.

(6.2) "DEA" means the United States Drug Enforcement Administration.

(7) "Deliver" or "delivery" means the actual, constructive, or attempted transfer from one person to another of a controlled substance, whether or not there is an agency relationship.

(8) "Dependent," "dependency," "physical dependency," "psychological dependency," or "psychic dependency" means and includes the state of dependence by an individual toward or upon a substance, arising from the use of that substance, being characterized by behavioral and other responses which include the loss of self-control with respect to that substance, or a strong compulsion to use that substance on a continuous basis in order to experience some psychic effect resulting from the use of that substance by that individual, or to avoid any discomfort occurring when the individual does not use that substance.

(9) "Dispense" means to deliver a controlled substance to an ultimate user or research subject by or pursuant to the lawful order of a practitioner, including the prescribing, administering, packaging, labeling, or compounding necessary to prepare the substance for that delivery, or the delivery of a controlled substance by a practitioner, acting in the normal course of his professional practice and in accordance with this article, or to a relative or representative of the person for whom the controlled substance is prescribed.

(10) "Dispenser" means a practitioner who dispenses.

(11) "Distribute" means to deliver a controlled substance, other than by administering or dispensing it.

(12) "Distributor" means a person who distributes.

(12.05) "FDA" means the United States Food and Drug Administration.

(12.1) "Imitation controlled substance" means:

(A) A product specifically designed or manufactured to resemble the physical appearance of a controlled substance, such that a reasonable person of ordinary knowledge would not be able to distinguish the imitation from the controlled substance by outward appearances; or

(B) A product, not a controlled substance, which, by representations made and by dosage unit appearance, including color, shape, size, or markings, would lead a reasonable person to believe that, if ingested, the product would have a stimulant or depressant effect similar to or the same as that of one or more of the controlled substances included in Schedules I through V of Code Sections 16-13-25 through 16-13-29.

(13) "Immediate precursor" means a substance which the State Board of Pharmacy has found to be and by rule identifies as being the principal compound commonly used or produced primarily for use, and which is an immediate chemical intermediary used or likely to be used in the manufacture of a controlled substance, the control of which is necessary to prevent, curtail, or limit manufacture.

(14) "Isomers" means stereoisomers (optical isomers), geometrical isomers, and structural isomers (chain and positional isomers, but shall not include functional isomers).

(15) "Manufacture" means the production, preparation, propagation, compounding, conversion, or processing of a controlled substance, either directly or indirectly by extraction from substances of natural origin, or independently by means of chemical synthesis, and includes any packaging or repackaging of the substance or labeling or relabeling of its container, except that this term does not include the preparation, compounding, packaging, or labeling of a controlled substance:

(A) By a practitioner as an incident to his administering or dispensing of a controlled substance in the course of his professional practice; or

(B) By a practitioner or by his authorized agent under his supervision for the purpose of, or as an incident to, research, teaching, or chemical analysis and not for sale.

(16) "Marijuana" means all parts of the plant of the genus Cannabis, whether growing or not, the seeds thereof, the resin extracted from any part of such plant, and every compound, manufacture, salt, derivative, mixture, or preparation of such plant, its seeds, or resin; but shall not include samples as described in subparagraph (P) of paragraph (3) of Code Section 16-13-25 and shall not include the completely defoliated mature stalks of such plant, fiber produced from such stalks, oil, or cake, or the completely sterilized samples of seeds of the plant which are incapable of germination.

(17) "Narcotic drug" means any of the following, whether produced directly or indirectly by extraction from substances of vegetable origin, or independently by means of chemical synthesis, or by a combination of extraction and chemical synthesis:

(A) Opium and opiate, and any salt, compound, derivative, or preparation of opium or opiate;

(B) Any salt, compound, isomer, derivative, or preparation thereof which is chemically equivalent or identical with any of the substances referred to in subparagraph (A) of this paragraph, but not including the isoquinoline alkaloids of opium;

(C) Opium poppy and poppy straw;

(D) Coca leaves and any salt, compound, derivative, stereoisomers of cocaine, or preparation of coca leaves, and any salt, compound, stereoisomers of cocaine, derivative, or preparation thereof which is chemically equivalent or identical with any of these substances, but not including decocainized coca leaves or extractions of coca leaves which do not contain cocaine or ecgonine.

(18) "Opiate" means any substance having an addiction-forming or addiction-sustaining liability similar to morphine or being capable of conversion into a drug having addiction-forming or addiction-sustaining liability. It does not include, unless specifically designated as controlled under Code Section 16-13-22, the dextrorotatory isomer of 3-methoxy-n-methylmorphinan and its salts (dextromethorphan). It does include its racemic and levorotatory forms.

(19) "Opium poppy" means the plant of the species Papaver somniferum L., except its seeds.

(20) "Person" means an individual, corporation, government, or governmental subdivision or agency, business trust, estate, trust, partnership, or association, or any other legal entity.

(21) "Poppy straw" means all parts, except the seeds, of the opium poppy after mowing.

(22) "Potential for abuse" means and includes a substantial potential for a substance to be used by an individual to the extent of creating hazards to the health of the user or the safety of the public, or the substantial potential of a substance to cause an individual using that substance to become dependent upon that substance.

(23) "Practitioner" means:

(A) A physician, dentist, pharmacist, podiatrist, veterinarian, scientific investigator, or other person licensed, registered, or otherwise authorized under the laws of this state to distribute, dispense, conduct research with respect to, or to administer a controlled substance in the course of professional practice or research in this state;

(B) A pharmacy, hospital, or other institution licensed, registered, or otherwise authorized by law to distribute, dispense, conduct research with respect to, or to administer a controlled substance in the course of professional practice or research in this state;

(C) An advanced practice registered nurse acting pursuant to the authority of Code Section 43-34-25. For purposes of this chapter and Code Section 43-34-25, an advanced practice registered nurse is authorized to register with the federal Drug Enforcement Administration and appropriate state authorities; or

(D) A physician assistant acting pursuant to the authority of subsection (e.1) of Code Section 43-34-103. For purposes of this chapter and subsection (e.1) of Code Section 43-34-103, a physician assistant is authorized to register with the federal Drug Enforcement Administration and appropriate state authorities.

(24) "Production" includes the manufacture, planting, cultivation, growing, or harvesting of a controlled substance.

(25) "Registered" or "register" means registration as required by this article.

(26) "Registrant" means a person who is registered under this article.

(27) "State," when applied to a part of the United States, includes any state, district, commonwealth, territory, insular possession thereof, or any area subject to the legal authority of the United States.

(28) "Ultimate user" means a person who lawfully possesses a controlled substance for his own use, for the use of a member of his household, or for administering to an animal owned by him or by a member of his household or an agent or representative of the person.

(29) "Noncontrolled substance" means any drug or other substance other than a controlled substance as defined by paragraph (4) of this Code section.

## O.C.G.A. § 16-13-25.  Schedule I.

The controlled substances listed in this Code section are included in Schedule I:

(1) Any of the following opiates, including their isomers, esters, ethers, salts, and salts of isomers, esters, and ethers, unless specifically excepted, pursuant to this article, whenever the existence of these isomers, esters, ethers, and salts is possible within the specific chemical designation:

(A) Acetylmethadol;

(B) Allylprodine;

(C) Reserved;

(D) Alphameprodine;

(E) Alphamethadol;

(F) Benzethidine;

(G) Betacetylmethadol;

(H) Betameprodine;

(I) Betamethadol;

(J) Betaprodine;

(K) Clonitazene;

(L) Dextromoramide;

(M) Dextromorphan;

(N) Diampromide;

(O) Diethylthiambutene;

(P) Dimenoxadol;

(Q) Dimetheptanol;

(R) Dimethylthiambutene;

(S) Dioxaphetyl butyrate;

(T) Dipipanone;

(U) Ethylmethylthiambutene;

(V) Etonitazene;

(W) Etoxeridene;

(X) Furethidine;

(Y) Hydroxypethidine;

(Z) Ketobemidone;

(AA) Levomoramide;

(BB) Levophenacylmorphan;

(CC) Morpheridine;

(DD) Noracymethadol;

(EE) Norlevorphanol;

(FF) Normethadone;

(GG) Norpipanone;

(HH) Phenadoxone;

(II) Phenampromide;

(JJ) Phenomorphan;

(KK) Phenoperidine;

(LL) Piritramide;

(MM) Proheptazine;

(NN) Properidine;

(OO) Propiram;

(PP) Racemoramide;

(QQ) Trimeperidine;

(2) Any of the following opium derivatives, their salts, isomers, and salts of isomers, unless specifically excepted, whenever the existence of these salts, isomers, and salts of isomers is possible within the specific chemical designation:

(A) Acetorphine;

(B) Acetyldihydrocodeine;

(C) Benzylmorphine;

(D) Codeine methylbromide;

(E) Codeine-N-Oxide;

(F) Cyprenorphine;

(G) Desomorphine;

(H) Dihydromorphine;

(I) Etorphine;

(J) Heroin;

(K) Hydromorphinol;

(L) Methyldesorphine;

(M) Methyldihydromorphine;

(N) Morphine methylbromide;

(O) Morphine methylsulfonate;

(P) Morphine-N-Oxide;

(Q) Myrophine;

(R) Nicocodeine;

(S) Nicomorphine;

(T) Normorphine;

(U) Pholcodine;

(V) Thebacon;

(3) Any material, compound, mixture, or preparation which contains any quantity of the following hallucinogenic substances, their salts, isomers (whether optical, position, or geometrics), and salts of isomers, unless specifically excepted, whenever the existence of these salts, isomers, and salts of isomers is possible within the specific chemical designation:

(A) 3, 4-methylenedioxyamphetamine;

(B) 5-methoxy-3, 4-methylenedioxyamphetamine;

(C) 3, 4, 5-trimethoxyamphetamine;

(D) Bufotenine;

(E) Diethyltryptamine;

(F) Dimethyltryptamine;

(G) 4-methyl-2, 5-dimethoxyamphetamine;

(H) Ibogaine;

(I) Lysergic acid diethylamide;

(J) Mescaline;

(K) Peyote;

(L) N-ethyl-3-piperidyl benzilate;

(M) N-methyl-3-piperidyl benzilate;

(N) Psilocybin;

(O) Psilocyn (Psilocin);

(P) Tetrahydrocannabinols which shall include, but are not limited to:

(i) All synthetic or naturally produced samples containing more than 15 percent by weight of tetrahydrocannabinols; and

(ii) All synthetic or naturally produced tetrahydrocannabinol samples which do not contain plant material exhibiting the external morphological features of the plant cannabis;

(Q) 2, 5-dimethoxyamphetamine;

(R) 4-bromo-2, 5-dimethoxyamphetamine;

(S) 4-methoxyamphetamine;

(T) Cyanoethylamphetamine;

(U) (1-phenylcyclohexyl) ethylamine;

(V) 1-(1-phenylcyclohexyl) pyrrolidine;

(W) Phencyclidine;

(X) 1-piperidinocyclohexanecarbonitrile;

(Y) 1-phenyl-2-propanone (phenylacetone);

(Z) 3, 4-Methylenedioxymethamphetamine (MDMA);

(AA) 1-methyl-4-phenyl-4-propionoxypiperidine;

(BB) 1-(2-phenylethyl)-4-phenyl-4-acetyloxypiperidine;

(CC) 3-methylfentanyl;

(DD) N-ethyl-3, 4-methylenedioxyamphetamine;

(EE) Para-flurofentanyl;

(FF) 2,5-Dimethoxy-4-Ethylamphetamine;

(GG) Cathinone;

(HH) MPPP (1-Methyl-4-Phenyl-4-Propionoxypiperidine);

(II) PEPAP (1-(2-phenethyl)-4 phenyl-4-acetoxypiperide);

(JJ) Alpha-Methylthiofentanyl;

(KK) Acetyl-Alpha-Methylfentanyl;

(LL) 3-Methylthiofentanyl;

(MM) Beta-Hydroxyfentanyl;

(NN) Thiofentanyl;

(OO) 3,4-Methylenedioxy-N-Ethylamphetamine;

(PP) 4-Methylaminorex;

(QQ) N-Hydroxy-3,4-Methylenedioxyamphetamine;

(RR) Beta-Hydroxy-3-Methylfentanyl;

(SS) Chlorophenylpiperazine (CPP);

(TT) N, N-Dimethylamphetamine;

(UU) 1-(1-(2-thienyl) cyclohexy) pyrrolidine;

(VV) 4-Bromo-2,5-Dimethoxyphenethylamine (DMPE);

(WW) Alpha-Ethyltryptamine;

(XX) Methcathinone;

(YY) Aminorex;

(ZZ) 4-iodo-2,5-dimethoxyamphetamine;

(AAA) 4-chloro-2,5-dimethoxyamphetamine;

(4) Any material, compound, mixture, or preparation which contains any of the following substances having a stimulant effect on the central nervous system, including its salts, isomers, and salts of isomers, unless specifically excepted, whenever the existence of these salts, isomers, and salts of isomers is possible within the specific chemical designation:

(A) Fenethylline;

(B) N-(1-benzyl-4-piperidyl)-N-phenylpropanamide (benzyl-fentanyl);

(C) N-(1-(2-thienyl) methyl-4-piperidyl)-N-phenylpropanamide (thenylfentanyl);

(5) Any material, compound, mixture, or preparation which contains any quantity of the following substances, their salts, isomers (whether optical, position, or geometrics), and salts of isomers, unless specifically excepted, whenever the existence of these substances, their salts, isomers, and salts of isomers is possible within the specific chemical designation:

(A) Gamma hydroxybutyric acid (gamma hydroxy butyrate); provided, however, that this does not include any amount naturally and normally occurring in the human body; and

(B) Sodium oxybate, when the FDA approved form of this drug is not:

(i) In a container labeled in compliance with subsection (a) or (b) of Code Section 26-3-8; and

(ii) In the possession of:

(I) A registrant permitted to dispense the drug;

(II) Any person other than to whom the drug was prescribed; or

(III) Any person who attempts to or does unlawfully possess, sell, distribute, or give this drug to any other person;

(6) Notwithstanding the fact that Schedule I substances have no currently accepted medical use, the General Assembly recognizes certain of these substances which are currently accepted for certain limited medical uses in treatment in the United States but have a high potential for abuse. Accordingly, unless specifically excepted or unless listed in another schedule, any material, compound, mixture, or preparation which contains any quantity of methaqualone, including its salts, isomers, optical isomers, salts of their isomers, and salts of these optical isomers, is included in Schedule I;

(7) 2,5-Dimethoxy-4-(n)-propylthiophenethylamine (2C-T-7);

(8) 1-(3-Trifluoromethylphenyl) Piperazine (TFMPP);

(9) N-Benzylpiperazine (BZP);

(10) 5-Methoxy-N,N-Diisopropyltryptamine (5-MeO-DIPT);

(11) Alpha-Methyltryptamine (AMT).

(12) Any material, compound, mixture, or preparation which contains any quantity of the following substances, their salts, isomers (whether optical, positional, or geometric), homologues, and salts of isomers and homologues, unless specifically excepted, whenever the existence of these salts, isomers, homologues, and salts of isomers and homologues is possible within the specific chemical designation:

(A) 1-pentyl-3-(1-naphthoyl)indole (JWH-018);

(B) 1,1-dimethylheptyl-11-hydroxy-delta-8-tetrahydrocannabinol (HU-210; (6a, 10a)-9-(hydroxymethyl)-6,6-dimethyl-3-(2-methyloctan-2-yl)-6a,7,10,10a-tetrahydrobenzo[c]chromen-1-ol

(C) 2-(3-hydroxycyclohexyl)-5-(2-methyloctan-2-yl)phenol (CP 47,497).

## O.C.G.A. § 16-13-26. Schedule II.

The controlled substances listed in this Code section are included in Schedule II:

(1) Any of the following substances, or salts thereof, except those narcotic drugs specifically exempted or listed in other schedules, whether produced directly or indirectly by extraction from substances of vegetable origin, or independently by extraction from substances of vegetable origin, or independently by means of chemical synthesis, or by combination of extraction and chemical synthesis:

(A) Opium and opiate, and any salt, compound, derivative, or preparation of opium or opiate, excluding naloxone hydrochloride, but including the following:

(i) Raw opium;

(ii) Opium extracts;

(iii) Opium fluid extracts;

(iv) Powdered opium;

(v) Granulated opium;

(vi) Tincture of opium;

(vii) Codeine;

(viii) Ethylmorphine;

(ix) Hydrocodone;

(x) Hydromorphone;

(xi) Metopon;

(xii) Morphine;

(xiii) Oripavine;

(xiv) Oxycodone;

(xv) Oxymorphone;

(xvi) Thebaine;

(B) Any salt, compound, isomer, derivative, or preparation thereof which is chemically equivalent or identical with any of the substances referred to in subparagraph (A) of this paragraph, except that these substances shall not include the isoquinoline alkaloids of opium;

(C) Opium poppy and poppy straw;

(D) Cocaine, coca leaves, any salt, compound, derivative, stereoisomers of cocaine, or preparation of coca leaves, and any salt, compound, derivative, stereoisomers of cocaine, or preparation thereof which is chemically equivalent or identical with any of these substances, but not including decocainized coca leaves or extractions which do not contain cocaine or ecgonine;

(2) Any of the following opiates, including their isomers, esters, ethers, salts, and salts of isomers, whenever the existence of these isomers, esters, ethers, and salts is possible within the specific chemical designation:

(A) Alfentanil;

(A.1) Alphaprodine;

(B) Anileridine;

(C) Bezitramide;

(D) Dihydrocodeine;

(E) Diphenoxylate;

(F) Fentanyl;

(G) Isomethadone;

(G.5) Levo-alphacetylmethadol (some other names: levomethadyl acetate, LAAM);

(H) Levomethorphan;

(I) Levorphanol;

(J) Methazocine;

(K) Methadone;

(L) Methadone-Intermediate, 4-cyano-2-dimethylamino-4, 4-diphenyl butane;

(M) Moramide-Intermediate, 2-methyl-3-morpholino-1, 1-diphenyl-propane-carboxylic acid;

(N) Pethidine (meperidine);

(O) Pethidine-Intermediate-A, 4-cyano-1-methyl-4-phenylpiperidine;

(P) Pethidine-Intermediate-B, ethyl-4-phenylpiperidine-4-carboxylate;

(Q) Pethidine-Intermediate-C, 1-methyl-4-phenylpiperidine-4-carboxylic acid;

(R) Phenazocine;

(S) Piminodine;

(T) Racemethorphan;

(U) Racemorphan;

(U.1) Remifentanil;

(V) Sufentanil;

(V.1) Tapentadol;

(W) 4-anilino-N-phenethyl-4-piperidine (ANPP);

(3) Unless specifically excepted or unless listed in another schedule, any material, compound, mixture, or preparation which contains any quantity of the following substances included as having a stimulant effect on the central nervous system:

(A) Amphetamine, its salts, optical isomers, and salts of its optical isomers;

(B) Any substance which contains any quantity of methamphetamine, including its salts, isomers, and salts of isomers;

(C) Phenmetrazine and its salts;

(D) Methylphenidate, including its salts, isomers, and salts of isomers;

(E) Carfentanil;

(F) Nabilone;

(G) Lisdexamfetamine;

(4) Unless specifically excepted or unless listed in another schedule, any material, compound, mixture, or preparation which contains any of the following substances included as having a depressant effect on the central nervous system, including its salts, isomers, and salts of isomers whenever the existence of such salts, isomers, and salts of isomers is possible within the specific chemical designation:

(A) Amobarbital;

(A.5) Glutethimide;

(B) Secobarbital;

(C) Pentobarbital.

## O.C.G.A. § 16-13-27.  Schedule III.

The controlled substances listed in this Code section are included in Schedule III:

(1) Unless specifically excepted or unless listed in another schedule, any material, compound, mixture, or preparation which contains any quantity of the following substances, included as having a stimulant effect on the central nervous system, including its salts, isomers (whether optical, position, or geometric), and salts of such isomers whenever the existence of such salts, isomers, and salts of isomers is possible within the specific chemical designation:

(A) Those compounds, mixtures, or preparations in dosage unit forms containing any stimulant substances which are listed as excepted compounds by the State Board of Pharmacy pursuant to this article, and any other drug of quantitative composition so excepted or which is the same except that it contains a lesser quantity of controlled substances;

(B) Benzphetamine;

(C) Chlorphentermine;

(D) Clortermine;

(E) Phendimetrazine;

(2) Unless specifically excepted or unless listed in another schedule, any material, compound, mixture, or preparation which contains any quantity of the following substances included as having a depressant effect on the central nervous system:

(A) Any compound, mixture, or preparation containing amobarbital, secobarbital, pentobarbital, or any salts thereof and one or more active medicinal ingredients which are not listed in any schedule;

(B) Any suppository dosage form containing amobarbital, secobarbital, pentobarbital, or any salt of any of these drugs and approved by the State Board of Pharmacy for marketing only as a suppository;

(C) Any substance which contains any quantity of a derivative of barbituric acid or any salt thereof;

(D) Chlorhexadol;

(E) Reserved;

(F) Lysergic acid;

(G) Lysergic acid amide;

(H) Methyprylon;

(I) Sulfondiethylmethane;

(J) Sulfonethylmethane;

(K) Sulfonmethane;

(L) Tiletamine/Zolozepam (Telazol);

(3) Nalorphine;

(4) Unless specifically excepted or unless listed in another schedule, any material, compound, mixture, or preparation containing limited quantities of the following narcotic drugs, or any salts thereof:

(A) Not more than 1.8 grams of codeine, or any of its salts, per 100 milliliters or not more than 90 milligrams per dosage unit, with an equal or greater quantity of an isoquinoline alkaloid of opium;

(B) Not more than 1.8 grams of codeine, or any of its salts, per 100 milliliters or not more than 90 milligrams per dosage unit, with one or more active, nonnarcotic ingredients in recognized therapeutic amounts;

(C) Not more than 300 milligrams of dihydrocodeinone (hydrocodone), or any of its salts, per 100 milliliters or not more than 15 milligrams per dosage unit, with a fourfold or greater quantity of an isoquinoline alkaloid of opium;

(D) Not more than 300 milligrams of dihydrocodeinone (hydrocodone), or any of its salts, per 100 milliliters or not more than 15 milligrams per dosage unit, with one or more active, nonnarcotic ingredients in recognized therapeutic amounts;

(E) Not more than 1.8 grams of dihydrocodeine, or any of its salts, per 100 milliliters or not more than 90 milligrams per dosage unit, with one or more active, nonnarcotic ingredients in recognized therapeutic amounts;

(F) Not more than 300 milligrams of ethylmorphine, or any of its salts, per 100 milliliters or not more than 15 milligrams per dosage unit, with one or more active, nonnarcotic ingredients in recognized therapeutic amounts;

(G) Not more than 500 milligrams of opium per 100 milliliters or per 100 grams, or not more than 25 milligrams per dosage unit, with one or more active, nonnarcotic ingredients in recognized therapeutic amounts;

(H) Not more than 50 milligrams of morphine, or any of its salts, per 100 milliliters or per 100 grams with one or more active, nonnarcotic ingredients in recognized therapeutic amounts;

(5) The State Board of Pharmacy may except by rule any compound, mixture, or preparation containing any stimulant or depressant substance listed in paragraphs (1) and (2) of this Code section from the application of all or any part of this article if the compound, mixture, or preparation contains one or more active, medicinal ingredients not having a stimulant or depressant effect on the central nervous system, and if the admixtures are included therein in combinations, quantity, proportion, or concentration that vitiate the potential for abuse of the substances which have a stimulant or depressant effect on the central nervous system;

(6) Any anabolic steroid or any salt, ester, or isomer of a drug or substance described or listed in this paragraph, if that salt, ester, or isomer promotes muscle growth. Such term does not include an anabolic steroid which is expressly intended for administration through implants to cattle or other nonhuman species and which has been approved by the secretary of health and human services for such administration:

(A) Boldenone;

(A.5) Boldione (Androsta-1,4-diene-3,17-dione);

(B) Chlorotestosterone;

(C) Clostebol;

(D) Dehydrochlormethyltestosterone;

(D.1) Desoxymethyltestosterone (17a-methyl-5a-androst-2-en-17-ol, madol);

(E) Dihydrotestosterone;

(F) Drostanolone;

(G) Ethylestrenol;

(H) Fluoxymesterone;

(I) Formebolone;

(J) Mesterolone;

(K) Methandienone;

(L) Methandranone;

(M) Methandriol;

(N) Methandrostenolone;

(O) Methenolone;

(P) Methyltestosterone;

(Q) Mibolerone;

(R) Nandrolone;

(S) Norethandrolone;

(T) Oxandrolone;

(U) Oxymesterone;

(V) Oxymetholone;

(W) Stanolone;

(X) Stanozolol;

(Y) Testolactone;

(Z) Testosterone;

(AA) Trenbolone;

(BB) 19-nor-4,9(10)-androstadienedione (estra-4,9(10)-diene-3,17-dione);

(7) Ketamine;

(8) Dronabinol (synthetic) in sesame oil and encapsulated in a U.S. Food and Drug Administration approved drug product also known as Marinol;

(9) Sodium oxybate, when the FDA approved form of this drug is in a container labeled in compliance with subsection (a) or (b) of Code Section 26-3-8, in the possession of a registrant permitted to dispense the drug, or in the possession of a person to whom it has been lawfully prescribed;

(10) Buprenorphine;

(11) Embutramide.

## O.C.G.A. § 16-13-27.1. Exemptions from Schedule III.

The following anabolic steroid containing compounds, mixtures, or preparations have been exempted as Schedule III Controlled Substances by the United States Drug Enforcement Administration, as listed in 21 C.F.R. 1308.34, and are therefore exempted from paragraph (6) of Code Section 16-13-27:

TABLE OF EXEMPT ANABOLIC STEROID PRODUCTS

Trade Name Company
Androgen LA Forest Pharmaceuticals, St. Louis, MO
Andro-Estro 90-4 Rugby Labs, Rockville Centre, NY
depANDROGYN Forest Pharmaceuticals, St. Louis, MO
DEPO-T.E. Quality Research Pharm, Carmel, IN
depTESTROGEN Maroca Pharm, Phoenix, AZ
Duomone Winitec Pharm, Pacific, MO
DURATESTRIN W. E. Hauck, Alpharetta, GA
DUO-SPAN II Premedics Labs, Gardena, CA
Estratest Solvay Pharmaceuticals, Marietta, GA
Estratest HS Solvay Pharmaceuticals, Marietta, GA
PAN ESTRA TEST Pan American Labs, Covington, LA
Premarin 1.25mg with Methyltestosterone Ayerst Labs, Inc. New York, NY
Premarin 0.625mg with Methyltestosterone Ayerst Labs, Inc. New York, NY
TEST-ESTRO Cypionates Rugby Labs, Rockville Centre, NY
Testosterone Cyp 50Estradiol Cyp 2 I.D.E. Interstate, Amityville, NY
Testosterone Cypionate-Estradiol Cypionate Injection Best Generics, N. Miami Beach, FL
Testosterone Cypionate-Estradiol Cypionate Injection Schein Pharm, Port Washington, NY
Testosterone Cypionate-Estradiol Cypionate Injection Steris Labs, Inc., Phoenix, AZ
Testosterone Cypionate-Estradiol Valerate Injection Schein Pharm, Port Washington, NY
Testosterone Enanthate-Estradiol Valerate Injection Steris Labs, Inc. Phoenix, AZ

## O.C.G.A. § 16-13-28. Schedule IV.

(a) The controlled substances listed in this Code section are included in Schedule IV. Unless specifically excepted or unless listed in another schedule, any material, compound, mixture, or preparation which contains any quantity of the following substances, including its salts, isomers, and salts of isomers whenever the existence of such salts, isomers, and salts of isomers is possible within the specified chemical designation, included as having a stimulant or depressant effect on the central nervous system or a hallucinogenic effect:

 (1) Alprazolam;

 (1.5) Armodafinil;

 (2) Barbital;

 (2.1) Bromazepam;

 (2.15) Butorphanol;

 (2.2) Camazepam;

 (2.25) Carisoprodol;

 (2.3) Cathine;

 (3) Chloral betaine;

 (4) Chloral hydrate;

 (5) Chlordiazepoxide, but not including librax (chlordiazepoxide hydrochloride and clidinium bromide) or menrium (chlordiazepoxide and water soluble esterified estrogens);

 (5.1) Clobazam;

 (6) Clonazepam;

 (7) Clorazepate;

 (7.1) Clotiazepam;

 (7.2) Cloxazolam;

 (7.3) Delorazepam;

 (8) Desmethyldiazepam;

 (8.5) Dexfenfluramine;

 (9) Reserved;

 (10) Diazepam;

 (11) Diethylpropion;

 (11.05) Difenoxin;

 (11.1) Estazolam;

 (12) Ethchlorvynol;

 (13) Ethinamate;

 (13.1) Ethyl loflazepate;

 (13.2) Fencamfamin;

 (14) Fenfluramine;

 (14.1) Flunitrazepam;

 (14.2) Fenproporex;

 (15) Flurazepam;

 (15.3) Fospropofol;

 (16) Halazepam;

 (16.1) Haloxazolam;

 (16.15) Indiplon;

 (16.2) Ketazolam;

 (16.3) Lometazepam;

 (16.4) Loprazolam;

 (17) Lorazepam;

 (18) Mazindol;

 (19) Mebutamate;

 (19.1) Medazepam;

 (19.2) Mefenorex;

 (20) Meprobamate;

 (21) Methohexital;

(22) Methylphenobarbital;

(22.1) Midazolam;

(22.15) Modafinil;

(22.2) Nimetazepam;

(22.3) Nitrazepam;

(22.4) Nordiazepam;

(23) Oxazepam;

(23.1) Oxazolam;

(24) Paraldehyde;

(25) Pemoline;

(26) Pentazocine;

(27) Petrichloral;

(28) Phenobarbital;

(29) Phentermine;

(29.1) Pipradrol;

(30) Prazepam;

(30.05) Propoxyphene (including all salts and optical isomers);

(30.1) Quazepam;

(30.2) Sibutramine;

(30.3) SPA (-)-1-dimethylamino-1, 2-diphenylethane;

(31) Temazepam;

(32) Triazolam;

(32.5) Zaleplon;

(33) Zolpidem;

(34) Zopiclone.

(b) The State Board of Pharmacy may except by rule any compound, mixture, or preparation containing any depressant, stimulant, or hallucinogenic substance listed in subsection (a) of this Code section from the application of all or any part of this article if the compound, mixture, or preparation contains one or more active, medicinal ingredients not having a depressant or stimulant effect on the central nervous system, and if the admixtures are included therein in combinations, quantity, proportion, or concentration that vitiate the potential for abuse of the substances which have a depressant or stimulant effect on the central nervous system.

### O.C.G.A. § 16-13-29. Schedule V.

The controlled substances listed in this Code section are included in Schedule V:

(1) Any compound, mixture, or preparation containing limited quantities of any of the following narcotic drugs, or salts thereof, which also contains one or more nonnarcotic, active, medicinal ingredients in sufficient proportion to confer upon the compound, mixture, or preparation valuable medicinal qualities other than those possessed by the narcotic drug alone:

(A) Not more than 200 milligrams of codeine, or any of its salts, per 100 milliliters or per 100 grams;

(B) Not more than 100 milligrams of dihydrocodeine, or any of its salts, per 100 milliliters or per 100 grams;

(C) Not more than 100 milligrams of ethylmorphine, or any of its salts, per 100 milliliters or per 100 grams;

(D) Not more than 2.5 milligrams of diphenoxylate and not less than 25 micrograms of atropine sulfate per dosage unit;

(E) Not more than 100 milligrams of opium per 100 milliliters or per 100 grams;

(2) Lacosamide;

(3) Pregabalin; or

(4) Pyrovalerone.

## O.C.G.A. § 16-13-49. Forfeitures.

(a) As used in this Code section, the term:

(1) "Controlled substance" shall have the same meaning as provided in paragraph (4) of Code Section 16-13-21 and shall also include marijuana as such term is defined in paragraph (16) of Code Section 16-13-21, notwithstanding any other provisions of this article.

(2) "Costs" means, but is not limited to:

(A) All expenses associated with the seizure, towing, storage, maintenance, custody, preservation, operation, or sale of the property; and

(B) Satisfaction of any security interest or lien not subject to forfeiture under this Code section.

(3) "Court costs" means, but is not limited to:

(A) All court costs, including the costs of advertisement, transcripts, and court reporter fees; and

(B) Payment of receivers, conservators, appraisers, accountants, or trustees appointed by the court pursuant to this Code section.

(4) "Enterprise" means any person, sole proprietorship, partnership, corporation, trust, association, or other legal entity created under the laws of this state, of the United States or any of the several states of the United States, or of any foreign nation or a group of individuals associated in fact although not a legal entity and includes illicit as well as licit enterprises and governmental as well as other entities.

(5) "Governmental agency" means any department, office, council, commission, committee, authority, board, bureau, or division of the executive, judicial, or legislative branch of a state, the United States, or any political subdivision thereof.

(6) "Interest holder" means a secured party within the meaning of Code Section 11-9-102 or the beneficiary of a perfected encumbrance pertaining to an interest in property.

(7) "Owner" means a person, other than an interest holder, who has an interest in property and is in compliance with any statute requiring its recordation or reflection in public records in order to perfect the interest against a bona fide purchaser for value.

(8) "Proceeds" means property derived directly or indirectly from, maintained by, or realized through an act or omission and includes any benefit, interest, or property of any kind without reduction for expenses incurred for acquisition, maintenance, or any other purpose.

(9) "Property" means anything of value and includes any interest in anything of value, including real property and any fixtures thereon, and tangible and intangible personal property, including but not limited to currency, instruments, securities, or any other kind of privilege, interest, claim, or right.

(10) "United States" includes its territories, possessions, and dominions and the District of Columbia.

(b)(1) An action filed pursuant to this Code section shall be filed in the name of the State of Georgia and may be brought:

(A) In the case of an in rem action, by the district attorney for the judicial circuit where the property is located;

(B) In the case of an in personam action, by the district attorney for the judicial circuit in which the defendant resides; or

(C) By the district attorney having jurisdiction over any offense which arose out of the same conduct which made the property subject to forfeiture.

Such district attorney may bring an action pursuant to this Code section in any superior court of this state.

(2) If more than one district attorney has jurisdiction to file an action pursuant to this Code section, the district attorney having primary jurisdiction over a violation of this article shall, in the event of a conflict, have priority over any other district attorney.

(3) Any action brought pursuant to this Code section may be compromised or settled in the same manner as other civil actions.

(c) An action for forfeiture brought pursuant to this Code section shall be tried:

(1) If the action is in rem against real property, in the county where the property is located, except where a single tract is divided by a county line, in which case the superior court of either county shall have jurisdiction;

(2) If the action is in rem against tangible or intangible personal property, in any county where the property is located or will be during the pendency of the action; or

(3) If the action is in personam, as provided by law.

(d) The following are declared to be contraband and no person shall have a property right in them:

(1) All controlled substances, raw materials, or controlled substance analogs that have been manufactured, distributed, dispensed, possessed, or acquired in violation of this article;

(2) All property which is, directly or indirectly, used or intended for use in any manner to facilitate a violation of this article or any proceeds derived or realized therefrom;

(3) All property located in this state which was, directly or indirectly, used or intended for use in any manner to facilitate a violation of this article or of the laws of the United States or any of the several states relating to controlled substances which is punishable by imprisonment for more than one year or any proceeds derived or realized therefrom;

(4) All weapons possessed, used, or available for use in any manner to facilitate a violation of this article or any of the laws of the United States or any of the several states relating to controlled substances which is punishable by imprisonment for more than one year;

(5) Any interest, security, claim, or property or contractual right of any kind affording a source of influence over any enterprise that a person has established, operated, controlled, conducted, or participated in the conduct of in violation of this article or any of the laws of the United States or any of the several states relating to controlled substances which is punishable by imprisonment for more than one year or any proceeds derived or realized therefrom; and

(6) All moneys, negotiable instruments, securities, or other things of value which are found in close proximity to any controlled substance or marijuana or other property which is subject to forfeiture under this subsection.

(e)(1) A property interest shall not be subject to forfeiture under this Code section if the owner of such interest or interest holder establishes that the owner or interest holder:

(A) Is not legally accountable for the conduct giving rise to its forfeiture, did not consent to it, and did not know and could not reasonably have known of the conduct or that it was likely to occur;

(B) Had not acquired and did not stand to acquire substantial proceeds from the conduct giving rise to its forfeiture other than as an interest holder in an arm's length commercial transaction;

(C) With respect to conveyances for transportation only, did not hold the property jointly, in common, or in community with a person whose conduct gave rise to its forfeiture;

(D) Does not hold the property for the benefit of or as nominee for any person whose conduct gave rise to its forfeiture, and, if the owner or interest holder acquired the interest through any such person, the owner or interest holder acquired it as a bona fide purchaser for value without knowingly taking part in an illegal transaction; and

(E) Acquired the interest:

(i) Before the completion of the conduct giving rise to its forfeiture, and the person whose conduct gave rise to its forfeiture did not have the authority to convey the interest to a bona fide

222

purchaser for value at the time of the conduct; or

(ii) After the completion of the conduct giving rise to its forfeiture:

(I) As a bona fide purchaser for value without knowingly taking part in an illegal transaction;

(II) Before the filing of a lien on it and before the effective date of a notice of pending forfeiture relating to it and without notice of its seizure for forfeiture under this article; and

(III) At the time the interest was acquired, was reasonably without cause to believe that the property was subject to forfeiture or likely to become subject to forfeiture under this article.

(2) A property interest shall not be subject to forfeiture under this Code section for a violation involving only one gram or less of a mixture containing cocaine or four ounces or less of marijuana unless said property was used to facilitate a transaction in or a purchase of or sale of a controlled substance or marijuana.

(f) A rented or leased vehicle shall not be subject to forfeiture unless it is established in forfeiture proceedings that the owner of the rented or leased vehicle is legally accountable for the conduct which would otherwise subject the vehicle to forfeiture, consented to the conduct, or knew or reasonably should have known of the conduct or that it was likely to occur. Upon learning of the address or phone number of the company which owns any rented or leased vehicle which is present at the scene of an arrest or other action taken pursuant to this Code section, the duly authorized authorities shall immediately contact the company to inform it that the vehicle is available for the company to take possession.

(g)(1) Property which is subject to forfeiture under this Code section may be seized by the director of the Georgia Drugs and Narcotics Agency or any duly authorized agent or drug agent of this state or by any law enforcement officer of this state or of any political subdivision thereof who has power to make arrests or execute process or a search warrant issued by any court having jurisdiction over the property. A search warrant authorizing seizure of property which is subject to forfeiture pursuant to this Code section may be issued on an affidavit demonstrating that probable cause exists for its forfeiture or that the property has been the subject of a previous final judgment of forfeiture in the courts of this state, any other state, or the United States. The court may order that the property be seized on such terms and conditions as are reasonable.

(2) Property which is subject to forfeiture under this Code section may be seized without process if there is probable cause to believe that the property is subject to forfeiture under this article or the seizure is incident to an arrest or search pursuant to a search warrant or to an inspection under an inspection warrant.

(3) The court's jurisdiction over forfeiture proceedings is not affected by a seizure in violation of the Constitution of Georgia or the United States Constitution made with process or in a good faith belief of probable cause.

(h)(1) When property is seized pursuant to this article, the sheriff, drug agent, or law enforcement officer seizing the same shall report the fact of seizure, in writing, within 20 days thereof to the district attorney of the judicial circuit having jurisdiction in the county where the seizure was made.

(2) Within 60 days from the date of seizure, a complaint for forfeiture shall be initiated as provided for in subsection (n), (o), or (p) of this Code section.

(3) If the state fails to initiate forfeiture proceedings against property seized for forfeiture by notice of pending forfeiture within the time limits specified in paragraphs (1) and (2) of this subsection, the property must be released on the request of an owner or interest holder, pending further proceedings pursuant to this Code section, unless the property is being held as evidence.

(i)(1) Seizure of property by a law enforcement officer constitutes notice of such seizure to any person who was present at the time of seizure who may assert an interest in the property.

(2) When property is seized pursuant to this article, the district attorney or the sheriff, drug agent, or law enforcement officer seizing the same shall give notice of the seizure to any owner or

interest holder who is not present at the time of seizure by personal service, publication, or the mailing of written notice:

(A) If the owner's or interest holder's name and current address are known, by either personal service or mailing a copy of the notice by certified mail or statutory overnight delivery to that address;

(B) If the owner's or interest holder's name and address are required by law to be on record with a government agency to perfect an interest in the property but the owner's or interest holder's current address is not known, by mailing a copy of the notice by certified mail or statutory overnight delivery, return receipt requested, to any address on the record; or

(C) If the owner's or interest holder's address is not known and is not on record as provided in subparagraph (B) of this paragraph or the owner's or interest holder's interest is not known, by publication in two consecutive issues of a newspaper of general circulation in the county in which the seizure occurs.

(3) Notice of seizure must include a description of the property, the date and place of seizure, the conduct giving rise to forfeiture, and the violation of law alleged.

(j) A district attorney may file, without a filing fee, a lien for forfeiture of property upon the initiation of any civil or criminal proceeding under this article or upon seizure for forfeiture. The filing constitutes notice to any person claiming an interest in the property owned by the named person. The filing shall include the following:

(1) The lien notice must set forth:

(A) The name of the person and, in the discretion of the state, any alias and any corporations, partnerships, trusts, or other entities, including nominees, that are either owned entirely or in part or controlled by the person; and

(B) The description of the property, the criminal or civil proceeding that has been brought under this article, the amount claimed by the state, the name of the court where the proceeding or action has been brought, and the case number of the proceeding or action if known at the time of filing;

(2) A lien under this subsection applies to the described property and to one named person and to any aliases, fictitious names, or other names, including names of corporations, partnerships, trusts, or other entities, that are either owned entirely or in part or controlled by the named person and any interest in real property owned or controlled by the named person. A separate lien for forfeiture of property must be filed for any other person;

(3) The lien creates, upon filing, a lien in favor of the state as it relates to the seized property or to the named person or related entities with respect to said property. The lien secures the amount of potential liability for civil judgment and, if applicable, the fair market value of seized property relating to all proceedings under this article enforcing the lien. The forfeiture lien referred to in this subsection must be filed in accordance with the provisions of the laws in this state pertaining to the type of property that is subject to the lien. The state may amend or release, in whole or in part, a lien filed under this subsection at any time by filing, without a filing fee, an amended lien in accordance with this subsection which identifies the lien amended. The state, as soon as practical after filing a lien, shall furnish to any person named in the lien a notice of the filing of the lien. Failure to furnish notice under this subsection does not invalidate or otherwise affect a lien filed in accordance with this subsection;

(4) Upon entry of judgment in favor of the state, the state may proceed to execute on the lien as in the case of any other judgment;

(5) A trustee, constructive or otherwise, who has notice that a lien for forfeiture of property, a notice of pending forfeiture, or a civil forfeiture proceeding has been filed against the property or against any person or entity for whom the person holds title or appears as the owner of record shall furnish, within ten days, to the district attorney or his designee the following information:

(A) The name and address of the person or entity for whom the property is held;

(B) The names and addresses of all beneficiaries for whose benefit legal title to the seized property, or property of the named person or related entity, is held; and

(C) A copy of the applicable trust agreement or other instrument, if any, under which the trustee or other person holds legal title or appears as the owner of record of the property; and

(6) A trustee, constructive or otherwise, who fails to comply with this subsection shall be guilty of a misdemeanor.

(k) Property taken or detained under this Code section is not subject to replevin, conveyance, sequestration, or attachment. The seizing law enforcement agency or the district attorney may authorize the release of the property if the forfeiture or retention is unnecessary or may transfer the action to another agency or district attorney by discontinuing forfeiture proceedings in favor of forfeiture proceedings initiated by the other law enforcement agency or district attorney. An action under this Code section may be consolidated with any other action or proceeding under this article relating to the same property on motion by an interest holder and must be so consolidated on motion by the district attorney in either proceeding or action. The property is deemed to be in the custody of the State of Georgia subject only to the orders and decrees of the superior court having jurisdiction over the forfeiture proceedings.

(l)(1) If property is seized under this article, the district attorney may:

(A) Remove the property to a place designated by the superior court having jurisdiction over the forfeiture proceeding;

(B) Place the property under constructive seizure by posting notice of pending forfeiture, by giving notice of pending forfeiture to its owners and interest holders, or by filing notice of seizure in any appropriate public record relating to the property;

(C) Remove the property to a storage area, within the jurisdiction of the court, for safekeeping or, if the property is a negotiable instrument or money and is not needed for evidentiary purposes, the district attorney may authorize its being deposited in an interest-bearing account in a financial institution in this state. Any accrued interest shall follow the principal in any judgment with respect thereto;

(D) Provide for another governmental agency, a receiver appointed by the court pursuant to Chapter 8 of Title 9, an owner, or an interest holder to take custody of the property and remove it to an appropriate location within the county where the property was seized; or

(E) Require the sheriff or chief of police of the political subdivision where the property was seized to take custody of the property and remove it to an appropriate location for disposition in accordance with law.

(2) If any property which has been attached or seized pursuant to this Code section is perishable or is liable to perish, waste, or be greatly reduced in value by keeping or if the expense of keeping the same is excessive or disproportionate to the value thereof, the court, upon motion of the state, a claimant, or the custodian, may order the property or any portion thereof to be sold upon such terms and conditions as may be prescribed by the court; and the proceeds shall be paid into the registry of the court pending final disposition of the action.

(m) As soon as possible, but not more than 30 days after the seizure of property, the seizing law enforcement agency shall conduct an inventory and estimate the value of the property seized.

(n) If the estimated value of personal property seized is $ 25,000.00 or less, the district attorney may elect to proceed under the provisions of this subsection in the following manner:

(1) Notice of the seizure of such property shall be posted in a prominent location in the courthouse of the county in which the property was seized. Such notice shall include a description of the property, the date and place of seizure, the conduct giving rise to forfeiture, a statement that the owner of such property has 30 days within which a claim must be filed, and the violation of law alleged;

(2) A copy of the notice, which shall include a statement that the owner of such property has 30 days within which a claim must be filed, shall be served upon an owner, interest holder, or person in possession of the property at the time of seizure as provided in subsection (i) of this Code

section and shall be published for at least three successive weeks in a newspaper of general circulation in the county where the seizure was made;

(3) The owner or interest holder may file a claim within 30 days after the second publication of the notice of forfeiture by sending the claim to the seizing law enforcement agency and to the district attorney by certified mail or statutory overnight delivery, return receipt requested;

(4) The claim must be signed by the owner or interest holder under penalty of perjury and must set forth:

(A) The caption of the proceedings as set forth on the notice of pending forfeiture and the name of the claimant;

(B) The address at which the claimant will accept mail;

(C) The nature and extent of the claimant's interest in the property;

(D) The date, identity of the transferor, and circumstances of the claimant's acquisition of the interest in the property;

(E) The specific provision of this Code section relied on in asserting that the property is not subject to forfeiture;

(F) All essential facts supporting each assertion; and

(G) The precise relief sought;

(5) If a claim is filed, the district attorney shall file a complaint for forfeiture as provided in subsection (o) or (p) of this Code section within 30 days of the actual receipt of the claim. A person who files a claim shall be joined as a party; and

(6) If no claim is filed within 30 days after the second publication of the notice of forfeiture, all right, title, and interest in the property is forfeited to the state and the district attorney shall dispose of the property as provided in subsection (u) of this Code section.

(o) In rem proceedings.

(1) In actions in rem, the property which is the subject of the action shall be named as the defendant. The complaint shall be verified on oath or affirmation by a duly authorized agent of the state in a manner required by the laws of this state. Such complaint shall describe the property with reasonable particularity; state that it is located within the county or will be located within the county during the pendency of the action; state its present custodian; state the name of the owner or interest holder, if known; allege the essential elements of the violation which is claimed to exist; state the place of seizure, if the property was seized; and conclude with a prayer of due process to enforce the forfeiture.

(2) A copy of the complaint and summons shall be served on any person known to be an owner or interest holder and any person who is in possession of the property.

(A) Service of the complaint and summons shall be as provided in subsections (a), (b), (c), and (e) of Code Section 9-11-4.

(B) If real property is the subject of the action or the owner or interest holder is unknown or resides out of the state or departs the state or cannot after due diligence be found within the state or conceals himself so as to avoid service, notice of the proceeding shall be published once a week for two successive weeks in the newspaper in which the sheriff's advertisements are published. Such publication shall be deemed notice to any and all persons having an interest in or right affected by such proceeding and from any sale of the property resulting therefrom, but shall not constitute notice to an interest holder unless that person is unknown or resides out of the state or departs the state or cannot after due diligence be found within the state or conceals himself to avoid service.

(C) If tangible property which has not been seized is the subject of the action, the court may order the sheriff or another law enforcement officer to take possession of the property. If the character or situation of the property is such that the taking of actual possession is impracticable, the sheriff shall execute process by affixing a copy of the complaint and summons to the property in a conspicuous place and by leaving another copy of the complaint and summons with the person having possession or his agent. In cases involving a vessel or aircraft, the sheriff or other law enforcement officer is authorized to make a written request with the appropriate governmental agency not to permit the departure of such vessel or aircraft until notified by the sheriff or his deputy that the vessel or aircraft has been released.

(3) An owner of or interest holder in the property may file an answer asserting a claim against the property in the action in rem. Any such answer shall be filed within 30 days after the service of the summons and complaint. Where service is made by publication and personal service has not been made, an owner or interest holder shall file an answer within 30 days of the date of final publication. An answer must be verified by the owner or interest holder under penalty of perjury. In addition to complying with the general rules applicable to an answer in civil actions, the answer must set forth:

(A) The caption of the proceedings as set forth in the complaint and the name of the claimant;

(B) The address at which the claimant will accept mail;

(C) The nature and extent of the claimant's interest in the property;

(D) The date, identity of transferor, and circumstances of the claimant's acquisition of the interest in the property;

(E) The specific provision of this Code section relied on in asserting that the property is not subject to forfeiture;

(F) All essential facts supporting each assertion; and

(G) The precise relief sought.

(4) If at the expiration of the period set forth in paragraph (3) of this subsection no answer has been filed, the court shall order the disposition of the seized property as provided for in this Code section.

(5) If an answer is filed, a hearing must be held within 60 days after service of the complaint unless continued for good cause and must be held by the court without a jury.

(6) An action in rem may be brought by the state in addition to or in lieu of any other in rem or in personam action brought pursuant to this title.

(p) In personam proceedings.

(1) The complaint shall be verified on oath or affirmation by a duly authorized agent of the state in a manner required by the laws of this state. It shall describe with reasonable particularity the property which is sought to be forfeited; state its present custodian; state the name of the owner or interest holder, if known; allege the essential elements of the violation which is claimed to exist; state the place of seizure, if the property was seized; and conclude with a prayer of due process to enforce the forfeiture.

(2) Service of the complaint and summons shall be as follows:

(A) Except as otherwise provided in this subsection, service of the complaint and summons shall be as provided by subsections (a), (b), (c), and (d) of Code Section 9-11-4; and

(B) If the defendant is unknown or resides out of the state or departs the state or cannot after due diligence be found within the state or conceals himself so as to avoid service, notice of the proceedings shall be published once a week for two successive weeks in the newspaper in which the sheriff's advertisements are published. Such publication shall be deemed sufficient notice to any such defendant.

(3) A defendant shall file a verified answer within 30 days after the service of the summons and complaint. Where service is made by publication and personal service has not been made, a defendant shall file such answer within 30 days of the date of final publication. In addition to complying with the general rules applicable to an answer in civil actions, the answer must contain all of the elements set forth in paragraph (3) of subsection (o) of this Code section.

(4) Any interest holder or person in possession of the property may join any action brought pursuant to this subsection as provided by Chapter 11 of Title 9, known as the "Georgia Civil Practice

Act."

(5) If at the expiration of the period set forth in paragraph (3) of this subsection no answer has been filed, the court shall order the disposition of the seized property as provided for in this Code section.

(6) If an answer is filed, a hearing must be held within 60 days after service of the complaint unless continued for good cause and must be held by the court without a jury.

(7) On a determination of liability of a person for conduct giving rise to forfeiture under this Code section, the court must enter a judgment of forfeiture of the property described in the complaint and must also authorize the district attorney or his agent or any law enforcement officer or peace officer to seize all property ordered to be forfeited which was not previously seized or was not then under seizure. Following the entry of an order declaring the property forfeited, the court, on application of the state, may enter any appropriate order to protect the interest of the state in the property ordered to be forfeited.

(8) Except as provided in this subsection, no person claiming an interest in property subject to forfeiture under this Code section may intervene in a trial or appeal of a criminal action or in an in personam civil action involving the forfeiture of the property.

(q) In conjunction with any civil or criminal action brought pursuant to this article:

(1) The court, on application of the district attorney, may enter any restraining order or injunction; require the execution of satisfactory performance bonds; appoint receivers, conservators, appraisers, accountants, or trustees; or take any action to seize, secure, maintain, or preserve the availability of property subject to forfeiture under this article, including issuing a warrant for its seizure and writ of attachment, whether before or after the filing of a complaint for forfeiture;

(2) A temporary restraining order under this Code section may be entered on application of the district attorney, without notice or an opportunity for a hearing, if the district attorney demonstrates that:

(A) There is probable cause to believe that the property with respect to which the order is sought, in the event of final judgment or conviction, would be subject to forfeiture under this title; and

(B) Provision of notice would jeopardize the availability of the property for forfeiture;

(3) Notice of the entry of a restraining order and an opportunity for a hearing must be afforded to persons known to have an interest in the property. The hearing must be held at the earliest possible date consistent with the date set in subsection (b) of Code Section 9-11-65 and is limited to the issues of whether:

(A) There is a probability that the state will prevail on the issue of forfeiture and that failure to enter the order will result in the property's being destroyed, conveyed, encumbered, removed from the jurisdiction of the court, concealed, or otherwise made unavailable for forfeiture; and

(B) The need to preserve the availability of property through the entry of the requested order outweighs the hardship on any owner or interest holder against whom the order is to be entered;

(4) If property is seized for forfeiture or a forfeiture lien is filed without a previous judicial determination of probable cause or order of forfeiture or a hearing under paragraph (2) of this subsection, the court, on an application filed by an owner of or interest holder in the property within 30 days after notice of its seizure or lien or actual knowledge of such seizure or lien, whichever is earlier, and complying with the requirements for an answer to an in rem complaint, and after five days' notice to the district attorney of the judicial circuit where the property was seized or, in the case of a forfeiture lien, to the district attorney filing such lien, may issue an order to show cause to the seizing law enforcement agency for a hearing on the sole issue of whether probable cause for forfeiture of the property then exists. The hearing must be held within 30 days unless continued for good cause on motion of either party. If the court finds that there is no probable cause for forfeiture of the property, the property must be released pending the outcome of a judicial proceeding which may be filed pursuant

to this Code section; and

(5) The court may order property that has been seized for forfeiture to be sold to satisfy a specified interest of any interest holder, on motion of any party, and after notice and a hearing, on the conditions that:

(A) The interest holder has filed a proper claim and:

(i) Is authorized to do business in this state and is under the jurisdiction of a governmental agency of this state or of the United States which regulates financial institutions, securities, insurance, or real estate; or

(ii) Has an interest that the district attorney has stipulated is exempt from forfeiture;

(B) The interest holder must dispose of the property by commercially reasonable public sale and apply the proceeds first to its interest and then to its reasonable expenses incurred in connection with the sale or disposal; and

(C) The balance of the proceeds, if any, must be returned to the actual or constructive custody of the court, in an interest-bearing account, subject to further proceedings under this Code section.

(r) A defendant convicted in any criminal proceeding is precluded from later denying the essential allegations of the criminal offense of which the defendant was convicted in any proceeding pursuant to this Code section, regardless of the pendency of an appeal from that conviction; however, evidence of the pendency of an appeal is admissible. For the purposes of this Code section, a conviction results from a verdict or plea of guilty, including a plea of nolo contendere.

(s) In hearings and determinations pursuant to this Code section:

(1) The court may receive and consider, in making any determination of probable cause or reasonable cause, all evidence admissible in determining probable cause at a preliminary hearing or by a magistrate pursuant to Article 1 of Chapter 5 of Title 17, together with inferences therefrom;

(2) The fact that money or a negotiable instrument was found in proximity to contraband or to an instrumentality of conduct giving rise to forfeiture authorizes the trier of the fact to infer that the money or negotiable instrument was the proceeds of conduct giving rise to forfeiture or was used or intended to be used to facilitate such conduct; and

(3) There is a rebuttable presumption that any property of a person is subject to forfeiture under this Code section if the state establishes probable cause to believe that:

(A) The person has engaged in conduct giving rise to forfeiture;

(B) The property was acquired by the person during the period of the conduct giving rise to forfeiture or within a reasonable time after the period; and

(C) There was no likely source for the property other than the conduct giving rise to forfeiture.

(t)(1) All property declared to be forfeited under this Code section vests in this state at the time of commission of the conduct giving rise to forfeiture together with the proceeds of the property after that time. Any property or proceeds transferred later to any person remain subject to forfeiture and thereafter must be ordered to be forfeited unless the transferee claims and establishes in a hearing under this Code section that the transferee is a bona fide purchaser for value and the transferee's interest is exempt under subsection (e) of this Code section.

(2) On entry of judgment for a person claiming an interest in the property that is subject to proceedings to forfeit property under this Code section, the court shall order that the property or interest in property be released or delivered promptly to that person free of liens and encumbrances, as provided under this article.

(3) The court shall order a claimant who fails to establish that a substantial portion of the claimant's interest is exempt from forfeiture under subsection (e) of this Code section to pay the reasonable costs relating to the disproving of the claim which were incurred by the state, including costs for investigation, prosecution, and attorneys' fees.

(u)(1) Whenever property is forfeited under this article, any property which is required by law to be destroyed or which is harmful to the public shall, when no longer needed for evidentiary purposes, be destroyed or forwarded to the Division of Forensic Sciences of the Georgia Bureau of Investigation or any other agency of state or local government for destruction or for any medical or scientific use not prohibited under the laws of the United States or this state.

(2) When property, other than money or real property, is forfeited under this article, the court may:

(A) Order the property to be sold, with the proceeds of the sale to be distributed as provided in paragraph (4) of this subsection; or

(B) Provide for the in-kind distribution of the property as provided for in paragraph (4) of this subsection.

(2.1) When real property is forfeited, the court may order that:

(A) The real property be turned over to the state;

(B) The appropriate political subdivision take charge of the property and:

(i) Sell the property with such conditions as the court deems proper, and distribute the proceeds in such manner as the court so orders; or

(ii) Hold the property for use by one or more law enforcement agencies;

(C) The real property be turned over to an appropriate political subdivision without restrictions;

(D) The real property be deeded to a land bank authority as provided in Article 4 of Chapter 4 of Title 48; or

(E) The real property be disposed of in such other manner as the court deems proper.

(3) Where property is to be sold pursuant to this subsection, the court may direct that such property be sold by:

(A) Judicial sale as provided in Article 7 of Chapter 13 of Title 9; provided, however, that the court may establish a minimum acceptable price for such property; or

(B) Any commercially feasible means, including, but not limited to, in the case of real property, listing such property with a licensed real estate broker, selected by the district attorney through competitive bids.

(4) All money and property forfeited in the same forfeiture proceeding shall be pooled together for distribution as follows:

(A) A fair market value shall be assigned to all items of property other than money in such pool; and a total value shall be established for the pool by adding together the fair market value of all such property in the pool and the amount of money in the pool;

(B) All costs, including court costs, shall be paid and the remaining pool shall be distributed pro rata to the state and to local governments, according to the role which their law enforcement agencies played in the seizure of the assets; provided, however, that the amount distributed to the state shall not exceed 25 percent of the amount distributed; county governments are authorized upon request of the district attorney to provide for payment of any and all necessary expenses for the operation of the office from the said forfeiture pool up to 10 percent of the amount distributed, in addition to any other expenses paid by the county to the district attorney's office.

(C) An order of distribution provided for in this subsection shall be submitted by the district attorney to the court for approval; and

(D)(i) Property and money distributed to a local government shall be passed through to the local law enforcement agency until the sum equals 33 1/3 percent of the amount of local funds appropriated or otherwise made available to such agency for the fiscal year in which such funds are distributed. Proceeds received may be used for any official law enforcement purpose except for the payment of salaries or rewards to law enforcement personnel, at the discretion of the chief officer of the local law enforcement agency, or may be used to fund victim-witness assistance programs or a state law enforcement museum. Such property shall not be used to supplant any other local, state, or federal funds appropriated for staff or operations.

(ii) The local governing authority shall expend any remaining proceeds for any law enforcement purpose; for the representation of indigents in criminal cases; for drug treatment, rehabilitation, prevention, or education or any other program which responds to problems created by drug or substance abuse; for use as matching funds for grant programs related to drug treatment or prevention; to fund victim-witness assistance programs; or for any combination of the foregoing. If real property is distributed to a local government, the local government may transfer the real property to a land bank authority as provided in Article 4 of Chapter 4 of Title 48.

(iii) Any local law enforcement agency receiving property under this subsection shall submit an annual report to the local governing authority. The report shall be submitted with the agency's budget request and shall itemize the property received during the fiscal year and the utilization made thereof.

(iv) Money distributed to the state pursuant to this subsection shall be paid into the general fund of the state treasury, it being the intent of the General Assembly that the same be used, subject to appropriation from the general fund in the manner provided by law for representation of indigents in criminal cases; for funding of the Crime Victims Emergency Fund; for law enforcement and prosecution agency programs and particularly for funding of advanced drug investigation and prosecution training for law enforcement officers and prosecuting attorneys; for drug treatment, rehabilitation, prevention, or education or any other program which responds to problems created by drug or substance abuse; for use as matching funds for grant programs related to drug treatment or prevention; or for financing the judicial system of the state.

(v) Property distributed in kind to the state pursuant to this subsection may be designated by the Attorney General, with the approval of the court, for use by such agency or officer of the state as may be appropriate or, otherwise, shall be turned over to the Department of Administrative Services for such use or disposition as may be determined by the commissioner of the Department of Administrative Services.

(v) An acquittal or dismissal in a criminal proceeding does not preclude civil proceedings under this article.

(w) For good cause shown, the court may stay civil forfeiture proceedings during the criminal trial resulting from a related indictment or information alleging a violation of this article.

(x)(1) The court shall order the forfeiture of any property of a claimant or defendant up to the value of property found by the court to be subject to forfeiture under the provisions of this Code section if any of the forfeited property:

(A) Cannot be located;

(B) Has been transferred or conveyed to, sold to, or deposited with a third party;

(C) Is beyond the jurisdiction of the court;

(D) Has been substantially diminished in value while not in the actual physical custody of the receiver or governmental agency directed to maintain custody of the property; or

(E) Has been commingled with other property that cannot be divided without difficulty.

(2) In addition to any other remedy provided for by law, a district attorney on behalf of the state may institute an action in any court of this state or of the United States or any of the several states against any person acting with knowledge or any person to whom notice of a lien for forfeiture of property has been provided in accordance with subsection (j) of this Code section; to whom notice of seizure has been provided in accordance with subsection (i) of this Code section; or to whom notice of a civil proceeding alleging conduct giving rise to forfeiture under this Code section has been provided, if property subject to forfeiture is conveyed, alienated, disposed of, or otherwise rendered unavailable for forfeiture after the filing of a forfeiture lien notice or notice of seizure or after the filing and notice of a civil proceeding alleging conduct giving rise to forfeiture under this Code section, as the case may

be. The state may recover judgment in an amount equal to the value of the lien but not to exceed the fair market value of the property or, if there is no lien, in an amount not to exceed the fair market value of the property, together with reasonable investigative expenses and attorneys' fees. If a civil proceeding is pending, the action must be heard by the court in which the civil proceeding is pending.

(3) A district attorney may file and prosecute in any of the courts of this state or of the United States or of any of the several states such civil actions as may be necessary to enforce any judgment rendered pursuant to this Code section.

(4) No person claiming an interest in property subject to forfeiture under this article may commence or maintain any action against the state concerning the validity of the alleged interest other than as provided in this Code section. Except as specifically authorized by this Code section, no person claiming an interest in such property may file any counterclaim or cross-claim to any action brought pursuant to this Code section.

(5) A civil action under this article must be commenced within five years after the last conduct giving rise to forfeiture or to the claim for relief became known or should have become known, excluding any time during which either the property or defendant is out of the state or in confinement or during which criminal proceedings relating to the same conduct are in progress.

(y) Controlled substances included in Schedule I which are contraband and any controlled substance whose owners are unknown are summarily forfeited to the state. The court may include in any judgment of conviction under this article an order forfeiting any controlled substance involved in the offense to the extent of the defendant's interest.

(z) This Code section must be liberally construed to effectuate its remedial purposes.

## Chapter 16. Forfeiture of Property Used in Burglary or Armed Robbery

### O.C.G.A. § 16-16-2. Forfeiture of Tangible Things Used or Intended for Use in Commission of Armed Robbery or Burglary.

(a) All motor vehicles, tools, and weapons which are used or intended for use in any manner in the commission of or to facilitate the commission of a burglary or armed robbery are subject to forfeiture under this chapter, but:

(1) No motor vehicle used by any person as a common carrier in the transaction of business as a common carrier is subject to forfeiture under this Code section unless it appears that the owner or other person in charge of the motor vehicle is a consenting party or privy to the commission of a burglary or armed robbery;

(2) No motor vehicle is subject to forfeiture under this Code section by reason of any act or omission established by the owner thereof to have been committed or omitted without his or her knowledge or consent, and any co-owner of a motor vehicle without knowledge of or consent to the act or omission is protected to the extent of the interest of such co-owner; and

(3) A forfeiture of a motor vehicle encumbered by a bona fide security interest is subject to the interest of the secured party if he or she neither had knowledge of or nor consented to the act or omission.

(b) Property subject to forfeiture under this chapter may be seized by any law enforcement officer of this state or any political subdivision thereof who has the power to make arrests upon process issued by any court having jurisdiction over the property. Seizure without process or warrant may be made if:

(1) The seizure is incident to an arrest or a search under a search warrant;

(2) The property subject to seizure has been the subject of a prior judgment in favor of the state in a criminal injunction or forfeiture proceeding based upon this chapter; or

(3) If probable cause exists that the vehicle, tool, or weapon is subject to seizure.

(c) Property taken or detained under this Code section shall not be subject to replevin but is deemed to be in the custody of the superior court wherein the seizure was made or in custody of the superior court where it can be proven that the burglary or armed robbery was committed, subject only to the orders and decrees of the court having jurisdiction over the forfeiture proceedings. When property is seized under this chapter, law enforcement officers seizing such property shall:

(1) Place the property under seal;

(2) Remove the property to a place designated by the judge of the superior court having jurisdiction over the forfeiture as set out in this subsection; or

(3) Deliver such property to the sheriff or police chief of the county in which the seizure occurred, and the sheriff or police chief shall take custody of the property and remove it to an appropriate location for disposition in accordance with law.

(d) When property is seized under this chapter, the sheriff or law enforcement officer seizing the same shall report the fact of seizure, within 20 days thereof, to the district attorney of the judicial circuit having jurisdiction in the county where the seizure was made. Within 60 days from the date he or she receives notice of the seizure, the district attorney of the judicial circuit shall cause to be filed in the superior court of the county in which the property is seized or detained an in rem complaint for forfeiture of such property as provided for in this Code section. The proceedings shall be brought in the name of the state by the district attorney of the circuit in which the property was seized, and the complaint shall be verified by a duly authorized agent of the state in a manner required by the law of this state. The complaint shall describe the property, state its location, state its present custodian, state the name of the owner, if known to the duly authorized agent of the state, allege the essential elements of the violation upon which the forfeiture is based, and shall conclude with a prayer of due process to enforce the forfeiture. Upon the filing of such a complaint, the court shall promptly cause process to issue to the present custodian in possession of the property described in the complaint, commanding him or her to seize the property described in the complaint and to hold that property for further order of the court. A copy of the complaint shall be served on the owner or lessee, if known. A copy of the complaint shall also be served upon any person having a duly recorded security interest in or lien upon that property. If the owner or lessee is unknown or resides out of the state or departs the state or cannot after due diligence be found within the state or conceals himself or herself so as to avoid service, notice of the proceedings shall be published once a week for two weeks in the newspaper in which the sheriff's advertisements are published. Such publication shall be deemed notice to any and all persons having an interest in or right affected by such proceeding and from any sale of the property resulting therefrom but shall not constitute notice to any person having a duly recorded security interest in or lien upon such property and required to be served under this Code section unless that person is unknown or resides out of the state or departs the state or cannot after due diligence be found within the state or conceals himself or herself to avoid service. An owner of or interest holder in the property may file an answer asserting a claim against the property in the action in rem. Any such answer shall be filed within 30 days after the service of the summons and complaint. Where service is made by publication and personal service has not been made, an owner or interest holder shall file an answer within 30 days of the date of final publication. An answer must be verified by the owner or interest holder under penalty of perjury. In addition to complying with the general rules applicable to an answer in civil actions, the answer must set forth:

(1) The caption of the proceedings as set forth in the complaint and the name of the claimant;

(2) The address at which the claimant will accept mail;

(3) The nature and extent of the claimant's interest in the property;

(4) The date, identity of transferor, and circumstances of the claimant's acquisition of the interest in the property;

(5) The specific provision of this Code section relied on in asserting that the property is not subject to forfeiture;

(6) All essential facts supporting each assertion; and

(7) The precise relief sought.

If at the expiration of the period set forth in this subsection no answer has been filed, the court shall order the disposition of the seized property as provided for in this Code section. If an answer is filed, a hearing must be held within 60 days after service of the complaint unless continued for good cause and must be held by the court without a jury. If the court determines that a claimant defending the complaint knew or by the exercise of ordinary care should have known that the property was to be used for an unlawful purpose subjecting it to forfeiture under this chapter, the court shall order the disposition of the seized property as provided in this Code section and that claimant shall have no claim upon the property or proceeds from the sale thereof.

(e) (1) When property is forfeited under this chapter, the judge of the superior court in the county where the seizure was made or in the county in which it can be proven that the burglary or armed robbery was committed may dispose of the property by issuing an order to:

(A) Retain it for official use by any agency of this state or any political subdivision thereof;

(B) Sell that which is not required to be destroyed by law and which is not harmful to the public. The proceeds shall be used for payment of all proper expenses of the proceedings for forfeiture and sale, including but not limited to the expenses of seizure, maintenance of custody, advertising, and court costs; or

(C) Require the sheriff or police chief of the county in which the seizure occurred to take custody of the property and remove it for disposition in accordance with law.

(2) (A) Money, currency, or proceeds which are realized from the sale or disposition of forfeited property shall after satisfaction of the interest of secured parties and after payment of all costs vest in the local political subdivision whose law enforcement officers seized it. If the property was seized by a municipal law enforcement agency then the money, currency, or proceeds realized from the sale or disposition of the property shall vest in that municipality. If the property was seized by a county law enforcement agency, then the money, currency, or proceeds realized from the sale or disposition of the property shall vest in that county. If the property was seized by joint action of a county law enforcement agency and a municipal law enforcement agency, then the money, currency, or proceeds realized from the sale or disposition of the property shall vest in that county and that municipality and shall be divided equally between the county and municipality. If the property was seized by a state law enforcement agency, then the money, currency, or proceeds realized from the sale or disposition of the property shall vest in the county where the condemnation proceedings are filed. Except as otherwise provided in subparagraph (B) of paragraph (1) of this subsection for payment of all costs, the local government in which the money, currency, or proceeds realized from the forfeited property vests shall expend or use such funds or proceeds received for any official law enforcement purpose except for the payment of salaries or rewards to law enforcement personnel, at the discretion of the chief officer of the local law enforcement agency, or to fund victim-witness assistance programs. Such property shall not be used to supplant any other local, state, or federal funds appropriated for staff or operations.

(B) Any local law enforcement agency receiving property under this subsection shall submit an annual report to the local governing authority. The report shall be submitted with the agency's budget request and shall itemize the property received during the fiscal year and the utilization made thereof.

## Title 17. Criminal Procedure
## Chapter 4. Arrest of Persons
## Article 2. Arrest by Law Enforcement Officers Generally

### O.C.G.A. § 17-4-20. Warrantless Arrest, and Use of Deadly Force.

(a) An arrest for a crime may be made by a law enforcement officer either under a warrant or without a warrant if the offense is committed in such officer's presence or within such officer's immediate knowledge; if the offender is endeavoring to escape; if the officer has probable cause to believe that an act of family violence, as defined in Code Section 19-13-1, has been committed; if the officer has probable cause to believe that an offense involving physical abuse has been committed against a vulnerable adult, who shall be for the purposes of this subsection a person 18 years old or older who is unable to protect himself or herself from physical or mental abuse because of a physical or mental impairment; or for other cause if there is likely to be failure of justice for want of a judicial officer to issue a warrant.

(b) Sheriffs and peace officers who are appointed or employed in conformity with Chapter 8 of Title 35 may use deadly force to apprehend a suspected felon only when the officer reasonably believes that the suspect possesses a deadly weapon or any object, device, or instrument which, when used offensively against a person, is likely to or actually does result in serious bodily injury; when the officer reasonably believes that the suspect poses an immediate threat of physical violence to the officer or others; or when there is probable cause to believe that the suspect has committed a crime involving the infliction or threatened infliction of serious physical harm. Nothing in this Code section shall be construed so as to restrict such sheriffs or peace officers from the use of such reasonable nondeadly force as may be necessary to apprehend and arrest a suspected felon or misdemeanant.

(c) Nothing in this Code section shall be construed so as to restrict the use of deadly force by employees of state and county correctional institutions, jails, and other places of lawful confinement or by peace officers of any agency in the State of Georgia when reasonably necessary to prevent escapes or apprehend escapees from such institutions.

(d) No law enforcement agency of this state or of any political subdivision of this state shall adopt or promulgate any rule, regulation, or policy which prohibits a peace officer from using that degree of force to apprehend a suspected felon which is allowed by the statutory and case law of this state.

(e) Each peace officer shall be provided with a copy of this Code section. Training regarding elder abuse, abuse of vulnerable adults, and the requirements of this Code section should be offered as part of at least one in-service training program each year conducted by or on behalf of each law enforcement department and agency in this state.

(f) A nuclear power facility security officer, including a contract security officer, employed by a federally licensed nuclear power facility or licensee thereof for the purpose of securing that facility shall have the authority to:

(1) Threaten or use force against another in defense of a federally licensed nuclear power facility and the persons therein as provided for under Code Sections 16-3-21 and 16-3-23;

(2) Search any person on the premises of the nuclear power facility or the properties adjacent to the facility if the facility is under imminent threat or danger pursuant to a written agreement entered into with the local enforcement agency having jurisdiction over the facility for the purpose of determining if such person possesses unauthorized weapons, explosives, or other similarly prohibited material; provided, however, that if such person objects to any search, he or she shall be detained as provided in paragraph (3) of this subsection or shall be required to immediately vacate the premises. Any person refusing to submit to a search and refusing to vacate the premises of a facility upon the request of a security officer as provided for in this Code section shall be guilty of a misdemeanor; and

(3) In accordance with a nuclear security plan approved by the United States Nuclear Regulatory Commission or other federal agency authorized to regulate nuclear facility security, detain any person located on the premises of a nuclear power facility or on the properties adjacent thereto if the facility is under imminent threat or danger pursuant to a written agreement entered into with the local law enforcement agency having jurisdiction over the facility, where there is reasonable suspicion to believe that such person poses a threat to the security of the nuclear power facility, regardless of whether such prohibited act occurred in the officer's presence. In the event of such detention, the law

enforcement agency having jurisdiction over the facility shall be immediately contacted. The detention shall not exceed the amount of time reasonably necessary to allow for law enforcement officers to arrive at the facility.

## Chapter 5. Searches and Seizures
## Article 3. Disposition of Property Seized

### O.C.G.A. § 17-5-51. Weapons Declared to be Contraband; Forfeiture of Same; Motor Vehicles Excepted.

Any device which is used as a weapon in the commission of any crime against any person or any attempt to commit any crime against any person, any weapon the possession or carrying of which constitutes a crime or delinquent act, and any weapon for which a person has been convicted of violating Code Section 16-11-126 are declared to be contraband and are forfeited. For the purposes of this article, a motor vehicle shall not be deemed to be a weapon or device and shall not be contraband or forfeited under this article; provided, however, this exception shall not be construed to prohibit the seizure, condemnation, and sale of motor vehicles used in the illegal transportation of alcoholic beverages.

### O.C.G.A. § 17-5-52. Sale or Destruction of Confiscated Weapons.

(a) When a final judgment is entered finding a defendant guilty of the commission or attempted commission of a crime against any person or guilty of the commission of a crime or delinquent act involving the illegal possession or carrying of a weapon, any device which was used as a weapon in the commission of the crime or delinquent act shall be turned over by the person having custody of the weapon or device to the sheriff, chief of police, or other executive officer of the law enforcement agency that originally confiscated the weapon or device when the weapon or device is no longer needed for evidentiary purposes. Within 90 days after receiving the weapon or device, the sheriff, chief of police, or other executive officer of the law enforcement agency shall retain the weapon or device for use in law enforcement, destroy the same, or sell the weapon or device pursuant to judicial sale as provided in Article 7 of Chapter 13 of Title 9 or by any commercially feasible means, provided that, if the weapon or device used as a weapon in the crime is not the property of the defendant, there shall be no forfeiture of such weapon or device.

(b) The proceeds derived from all sales of such weapons or devices, after deducting the costs of the advertising and the sale, shall be turned in to the treasury of the county or the municipal corporation that sold the weapon or device. The proceeds derived from the sale of such weapons or devices confiscated by a state law enforcement agency shall be paid into the state treasury.

(c) Any law enforcement agency that retains, destroys, or sells any weapon or device pursuant to this Code section shall maintain records that include an accurate description of each weapon or device along with records of whether each weapon or device was retained, sold, or destroyed.

### O.C.G.A. § 17-5-53. Confiscated or Forfeited Weapons with Historical or Instructional Value.

(a) After a forfeiture of a device used in a crime, in the event the director of the Division of Archives and History or the commissioner of public safety, in that order or priority, shall desire to receive and retain a device described in Code Section 17-5-51 for historical or instructional purposes of his or her division or department and gives written notice thereof to the sheriff, either prior to the sheriff's advertisement of the device for sale or within ten days thereafter, the sheriff shall forthwith deliver the device to the requesting division or department which shall retain the device for such purposes. A device delivered to either the division or the department in accordance with this Code section shall become the property of the state.

(b) This Code section shall prevail over Code Section 17-5-52.

## Chapter 10. Sentence and Punishment
### Article 1. Procedure for Sentencing and Imposition of Punishment

### O.C.G.A. § 17-10-3. Punishment for Misdemeanors.

(a) Except as otherwise provided by law, every crime declared to be a misdemeanor shall be punished as follows:

(1) By a fine not to exceed $ 1,000.00 or by confinement in the county or other jail, county correctional institution, or such other places as counties may provide for maintenance of county inmates, for a total term not to exceed 12 months, or both;

(2) By confinement under the jurisdiction of the Board of Corrections in a state probation detention center or diversion center pursuant to Code Sections 42-8-35.4 and 42-8-35.5, for a determinate term of months which shall not exceed a total term of 12 months; or

(3) If the crime was committed by an inmate within the confines of a state correctional institution, by confinement under the jurisdiction of the Board of Corrections in a state correctional institution or such other institution as the Department of Corrections may direct for a term which shall not exceed 12 months.

(b) Either the punishment provided in paragraph (1) or (2) of subsection (a) of this Code section, but not both, may be imposed in the discretion of the sentencing judge. Misdemeanor punishment imposed under either paragraph may be subject to suspension or probation. The sentencing courts shall retain jurisdiction to amend, modify, alter, suspend, or probate sentences under paragraph (1) of subsection (a) of this Code section at any time, but in no instance shall any sentence under the paragraph be modified in a manner to place a county inmate under the jurisdiction of the Board of Corrections, except as provided in paragraph (2) of subsection (a) of this Code section.

(c) In all misdemeanor cases in which, upon conviction, a six-month sentence or less is imposed, it is within the authority and discretion of the sentencing judge to allow the sentence to be served on weekends by weekend confinement or during the nonworking hours of the defendant. A weekend shall commence and shall end in the discretion of the sentencing judge, and the nonworking hours of the defendant shall be determined in the discretion of the sentencing judge; provided, however, that the judge shall retain plenary control of the defendant at all times during the sentence period. A weekend term shall be counted as serving two days of the full sentence. Confinement during the nonworking hours of a defendant during any day may be counted as serving a full day of the sentence.

(d) In addition to or instead of any other penalty provided for the punishment of a misdemeanor involving a traffic offense, or punishment of a municipal ordinance involving a traffic offense, with the exception of habitual offenders sentenced under Code Section 17-10-7, a judge may impose any one or more of the following sentences:

(1) Reexamination by the Department of Driver Services when the judge has good cause to believe that the convicted licensed driver is incompetent or otherwise not qualified to be licensed;

(2) Attendance at, and satisfactory completion of, a driver improvement course meeting standards approved by the court;

(3) Within the limits of the authority of the charter powers of a municipality or the punishment prescribed by law in other courts, imprisonment at times specified by the court or release from imprisonment upon such conditions and at such times as may be specified; or

(4) Probation or suspension of all or any part of a penalty upon such terms and conditions as may be prescribed by the judge. The conditions may include driving with no further motor vehicle violations during a specified time unless the driving privileges have been or will be otherwise suspended or revoked by law; reporting periodically to the court or a specified agency; and performing, or

refraining from performing, such acts as may be ordered by the judge.

(e) Any sentence imposed under subsection (d) of this Code section shall be reported to the Department of Driver Services as prescribed by law.

(f) The Department of Corrections shall lack jurisdiction to supervise misdemeanor offenders, except when the sentence is made concurrent to a probated felony sentence or when the sentence is accepted pursuant to Code Section 42-9-71. Except as provided in this subsection, the Department of Corrections shall lack jurisdiction to confine misdemeanor offenders.

(g) This Code section will have no effect upon any offender convicted of a misdemeanor offense prior January 1, 2001, and sentenced to confinement under the jurisdiction of the Board of Corrections or to the supervision of the Department of Corrections.

## Title 20.  Education.
### Chapter 2.  Elementary and Secondary Education
### Article 16.  Students
### Part 2.  Discipline
### Subpart 2.  Public Disciplinary Tribunals

### O.C.G.A. § 20-2-751.  Definitions.

As used in this subpart, the term:

(1) "Expulsion" means expulsion of a student from a public school beyond the current school quarter or semester.

(2) "Long-term suspension" means the suspension of a student from a public school for more than ten school days but not beyond the current school quarter or semester.

(3) "Short-term suspension" means the suspension of a student from a public school for not more than ten school days.

(4) "Weapon" means a firearm as such term is defined in Section 921 of Title 18 of the United States Code.

### O.C.G.A. § 20-2-751.1.  Local Boards of Education to Establish Policy Requiring Expulsion from School for Those Students Who Bring Weapon to School.

(a) Each local board of education shall establish a policy requiring the expulsion from school for a period of not less than one calendar year of any student who is determined, pursuant to this subpart, to have brought a weapon to school.

(b) The local board of education shall have the authority to modify such expulsion requirement as provided in subsection (a) of this Code section on a case-by-case basis.

(c) A hearing officer, tribunal, panel, superintendent, or local board of education shall be authorized to place a student determined to have brought a weapon to school in an alternative educational setting.

(d) Nothing in this Code section shall infringe on any right provided to students with Individualized Education Programs pursuant to the federal Individuals with Disabilities Education Act, Section 504 of the federal Rehabilitation Act of 1973, or the federal Americans with Disabilities Act.

### O.C.G.A. § 20-2-751.5.  Provisions to be Included in Student Code of Conduct.

(a) Each student code of conduct shall contain provisions that address the following conduct of students during school hours, at school related functions, and on the school bus in a manner that is appropriate to the age of the student:

(1) Verbal assault, including threatened violence, of teachers, administrators, and other school personnel;

(2) Physical assault or battery of teachers, administrators, and other school personnel;

(3) Disrespectful conduct toward teachers, administrators, and other school personnel, including use of vulgar or profane language;

(4) Verbal assault of other students, including threatened violence or sexual harassment as defined pursuant to Title IX of the Education Amendments of 1972;

(5) Physical assault or battery of other students, including sexual harassment as defined pursuant to Title IX of the Education Amendments of 1972;

(6) Disrespectful conduct toward other students, including use of vulgar or profane language;

(7) Verbal assault of, physical assault or battery of, and disrespectful conduct, including use of vulgar or profane language, toward persons attending school related functions;

(8) Failure to comply with compulsory attendance as required under Code Section 20-2-690.1;

(9) Willful or malicious damage to real or personal property of the school or to personal property of any person legitimately at the school;

(10) Inciting, advising, or counseling of others to engage in prohibited acts;

(11) Marking, defacing, or destroying school property;

(12) Possession of a weapon, as provided for in Code Section 16-11-127.1;

(13) Unlawful use or possession of illegal drugs or alcohol;

(14) Willful and persistent violation of the student code of conduct;

(15) Bullying as defined by Code Section 20-2-751.4;

(16) Marking, defacing, or destroying the property of another student; and

(17) Falsifying, misrepresenting, omitting, or erroneously reporting information regarding instances of alleged inappropriate behavior by a teacher, administrator, or other school employee toward a student.

With regard to paragraphs (9), (11), and (17) of this subsection, each student code of conduct shall also contain provisions that address conduct of students during off-school hours.

(b)(1) In addition to the requirements contained in subsection (a) of this Code section, each student code of conduct shall include comprehensive and specific provisions prescribing and governing student conduct and safety rules on all public school buses. The specific provisions shall include but not be limited to:

(A) Students shall be prohibited from acts of physical violence as defined by Code Section 20-2-751.6, bullying as defined by subsection (a) of Code Section 20-2-751.4, physical assault or battery of other persons on the school bus, verbal assault of other persons on the school bus, disrespectful conduct toward the school bus driver or other persons on the school bus, and other unruly behavior;

(B) Students shall be prohibited from using any electronic devices during the operation of a school bus, including but not limited to cell phones; pagers; audible radios, tape or compact disc players without headphones; or any other electronic device in a manner that might interfere with the school bus communications equipment or the school bus driver's operation of the school bus; and

(C) Students shall be prohibited from using mirrors, lasers, flash cameras, or any other lights or reflective devises in a manner that might interfere with the school bus driver's operation of the school bus.

(2) If a student is found to have engaged in physical acts of violence as defined by Code Section 20-2-751.6, the student shall be subject to the penalties set forth in such Code section. If a student is found to have engaged in bullying as defined by subsection (a) of Code Section 20-2-751.4 or in physical assault or battery of another person on the school bus, the local school board policy shall require a meeting of the parent or guardian of the student and appropriate school district officials to form a school bus behavior contract for the student. Such contract shall provide for progressive age-appropriate discipline, penalties, and restrictions for student misconduct on the bus. Contract provisions may include but shall not be not limited to assigned seating, ongoing parental involvement, and suspension from riding the bus. This subsection is not to be construed to limit the instances when

a school code of conduct or local board of education may require use of a student bus behavior contract.

(c) Each student code of conduct shall also contain provisions that address any off-campus behavior of a student which could result in the student being criminally charged with a felony and which makes the student's continued presence at school a potential danger to persons or property at the school or which disrupts the educational process.

(d) Local board policies relating to student codes of conduct shall provide that each local school superintendent shall fully support the authority of principals and teachers in the school system to remove a student from the classroom pursuant to Code Section 20-2-738, including establishing and disseminating procedures. It is the policy of this state that it is preferable to reassign disruptive students to alternative educational settings rather than to suspend or expel such students from school.

(e) Any student handbook which is prepared by a local board or school shall include a copy of the student code of conduct for that school or be accompanied by a copy of the student code of conduct for that school as annually distributed pursuant to Code Section 20-2-736. When distributing a student code of conduct, a local school shall include a form for acknowledgment of the student's parent or guardian's receipt of the code, and the local school shall solicit or require that the form be signed and returned to the school.

## Article 27.  Loitering or Disrupting Schools

### O.C.G.A. § 20-2-1184.  School Personnel to Report Crimes.

(a) Any teacher or other person employed at any public or private elementary or secondary school or any dean or public safety officer employed by a college or university who has reasonable cause to believe that a student at that school has committed any act upon school property or at any school function, which act is prohibited by any of the following:

(1) Code Section 16-5-21, relating to aggravated assault if a firearm is involved;

(2) Code Section 16-5-24, relating to aggravated battery;

(3) Chapter 6 of Title 16, relating to sexual offenses;

(4) Code Section 16-11-127, relating to carrying a weapon or long gun in an unauthorized location;

(5) Code Section 16-11-127.1, relating to carrying weapons at school functions or on school property or within school safety zones;

(6) Code Section 16-11-132, relating to the illegal possession of a handgun by a person under 18 years of age; or

(7) Code Section 16-13-30, relating to possession and other activities regarding marijuana and controlled substances, shall immediately report the act and the name of the student to the principal or president of that school or the principal's or president's designee.

(b) The principal or designee who receives a report made pursuant to subsection (a) of this Code section who has reasonable cause to believe that the report is valid shall make an oral report thereof immediately by telephone or otherwise to the appropriate school system superintendent and to the appropriate police authority and district attorney.

(c) Any person participating in the making of a report or causing a report to be made as authorized or required pursuant to this Code section or participating in any judicial proceeding or any other proceeding resulting therefrom shall in so doing be immune from any civil or criminal liability that might otherwise be incurred or imposed, providing such participation pursuant to this Code section is made in good faith.

(d) Any person required to make a report pursuant to this Code section who knowingly and willfully fails to do so shall be guilty of a misdemeanor.

## Chapter 8. Campus Policemen

### O.C.G.A. § 20-8-5. School Security Personnel Law Enforcement Powers.

(a) In each public school system in this state, school security personnel employed by the board of education of a county or an independent board of education of a municipality for the various public schools thereof who are certified pursuant to subsection (b) of this Code section and who are authorized by the board of education of that county or the independent board of education of that municipality shall have the same law enforcement powers on school property, including the power of arrest, as law enforcement officers of that respective county or municipality.

(b) As a condition precedent to the exercise of law enforcement powers pursuant to subsection (a) of this Code section, school security personnel must be certified by the Georgia Peace Officer Standards and Training Council as having met the qualifications and having completed the basic training requirements for a peace officer under Chapter 8 of Title 35. The certification of school security personnel by the Georgia Peace Officer Standards and Training Council does not require that such security personnel exercise the powers provided in subsection (a) of this Code section.

(c) The provisions of this Code section shall not prohibit a board of education of a county or an independent board of education of a municipality from employing school security personnel without law enforcement powers.

(d) School security personnel who are certified by the Georgia Peace Officer Standards and Training Council may be authorized by a local board of education to carry a standard issue firearm or weapon generally used for law enforcement purposes for the purpose of carrying out law enforcement duties.

## Title 21. Elections
## Chapter 2. Elections and Primaries Generally
## Article 2. Preparation for and Conduct of Primaries and Elections
## Part 1. General Provisions

### O.C.G.A. § 21-2-413. Regulations for Polling Places.

(a) No elector shall be allowed to occupy a voting compartment or voting machine booth already occupied by another except when giving assistance as permitted by this chapter.

(b) No elector shall remain in a voting compartment or voting machine booth an unreasonable length of time; and, if such elector shall refuse to leave after such period, he or she shall be removed by the poll officers.

(c) No elector except a poll officer or poll watcher shall reenter the enclosed space after he or she has once left it except to give assistance as provided by this chapter.

(d) No person, when within the polling place, shall electioneer or solicit votes for any political party or body or candidate or question, nor shall any written or printed matter be posted within the room, except as required by this chapter. The prohibitions contained within Code Section 21-2-414 shall be equally applicable within the polling place and no elector shall violate the provisions of Code Section 21-2-414.

(e) No elector shall use photographic or other electronic monitoring or recording devices or cellular telephones while such elector is within the enclosed space in a polling place.

(f) All persons except poll officers, poll watchers, persons in the course of voting and such persons' children under 18 years of age or any child who is 12 years of age or younger accompanying such persons, persons lawfully giving assistance to electors, duly authorized investigators of the State Election Board, and peace officers when necessary for the preservation of order, must remain outside the enclosed space during the progress of the voting. Notwithstanding any other provision of this chapter, any elector shall be permitted to be accompanied into the enclosed area and into a voting compartment or voting machine booth while voting by such elector's child or children under 18 years of age or any child who is 12 years of age or younger unless the poll manager or an assistant manager determines in his or her sole discretion that such child or children are causing a disturbance or are interfering with the conduct of voting. Children accompanying an elector in the enclosed space pursuant to this subsection shall not in any manner handle any ballot nor operate any function of the voting equipment under any circumstances.

(g) When the hour for closing the polls shall arrive, all electors who have already qualified and are inside the enclosed space shall be permitted to vote; and, in addition thereto, all electors who are then in the polling place outside the enclosed space, or then in line outside the polling place, waiting to vote, shall be permitted to do so if found qualified, but no other persons shall be permitted to vote.

(h) It shall be the duty of the chief manager to secure the observances of this Code section, to keep order in the polling place, and to see that no more persons are admitted within the enclosed space than are permitted by this chapter. Further, from the time a polling place is opened until the ballots are delivered to the superintendent, the ballots shall be in the custody of at least two poll officers at all times.

(i) No person except peace officers regularly employed by the federal, state, county, or municipal government or certified security guards shall be permitted to carry firearms within 150 feet of any polling place.

## Title 27. Game and Fish
## Chapter 1. General Provisions

### O.C.G.A. § 27-1-3. Hunting and Fishing Regulations.

(a) The General Assembly recognizes that hunting and fishing and the taking of wildlife are a valued part of the cultural heritage of the State of Georgia. The General Assembly further recognizes that such activities play an essential role in the state's economy and in funding the state's management programs for game and nongame species alike, and that such activities have also come to play an important and sometimes critical role in the biological management of certain natural communities within this state. In recognition of this cultural heritage and the tradition of stewardship it embodies, and of the important role that hunting and fishing and the taking of wildlife play in the state's economy and in the preservation and management of the state's natural communities, the General Assembly declares that Georgia citizens have the right to take fish and wildlife, subject to the laws and regulations adopted by the board for the public good and general welfare, which laws and regulations should be vigorously enforced. The General Assembly further declares that the state's wildlife resources should be managed in accordance with sound principles of wildlife management, using all appropriate tools, including hunting, fishing, and the taking of wildlife.

(b) The ownership of, jurisdiction over, and control of all wildlife, as defined in this title, are declared to be in the State of Georgia, in its sovereign capacity, to be controlled, regulated, and disposed of in accordance with this title. Wildlife is held in trust by the state for the benefit of its citizens and shall not be reduced to private ownership except as specifically provided for in this title. All wildlife of the State of Georgia is declared to be within the custody of the department for purposes of management and regulation in accordance with this title. However, the State of Georgia, the department, and the board shall be immune from suit and shall not be liable for any damage to life, person, or property caused directly or indirectly by any wildlife.

(c)(1) To the greatest practical extent, department land management decisions and actions shall not result in any net loss of land acreage available for hunting opportunities on department managed state owned lands that exists on July 1, 2005.

(2) The department has the authority and the responsibility to work with cooperating sportsmen, conservation groups, and others to encourage participation in hunting and fishing at a level

to ensure continuation of such activities in perpetuity and no net loss of hunting and fishing opportunity on state owned lands. Further, the department is authorized to promote and encourage hunting, fishing, and other wildlife associated recreation on state managed wildlife areas, public fishing areas, federally owned or managed forests, and other suitable public and private lands of this state.

(d) To hunt, trap, or fish, as defined in this title, or to possess or transport wildlife is declared to be a right to be exercised only in accordance with the laws governing such right. Every person exercising this right does so subject to the authority of the state to regulate hunting, trapping, and fishing for the public good and general welfare; and it shall be unlawful for any person exercising the right of hunting, trapping, fishing, possessing, or transporting wildlife to refuse to permit authorized employees of the department to inspect and count such wildlife to ascertain whether the requirements of the wildlife laws and regulations are being faithfully complied with. Any person who hunts, traps, fishes, possesses, or transports wildlife in violation of the wildlife laws and regulations violates the conditions under which this right is extended; and any wildlife then on his person or within his immediate possession is deemed to be wildlife possessed in violation of the law and is subject to seizure by the department pursuant to Code Section 27-1-21. Nothing in this subsection shall be construed to reduce, infringe upon, or diminish the rights of private property owners as otherwise provided by general law.

(e) It shall be unlawful to hunt, trap, or fish except during an open season for the taking of wildlife, as such open seasons may be established by law or by rules and regulations promulgated by the board or as otherwise provided by law.

(f) It shall be unlawful to hunt, trap, or fish except in compliance with the bag, creel, size, and possession limits and except in accordance with such legal methods and weapons and except at such times and places as may be established by law or by rules and regulations promulgated by the board.

(g) It shall be unlawful to hunt, trap, or fish for any game species after having obtained the daily or season bag or creel limit for that species.

(h) Except as otherwise provided by general law, the power and duty to promulgate rules and regulations relating to hunting, trapping, and fishing rests solely with the board. No political subdivision of the state may regulate hunting, trapping, or fishing by local ordinance; provided, however, that a local government shall not be prohibited from exercising its management rights over real property owned or leased by it for purposes of prohibiting hunting, fishing, or trapping upon the property or for purposes of setting times when access to the property for purposes of hunting, fishing, or trapping in accordance with this title may be permitted. Nothing contained in this Code section shall prohibit municipalities or counties, by ordinance, resolution, or other enactment, from reasonably limiting or prohibiting the discharge of firearms within the boundaries of the political subdivision for purposes of public safety.

(i) A person who takes any wildlife in violation of this title commits the offense of theft by taking. A person who hunts, traps, or fishes in violation of this title commits the offense of criminal attempt. Any person who violates any provision of this Code section shall be guilty of a misdemeanor.

(j) If any court finds that any criminal violation of the provisions of this title is so egregious as to display a willful and reckless disregard for the wildlife of this state, the court may, in its discretion, suspend the violator's right to hunt, fish, trap, possess, or transport wildlife in this state for a period not to exceed five years. Any person who hunts, fishes, traps, possesses, or transports wildlife in this state in violation of such suspension of rights shall be guilty of a misdemeanor of a high and aggravated nature and upon conviction thereof shall be punished by a fine of not less than $1,500.00 nor more than $5,000.00 or imprisonment for a period not exceeding 12 months or both.

## O.C.G.A. § 27-1-36. Civil Enforcement by Department of Natural Resources.

(a) As an alternative to criminal enforcement pursuant to Code Section 27-1-38, the department, in order to enforce this title or any rules and regulations promulgated pursuant thereto, may employ any one or any combination of the following methods:

(1) Any person who violates any provisions of this title or any regulations or orders promulgated and administered thereunder shall be liable civilly for a penalty in an amount of up to $1,000.00 for each and every violation thereof, the penalty to be recoverable by a civil action brought in the name of the commissioner by the district attorney of the county in which the alleged violator resides. The commissioner on his motion may or upon complaint of any interested party charging a violation shall refer the matter directly to the district attorney of the county in which the alleged violator resides. The proceeds from all civil penalties arising from enforcement of the wildlife laws, regulations, and orders pursuant to this Code section shall be used in the manner prescribed in Code Section 27-1-14;

(2) Whenever the commissioner determines that any person has violated any provision of this title or any regulations or orders promulgated under this title, the commissioner may issue an administrative order imposing a civil penalty not to exceed $1,000.00 for the violation. Any person who is aggrieved or adversely affected by any such order shall, upon petition within 30 days after the issuance of such order, have a right to a hearing before an administrative law judge appointed by the Board of Natural Resources. The hearing before the administrative law judge shall be conducted in accordance with Chapter 13 of Title 50, the "Georgia Administrative Procedure Act," and the rules and regulations adopted by the board pursuant thereto. The decision of the administrative law judge shall constitute the final decision of the board and any party to the hearing, including the commissioner, shall have the right of judicial review thereof in accordance with Chapter 13 of Title 50; or

(3) All civil penalties recovered by the department as provided in this Code section shall be paid into the state treasury. The commissioner may file in the superior court in the county in which the person under order resides or, if the person is a corporation, in the county in which the corporation maintains its principal place of business, or in the county in which the violation occurred, a certified copy of a final order of the commissioner or the administrative law judge unappealed from or of a final order of the administrative law judge affirmed upon appeal, whereupon the court shall render judgment in accordance therewith and notify the parties. The judgment shall have the same effect, and all proceedings in relation thereto shall thereafter be the same, as though the judgment had been rendered in an action duly heard and determined by the court.

(b) The civil penalty prescribed in this Code section shall be concurrent with, alternative to, and cumulative of any and all other civil, criminal, or alternative rights, remedies, forfeitures, or penalties provided, allowed, or available to the commissioner with respect to any violation of this title and any regulations or orders promulgated pursuant thereto; provided, however, that in no instance shall the department be authorized to proceed against any person under both Code Section 27-1-38 and this Code section for any single violation of the wildlife laws, rules, and regulations.

### O.C.G.A. § 27-1-38. Penalties for Violations.

Unless otherwise specifically provided, any person who violates any of the provisions of this title shall be guilty of a misdemeanor; provided, however, that unless otherwise specifically provided, any person who violates any of the provisions of this title or any rule or regulation promulgated pursuant thereto relating to the possession or use of fishing gear on trawlers shall be a misdemeanor of a high and aggravated nature and shall be fined $ 1,000.00 for the first offense, $ 3,000.00 for the second offense, and $ 5,000.00 for the third and each subsequent offense.

## Chapter 2. Licenses, Permits, and Stamps Generally
### Article 1. Hunting, Trapping, or Fishing

### O.C.G.A. § 27-2-5. Hunter Education Course Requirements.

(a) It shall be unlawful for any person born on or after January 1, 1961, to procure a hunting license or to hunt by means of weapons in this state unless that person has been issued a certificate or other evidence the department deems acceptable which indicates satisfactory completion of a hunter education course as prescribed by the board. Persons ages 16 through 25 shall provide such certificate or other evidence to the issuing agent at the time of purchase of a hunting license. All persons required by this subsection to complete a hunter education course, by signing such license, by receiving a temporary license identification number, or by receiving a license from a telephone license agent, Internet license agent, or other vendor, shall certify their compliance with this subsection.

(b) It shall be unlawful for any person authorized to issue hunting licenses in this state to issue a hunting license to any person age 16 through 25 unless that license agent shall have been provided with a certificate showing the license applicant has satisfactorily completed a hunter education course as prescribed by the board, or to any other person born on or after January 1, 1961, unless such person provides such other evidence of completion of a hunter education course as the department deems acceptable. Internet and telephone license agents may accept a valid hunter education certificate number as fulfillment of this requirement.

(c) It shall be unlawful for any person age 16 through 25 who is not required by law to obtain a hunting license to hunt in this state unless that person carries on his or her person while hunting a certificate attesting to that person's satisfactory completion of a hunter education course as prescribed by the board. Such person shall present his or her certificate to a conservation ranger or deputy conservation ranger for inspection upon demand.

(d) Any person who is age 12 through 15 shall satisfactorily complete a hunter education course as a prerequisite to hunting with a weapon in this state. It shall be unlawful for any adult to permit his or her child or ward age 12 through 15 to hunt with a weapon unless the child has a certificate attesting to his or her satisfactory completion of such course on his or her person; provided, however, that a hunter education course is not required for a child age 12 through 15 years who is hunting under adult supervision by a licensed adult hunter.

(e) Any person applying for an annual nonresident hunting/fishing license may provide a certificate of completion or such other evidence of completion the department deems acceptable of the official hunter education or hunter safety course of such person's state of residence if that course shall have been approved by the department. Those persons applying for a hunting license other than a season hunting license shall not be required to exhibit such a certificate or to complete a hunter education course in order to obtain the license.

(f) By rule or regulation, the board shall prescribe a course of instruction in competency and safety in hunting and in the handling of weapons. The board shall also prescribe procedures whereby competent residents of this state shall be certified as hunter education instructors. The board may provide, by rule or regulation, for charging reasonable fees for the issuance by the department of duplicate certificates of completion of a hunter education course and for hunter education courses in order to defray the expenses of conducting such courses. Any such fees shall be deemed as "other income" of the department for purposes of subsection (c) of Code Section 27-1-13.

(g) Any person violating any provision of this Code section shall be guilty of a misdemeanor; provided, however, that this subsection shall not apply to any person under the age of 16.

(h) The requirements of subsections (c) and (d) of this Code section shall not apply to any person hunting on his or her own land or that of his or her parents or legal guardian or to persons permitting a child or ward aged 12 through 15 years to hunt on the parent's or guardian's own land.

## O.C.G.A. § 27-2-16. Commercial Quail Breeder Permits.

(a) It shall be unlawful for any person to engage in the business of propagating quail for food, restocking, propagation, or other commercial purposes unless the quail are pen raised quail and unless the person has obtained a commercial quail breeder permit as provided in Code Section 27-2-23. For purposes of this Code section, the term "pen raised quail" means a quail that has been hatched from an egg laid by a quail confined in a pen or coop.

(b) Each person holding a commercial quail breeder permit shall keep records, in a suitably bound book, of all bird carcasses sold, to whom sold, and the number sold.

(c) It shall be unlawful to sell the carcass of any pen raised quail unless the carcass has been stamped with the following information:

Ga. Department of Natural Resources
Comm. Quail Permit
No. _____
(Name of Breeder)
Permit expires (date) ,

(d) It shall be unlawful to sell pen raised quail which have been killed with a firearm.

(e) It shall be unlawful to transport any pen raised quail without meeting the requirements of this title relating to the transportation of wildlife, provided that nothing in this subsection shall be construed to limit the number of pen raised quail which may be transported in this state.

## O.C.G.A. § 27-2-25.1. Penalties for Negligent Killing or Injuring Another Person While Hunting.

(a) The General Assembly has heretofore found and declared that hunting is a privilege to be exercised only in accordance with the law granting such privilege. The General Assembly now specifically finds and declares that while the act of hunting is an enjoyable and beneficial form of recreation, it can be dangerous not only to the hunter himself but also to other persons if due care is not exercised. Therefore, the General Assembly declares that all persons who refuse or fail to exercise such due care may have their hunting privileges suspended as provided in this Code section.

(b) Any person engaged in the act of hunting who by the use of a weapon kills or injures another person or persons, whether or not such other person or persons are likewise engaged in the act of hunting, shall notify the department or any appropriate law enforcement officer who shall then notify the department immediately after such occurrence. Any person who fails so to notify the department or such law enforcement officer shall be guilty of a misdemeanor.

(c) Upon notification of such a death or injury, whether by the hunter or by some other person, the department shall immediately initiate an investigation of such incident and submit a report to the commissioner. If the commissioner determines culpable negligence on the part of the person causing the death or injury and that such negligence was the proximate cause of such death or injury, the commissioner may suspend that person's hunting privileges for a specified period of time not to exceed ten years. Any such determination to suspend shall be subject to review as provided for in this Code section. When the commissioner shall decide to suspend said person's hunting privileges, the commissioner must notify such person of said suspension and of his right to a hearing to contest the commissioner's determination. The notification from the commissioner to the person whose license is being suspended shall be by certified mail or statutory overnight delivery with return receipt requested; or, in lieu thereof, notice may be given by personal service upon such person. Upon such notice, any such hunting privileges shall be revoked by such notice and such person shall surrender his or her hunting license, if any, to the department within ten days of such notification. For the purposes of this article, notice given by certified mail or statutory overnight delivery with return receipt requested mailed to the person's last known address shall be prima-facie evidence that such person received the required notice.

(d) The person so notified may request an administrative hearing before an administrative law judge appointed by the board within 30 days of receipt of the notice. If no hearing is requested within the 30 day period, the right to a hearing shall have been waived and the hunting privileges of the person shall stand suspended as prescribed by the commissioner's notice. If, following the administrative hearing, there is a determination that such person was negligent and that such negligence was the proximate cause of the death or injury, the hunting privileges of such person may be suspended for a period of up to ten years. The period of time that such privileges are suspended shall be commensurate with the degree of negligence and the severity of the injury. If there is a determination of no negligence or that the negligence was not the proximate cause of the death or injury, the person's hunting privileges shall be restored. The provisions of Code Section 27-2-27 shall not be applicable to a suspension under this Code section.

(e) Any person whose hunting privileges have been suspended under this Code section and who engages in the act of hunting during such period of suspension shall be guilty of a misdemeanor of a high and aggravated nature and shall be punished by a fine of not more than $ 5,000.00 or by imprisonment for not more than 12 months, or both. Any person whose hunting privileges have been suspended under this Code section shall complete a course of instruction in competency and safety in hunting and in the handling of weapons provided for in Code Section 27-2-5 prior to any subsequent exercise of his hunting privileges.

(f) As used in this Code section, the term:

(1) "License" means any and all licenses, permits, or stamps as required by law for hunting in this state.

(2) "Hunting privileges" means the exercise of the privilege of hunting whether such privilege is bestowed by license or otherwise.

(3) "Suspend" means the suspension or revocation of any existing license or hunting privileges and the suspension or revocation of the privilege of obtaining any new license or hunting privileges.

(g) The hearing before an administrative law judge and any judicial review shall be conducted in accordance with Chapter 13 of Title 50 and applicable rules and regulations of the board.

(h) The proceedings provided for by this Code section shall be in addition to and not in lieu of any civil or criminal action or actions provided for by law and the final decision of this proceeding shall not constitute res judicata as to any such civil or criminal action or actions and shall not be admissible as evidence in any such civil or criminal action or actions.

## Chapter 3. Wildlife Generally
## Article 1. Hunting
## Part 1. General Provisions

### O.C.G.A. § 27-3-1.1. Prohibited Acts in Wildlife Management Area.

It shall be unlawful for any person on any wildlife management area owned or operated by the department:

(1) To possess a firearm other than a handgun, as such term is defined in Code Section 16-11-125.1, during a closed hunting season for that area unless such firearm is unloaded and stored in a motor vehicle so as not to be readily accessible or to possess a handgun during a closed hunting season for that area unless such person possesses a valid weapons carry license issued pursuant to Code Section 16-11-129;

(2) To possess a loaded firearm other than a handgun, as such term is defined in Code Section 16-11-125.1, in a motor vehicle during a legal open hunting season for that area or to possess a loaded handgun in a motor vehicle during a legal open season for that area unless such person possesses a valid weapons carry license issued pursuant to Code Section 16-11-129;

(3) To be under the influence of drugs, intoxicating liquors, beers, or wines. The determination of whether any person is under the influence of drugs or intoxicating liquors, beers, or wines may be made in accordance with Code Section 27-3-7;

(4) To hunt within 50 yards of any road which receives regular maintenance for the purpose of public vehicular access;

(5) To target practice, except where an authorized shooting range is made available by the department, and then only in a manner consistent with the rules for shooting ranges promulgated by the board;

(6) To drive a vehicle around a closed gate, cable, sign, or other structure or device intended to prevent vehicular access to a road entering onto or within such an area;

(7) To hunt within any posted safety zone;

(8) To camp upon or drive a motor vehicle over any permanent pasture or area planted in crops;

(9) While hunting bears in any such area opened to bear hunting, to kill a female bear with a cub or cubs or to kill a cub weighing less than 75 pounds;

(10) To fail to report if he or she kills a deer, bear, or turkey in the manner specified by the rules of the department for that wildlife management area on the date killed to the state game and fish checking station on the area;

(11) To construct any tree stand or to hunt from any tree stand except a portable or natural tree stand; or

(12) To trap except with a special trapping permit issued by the department.

## O.C.G.A. § 27-3-4. Legal Weapons for Hunting.

It shall be unlawful to hunt wildlife with any weapon, except that:

(1) Longbows, recurve bows, crossbows, and compound bows may be used for taking small game, feral hogs, or big game. Arrows for hunting deer, bear, and feral hogs must be broadhead type;

(2) During primitive weapon hunts or primitive weapons seasons:

(A) longbows, recurve bows, crossbows, compound bows, muzzleloading firearms of .44 caliber or larger, and muzzleloading shotguns of 20 gauge or larger loaded with single shot may be used; and,

(B) Youth under 16 years of age may hunt deer with any firearm legal for hunting deer.

(3) Firearms for hunting deer, bear, and feral hogs are limited to 20 gauge shotguns or larger shotguns loaded with slugs or buckshot (except that no buckshot is permitted on state wildlife management areas unless otherwise specified), muzzleloading firearms of .44 caliber or larger, and center-fire firearms .22 caliber or larger; provided, however, that firearms for hunting feral hogs, other than those weapons specified in this paragraph, may be authorized by rule or regulation of the board. Bullets used in all center-fire rifles and handguns must be of the expanding type;

(4) Weapons for hunting small game shall be limited to shotguns with shot shell size of no greater than 3 1/2 inches in length with No. 2 lead shot or smaller or federally approved nontoxic shot size of F or smaller shot, .22 caliber or smaller rimfire firearms, air rifles, muzzleloading firearms, longbows, recurve bows, crossbows, and compound bows; provided, however, that nothing contained in this paragraph shall permit the taking of protected species;

(5)(A) For hunting deer, feral hogs, and bear, shotguns shall be limited to a capacity of not more than five shells in the magazine and chamber combined. If a plug is necessary to so limit the capacity, the plug shall be of one piece, incapable of being removed through the loading end of the magazine.

(B) For hunting all other game animals, shotguns shall be limited to a capacity of not more than three shells in the magazine and chamber combined. If a plug is necessary to so limit the capacity, the plug shall be of one piece, incapable of being removed through the loading end of the magazine;

(6) It shall be unlawful to hunt turkey with any weapons except shotguns using No. 2 shot or smaller, muzzleloading firearms, longbows, crossbows, recurve bows, or compound bows. Any person taking turkey in violation of this paragraph shall be guilty of a misdemeanor and, upon conviction

thereof, shall be punished as for a misdemeanor, except that a fine imposed for such violation shall not be less than $ 250.00;

(7) Weapons for hunting alligators shall be limited to hand-held ropes or snares, snatch hooks, harpoons, gigs, or arrows with restraining lines attached. Lawfully restrained alligators may be killed with any caliber handgun or bangstick and shall be killed immediately before transporting;

(8) There are no firearms restrictions for taking nongame animals or nongame birds; and

(9) The use of silencers for hunting within this state is prohibited.

## O.C.G.A. § 27-3-6. Possession of Centerfire or Rimfire Firearm While Bow Hunting or Hunting with Muzzleloading Firearm.

It shall be unlawful for any person to possess any center-fire or rimfire firearm other than a handgun, as such term is defined in Code Section 16-11-125.1, while hunting with a bow and arrow during archery or primitive weapons season for deer or while hunting with a muzzleloading firearm during a primitive weapons season for deer or to possess a loaded handgun while hunting with a bow and arrow during archery or primitive weapons season for deer or while hunting with a muzzleloading firearm during primitive weapons season for deer unless such person possesses a valid weapons carry license issued pursuant to Code Section 16-11-129.

## O.C.G.A. § 27-3-7. Hunting While Under the Influence.

(a) As used in this Code section, the term "hunt" or "hunting" means the act of hunting, as such term is defined in Code Section 27-1-2, while in possession of or using a firearm, bow, or any other device which serves to launch a projectile.

(b) A person shall not hunt while:

(1) Under the influence of alcohol to the extent that it is less safe for the person to hunt;

(2) Under the influence of any drug to the extent that it is less safe for the person to hunt;

(3) Under the combined influence of alcohol and any drug to the extent that it is less safe for the person to hunt;

(4) The person's alcohol concentration is 0.10 grams or more at any time within three hours after such hunting from alcohol consumed before such hunting ended; or

(5) Subject to the provisions of subsection (c) of this Code section, there is any amount of marijuana or a controlled substance, as defined in Code Section 16-13-21, present in the person's blood or urine, or both, including the metabolites and derivatives of each or both without regard to whether or not any alcohol is present in the person's breath or blood.

(c) The fact that any person charged with violating this Code section is or has been legally entitled to use a drug shall not constitute a defense against any charge of violating this Code section; provided, however, that such person shall not be in violation of this Code section unless such person is rendered incapable of hunting safely as a result of using a drug other than alcohol which such person is legally entitled to use.

(d) Upon the trial of any civil or criminal action or proceeding arising out of acts alleged to have been committed by any person in violation of subsection (b) of this Code section, evidence of the amount of alcohol or drug in a person's blood, urine, breath, or other bodily substance at the alleged time, as determined by a chemical analysis of the person's blood, urine, breath, or other bodily substance shall be admissible. Where such a chemical test is made, the following provisions shall apply:

(1) Chemical analysis of the person's blood, urine, breath, or other bodily substance, to be considered valid under this Code section, shall have been performed according to methods approved by the Division of Forensic Sciences of the Georgia Bureau of Investigation on a machine which was operated with all the electronic and operating components prescribed by its manufacturer properly attached and in good working order and by an individual possessing a valid permit issued by the Division of Forensic Sciences for this purpose. The Division of Forensic Sciences of the Georgia Bureau of

Investigation shall approve satisfactory techniques or methods to ascertain the qualifications and competence of individuals to conduct analyses and to issue permits, along with requirements for properly operating and maintaining any testing instruments, and to issue certificates certifying that instruments have met those requirements, which certificates and permits shall be subject to termination or revocation at the discretion of the Division of Forensic Sciences;

(2) When a person undergoes a chemical test at the request of a law enforcement officer, only a physician, registered nurse, laboratory technician, emergency medical technician, or other qualified person may withdraw blood for the purpose of determining the alcoholic content therein, provided that this limitation shall not apply to the taking of breath or urine specimens. No physician, registered nurse, or other qualified person or employer thereof shall incur any civil or criminal liability as a result of the medically proper obtaining of such blood specimens when requested in writing by a law enforcement officer;

(3) The person tested may have a physician or a qualified technician, chemist, registered nurse, or other qualified person of his or her own choosing administer a chemical test or tests in addition to any administered at the direction of a law enforcement officer. The justifiable failure or inability to obtain an additional test shall not preclude the admission of evidence relating to the test or tests taken at the direction of a law enforcement officer; and

(4) Upon the request of the person who shall submit to a chemical test or tests at the request of a law enforcement officer, full information concerning the test or tests shall be made available to such person or such person's attorney. The arresting officer at the time of arrest shall advise the person arrested of his or her rights to a chemical test or tests according to this Code section.

(e) In the event of a hunting accident involving a fatality, the investigating coroner or medical examiner having jurisdiction shall direct that a chemical blood test to determine the blood alcohol concentration or the presence of drugs be performed on the dead person and that the results of such test be properly recorded on his or her report.

(f) Upon the trial of any civil or criminal action or proceeding arising out of acts alleged to have been committed by any person hunting in violation of subsection (b) of this Code section, the amount of alcohol in the person's blood at the time alleged, as shown by chemical analysis of the person's blood, urine, breath, or other bodily substance, shall give rise to the following presumptions:

(1) If there was at that time a blood alcohol concentration of 0.05 grams or less, it shall be presumed that the person was not under the influence of alcohol, as prohibited by paragraphs (1), (2), and (3) of subsection (b) of this Code section;

(2) If there was at that time a blood alcohol concentration in excess of 0.05 grams but less than 0.08 grams, such fact shall not give rise to any presumption that the person was or was not under the influence of alcohol, as prohibited by paragraphs (1), (2), and (3) of subsection (b) of this Code section, but such fact may be considered with other competent evidence in determining whether the person was under the influence of alcohol, as prohibited by paragraphs (1), (2), and (3) of subsection (b) of this Code section;

(3) If there was at that time a blood alcohol concentration of 0.08 grams or more, it shall be presumed that the person was under the influence of alcohol, as prohibited by paragraphs (1), (2), and (3) of subsection (b) of this Code section; and

(4) If there was at that time or within three hours after hunting, from alcohol consumed before such hunting ended, a blood alcohol concentration of 0.10 or more grams, the person shall be in violation of paragraph (4) of subsection (b) of this Code section.

(g)(1) Any person who exercises the privilege of hunting in this state shall be deemed to have given consent, subject to subsection (d) of this Code section, to a chemical test or tests of his or her blood, breath, urine, or other bodily substances for the purpose of determining the presence of alcohol or any other drug, if arrested for any offense arising out of acts alleged to have been committed while such person was hunting in violation of subsection (b) of this Code section. Subject to subsection (d) of this Code section, the requesting law enforcement officer shall designate which test or tests shall be administered.

(2) At the time a chemical test or tests are requested, the arresting officer shall read to the person the following implied consent warning:

"Georgia law requires you to submit to state administered chemical tests of your blood, breath, urine, or other bodily substances for the purpose of determining if you are under the influence of alcohol or drugs. If you refuse this testing and you are convicted of hunting while under the influence of alcohol or drugs, your privilege to hunt in this state will be suspended for a period of two years. Your refusal to submit to the required testing may be offered into evidence against you at trial. If you consent to the test, the results may be offered into evidence against you. After first submitting to the required state tests, you are entitled to additional chemical tests of your blood, breath, urine, or other bodily substances at your own expense and from qualified personnel of your own choosing. Will you submit to the state administered chemical tests of your (designate which tests) under the implied consent law?"

(h) Any person who is dead, unconscious, or otherwise in a condition rendering such person incapable of refusal shall be deemed not to have withdrawn the consent provided by subsection (g) of this Code section, and the test or tests may be administered, subject to subsection (d) of this Code section.

(i)(1) If a person refuses, upon the request of a law enforcement officer, to submit to a chemical test designated by the law enforcement officer as provided in subsection (g) of this Code section, no test shall be given; provided, however, that subject to the provisions of paragraphs (2) and (3) of this subsection, such refusal shall be admissible in any legal action; and provided, further, that upon conviction of a violation of subsection (b) of this Code section, in addition to any other punishment imposed, such person's privileges to hunt in this state shall be suspended by operation of law for a period of two years. The fact that such person was not in possession of a valid hunting license at the time of the violation shall have no effect on the suspension of his or her hunting privilege.

(2) If in any legal action a party desires to present evidence of the refusal of a person charged with violating subsection (b) of this Code section to submit to a chemical test designated by a law enforcement officer as provided in subsection (g) of this Code section, the party desiring to present such evidence shall request the judge presiding over such legal proceeding to hold a hearing to determine the admissibility of such evidence after notice to the person alleged to have refused to submit to such testing and to the law enforcement officer.

(3) The scope of the hearing shall be limited to the following issues:

(A) Whether the law enforcement officer had reasonable grounds to believe the person was hunting while under the influence of alcohol or a controlled substance and was lawfully placed under arrest for violating subsection (b) of this Code section;

(B) Whether at the time of the request for the test or tests the officer informed the person of the person's implied consent rights and the consequence of submitting or refusing to submit to such test; and

(C) Whether the person refused to submit to the test.

(4) It shall be unlawful during any period of a person's hunting privilege suspension for such person to:

(A) Hunt without a license in violation of Code Section 27-2-1;

(B) Possess a current Georgia hunting license; or

(C) Hunt in any situation where a hunting license is not required.

(5) Any person convicted of hunting while intoxicated while his or her hunting privileges are suspended pursuant to this subsection shall be guilty of a misdemeanor.

**O.C.G.A. § 27-3-10.  Hunting on or Discharging Weapon From or Across Public Road Prohibited.**

(a) It shall be unlawful for any person to hunt, with or without dogs, any wildlife upon any public road in this state. It shall also be unlawful for any person while hunting to discharge any weapon from or across any public road in this state.

(b) Any person who violates the provisions of subsection (a) of this Code section shall be guilty of a misdemeanor and, upon conviction thereof, shall be punished by a fine of not less than $50.00 and not more than $1,000.00 and, in the discretion of the sentencing court, imprisonment for not more than 12 months; provided, however, that such fine shall not be subject to suspension, stay, or probation except that if the court finds that payment of such fine would impose great economic hardship upon the defendant, the court may order such fine paid in installments.

**O.C.G.A. § 27-3-11 Repealed.**

**O.C.G.A. § 27-3-12.  Prohibited Means of Hunting.**

(a) It shall be unlawful to hunt any wild animal, game animal, or game bird by means of drugs, poisons, chemicals, smoke, gas, explosives, recorded calls or sounds, or recorded and electronically imitated or amplified sounds or calls. It shall also be unlawful to use electronic communications equipment for the purpose of facilitating pursuit of any wild animal, game bird, or game animal.

(b)(1) As used in this subsection, the term "computer assisted remote hunting" means the use of a computer or other device, equipment, hardware, or software to control remotely the aiming and discharge of a firearm or other weapon so as to allow a person not holding that firearm or other weapon to hunt or shoot a wild animal or any wildlife.

(2) It shall be unlawful for any person, firm, partnership, or association to engage in computer assisted remote hunting or provide or operate a facility that allows others to engage in computer assisted remote hunting if the wild animal or wildlife being hunted or shot is located in this state.

(3)(A) Any person violating the provisions of this subsection shall be guilty of a misdemeanor of a high and aggravated nature and upon conviction thereof shall be punished by a fine of not less than $1,000.00 and not more than $5,000.00, imprisonment for a term not to exceed 12 months, or both such fine and imprisonment.

(B) Any equipment used or intended for use in a violation of this Code section, excluding motor vehicles, is declared to be contraband and shall be forfeited to the state.

(C) The hunting and fishing privileges of any person convicted of violating this subsection shall be suspended for three years.

**O.C.G.A. § 27-3-16.  Training of Hunting Dogs.**

(a) It shall be unlawful for any person to have in his or her possession any firearms, axes, climbers, or other equipment for taking game while training hunting dogs, provided that handguns with blank ammunition or shot cartridges may be used for training hunting dogs, and shotguns with number six shot or smaller shot may be used while training pointing, flushing, and retrieving dogs using pen raised quail and pigeons.

(b) There is no closed season for training hunting dogs, except as otherwise provided.

(c) It shall be unlawful to run deer with dogs, except during the lawful open season for hunting deer with dogs.

(d) It shall be unlawful to take game by any means while training hunting dogs, except during the lawful open seasons for such game; provided, however, that pen raised quail may be taken at any time for training hunting dogs if the dog trainer maintains proof of purchase of pen raised quail.

(e) It shall be unlawful for any person to train hunting dogs on property other than that owned by such person or his immediate family unless such person has a hunting license in his immediate possession.

## O.C.G.A. § 27-3-19. Hunting and Taking Alligators.

(a) Except as provided in Code Section 27-3-15, it shall be unlawful for any person to hunt alligators within this state. The display or use of a light in any area closed to alligator hunting by any person not otherwise authorized to do so by regulations of the board in a place which alligators might be known to inhabit and in a manner capable of disclosing the presence of alligators, together with the possession of firearms, spear guns, gigs, harpoons, or other such equipment customarily used for the taking of alligators, during the period between one-half hour after sunset and one-half hour before sunrise shall be considered prima-facie evidence of an intent to violate this subsection.

(b) Any person who violates the provisions of subsection (a) of this Code section shall be guilty of a misdemeanor and, upon conviction thereof, shall be punished by a fine of not less than $500.00 and, in the discretion of the sentencing court, imprisonment for not more than 12 months; provided, however, that such fine shall not be subject to suspension, stay, or probation except that if the court finds that payment of such fine would impose great economic hardship upon the defendant, the court may order such fine paid in installments.

(c)(1) It shall be unlawful for any person to possess, buy, or sell in this state the untanned hide or skin or alligator products from an alligator not lawfully taken under the authority of Code Section 27-3-15. All such hides, skins, and alligators not lawfully taken are declared to be contraband and shall be seized and disposed of as directed by the commissioner. Possession in a store, warehouse, or retail place of business of such untanned hides or skins or alligator products not lawfully taken shall be prima-facie evidence of violation of this subsection. This subsection shall not apply to alligator products made from hides or skins of alligators produced on farms licensed under this title or from hides or skins of alligators lawfully possessed, taken, or acquired outside or inside this state, nor shall any provision of this subsection be construed so as to prohibit the preparation, processing, or manufacturing of such commercially grown or lawfully possessed, taken, or acquired alligator hides or the storage or sale of products made therefrom, subject to rules and regulations promulgated by the board.

(2) It shall be unlawful for any person to gather alligator eggs from the wild or possess alligator eggs gathered from the wild in this state except pursuant to permit issued by the department for such purpose. The board shall establish the conditions of such permits by such rules or regulations as are reasonable and necessary under sound game management practices, which shall include without limitation specification of when and where such eggs may be gathered, limits on the number of eggs that may be gathered, the placement of gathered eggs in incubators, return of a minimum percentage and size of hatchlings from gathered eggs to the wild, and permit fees in such amounts as are necessary to cover the cost of administration. This paragraph shall not apply to the collection of alligator eggs from an alligator farm licensed under this title.

(d)(1) It shall be unlawful to possess or transport into this state any untanned alligator hide, skin, or alligator product from any place in which the taking of alligators is prohibited.

(2) It shall be unlawful to possess or transport into this state any alligator eggs gathered from the wild from any place where such gathering of alligator eggs from the wild is prohibited.

(3) All such hides, skins, alligator products, and alligator eggs are declared to be contraband and shall be seized and disposed of in accordance with Code Section 27-1-21.

(4) Notwithstanding any other provision to the contrary, it shall be lawful to possess and transport into this state any untanned alligator hide, skin, alligator product, or alligator egg which was lawfully taken and transported and which is accompanied by a bill of sale, bill of lading, invoice, or permit.

(e) Any person who possesses any untanned alligator hide, skin, alligator product, or alligator

253

egg from any place in which the taking of alligators is lawful, the gathering of alligator eggs from the wild is lawful, or from an alligator farm licensed under this title shall retain such receipts, invoices, bills of lading, permits, or other indicia of lawful possession, taking, or acquisition as are necessary to indicate clearly at all times the place of origin of the specific untanned alligator hides, skins, alligator products, or alligator eggs possessed.

(f) The hunting privileges of a person found guilty of hunting alligators at night in violation of subsection (a) of this Code section shall be suspended by the court of jurisdiction for a period not less than two years.

## O.C.G.A. § 27-3-24. Hunting Feral Dogs.

(a) It shall be unlawful to hunt, or engage in the hunting of, feral hogs:

(1) Upon the lands of another or enter upon the lands of another in pursuit of feral hogs without first obtaining permission from the landowner or lessee of such land or the lessee of the game rights of such land;

(2) Upon any land which is posted without having the permission required by paragraph (1) of this subsection in writing and carried upon the person;

(3) Upon, over, around, or near any land or place upon which any corn, wheat, or other grains, salts, apples, or other feeds or bait which would constitute a lure, attraction, or enticement for any feral hog has been placed, exposed, deposited, distributed, or scattered or upon, over, around, or near any such place for a period of ten days following the complete removal of all such feed or bait; provided, however, this paragraph shall not prohibit the use of bait described in this paragraph for the purpose of trapping feral hogs or hunting feral hogs by means other than a firearm or bow and arrow;

(4) From within a vehicle or while riding on a vehicle at night and with the use of a light;

(5) At night with a light, except that a light which is carried on the person of a hunter, affixed to a helmet or hat worn by a hunter, or part of a belt system worn by a hunter may be used for locating feral hogs; or

(6) During the firearms deer season unless the hunter and each person accompanying the hunter are wearing a total of at least 500 square inches of daylight fluorescent orange material as an outer garment and such material or garment is worn above the waistline, and may include a head covering.

(b) The Board of Natural Resources is authorized by rules or regulations to control and regulate the hunting or taking of feral hogs on wildlife management areas.

## Part 2. Deer

## O.C.G.A. § 27-3-41. Persons Under 12 Prohibited from Hunting Wildlife Alone.

(a) It shall be unlawful for any person who is under 12 years of age to hunt any wildlife in this state unless such person is under the direct supervision of an adult during the period in which such person is hunting.

(b) It shall be unlawful for any person to cause or knowingly permit such person's child or ward who is less than 12 years of age to hunt any wildlife with a weapon in this state unless such child or ward is under adult supervision.

## Article 2. Trapping, Trappers, and Fur Dealers

## O.C.G.A. § 27-3-63. Unlawful Trapping Activities.

(a) It shall be unlawful for any person to:

(1) Trap any wildlife upon the right of way of any public road or highway of this state; provided, however, that this paragraph shall not apply to any person licensed as required by Code

Section 27-3-60 who traps beaver upon the right of way of any state highway, county road, or municipal street as an authorized agent, employee, or contractor of the state, county, or municipality for the purpose of preventing, reducing, or stopping damage to such highway, road, or street resulting from beaver activity;

(2) Set, place, or bait any trap for the purpose of taking any wildlife upon the land or in the waters adjoining the land of any other person, except during the open trapping season for such wildlife, and then only after obtaining the written consent of the owner of the land, which written consent shall be carried upon the trapper's person while engaged in trapping;

(3) Trap any wildlife without inspecting the traps used for such purpose at least once during each 24 hour period and removing from the traps any wildlife caught therein;

(4) Trap any wildlife by the use of any trap or other device which is not legibly etched, stamped, or tagged by affixing a stamped metal tag showing the owner's permanent trapper's identification number as provided by the department or the owner's name. In the event that a trap or other device etched or stamped with the owner's permanent trapper's identification number or name is being used in the field by another, such trap or device must have attached to it a stamped metal tag with the user's permanent trapper's identification number or name. Any trap or other device found in use in the field which is not etched, stamped, or tagged as required by this paragraph may be confiscated and destroyed by the department through its officers and conservation rangers;

(5) Ship or otherwise remove or cause to be removed from this state any raw or undressed hide, fur, pelt, or skin of any fur-bearing animal without first making a report to the department of the removal on forms to be furnished by the department for such purpose;

(6) Fail to carry a weapon of .22 caliber rimfire while tending traps and to fail to use such weapon to dispatch any fur-bearing animal found in a trap, which animal is to be taken by the person;

(7) Fail to carry a choke stick or similar device while tending traps, which device shall be used for releasing domestic animals;

(8) Set on land any trap with a jaw opening larger than 5 3/4 inches, provided that nothing in this Code section shall be construed to restrict the type of trap which may be used in water;

(9) Sell the fur, hide, or pelt of any domestic dog or cat caught by a trap;

(10) Sell the raw, undressed fur, hide, skin, or pelt of any fur-bearing animal unless the person has a current valid commercial trapping license or fur dealer license; or

(11) Set any body-gripping trap (as opposed to a leg-hold trap) of a size in excess of 9 1/2 inches square except in water or on land within ten feet of water, including swamps, marshes, and tidal areas.

(b) Any person who violates subsection (a) of this Code section shall be guilty of a misdemeanor and shall be punished as for a misdemeanor, subject to a minimum punishment as follows:

(1) For the first offense, the offender shall be fined not less than $100.00, except that this minimum fine shall not apply to the offender if he is 17 years of age or younger;

(2) For a second offense within a two-year period after the first offense, the offender shall be fined not less than $300.00; or

(3) For a third offense and for each subsequent offense within a two-year period after the first offense, the offender shall be fined not less than $750.00.

## O.C.G.A. § 27-3-64. Killing Mink or Otter with Firearms is Prohibited.

It shall be unlawful to use any kind of firearm to kill or injure mink or otter or to possess or sell any mink or otter, or the pelt thereof, which was killed by any kind of firearm, provided that nothing in this Code section shall prevent a person from dispatching a mink or otter found in a trap or from killing any mink or otter while it is destroying or damaging, or about to destroy or damage, the person's crops, domestic fowl, or other personal property.

# Chapter 4. Fish
## Article 1. General Provisions

**O.C.G.A. § 27-4-8. Unlawful to Use Firearms and Other Devices to Take Fish.**

It shall be unlawful for any person to use any firearm, battery, generator or other similar device or any dynamite, explosives, or destructive substances, including poisons, walnut hulls, and lime, for the purpose of catching, killing, taking, or harming fish. The possession of any of the foregoing devices or substances, except firearms, in any boat on the fresh waters of this state shall be deemed prima-facie evidence of guilt under this Code section; provided, however, this provision shall not apply to batteries used to operate motors or lights.

**O.C.G.A. § 27-4-11.1. Public Fishing Areas.**

(a) It shall be unlawful for any person on any public fishing area owned or operated by the department:

(1) To possess a firearm other than a handgun, as such term is defined in Code Section 16-11-125.1, during a closed hunting season for that area unless such firearm is unloaded and stored in a motor vehicle so as not to be readily accessible or to possess a handgun during closed hunting season for that area unless such person possesses a valid weapons carry license issued pursuant to Code Section 16-11-129;

(2) To possess a loaded firearm other than a handgun, as such term is defined in Code Section 16-11-125.1, in a motor vehicle during a legal open hunting season for that area or to possess a loaded handgun in a motor vehicle during a legal open hunting season for that area unless such person possesses a valid weapons carry license issued pursuant to Code Section 16-11-129; or

(3) To be under the influence of drugs, intoxicating liquors, beers, or wines. The determination of whether any person is under the influence of drugs or intoxicating liquors, beers, or wines may be made in accordance with the provisions of Chapter 3 of this title relating to hunting while under the influence of drugs or alcohol.

(b) It shall be unlawful for any person to fish at any time in any pond or lake on a public fishing area owned or operated by the department which has been posted "closed" by the department for purposes of fisheries management or to take or possess any species or any size of any species or to exceed the creel limit of any species at any time from any pond or lake on a public fishing area which has been posted with a sign which states that that species or size may not be taken or that creel limit exceeded. Creel and size limits posted as permissible must be within the limits set forth in Code Section 27-4-10 and, if applicable, the limits set by the board pursuant to subsection (c) of this Code section.

(c) It shall be unlawful for any person to take in one day or to possess at any one time any number of fish caught from public fishing areas except in compliance with limits set by rule and regulation of the board, which limits shall not be more than the maximum limit for that species set forth in Code Section 27-4-10.

(d) It shall be unlawful for any person to fish or to be present on any public fishing area except in accordance with rules and regulations established by the board for the use of such area. The board shall have the authority to adopt rules and regulations governing methods of fishing; to regulate the operation and use of vessels; to close the area or certain ponds or lakes of the area to vessels; and to regulate other matters that the board deems necessary for the safe operation and sound management of the area.

(e) It shall be unlawful on any public fishing area for any person to drive or otherwise operate a vehicle on any road posted "closed" to vehicular access, to drive around a closed gate or cable blocking a road, or to drive on any road that is not improved in that it is not receiving maintenance for the purpose of vehicular access. It shall be unlawful for any person to park a vehicle at any place within a public fishing area, including upon the right of way of any county, state, or federal highway which traverses the public fishing area, where signs placed at the direction of the commissioner or his or her designee prohibit parking.

(f) It shall be unlawful for any person to camp anywhere on any public fishing area except in those areas designated by appropriate signs as camping areas.

(g) It shall be unlawful for persons under 14 years of age to enter or remain upon any public fishing area unless such person is under adult supervision. It shall be unlawful for any person to cause or knowingly to permit his or her ward who is under 14 years of age to enter or remain upon any public fishing area unless such child or ward is under adult supervision.

(h) It shall be unlawful for any person who has fished at a public fishing area to refuse to allow department personnel to count, measure, and weigh his or her catch.

## Article 2.  Noncommercial Fishing
## Part 1.  General Provisions

### O.C.G.A. § 27-4-33.  Spearing of Fish.

(a) It shall be unlawful to spear game fish and all species of catfish in the fresh waters of this state except as provided in this Code section; provided, however, other species of nongame fish may be speared solely for the purpose of sport, provided the person engaged in the act of spearing is completely submerged.

(b) "Spearing" as used in this Code section shall be limited to the use of a spear or similar instrument that is held in the hand of the person using the same and the use of a weapon other than a firearm which propels or forces a projectile or similar device therefrom, to which a wire, rope, line, cord, or other means of recovering the projectile or similar device is attached, which wire, rope, line, cord, or other means is secured to the weapon or the person using the weapon.

(c) It shall also be unlawful for any person to engage in the spearing of fish in the fresh waters of this state without a resident or nonresident fishing license as provided in Code Section 27-2-23.

(d) It shall be unlawful to use spears with poisonous or exploding heads.

(e) It shall be unlawful to discharge spears into waters nearer than 150 feet to anyone engaged in any other means of recreation.

(f) Any game fish, except channel catfish and flathead catfish taken under the provisions of subsection (g) of this Code section, with an open wound and in the possession of a person fishing with a spear shall be prima-facie evidence of taking and possessing fish illegally.

(g) It shall be unlawful to take channel catfish and flathead catfish anywhere in the Savannah River, including its tributaries and impoundments within the Savannah River Basin, by means of spearing, except under the following conditions:

(1) The taking of channel catfish and flathead catfish in the Savannah River, including its tributaries and impoundments within the Savannah River Basin, by spear shall be legal at any time of the day and at night by the use of a light; and

(2) All spears used pursuant to this subsection must be equipped with barbs or contain devices on the point to act as a harpoon for recovering fish and must be attached to the person using the spear or to the weapon by a rope, line, or cord sufficient for recovering the spear and channel catfish or flathead catfish.

# Title 28. General Assembly
## Chapter 5. Financial Affairs
### Article 4. Claims Advisory Board
#### Part 3. Compensation of Persons for Injuries Sustained While Preventing Crime or While Aiding Officers of the Law

**O.C.G.A. § 28-5-104. Applicability of Law; Compensation Limits.**

(a) In no event shall the board recommend that compensation be awarded to:

(1) Any victim of a criminal act not provided for in Code Section 28-5-100;

(2) Anyone who:

(A) Is a spouse, parent, grandparent, child (natural or adopted), grandchild, brother, sister, half brother, half sister, or parent of the spouse of the offender;

(B) Was, at the time of the personal injury or death of the victim, living with the offender as a member of his or her family or household or maintaining a sexual relationship, whether illicit or not, with such person or with any member of the family of such person;

(C) Violated a penal law of this state which violation caused or contributed to his or her injuries or death; or

(D) Was injured as a result of the operation of a motor vehicle, boat, or airplane, unless the same was used as a weapon in a deliberate attempt to run the victim down;

(3) Any officer of the law injured in the performance of his or her official duties; or

(4) Any person who is or was at the time of the alleged loss an inmate in the custody of the Department of Corrections.

(b) No compensation shall be recommended by the board in an amount exceeding $5,000.00 per claim.

(c) The board shall, in an advisory way only, recommend to the General Assembly payment of compensation and the amount thereof; and the General Assembly shall act on such recommendation in accordance with law and the rules of the House and Senate for action upon such resolutions.

# Title 33. Insurance
## Chapter 24. Insurance Generally
### Article 1. General Provisions

**O.C.G.A. § 33-24-30.1. Prohibition of Denial of Coverage Based on Firearms on Property.**

No policy of insurance issued or delivered in this state covering any loss, damage, expense, or liability shall exclude or deny coverage because the insured, members of the insured's family, or employees of the insured will keep or carry in a lawful manner firearms on the property or premises of the insured.

# Title 35. Law Enforcement Officers and Agencies
## Chapter 2. Department of Public Safety
### Article 2. Georgia State Patrol

**O.C.G.A. § 35-2-49.1. Disability from Injuries Incurred in the Line of Duty.**

(a) As used in this Code section, the term "disability" means a disability that prevents an individual from working as a law enforcement officer.

(b) When a member of the Uniform Division of the Department of Public Safety leaves the Uniform Division as a result of a disability arising in the line of duty, such member of the Uniform Division shall be entitled as part of such officer's compensation to retain his or her weapon and badge in accordance with regulations promulgated by the commissioner.

## O.C.G.A. § 35-3-4.  Duties, Fingerprinting, and Photographs.

(a) It shall be the duty of the bureau to:

(1) Take, receive, and forward fingerprints, photographs, descriptions, and measurements of persons in cooperation with the bureaus and departments of other states and of the United States;

(2) Exchange information relating to crime and criminals;

(3) Keep permanent files and records of such information procured or received;

(4) Provide for the scientific investigation of articles used in committing crimes or articles, fingerprints, or bloodstains found at the scene of a crime;

(5) Provide for the testing and identification of weapons and projectiles fired therefrom;

(6) Acquire, collect, classify, and preserve any information which would assist in the identification of any deceased individual who has not been identified after the discovery of such deceased individual;

(7) Acquire, collect, classify, and preserve immediately any information which would assist in the location of any missing person, including any minor, and provide confirmation as to any entry for such a person to the parent, legal guardian, or next of kin of that person and the bureau shall acquire, collect, classify, and preserve such information from such parent, guardian, or next of kin;

(8) Exchange such records and information as provided in paragraphs (6) and (7) of this subsection with, and for the official use of, authorized officials of the federal government, the states, cities, counties, and penal and other institutions. With respect to missing minors, such information shall be transmitted immediately to other law enforcement agencies;

(9) Identify and investigate violations of Article 4 of Chapter 7 of Title 16;

(10) Identify and investigate violations of Part 2 of Article 3 of Chapter 12 of Title 16, relating to offenses related to minors; or

(11) Identify and investigate violations of Article 8 of Chapter 9 of Title 16.

(b) In addition to the duties provided in subsection (a) of this Code section, the members of the bureau shall have and are vested with the same authority, powers, and duties as are possessed by the members of the Uniform Division of the Department of Public Safety under this title.

(12) Identify and investigate violations of Article 5 of Chapter 8 of Title 16.

## O.C.G.A. § 35-3-11.  Agents Under Merit System.

(a) All agents of the bureau shall be governed by such rules of position, classification, appointment, promotion, demotion, transfer, dismissal, qualification, compensation, seniority privileges, tenure, and other employment standards as may now or hereafter be established under such merit system controls as may be authorized by Chapter 20 of Title 45, relating to the State Personnel Board and the State Personnel Administration.

(b) This Code section shall not apply to narcotics agents as provided for in Code Section 35-3-9.

(c) As used in this subsection, the term "disability" means a disability that prevents an individual from working as a law enforcement officer. When an agent of the bureau leaves the bureau as a result of a disability arising in the line of duty, such agent shall be entitled as part of such agent's compensation to retain his or her weapon and badge pursuant to regulations promulgated by the director.

# Article 2. Georgia Crime Information Center

## O.C.G.A. § 35-3-33. Functions.

(a) The center shall:

(1) Obtain and file fingerprints, descriptions, photographs, and any other pertinent identifying data on persons who:

(A) Have been or are hereafter arrested or taken into custody in this state:

(i) For an offense which is a felony;

(ii) For an offense which is a misdemeanor or a violation of an ordinance involving burglary tools, commercial gambling, dealing in gambling devices, contributing to the delinquency of a child, dealing in stolen property, dangerous drugs, marijuana, narcotics, firearms, dangerous weapons, explosives, pandering, prostitution, sex offenses where children are victims, or worthless checks;

(iii) For an offense charged as disorderly conduct but which relates to an act connected with one or more of the offenses under division (ii) of this subparagraph;

(iv) As a fugitive from justice; or

(v) For any other offense designated by the Attorney General;

(B) Are or become career criminals, well-known offenders, or habitual offenders;

(C) Are currently or become confined to any prison, penitentiary, or other penal institution;

(D) Are unidentified human corpses found in this state; or

(E) Are children who are charged with an offense that if committed by an adult would be a felony or are children whose cases are transferred from a juvenile court to another court for prosecution;

(2) Compare all fingerprint and other identifying data received with those already on file and, whether or not a criminal record is found for a person, at once inform the requesting agency or arresting officer of such facts as may be disseminated consistent with applicable security and privacy laws and regulations. A log shall be maintained of all disseminations made of each individual criminal history including at least the date and recipient of such information;

(3) Provide a uniform crime reporting system for the periodic collection, analysis, and reporting of crimes reported to and otherwise processed by any and all law enforcement agencies within the state, as defined and provided for in this article;

(4) Periodically conduct audits of crime reporting practices of criminal justice agencies to ensure compliance with the standards of national and state uniform crime reporting systems and to ensure reporting of criminal arrests, dispositions, and custodial information;

(5) Develop, operate, and maintain an information system which will support the collection, storage, retrieval, and dissemination of all crime and offender data described in this article consistent with those principles of scope, security, and responsiveness prescribed by this article;

(6) Cooperate with all criminal justice agencies within the state in providing those forms, procedures, standards, and related training assistance necessary for the uniform operation of the center;

(7) Offer assistance and, when practicable, instruction to all criminal justice agencies in establishing efficient local records systems;

(8) Compile statistics on the nature and extent of crime in the state and compile other data related to planning for and operating criminal justice agencies, provided that such statistics do not identify persons, and make available all such statistical information obtained to the Governor, the General Assembly, and any other governmental agencies whose primary responsibilities include the planning, development, or execution of crime reduction programs. Access to such information by the latter governmental agencies will be on an individual, written request basis wherein must be demonstrated a need to know, the intent of any analyses, dissemination of such analyses, and any security provisions deemed necessary by the center;

(9) Periodically publish in print or electronically statistics, no less frequently than annually,

that do not identify persons and report such information to the Governor, the General Assembly, state and local criminal justice agencies, and the general public. Such information shall accurately reflect the level and nature of crime in the state and the operations in general of the different types of agencies within the criminal justice system;

(10) Make available, upon request, to all local and state criminal justice agencies, all federal criminal justice agencies, and criminal justice agencies in other states any information in the files of the center which will aid these agencies in the performance of their official duties. For this purpose the center shall operate on a 24 hour basis, seven days a week. Such information when authorized by the council may also be made available to any other agency of the state or political subdivision of the state and to any other federal agency upon assurance by the agency concerned that the information is to be used for official purposes only in the prevention or detection of crime or the apprehension of criminal offenders;

(11) Cooperate with other agencies of the state, the crime information agencies of other states, and the Uniform Crime Reports and National Crime Information Center systems of the Federal Bureau of Investigation in developing and conducting an interstate, national, and international system of criminal identification, records, and statistics;

(12) Provide the administrative mechanisms and procedures necessary to respond to those individuals who file requests to view their own records as provided for in this article and to cooperate in the correction of the central center records and those of contributing agencies when their accuracy has been successfully challenged either through the related contributing agencies or by court order issued on behalf of the individual;

(13) Institute the necessary measures in the design, implementation, and continued operation of the criminal justice information system to ensure the privacy and security of the system. This will include establishing complete control over use and access of the system and restricting its integral resources and facilities to those either possessed or procured and controlled by criminal justice agencies as defined in this article. Such security measures must meet standards to be set by the council as well as those set by the nationally operated systems for interstate sharing of information;

(14) Provide availability, by means of data processing, to files listing motor vehicle drivers' license numbers, motor vehicle registration numbers, wanted and stolen motor vehicles, outstanding warrants, identifiable stolen property, and such other files as may be of general assistance to criminal justice agencies; and

(15) Receive and process fingerprints from the Supreme Court of Georgia Office of Bar Admissions for the purpose of determining whether or not an applicant for admission to the State Bar of Georgia has a criminal record. The processing shall include submission of fingerprints to the Georgia Bureau of Investigation and the Federal Bureau of Investigation for comparison to each of their respective files and data bases.

(b) Criminal justice agencies shall furnish upon written request and without charge to any local fire department in this state a copy, processed under purpose code "E", of the criminal history record information of an applicant for employment.

(c) The provisions of this article notwithstanding, information and records of children shall only be inspected and disclosed as provided in Code Sections 15-11-82 and 15-11-83. Such records and information shall be destroyed according to the procedures outlined in Code Sections 15-11-79.2 and 15-11-81.

## O.C.G.A. § 35-3-37. Inspection of Records.

(a) Nothing in this article shall be construed so as to authorize any person, agency, corporation, or other legal entity to invade the privacy of any citizen as defined by the General Assembly or the courts other than to the extent provided in this article.

(b) The center shall make a person's criminal records available for inspection by such person or his or her attorney upon written application to the center. Should the person or his or her attorney contest the accuracy of any portion of the records, it shall be mandatory upon the center to make available to the person or such person's attorney a copy of the contested record upon written application identifying the portion of the record contested and showing the reason for the contest of accuracy. Forms, procedures, identification, and other related aspects pertinent to access to records may be prescribed by the center.

(c) If an individual believes his or her criminal records to be inaccurate or incomplete, he or she may request the original agency having custody or control of the detail records to purge, modify, or supplement them and to notify the center of such changes. Should the agency decline to act or should the individual believe the agency's decision to be unsatisfactory, the individual or his or her attorney may, within 30 days of such decision, enter an appeal to the superior court of the county of his or her residence or to the court in the county where the agency exists, with notice to the agency, to acquire an order by the court that the subject information be expunged, modified, or supplemented by the agency of record. The court shall conduct a de novo hearing and may order such relief as it finds to be required by law. Such appeals shall be entered in the same manner as appeals are entered from the probate court, except that the appellant shall not be required to post bond or pay the costs in advance. If the aggrieved person desires, the appeal may be heard by the judge at the first term or in chambers. A notice sent by registered or certified mail or statutory overnight delivery shall be sufficient service on the agency having custody or control of disputed record that such appeal has been entered. Should the record in question be found to be inaccurate, incomplete, or misleading as set forth in paragraph (3) of subsection (d) of this Code section, the court shall order it to be appropriately expunged, modified, or supplemented by an explanatory notation. Each agency or individual in the state with custody, possession, or control of any such record shall promptly cause each and every copy thereof in his or her custody, possession, or control to be altered in accordance with the court's order. Notification of each such deletion, amendment, and supplementary notation shall be promptly disseminated to any individuals or agencies, including the center, to which the records in question have been communicated, as well as to the individual whose records have been ordered so altered.

(d)(1) An individual who was:

(A) Arrested for an offense under the laws of this state but subsequent to such arrest is released by the arresting agency without such offense being referred to the prosecuting attorney for prosecution; or

(B) After such offense referred to the proper prosecuting attorney, and the prosecuting attorney dismisses the charges without seeking an indictment or filing an accusation may request the original agency in writing to expunge the records of such arrest, including any fingerprints or photographs of the individual taken in conjunction with such arrest, from the agency files. Such request shall be in such form as the center shall prescribe. Reasonable fees shall be charged by the original agency and the center for the actual costs of the purging of such records, provided that such fees shall not exceed $50.00.

(2) Upon receipt of such written request, the agency shall provide a copy of the request to the proper prosecuting attorney. Upon receipt of a copy of the request to expunge a criminal record, the prosecuting attorney shall promptly review the request to determine if it meets the criteria for expungement set forth in paragraph (3) of this subsection. If the request meets those criteria, the prosecuting attorney shall review the records of the arrest to determine if any of the material contained therein must be preserved in order to protect the constitutional rights of an accused under Brady v. Maryland.

(3) An individual has the right to have his or her record of such arrest expunged, including any fingerprints or photographs of the individual taken in conjunction with such arrest, if the prosecuting attorney determines that the following criteria have been satisfied:

(A) The charge was dismissed under the conditions set forth in paragraph (1) of this subsection;

(B) No other criminal charges are pending against the individual; and

(C) The individual has not been previously convicted of the same or similar offense under the laws of this state, the United States, or any other state within the last five years, excluding any period of incarceration.

(4) The agency shall expunge the record by destroying the fingerprint cards, photographs, and documents relating exclusively to such person. Any material which cannot be physically destroyed or which the prosecuting attorney determines must be preserved under Brady v. Maryland shall be restricted by the agency and shall not be subject to disclosure to any person except by direction of the prosecuting attorney or as ordered by a court of record of this state.

(5) It shall be the duty of the agency to notify promptly the center of any records which are expunged pursuant to this subsection. Upon receipt of notice from an agency that a record has been expunged, the center shall, within a reasonable time, restrict access to the criminal history of such person relating to such charge. Records for which access is restricted pursuant to this subsection shall be made available only to criminal justice officials upon written application for official judicial law enforcement or criminal investigative purposes.

(6) If the agency declines to expunge such arrest record, the individual may file an action in the superior court where the agency is located as provided in Code Section 50-13-19. A decision of the agency shall be upheld only if it is determined by clear and convincing evidence that the individual did not meet the criteria set forth in paragraph (3) of this subsection or subparagraphs (A) through (G) of paragraph (7) of this subsection. The court in its discretion may award reasonable court costs including attorney's fees to the individual if he or she prevails in the appellate process. Any such action shall be served upon the agency, the center, the prosecuting attorney having jurisdiction over the offense sought to be expunged, and the Attorney General who may become parties to the action.

(7) After the filing of an indictment or an accusation, a record shall not be expunged if the prosecuting attorney shows that the charges were nolle prossed, dead docketed, or otherwise dismissed because:

(A) Of a plea agreement resulting in a conviction for an offense arising out of the same underlying transaction or occurrence as the conviction;

(B) The government was barred from introducing material evidence against the individual on legal grounds including but not limited to the grant of a motion to suppress or motion in limine;

(C) A material witness refused to testify or was unavailable to testify against the individual unless such witness refused to testify based on his or her statutory right to do so;

(D) The individual was incarcerated on other criminal charges and the prosecuting attorney elected not to prosecute for reasons of judicial economy;

(E) The individual successfully completed a pretrial diversion program, the terms of which did not specifically provide for expungement of the arrest record;

(F) The conduct which resulted in the arrest of the individual was part of a pattern of criminal activity which was prosecuted in another court of this state, the United States, another state, or foreign nation; or

(G) The individual had diplomatic, consular, or similar immunity or inviolability from arrest or prosecution.

(8) If the prosecuting attorney having jurisdiction determines that the records should not be expunged because the criteria set forth in paragraph (3) or subparagraphs (A) through (G) of paragraph (7) of this subsection were not met, and the agency or center fails to follow the prosecuting attorney's recommendation, the prosecuting attorney having jurisdiction over the offense sought to be expunged or the Attorney General may appeal a decision by the agency or center to expunge a criminal history as provided in Code Section 50-13-19.

(9) An individual who has been indicted or charged by accusation that was subsequently

dismissed, dead docketed, or nolle prossed may request an expungement as provided by paragraphs (1) through (3) of this subsection; provided, however, that if the prosecuting attorney objects to the expungement request within 60 days after receiving a copy of said request from the agency, the agency shall decline to expunge and the individual shall have the right to appeal as provided by paragraph (6) of this subsection.

(10) Nothing in this subsection shall be construed as requiring the destruction of incident reports or other records that a crime was committed or reported to law enforcement. Further, nothing in this subsection shall be construed to apply to custodial records maintained by county or municipal jail or detention centers. It shall be the duty of the agency to take such action as may be reasonable to prevent disclosure of information to the public which would identify such person whose records were expunged.

(e) Agencies, including the center, at which criminal offender records are sought to be inspected may prescribe reasonable hours and places of inspection and may impose such additional procedures, fees not to exceed $3.00, or restrictions including fingerprinting as are reasonably necessary to assure the records' security, to verify the identities of those who seek to inspect them, and to maintain an orderly and efficient mechanism for inspection of records.

(f) The provisions of Chapter 13 of Title 50, the "Georgia Administrative Procedure Act," shall not apply to proceedings under this Code section.

(g) If the center has notified a firearms dealer that a person is prohibited from purchasing or possessing a handgun pursuant to Part 5 of Article 4 of Chapter 11 of Title 16 and if the prohibition is the result of such person's being involuntarily hospitalized within the immediately preceding five years, upon such person or his or her attorney making an application to inspect his or her records, the center shall provide the record of involuntary hospitalization and also inform the person or attorney of his or her right to a hearing before the judge of the probate court or superior court relative to such person's eligibility to possess or transport a handgun.

### Article 6. Division of Forensic Services

### O.C.G.A. § 35-3-151. Duties and Responsibilities.
The Division of Forensic Sciences of the Georgia Bureau of Investigation:

(1) Shall provide a state-wide system of laboratories dedicated to conducting forensic analysis of evidence submitted to the laboratory by law enforcement agencies, prosecuting attorneys, coroners, and medical examiners;

(2) Shall provide forensic services to the criminal justice system for the examination and analysis of evidence in the areas of medical examiner inquiries, latent fingerprints, photography, questioned documents, firearms and weapons, trace evidence, implied consent, blood alcohol, toxicology, chemistry, drugs, serology, DNA, and such other areas as the director may authorize or the board shall direct;

(3) Shall establish standards for the identification, collection, transportation, and analysis of forensic evidence;

(4) Shall facilitate independent testing or analysis of evidence within the possession, custody, or control of the division as provided in paragraph (3) of subsection (a) of Code Section 17-16-4, relating to discovery in criminal cases;

(5) Shall provide for and establish uniform fees as approved by the board to be paid to medical examiners, dentists, and other professionals for participating in medical examiners' inquiries or coroners' inquests pursuant to Article 2 of Chapter 16 of Title 45, known as the "Georgia Death Investigation Act";

(6) May assist in the training of law enforcement officers, prosecuting attorneys, coroners, and medical examiners as it relates to forensic sciences in cooperation with the Georgia Peace Officer

Standards and Training Council, the Prosecuting Attorneys' Council of the State of Georgia, and the Georgia Coroner's Training Council, as appropriate; and

(7) May assist in the training of judges and attorneys as it relates to forensic sciences in cooperation with the Institute of Continuing Judicial Education of Georgia and the Institute of Continuing Legal Education, as appropriate.

## Chapter 8. Employment and Training of Peace Officers.

### O.C.G.A. § 35-8-26. Tasers and Electronic Control Weapons.

(a) This Code section shall be known and may be cited as the "TASER and Electronic Control Weapons Act."

(b) It is the intent and purpose of the Georgia General Assembly to establish legal requirements for the official use of electronic control weapons and similar devices by law enforcement officers, including those officers employed in detention facilities, which requirements shall be consistent with generally accepted industry practices. It is the further intent of the General Assembly to require that such devices, commonly referred to as TASERS or stun-guns, which disrupt the central nervous system of the human body, be used for law enforcement purposes in a manner consistent with established standards and with federal and state constitutional provisions.

(c) A law enforcement unit authorizing the use of electronic control weapons or similar devices shall establish lawful written policies and directives providing for the use and deployment of such weapons and devices that are consistent with the training requirements established by the Georgia Peace Officer Standards and Training Council. The policies and directives required by this subsection shall be issued prior to the issuance of such devices.

(d) Prior to the official use of electronic control weapons or similar devices, peace officers authorized by the officer's law enforcement unit to use such devices shall be required to satisfactorily complete a course of instruction and certification requirements approved by the council. All persons certified to use electronic control weapons shall complete an update or refresher training course of such duration and at such time as may be prescribed by the council in order for their electronic control weapons certification to remain in force and effect.

(e) A department head authorizing the use of an electronic control weapon or similar device or a peace officer using an electronic control weapon or similar device in violation of this Code section shall be subject to disciplinary action as provided for in this chapter. The council is authorized to withdraw or suspend the certification to operate an electronic control weapon of any person for failure to meet the update or refresher requirements specified in this Code section or for violation of any portion of this chapter relating to conditions which may lead to the withdrawal, suspension, or probation of a peace officer's certification.

(f) The Georgia Public Safety Training Center shall provide council approved training to peace officers for the use of electronic control weapons and similar devices.

## Chapter 9. Special Policemen

### O.C.G.A. § 35-9-9. Powers and Duties.

(a) Each person appointed as a special policeman under Code Sections 35-9-2 through 35-9-8, this Code section, and Code Sections 35-9-10 through 35-9-12 shall:

(1) Be charged with the duty of protecting and preserving the property described in the application for his appointment;

(2) Have power to arrest all persons trespassing or committing offenses or crimes on the property described in the application for his appointment;

(3) Have and may exercise the powers of a peace officer, but only upon the property or in

connection with the property described in the application for his appointment; and

(4) Have power to possess and carry such firearms and other weapons while on duty as may be prescribed by the appointing authority.

(b) When on duty, a special policeman shall wear a metallic badge upon which shall be inscribed the words "special policeman."

(c) Whenever a person appointed as a special policeman shall change his residence, he shall forthwith give notice of his new address to the appointing authority.

## Title 37. Mental Health
## Chapter 1. Governing and Regulation of Mental Health
## Article 2. Powers and Duties of the Department of Behavioral Health and Developmental Disabilities

### O.C.G.A. § 37-1-27. Suicide Prevention Program.

(a) The General Assembly makes the following findings:

(1) Every year in Georgia, approximately 850 people die from suicide;

(2) More Georgians die from suicide than from homicide;

(3) More teenagers and young adults die from suicide than from cancer, heart disease, AIDS, birth defects, stroke, pneumonia, influenza, and chronic lung disease combined;

(4) Many who attempt suicide do not seek professional help after the attempt;

(5) In Georgia, three out of four suicide deaths involve a firearm;

(6) Factors such as aging, drug and alcohol abuse, unemployment, mental illness, isolation, and bullying in school contribute to causes of suicide; and

(7) Education is necessary to inform the public about the causes of suicide and the early intervention programs that are available.

(b) There is created the Suicide Prevention Program to be managed by the department.

(c) The department, in implementing the Suicide Prevention Program, shall:

(1) Establish a link between state agencies and offices, including but not limited to the Division of Aging Services and Division of Family and Children Services of the Department of Human Services, the Department of Community Health, local government agencies, health care providers, hospitals, nursing homes, and jails to collect data on suicide deaths and attempted suicides;

(2) Work with public officials to improve firearm safety;

(3) Improve education for nurses, judges, physician assistants, social workers, psychologists, and other counselors with regard to suicide education and prevention and expand educational resources for professionals working with those persons most at risk of suicide;

(4) Provide training and minimal screening tools for clergy, teachers and other educational staff, and correctional workers on how to identify and respond to persons at risk of suicide;

(5) Provide educational programs for family members of persons at an elevated risk of suicide;

(6) Develop standardized protocols to be used by the department in reviewing suicide death scene investigations;

(7) Work to increase the number of follow-back studies of suicides;

(8) Work to increase the number of hospitals that code for external causes of injury;

(9) Implement a state-wide reporting system for reporting suicides;

(10) Support pilot projects to link and analyze information on self-destructive behavior from various, distinct data systems; and

(11) Perform such other tasks as deemed appropriate to further suicide education and prevention in Georgia.

(d) The Suicide Prevention Program shall coordinate with and receive technical assistance from epidemiologists and other staff of the Division of Public Health of the Department of Community Health to support the research and outreach efforts related to this program.

## Title 38. Military, Emergency Management, and Veterans' Affairs
### Chapter 2. Military Affairs
### Article 2. Military Administration
### Part 5. Armories and Other Facilities

### O.C.G.A. § 38-2-194. Control of Armories and Other Facilities.

All armories and other facilities defined in Code Section 38-2-190 owned, leased, or maintained by the state or by the United States for use of the organized militia and all activities conducted therein shall be under the general charge and control of the adjutant general. Unless otherwise designated by the adjutant general, the unit commander shall be the officer in charge of the armory and other facilities occupied by his unit; provided, however, that, where two or more units occupy the same armory or facility, the senior unit commander shall be the officer in charge. The officer in charge shall be directly responsible to the adjutant general for carrying out this part and regulations issued pursuant thereto.

### Article 3. Personnel
### Part 4. Rights, Privileges, and Prohibitions

### O.C.G.A. § 38-2-277. Unauthorized Military Bodies.

(a) No body of men other than the organized militia, components of the armed forces of the United States, and bodies of the police and state constabulary and such other organizations as may be formed under this chapter shall associate themselves together as a military unit or parade or demonstrate in public with firearms.

(b) Associations wholly comprised of military personnel honorably discharged from the service of the United States and benevolent and secret organizations may parade in public with swords. Students in educational institutions where military science is a prescribed part of the course of instruction may drill or parade with firearms in public under the supervision of their instructors. This Code section shall not be construed to prevent parades in public with firearms by authorized organizations of the organized militia of any other state.

(c) No political subdivision of this state shall raise or appropriate any money toward arming, equipping, uniforming, or in any other way supporting, sustaining, or providing drill rooms or armories for any such unauthorized organizations.

(d) Any person who actively participates in an unauthorized military organization or who parades with any unauthorized body of men as set forth in subsection (a) of this Code section shall be guilty of a misdemeanor.

### Article 4. Active Duty Powers

### O.C.G.A. § 38-2-301. Closing Places Where Firearms and Ammunition is Sold.

(a) Whenever any force of the organized militia is or has been called out for the performance of any duty under Code Section 38-2-6, it shall be lawful for the commanding officer of the force, if in his judgment the maintenance of law and order in the area into which the force has been ordered will be promoted thereby, to close places where arms and ammunition are sold and all places where disorder is likely to occur.

(b) Any person who sells or dispenses arms or ammunition in violation of an order of a commanding officer under the authority of subsection (a) of this Code section or who maintains a place ordered to be closed under such authority shall be guilty of a felony and, upon conviction thereof, shall be punished by imprisonment for not less than two nor more than five years.

## Chapter 3. Emergency Management
### Article 3. Emergency Powers
### Part 1. Governor

### O.C.G.A. § 38-3-51. Emergency Powers of Governor.

(a) In the event of actual or impending emergency or disaster of natural or human origin, or pandemic influenza emergency, or impending or actual enemy attack, or a public health emergency, within or affecting this state or against the United States, the Governor may declare that a state of emergency or disaster exists. As a condition precedent to declaring that a state of emergency or disaster exists as a result of a public health emergency, the Governor shall issue a call for a special session of the General Assembly pursuant to Article V, Section II, Paragraph VII of the Constitution of Georgia, which session shall convene at 8:00 A.M. on the second day following the date of such declaration for the purpose of concurring with or terminating the public health emergency. The state of emergency or disaster shall continue until the Governor finds that the threat or danger has passed or the emergency or disaster has been dealt with, to the extent that emergency or disaster conditions no longer exist, and terminates the state of emergency or disaster. No state of emergency or disaster may continue for longer than 30 days unless renewed by the Governor. The General Assembly by concurrent resolution may terminate a state of emergency or disaster at any time. Thereupon, the Governor shall by appropriate action end the state of emergency or disaster.

(b) A declaration of a state of emergency or disaster shall activate the emergency and disaster response and recovery aspects of the state and local emergency or disaster plans applicable to the political subdivision or area in question and shall be authority for the deployment and use of any forces to which the plan or plans apply and for use or distribution of any supplies, equipment, and materials and facilities assembled, stockpiled, or arranged to be made available pursuant to Articles 1 through 3 of this chapter or any other law relating to emergencies or disasters.

(c) The Governor shall have and may exercise for such period as the state of emergency or disaster exists or continues the following additional emergency powers:

(1) To enforce all laws, rules, and regulations relating to emergency management and to assume direct operational control of all civil forces and helpers in the state;

(2) To seize, take for temporary use, or condemn property for the protection of the public in accordance with condemnation proceedings as provided by law;

(3) To sell, lend, give, or distribute all or any such property among the inhabitants of the state and to account to the proper agency for any funds received for the property; and

(4) To perform and exercise such other functions, powers, and duties as may be deemed necessary to promote and secure the safety and protection of the civilian population.

(d) In addition to any other emergency powers conferred upon the Governor by law, he may:

(1) Suspend any regulatory statute prescribing the procedures for conduct of state business, or the orders, rules, or regulations of any state agency, if strict compliance with any statute, order, rule, or regulation would in any way prevent, hinder, or delay necessary action in coping with the emergency or disaster;

(2) Utilize all available resources of the state government and of each political subdivision of the state as reasonably necessary to cope with the emergency or disaster;

(3) Transfer the direction, personnel, or functions of state departments and agencies or units thereof for the purpose of performing or facilitating emergency services;

(4) Commandeer or utilize any private property if he finds this necessary to cope with the emergency or disaster;

(4.1) Compel a health care facility to provide services or the use of its facility if such services or use are reasonable and necessary for emergency response. The use of such health care facility may include transferring the management and supervision of the health care facility to the Department of Community Health for a limited or unlimited period of time not extending beyond the termination of the public health emergency;

(5) Direct and compel the evacuation of all or part of the population from any stricken or threatened area within the state if he deems this action necessary for the preservation of life or other disaster mitigation, response, or recovery;

(6) Prescribe routes, modes of transportation, and destinations in connection with evacuation;

(7) Control ingress and egress to and from a disaster area, the movement of persons within the area, and the occupancy of premises therein;

(8) Suspend or limit the sale, dispensing, or transportation of alcoholic beverages, firearms, explosives, and combustibles; provided, however, that any limitation on firearms under this Code section shall not include an individual firearm owned by a private citizen which was legal and owned by that citizen prior to the declaration of state of emergency or disaster or thereafter acquired in compliance with all applicable laws of this state and the United States; and

(9) Make provision for the availability and use of temporary emergency housing.

(e) When the available funds are not sufficient for the purpose of paying the expenses incident to carrying out the provisions authorized by Articles 1 through 3 of this chapter, the Governor may transfer from any available fund in the state treasury such sum as may be necessary to meet the emergency or disaster; and the moneys so transferred shall be repaid to the fund from which transferred when moneys become available for that purpose by legislative appropriation or otherwise.

(f) In the event that the Governor proclaims an emergency or disaster, as defined by Articles 1 through 3 of this chapter, to be a catastrophe within the meaning of Article III, Section IX, Paragraph VI(b) of the Constitution of the state, the funds referred to in the paragraph may be utilized by the Governor for the purpose of carrying out the provisions authorized by Articles 1 through 3 of this chapter.

(g) In the event that the Governor proclaims an emergency or disaster, as defined in Articles 1 through 3 of this chapter, the Governor may provide welfare benefits to the citizens of this state in the form of grants to meet disaster related necessary expenses or serious needs of individuals or families adversely affected by an emergency or disaster in those cases where the individuals or families are unable to meet the expenses or needs from other means, provided that such grants are authorized only when matching federal funds are available for such purposes pursuant to the Disaster Relief Act of 1974 [FN1] (Pub. L. 93-288).

(h) If the Governor declares a state of emergency solely because of an energy emergency, he shall not have the authority to:

(1) Seize, take for temporary use, or condemn property other than energy resources as authorized by paragraph (2) of subsection (c) of this Code section;

(2) Sell, lend, give, or distribute property other than energy resources as authorized by paragraph (3) of subsection (c) of this Code section; or

(3) Commandeer or utilize property other than energy resources as authorized by paragraph (4) of subsection (d) of this Code section.

(i)(1) The Governor may direct the Department of Community Health to coordinate all matters pertaining to the response of the state to a public health emergency including without limitation:

(A) Planning and executing public health emergency assessments, mitigation, preparedness response, and recovery for the state;

(B) Coordinating public health emergency responses between state and local authorities;

(C) Collaborating with appropriate federal government authorities, elected officials of other states, private organizations, or private sector companies;

(D) Coordinating recovery operations and mitigation initiatives subsequent to public health emergencies;

(E) Organizing public information activities regarding state public health emergency response operations; and

(F) Providing for special identification for public health personnel involved in a public health emergency.

(2) The following due process procedures shall be applicable to any quarantine or vaccination program instituted pursuant to a declaration of a public health emergency:

(A) Consonant with maintenance of appropriate quarantine rules, the department shall permit access to counsel in person or by such other means as practicable that do not threaten the integrity of the quarantine;

(B) An order imposing a quarantine or a vaccination program may be appealed but shall not be stayed during the pendency of the challenge. The burden of proof shall be on the state to demonstrate that there exists a substantial risk of exposing other persons to imminent danger. With respect to vaccination, the state's burden of proof shall be met by clear and convincing evidence. With respect to quarantine, the state's burden of proof shall be met by a preponderance of the evidence;

(C) An individual or a class may challenge the order before any available judge of the state courts, the superior courts, the Court of Appeals, or the Supreme Court. Such judge, upon attestation of the exigency of the circumstances, may proceed ex parte with respect to the state or may appoint counsel to represent the interests of the state or other unrepresented parties. The judge hearing the matter may consolidate a multiplicity of cases or, on the motion of a party or of the court, proceed to determine the interests of a class or classes. The rules of evidence applicable to civil cases shall be applied to the fullest extent practicable taking into account the circumstances of the emergency. All parties shall have the right to subpoena and cross-examine witnesses, but in enforcement of its subpoena powers the court shall take into account the circumstances of the emergency. All proceedings shall be transcribed to the extent practicable. Filing fees shall be waived and all costs borne by the state;

(D) The judge hearing the matter may enter an appropriate order upholding or suspending the quarantine or vaccination order. With respect to vaccination, the order may be applicable on notice to the department or its agents administering the vaccination, or otherwise in the court's discretion. With respect to quarantines, the order shall be automatically stayed for 48 hours;

(E) The department or any party may appeal any order within 24 hours to the Court of Appeals, the Supreme Court, or to any available judge thereof in the event that circumstances render a full court unavailable. If the trial judge has proceeded ex parte or with counsel appointed for the state, the trial court shall either direct the filing of an appeal in its order or itself certify the order for appeal. Filing fees for appeal shall be waived, all costs shall be borne by the state, and such appeals shall be heard expeditiously; and

(F) No provisions of this paragraph shall be construed to limit or restrict the right of habeas corpus under the laws of the United States.

(j) Any individual, partnership, association, or corporation who acts in accordance with an order, rule, or regulation entered by the Governor pursuant to the authority granted by this Code section will not be held liable to any other individual, partnership, association, or corporation by reason thereof in any action seeking legal or equitable relief.

## Chapter 5. Drivers' Licenses
## Article 2. Issuance, Expiration, and Renewal of License

### O.C.G.A. § 40-5-22. Persons Not to be Issued License.

(a) Except as otherwise provided in this Code section, the department shall not issue any

Class C driver's license to any person who is under 18 years of age or Class M driver's license to any person who is under the age of 17 years, except that the department may, under subsection (a) of Code Section 40-5-24, issue a Class P instruction permit permitting the operation of a noncommercial Class C vehicle to any person who is at least 15 years of age, and may, under subsection (b) of Code Section 40-5-24, issue a Class D driver's license permitting the operation of a noncommercial Class C vehicle to any person who is at least 17 years of age. On and after January 1, 1985, the department shall not issue any driver's license to any person under 18 years of age unless such person presents a certificate or other evidence acceptable to the department which indicates satisfactory completion of an alcohol and drug course as prescribed in subsection (b) of Code Section 20-2-142; provided, however, that a person under 18 years of age who becomes a resident of this state and who has in his or her immediate possession a valid license issued to him or her in another state or country shall not be required to take or complete the alcohol and drug course. The department shall not issue a driver's license or a Class P instruction permit for the operation of a Class A or B vehicle or any commercial driver's license to any person who is under the age of 18 years.

(a.1)(1) The department shall not issue an instruction permit or driver's license to a person who is younger than 18 years of age unless at the time such minor submits an application for an instruction permit or driver's license the applicant presents acceptable proof that he or she has received a high school diploma, a general educational development (GED) diploma, a special diploma, or a certificate of high school completion or has terminated his or her secondary education and is enrolled in a postsecondary school, is pursuing a general educational development (GED) diploma, or the records of the department indicate that said applicant:

(A) Is enrolled in and not under expulsion from a public or private school and has satisfied relevant attendance requirements as set forth in paragraph (2) of this subsection for a period of one academic year prior to application for an instruction permit or driver's license; or

(B) Is enrolled in a home education program that satisfies the reporting requirements of all state laws governing such program.

The department shall notify such minor of his or her ineligibility for an instruction permit or driver's license at the time of such application.

(2) The department shall forthwith notify by certified mail or statutory overnight delivery, return receipt requested, any minor issued an instruction permit or driver's license in accordance with this subsection other than a minor who has terminated his or her secondary education and is enrolled in a postsecondary school or who is pursuing a general educational development (GED) diploma that such minor's instruction permit or driver's license is suspended subject to review as provided for in this subsection if the department receives notice that indicates that such minor:

(A) Has dropped out of school without graduating and has remained out of school for ten consecutive school days;

(B) Has ten or more school days of unexcused absences in the current academic year or ten or more school days of unexcused absences in the previous academic year; or

(C) Has been found in violation by a hearing officer, panel, or tribunal of one of the following offenses, has received a change in placement for committing one of the following offenses, or has waived his or her right to a hearing and pleaded guilty to one of the following offenses:

(i) Threatening, striking, or causing bodily harm to a teacher or other school personnel;

(ii) Possession or sale of drugs or alcohol on school property or at a school sponsored event;

(iii) Possession or use of a weapon on school property or at a school sponsored event. For purposes of this division, the term weapon shall have the same meaning as in Code Section 16-11-127.1 but shall not include any part of an archeological or cultural exhibit brought to school in connection with a school project;

(iv) Any sexual offense prohibited under Chapter 6 of Title 16; or

(v) Causing substantial physical or visible bodily harm to or seriously disfiguring another person, including another student.

Notice given by certified mail or statutory overnight delivery with return receipt requested mailed to the person's last known address shall be prima-facie evidence that such person received the required notice. Such notice shall include instructions to the minor to return immediately the instruction permit or driver's license to the department and information summarizing the minor's right to request an exemption from the provisions of this subsection. The minor so notified may request in writing a hearing within ten business days from the date of receipt of notice. Within 30 days after receiving a written request for a hearing, the department shall hold a hearing as provided for in Chapter 13 of Title 50, the Georgia Administrative Procedure Act. After such hearing, the department shall sustain its order of suspension or rescind such order. The department shall be authorized to grant an exemption from the provisions of this subsection to a minor, upon such minor's petition, if there is clear and convincing evidence that the enforcement of the provisions of this subsection upon such minor would create an undue hardship upon the minor or the minor's family or if there is clear and convincing evidence that the enforcement of the provisions of this subsection would act as a detriment to the health or welfare of the minor. Appeal from such hearing shall be in accordance with said chapter. If no hearing is requested within the ten business days specified above, the right to a hearing shall have been waived and the instruction permit or driver's license of the minor shall remain suspended. The suspension provided for in this paragraph shall be for a period of one year or shall end upon the date of such minor's eighteenth birthday or, if the suspension was imposed pursuant to subparagraph (A) of this paragraph, upon receipt of satisfactory proof that the minor is pursuing or has received a general educational development (GED) diploma, a high school diploma, a special diploma, a certificate of high school completion, or has terminated his or her secondary education and is enrolled in a postsecondary school, whichever comes first.

(3) The State Board of Education and the commissioner of driver services are authorized to promulgate rules and regulations to implement the provisions of this subsection.

(4) The Technical College System of Georgia shall be responsible for compliance and noncompliance data for students pursuing a general educational development (GED) diploma.

(a.2)(1) On and after January 1, 2002, the department shall not issue any initial Class D driver's license or, in the case of a person who has never been issued a Class D driver's license by the department or the equivalent thereof by any other jurisdiction, any initial Class C driver's license unless such person:

(A) Is at least 16 years of age and has completed an approved driver education course in a licensed private or public driver training school and in addition a cumulative total of at least 40 hours of other supervised driving experience including at least six hours at night, all of which is verified in writing signed before a person authorized to administer oaths by a parent or guardian of the applicant or by the applicant if such person is at least 18 years of age; or

(B) Is at least 17 years of age and has completed a cumulative total of at least 40 hours of supervised driving experience including at least six hours at night, and the same is verified in writing signed before a person authorized to administer oaths by a parent or guardian of the applicant or by the applicant if such person is at least 18 years of age; provided, however, that a person 17 years of age or older who becomes a resident of this state, who meets all of the qualifications for issuance of a Class C license with the exception of the completion of an approved driver education training course and at least 40 hours of supervised driving experience as required by this subsection, and who has in his or her immediate possession a valid license equivalent to a Class C license issued to him or her in another state or country shall be entitled to receive a Class C license.

(2) The commissioner shall by rule or regulation establish standards for approval of any driver education course for purposes of subparagraph (A) of paragraph (1) of this subsection, provided that such course shall be designed to educate young drivers about safe driving practices and the traffic laws of this state and to train young drivers in the safe operation of motor vehicles.

(3) For purposes of supervised driving experience under paragraph (1) of this subsection, supervision shall be provided by a person at least 21 years of age who is licensed as a driver for a commercial or noncommercial Class C vehicle, who is fit and capable of exercising control over the vehicle, and who is occupying a seat beside the driver.

(4) For the purposes of this Code section, the term "approved driver education training course" shall include those driver education training courses approved by the Department of Driver Services.

(5) For purposes of this Code section, the term approved driver education training course shall include instruction given in the course of a home education program that satisfies the reporting requirements of all state laws governing such programs, provided that such instruction utilizes a curriculum approved by the department.

(b)(1) Notwithstanding the provisions of subsection (a) of this Code section, any person 14 years of age who has a parent or guardian who is medically incapable of being licensed to operate a motor vehicle due to visual impairment may apply for and, subject to the approval of the commissioner, may be issued a restricted noncommercial Class P instruction permit for the operation of a noncommercial Class C vehicle. Any person permitted pursuant to this subsection shall be accompanied by such visually impaired parent or guardian whenever operating a motor vehicle.

(2) Notwithstanding the provisions of subsection (a) of this Code section, any person 15 years of age or older who has a parent or guardian who is medically incapable of being licensed to operate a motor vehicle due to physical impairment and has been issued an identification card containing the international handicapped symbol pursuant to Article 8 of this chapter may apply for and, subject to the approval of the commissioner, may be issued a restricted noncommercial Class P instruction permit for the operation of a noncommercial Class C vehicle. Any person permitted pursuant to this paragraph shall be accompanied whenever operating a motor vehicle by such physically impaired parent or guardian or by a person at least 21 years of age who is licensed as a driver for a commercial or noncommercial Class C vehicle, who is fit and capable of exercising control over the vehicle, and who is occupying a seat beside the driver. The department shall require satisfactory proof that the physically impaired parent or guardian previously held a valid driver's license in the State of Georgia, another state, or the District of Columbia before issuing an instructional permit pursuant to this paragraph.

(c) The department shall not issue any driver's license to nor renew the driver's license of any person:

(1) Whose license has been suspended during such suspension, or whose license has been revoked, except as otherwise provided in this chapter;

(2) Whose license is currently under suspension or revocation in any other jurisdiction upon grounds which would authorize the suspension or revocation of a license under this chapter;

(3) Who is a habitual user of alcohol or any drug to a degree rendering him or her incapable of safely driving a motor vehicle;

(4) Who has previously been adjudged to be afflicted with or suffering from any mental disability or disease and who has not at the time of application been restored to competency by the methods provided by law;

(5) Who is required by this chapter to take an examination, unless such person shall have successfully passed such examination;

(6) Who the commissioner has good cause to believe would not, by reason of physical or mental disability, be able to operate a motor vehicle with safety upon the highway; or

(7) Whose license issued by any other jurisdiction is suspended or revoked by such other jurisdiction during the period such license is suspended or revoked by such other jurisdiction.

## Title 41. Nuisances
## Chapter 1. General Provisions

**O.C.G.A. § 41-1-9. Shooting Ranges Not to be Deemed Nuisances Due to Changed Circumstances.**

(a) As used in this Code section, the term:

(1) "Person" means an individual, proprietorship, partnership, corporation, or unincorporated association.

(2) "Sport shooting range" or "range" means an area designated and operated by a person for the sport shooting of firearms and not available for such use by the general public without payment of a fee, membership contribution, or dues or by invitation of an authorized person, or any area so designated and operated by a unit of government, regardless of the terms of admission thereto.

(3) "Unit of government" means any of the departments, agencies, authorities, or political subdivisions of the state, cities, municipal corporations, townships, or villages and any of their respective departments, agencies, or authorities.

(b) No sport shooting range shall be or shall become a nuisance, either public or private, solely as a result of changed conditions in or around the locality of such range if the range has been in operation for one year since the date on which it commenced operation as a sport shooting range. Subsequent physical expansion of the range or expansion of the types of firearms in use at the range shall not establish a new date of commencement of operations for purposes of this Code section.

(c) No sport shooting range or unit of government or person owning, operating, or using a sport shooting range for the sport shooting of firearms shall be subject to any action for civil or criminal liability, damages, abatement, or injunctive relief resulting from or relating to noise generated by the operation of the range if the range remains in compliance with noise control or nuisance abatement rules, regulations, statutes, or ordinances applicable to the range on the date on which it commenced operation.

(d) No rules, regulations, statutes, or ordinances relating to noise control, noise pollution, or noise abatement adopted or enacted by a unit of government shall be applied retroactively to prohibit conduct at a sport shooting range, which conduct was lawful and being engaged in prior to the adoption or enactment of such rules, regulations, statutes, or ordinances.

## Title 42. Penal Institutions
## Chapter 4. Jails
## Article 1. General Provisions

**O.C.G.A. § 42-4-13. Smuggling Contraband to Inmates.**

(a) As used in this Code section, the term:

(1) "Alcoholic beverage" means and includes all alcohol, distilled spirits, beer, malt beverage, wine, or fortified wine.

(2) "Controlled substance" means a drug, substance, or immediate precursor as defined in Code Section 16-13-21.

(3) "Dangerous drug" has the same meaning as defined by Code Section 16-13-71.

(4) "Jail" means any county jail, municipal jail, or any jail or detention facility operated by a county, municipality, or a regional jail authority as authorized under Article 5 of this chapter.

(5) "Jailer" means the sheriff in the case of any county jail, or the chief of police if the jail is under the supervision of the chief of police of a municipality, or the warden, captain, administrator, superintendent, or other officer having supervision of any other jail, or the designee of such officer.

(b)(1) It shall be unlawful for an inmate of a jail to possess any controlled substance, dangerous drug, gun, pistol, or other dangerous weapon or marijuana.

(2) Any person who violates paragraph (1) of this subsection shall be guilty of a felony and, upon conviction thereof, shall be imprisoned for not less than one nor more than five years.

(3) Notwithstanding the provisions of this subsection, possession of a controlled substance, a dangerous drug, or marijuana shall be punished as provided in Chapter 13 of Title 16; provided, however, that the provisions of Code Section 16-13-2 shall not apply to a violation of paragraph (1) of this subsection.

(4) The provisions of this subsection shall not prohibit the lawful use or dispensing of a controlled substance or dangerous drug to an inmate with the knowledge and consent of the jailer when such use or dispensing is lawful under the provisions of Chapter 13 of Title 16.

(c)(1) Unless otherwise authorized by law, it shall be unlawful for an inmate of a jail to possess any alcoholic beverage.

(2) Any person who violates paragraph (1) of this subsection shall be guilty of a misdemeanor.

(d)(1)(A) It shall be unlawful for any person to come inside the guard lines established at any jail with, or to give or have delivered to an inmate of a jail, any controlled substance, dangerous drug, marijuana, or any gun, pistol, or other dangerous weapon without the knowledge and consent of the jailer or a law enforcement officer.

(B) It shall be unlawful for any person to come inside the guard lines established at any jail with, or to give or have delivered to an inmate of a jail, any alcoholic beverage without the knowledge and consent of the jailer or a law enforcement officer; provided, however, that the provisions of this subsection shall not apply to nor prohibit the use of an alcoholic beverage by a clergyman or priest in sacramental services only.

(2) Except as otherwise provided in paragraph (3) of this subsection, any person who violates subparagraph (A) of paragraph (1) of this subsection shall be guilty of a felony and, upon conviction thereof, shall be imprisoned for not less than one nor more than five years. Any person who violates subparagraph (B) of paragraph (1) of this subsection shall be guilty of a misdemeanor.

(3) Notwithstanding the provisions of paragraph (2) of this subsection, the possession, possession with intent to distribute, trafficking, or distribution of a controlled substance or marijuana shall be punished as provided in Chapter 13 of Title 16; provided, however, that the provisions of Code Section 16-13-2 shall not apply to a violation of subparagraph (A) of paragraph (1) of this subsection.

(e) It shall be unlawful for any person to obtain, to procure for, or to give to an inmate, or to bring within the guard lines, any other article or item without the knowledge and consent of the jailer or a law enforcement officer. Any person violating this subsection shall be guilty of a misdemeanor.

(f)(1) It shall be unlawful for any person to come inside the guard lines or be within any jail while under the influence of a controlled substance, dangerous drug, or marijuana without the knowledge and consent of the jailer or a law enforcement officer unless such person has a valid prescription for such controlled substance or dangerous drug issued by a person licensed under Chapter 11 or 34 of Title 43 and such prescribed substance is consumed only as authorized by the prescription. Any person convicted of a violation of this subsection shall be punished by imprisonment for not less than one nor more than four years.

(2) It shall be unlawful for any person to come inside the guard lines or be within any jail while under the influence of alcohol without the knowledge and consent of the jailer or a law enforcement officer. Any person violating this subsection shall be guilty of a misdemeanor.

(g) It shall be unlawful for any person to loiter where inmates are assigned after having been ordered by the jailer or a law enforcement officer to desist therefrom. Any person violating this subsection shall be guilty of a misdemeanor.

(h) It shall be unlawful for any person to attempt, conspire, or solicit another to commit any offense defined by this Code section and, upon conviction thereof, shall be punished by imprisonment not exceeding the maximum punishment prescribed for the offense, the commission of which was the object of the attempt, conspiracy, or solicitation.

(i) Any violation of this Code section shall constitute a separate offense.

(j) Perimeter guard lines shall be established at every jail by the jailer thereof. Such guard lines shall be clearly marked by signs on which shall be plainly stamped or written: "Guard line of _____." Signs shall also be placed at all entrances and exits for vehicles and pedestrians at the jail and at such intervals along the guard lines as will reasonably place all persons approaching the guard lines on notice of the location of the jail.

## Title 43. Professions and Businesses
## Chapter 16. Firearms Dealers

### O.C.G.A. § 43-16-1. Department of Public Safety.

As used in this chapter, the term 'department' means the Department of Public Safety.

### O.C.G.A. § 43-16-2. License for Dealers.

Any person, firm, retail dealer, wholesale dealer, pawnbroker, or corporation who shall sell, dispose of, or offer for sale or cause or permit to be sold, disposed of, or offered for sale any pistol, revolver, or short-barreled firearm of less than 15 inches in length, whether the same shall be his own property or whether he shall sell the same as an agent or employee of another, shall obtain from the department a license permitting the sale of such pistols, revolvers, and firearms. Nothing in this chapter shall apply to or prohibit the casual sales of the articles referred to in this Code section between individuals or bona fide gun collectors.

### O.C.G.A. § 43-16-3. Affidavit to be Included with Dealer Application.

Any person, firm, retail dealer, wholesale dealer, pawnbroker, or corporation who makes application for a license under this chapter must accompany such application with an affidavit of the applicant sworn to before an officer authorized by law to administer oaths, stating that the applicant is a citizen of the United States, has reached the age of 21 years, and has not been convicted of a felony.

### O.C.G.A. § 43-16-4. Reserved.

### O.C.G.A. § 43-16-5. Annual Dealer License Fee.

All annual license fees described by this chapter shall be paid to the department on or before July 1 of each year. The department shall issue its receipt for every payment. The annual license payment to acquire such license shall be $ 25.00 for the owner of any establishment which sells any firearms listed in Code Section 43-16-2. The annual employee license fee shall be $ 3.00.

### O.C.G.A. § 43-16-6. Disposition of Annual Dealer License Fees.

All fees derived under this chapter shall be paid into the general fund of the state treasury; and the funds necessary to pay the expense of administering this chapter shall be derived from appropriations made to the department.

### O.C.G.A. § 43-16-7. Display of Dealer License.

Every recipient of a license to sell any firearms listed in Code Section 43-16-2 shall keep such license conspicuously displayed on his business premises.

### O.C.G.A. § 43-16-8. Revocation of Dealer License for Nonpayment of Fee.

Should any licensee fail or neglect to pay his annual license fee on or before July 1 of every year, the department shall notify him that his license will be revoked. Unless the fee is paid in full before

August 1 of the same year, the department shall revoke the license.

## O.C.G.A. § 43-16-9. Reinstatement fee.

The owner of any establishment or employee thereof whose license for selling such firearms has been revoked for failure to pay the annual license fee may make application to the department for reinstatement. Such application shall be accompanied by a fee of $ 10.00, in addition to the regular license fee required. If the department shall find the applicant guilty only of default in payment of annual license fees, the license may be immediately reinstated.

## O.C.G.A. § 43-16-10. Revocation for Fraud, Violation of Ethics, or Crime.

The department shall have the power to revoke any license granted by it under this chapter to any person, firm, retail dealer, wholesale dealer, pawnbroker, or corporation, or any agent or employee thereof, found by the Board of Public Safety to be guilty of fraud or willful misrepresentation, or found guilty under the laws of this state of any crime involving moral turpitude, or found guilty of violating Code Section 16-11-101.

## O.C.G.A. § 43-16-10.1. Firearms Records.

(a) As a condition of any license issued pursuant to this chapter, each licensee shall be required to keep a record of the acquisition and disposition of firearms as provided in this Code section.

(b) The record required by subsection (a) of this Code section shall be identical in form and context to the firearms acquisition and disposition record required by Part 178 of Chapter 1 of Title 27 of the Code of Federal Regulations as it exists on July 1, 1988.

(c) The record required by subsection (a) of this Code section shall be maintained on the licensed premises and shall be open to the inspection of any duly authorized law enforcement officer during the ordinary hours of business or at any reasonable time. The record of each acquisition or disposition of a firearm shall be maintained for a period of not less than five years.

(d) The failure of a licensee to keep and maintain the records required by this Code section shall be grounds for revocation of the license.

## O.C.G.A. § 43-16-11. Revocation Proceedings.

All proceedings for the revocation of licenses issued under this chapter shall be governed by Chapter 13 of Title 50, the "Georgia Administrative Procedure Act."

## O.C.G.A. § 43-16-12. Punishment.

Any person, firm, or corporation who violates this chapter shall be guilty of a misdemeanor.

## Chapter 38. Operators of Private Detective Businesses and Private Security Businesses.

## O.C.G.A. § 43-38-10. Permits to Carry Firearms.

(a) The board may grant a permit to carry a pistol, revolver, or other firearm to any person who is at least 21 years of age and who is licensed or registered in accordance with this chapter and who meets the qualifications and training requirements set forth in this Code section and such other qualifications and training requirements as the board by rule may establish. The board shall have the authority to establish limits on type and caliber of such weapons by rule. Application for such permit and for renewal thereof shall be made on forms provided by the division director. No weapons permit issued under this Code section shall be transferable to another individual.

(b) No permit under this Code section shall be issued or renewed until the applicant has presented proof to the board that he is proficient in the use of firearms. The board shall have the authority to require periodic recertification of proficiency in the use of firearms and to refuse to renew a permit upon failure to comply with such requirement. The applicant shall present proof to the board that:

(1) He has demonstrated on the firearms range proficiency in the use of firearms by meeting such minimum qualifications on pistol and shotgun (if so armed) courses as the board may prescribe by rule; and

(2) He has received such other training and instruction in the use of firearms as the board may require by rule.

(c) All licensees and registrants under this chapter shall be required to obtain from the board a weapons permit under this Code section if a firearm is carried, or is to be carried, by such licensee or registrant while at or en route directly to and from his post or place of employment.

(d) Any licensee or registrant under this chapter meeting the qualifications and training requirements set out in this Code section may be issued an exposed weapons permit in accordance with this Code section and shall be authorized to carry such firearm in an open and fully exposed manner. Such carrying of a firearm shall be limited to the time the licensee or registrant is on duty or en route directly to and from his post or place of employment. No stopover en route to and from such post or place of employment is permitted under the terms of this Code section.

(e) Licensees or registrants under this chapter may apply to the board for a concealed weapons permit. Qualifications and training requirements for such permits and restrictions on such permits shall be established by appropriate rules of the board. The board shall, in its discretion, consider and approve each application for a concealed weapons permit on an individual basis.

(f) An individual issued a permit in accordance with this Code section shall be exempt from the following laws of this state:

(1) Code Section 16-11-126, relating to carrying a weapon;

(2) Code Section 16-11-127, relating to carrying a weapon or long gun in an unauthorized location; and

(3) Code Section 16-11-129, relating to licenses to carry weapons generally.

(g) The board shall have the power to deny a weapons permit to any applicant who fails to provide the information and supporting documentation required by this Code section or to refuse to renew a permit upon failure to comply with such weapons proficiency recertification requirements as the board may prescribe.

(h) The board shall have the authority to order the summary suspension of any weapons permit issued under this Code section, pending proceedings for revocation or other sanction, upon finding that the public health, safety, or welfare imperatively requires such emergency action, which finding shall be incorporated in its order.

(i) The board shall have the same power and authority to deny and sanction weapons permits under this Code section as that enumerated in Code Section 43-38-11, based on the same grounds as those enumerated in that Code section.

(j) A weapons permit issued under this Code section to any person whose license is suspended pursuant to subsection (f) of Code Section 43-38-6 or whose registration is suspended pursuant to subsection (g) of Code Section 43-38-7 shall be suspended at the same time as the suspension of the license or registration without a prior hearing as required in Code Section 43-38-11. A weapons permit shall be restored to a person upon the restoration of the person's license or registration.

## Title 49. Social Services
## Chapter 4A. Department of Juvenile Justice

### O.C.G.A. § 49-4A-11. Unlawful Assistance to Child in Custody of Department.

(a) Any person who shall knowingly aid, assist, or encourage any child or youth who has been committed to the department to escape or to attempt to escape its control or custody shall be guilty of a felony and, upon conviction thereof, shall be imprisoned for not less than one nor more than five years.

(b) Any person who shall knowingly harbor or shelter any child or youth who has escaped the lawful custody or control of the department shall be guilty of a felony and, upon conviction thereof, shall be imprisoned for not less than one nor more than five years.

(c) Any person who shall knowingly hinder the apprehension of any child under the lawful control or custody of the department who has been placed by the department in one of its institutions or facilities and who has escaped therefrom or who has been placed under supervision and is alleged to have broken the conditions thereof shall be guilty of a felony and, upon conviction thereof, shall be imprisoned for not less than one nor more than five years.

(d) Any person who shall knowingly provide to any child under the lawful control or custody of the department a gun, pistol, or any other weapon, any intoxicating liquor, any controlled substance listed in Code Section 16-13-27 as a Schedule III controlled substance, listed in Code Section 16-13-28 as a Schedule IV controlled substance, or listed in Code Section 16-13-29 as a Schedule V controlled substance, or an immediate precursor of any such controlled substance, or any dangerous drug as defined by Code Section 16-13-71, regardless of the amount, or any other harmful, hazardous, or illegal article or item which may be injurious to department personnel without the consent of the director of the institution providing care and supervision to the child shall be guilty of a felony and, upon conviction thereof, shall be imprisoned for not less than one nor more than five years.

(e) Any child who shall knowingly possess a gun, pistol, or any other weapon, any intoxicating liquor, any controlled substance listed in Code Section 16-13-27 as a Schedule III controlled substance, listed in Code Section 16-13-28 as a Schedule IV controlled substance, or listed in Code Section 16-13-29 as a Schedule V controlled substance, or an immediate precursor of any such controlled substance, or any dangerous drug as defined by Code Section 16-13-71, regardless of the amount, or any other harmful, hazardous, or illegal article or item which may be injurious to department personnel given to said child in violation of subsection (d) of this Code section while under the lawful custody or control of the department shall cause the department to file a delinquency petition in the court having jurisdiction; provided, however, if such person is 17 or older and is under the lawful custody or control of the department, such person shall be guilty of a felony and, upon conviction thereof, shall be imprisoned for not less than one nor more than five years.

## Title 50. State Government
## Chapter 18. State Printing and Documents
## Article 4. Inspection of Public Records

### O.C.G.A. § 50-18-72. Exception of Certain Records.

(a) Public disclosure shall not be required for records that are:

(1) Specifically required by federal statute or regulation to be kept confidential;

(2) Medical or veterinary records and similar files, the disclosure of which would be an invasion of personal privacy;

(3) Except as otherwise provided by law, records compiled for law enforcement or prosecution purposes to the extent that production of such records would disclose the identity of a confidential source, disclose confidential investigative or prosecution material which would endanger

the life or physical safety of any person or persons, or disclose the existence of a confidential surveillance or investigation;

(4) Records of law enforcement, prosecution, or regulatory agencies in any pending investigation or prosecution of criminal or unlawful activity, other than initial police arrest reports and initial incident reports; provided, however, that an investigation or prosecution shall no longer be deemed to be pending when all direct litigation involving said investigation and prosecution has become final or otherwise terminated;

(4.1) Individual Georgia Uniform Motor Vehicle Accident Reports, except upon the submission of a written statement of need by the requesting party, such statement to be provided to the custodian of records and to set forth the need for the report pursuant to this Code section; provided, however, that any person or entity whose name or identifying information is contained in a Georgia Uniform Motor Vehicle Accident Report shall be entitled, either personally or through a lawyer or other representative, to receive a copy of such report; and provided, further, that Georgia Uniform Motor Vehicle Accident Reports shall not be available in bulk for inspection or copying by any person absent a written statement showing the need for each such report pursuant to the requirements of this Code section. For the purposes of this subsection, the term "need" means that the natural person or legal entity who is requesting in person or by representative to inspect or copy the Georgia Uniform Motor Vehicle Accident Report:

(A) Has a personal, professional, or business connection with a party to the accident;

(B) Owns or leases an interest in property allegedly or actually damaged in the accident;

(C) Was allegedly or actually injured by the accident;

(D) Was a witness to the accident;

(E) Is the actual or alleged insurer of a party to the accident or of property actually or allegedly damaged by the accident;

(F) Is a prosecutor or a publicly employed law enforcement officer;

(G) Is alleged to be liable to another party as a result of the accident;

(H) Is an attorney stating that he or she needs the requested reports as part of a criminal case, or an investigation of a potential claim involving contentions that a roadway, railroad crossing, or intersection is unsafe;

(I) Is gathering information as a representative of a news media organization;

(J) Is conducting research in the public interest for such purposes as accident prevention, prevention of injuries or damages in accidents, determination of fault in an accident or accidents, or other similar purposes; provided, however, this subparagraph will apply only to accident reports on accidents that occurred more than 30 days prior to the request and which shall have the name, street address, telephone number, and driver's license number redacted; or

(K) Is a governmental official, entity, or agency, or an authorized agent thereof, requesting reports for the purpose of carrying out governmental functions or legitimate governmental duties;

(5) Records that consist of confidential evaluations submitted to, or examinations prepared by, a governmental agency and prepared in connection with the appointment or hiring of a public officer or employee; and records consisting of material obtained in investigations related to the suspension, firing, or investigation of complaints against public officers or employees until ten days after the same has been presented to the agency or an officer for action or the investigation is otherwise concluded or terminated, provided that this paragraph shall not be interpreted to make such investigatory records privileged;

(6)(A) Real estate appraisals, engineering or feasibility estimates, or other records made for or by the state or a local agency relative to the acquisition of real property until such time as the property has been acquired or the proposed transaction has been terminated or abandoned; and

(B) Engineers' cost estimates and pending, rejected, or deferred bids or proposals until such time as the final award of the contract is made or the project is terminated or abandoned. The provisions of this subparagraph shall apply whether the bid or proposal is received or prepared by the Department of Transportation pursuant to Article 4 of Chapter 2 of Title 32, by a county pursuant to Article 3 of Chapter 4 of Title 32, by a municipality pursuant to Article 4 of Chapter 4 of Title 32, or by a governmental entity pursuant to Article 2 of Chapter 91 of Title 36;

(7) Notwithstanding any other provision of this article, an agency shall not be required to release those portions of records which would identify persons applying for or under consideration for employment or appointment as executive head of an agency as that term is defined in paragraph (1) of subsection (a) of Code Section 50-14-1, or of a unit of the University System of Georgia; provided, however, that at least 14 calendar days prior to the meeting at which final action or vote is to be taken on the position, the agency shall release all documents which came into its possession with respect to as many as three persons under consideration whom the agency has determined to be the best qualified for the position and from among whom the agency intends to fill the position. Prior to the release of these documents, an agency may allow such a person to decline being considered further for the position rather than have documents pertaining to the person released. In that event, the agency shall release the documents of the next most qualified person under consideration who does not decline the position. If an agency has conducted its hiring or appointment process open to the public, it shall not be required to delay 14 days to take final action on the position. The agency shall not be required to release such records with respect to other applicants or persons under consideration, except at the request of any such person. Upon request, the hiring agency shall furnish the number of applicants and the composition of the list by such factors as race and sex. The agency shall not be allowed to avoid the provisions of this paragraph by the employment of a private person or agency to assist with the search or application process;

(8) Related to the provision of staff services to individual members of the General Assembly by the Legislative and Congressional Reapportionment Office, the Senate Research Office, or the House Research Office, provided that this exception shall not have any application with respect to records related to the provision of staff services to any committee or subcommittee or to any records which are or have been previously publicly disclosed by or pursuant to the direction of an individual member of the General Assembly;

(9) Records that are of historical research value which are given or sold to public archival institutions, public libraries, or libraries of a unit of the Board of Regents of the University System of Georgia when the owner or donor of such records wishes to place restrictions on access to the records. No restriction on access, however, may extend more than 75 years from the date of donation or sale. This exemption shall not apply to any records prepared in the course of the operation of state or local governments of the State of Georgia;

(10) Records that contain information from the Department of Natural Resources inventory and register relating to the location and character of a historic property or of historic properties as those terms are defined in Code Sections 12-3-50.1 and 12-3-50.2 if the Department of Natural Resources through its Division of Historic Preservation determines that disclosure will create a substantial risk of harm, theft, or destruction to the property or properties or the area or place where the property or properties are located;

(10.1) Records of farm water use by individual farms as determined by water-measuring devices installed pursuant to Code Section 12-5-31 or 12-5-105; provided, however, that compilations of such records for the 52 large watershed basins as identified by the eight-digit United States Geologic Survey hydrologic code or an aquifer that do not reveal farm water use by individual farms shall be subject to disclosure under this article;

(10.2) Agricultural or food system records, data, or information that are considered by the Georgia Department of Agriculture to be a part of the critical infrastructure, provided that nothing in this paragraph shall prevent the release of such records, data, or information to another state or federal agency if the release of such records, data, or information is necessary to prevent or control disease or to protect public health, safety, or welfare. As used in this paragraph, the term "critical infrastructure" shall have the same meaning as in 42 U.S.C. Section 5195c(e). Such records, data, or information shall be subject to disclosure only upon the order of a court of competent jurisdiction;

(10.3) Records, data, or information collected, recorded, or otherwise obtained that is deemed confidential by the Georgia Department of Agriculture for the purposes of the national animal identification system, provided that nothing in this paragraph shall prevent the release of such records, data, or information to another state or federal agency if the release of such records, data, or information is necessary to prevent or control disease or to protect public health, safety, or welfare. As used in this paragraph, the term "national animal identification program" means a national program intended to identify animals and track them as they come into contact with or commingle with animals other than herdmates from their premises of origin. Such records, data, or information shall be subject to disclosure only upon the order of a court of competent jurisdiction;

(11) Records that contain site specific information regarding the occurrence of rare species of plants or animals or the location of sensitive natural habitats on public or private property if the Department of Natural Resources determines that disclosure will create a substantial risk of harm, theft, or destruction to the species or habitats or the area or place where the species or habitats are located; provided, however, that the owner or owners of private property upon which rare species of plants or animals occur or upon which sensitive natural habitats are located shall be entitled to such information pursuant to this article;

(11.1) An individual's social security number and insurance or medical information in personnel records, which may be redacted from such records;

(11.2) Records that would reveal the names, home addresses, telephone numbers, security codes, e-mail addresses, or any other data or information developed, collected, or received by counties or municipalities in connection with neighborhood watch or public safety notification programs or with the installation, servicing, maintaining, operating, selling, or leasing of burglar alarm systems, fire alarm systems, or other electronic security systems; provided, however, that initial police reports and initial incident reports shall remain subject to disclosure pursuant to paragraph (4) of this subsection;

(11.3)(A) An individual's social security number, mother's birth name, credit card information, debit card information, bank account information, account number, including a utility account number, password used to access his or her account, financial data or information, and insurance or medical information in all records, and if technically feasible at reasonable cost, day and month of birth, which shall be redacted prior to disclosure of any record requested pursuant to this article; provided, however, that such information shall not be redacted from such records if the person or entity requesting such records requests such information in a writing signed under oath by such person or a person legally authorized to represent such entity which states that such person or entity is gathering information as a representative of a news media organization for use in connection with news gathering and reporting; and provided, further, that such access shall be limited to social security numbers and day and month of birth; and provided, further, that this news media organization exception for access to social security numbers and day and month of birth and the other protected information set forth in this subparagraph shall not apply to teachers, employees of a public school, or public employees as set forth in paragraph (13.1) of this subsection. For purposes of this subparagraph, the term "public employee" means any nonelected employee of the State of Georgia or its agencies, departments, or commissions or any county or municipality or its agencies, departments, or commissions.

(B) This paragraph shall have no application to:

(i) The disclosure of information contained in the records or papers of any court or derived therefrom including without limitation records maintained pursuant to Article 9 of Title 11;

(ii) The disclosure of information to a court, prosecutor, or publicly employed law enforcement officer, or authorized agent thereof, seeking records in an official capacity;

(iii) The disclosure of information to a public employee of this state, its political subdivisions, or the United States who is obtaining such information for administrative purposes, in which case, subject to applicable laws of the United States, further access to such information shall continue to be subject to the provisions of this paragraph;

(iv) The disclosure of information as authorized by the order of a court of competent jurisdiction upon good cause shown to have access to any or all of such information upon such conditions as may be set forth in such order;

(v) The disclosure of information to the individual in respect of whom such information is maintained, with the authorization thereof, or to an authorized agent thereof; provided, however, that the agency maintaining such information shall require proper identification of such individual or such individual's agent, or proof of authorization, as determined by such agency;

(vi) The disclosure of the day and month of birth and mother's birth name of a deceased individual;

(vii) The disclosure by an agency of credit or payment information in connection with a request by a consumer reporting agency as that term is defined under the federal Fair Credit Reporting Act (15 U.S.C. Section 1681, et seq.);

(viii) The disclosure by an agency of information in its records in connection with the agency's discharging or fulfilling of its duties and responsibilities, including, but not limited to, the collection of debts owed to the agency or individuals or entities whom the agency assists in the collection of debts owed to the individual or entity;

(ix) The disclosure of information necessary to comply with legal or regulatory requirements or for legitimate law enforcement purposes; or

(x) The disclosure of the date of birth within criminal records.

(C) Records and information disseminated pursuant to this paragraph may be used only by the authorized recipient and only for the authorized purpose. Any person who obtains records or information pursuant to the provisions of this paragraph and knowingly and willfully discloses, distributes, or sells such records or information to an unauthorized recipient or for an unauthorized purpose shall be guilty of a misdemeanor of a high and aggravated nature and upon conviction thereof shall be punished as provided in Code Section 17-10-4. Any person injured thereby shall have a cause of action for invasion of privacy. Any prosecution pursuant to this paragraph shall be in accordance with the procedure in subsection (b) of Code Section 50-18-74.

(D) In the event that the custodian of public records protected by this paragraph has good faith reason to believe that a pending request for such records has been made fraudulently, under false pretenses, or by means of false swearing, such custodian shall apply to the superior court of the county in which such records are maintained for a protective order limiting or prohibiting access to such records.

(E) This paragraph shall supplement and shall not supplant, overrule, replace, or otherwise modify or supersede any provision of statute, regulation, or law of the federal government or of this state as now or hereafter amended or enacted requiring, restricting, or prohibiting access to the information identified in subparagraph (A) of this paragraph and shall constitute only a regulation of the methods of such access where not otherwise provided for, restricted, or prohibited;

(12) Public records containing information that would disclose or might lead to the disclosure of any component in the process used to execute or adopt an electronic signature, if such disclosure would or might cause the electronic signature to cease being under the sole control of the person using it. For purposes of this paragraph, the term "electronic signature" has the same meaning as that term is defined in Code Section 10-12-2;

(13) Records that would reveal the home address or telephone number, social security number, or insurance or medical information of employees of the Department of Revenue, law enforcement officers, firefighters as defined in Code Section 25-4-2, judges, emergency medical

technicians and paramedics, scientists employed by the Division of Forensic Sciences of the Georgia Bureau of Investigation, correctional employees, and prosecutors or identification of immediate family members or dependents thereof;

(13.1) Records that reveal the home address, the home telephone number, the email address, or the social security number of or insurance or medical information about public employees or teachers and employees of a public school. For the purposes of this paragraph, the term "public school" means any school which is conducted within this state and which is under the authority and supervision of a duly elected county or independent board of education. Public disclosure shall also not be required for records that reveal the home address, the home telephone number, the e-mail address, or the social security number of or insurance or medical information about employees or teachers of a nonpublic school;

(13.2) Records that are kept by the probate court pertaining to guardianships and conservatorships except as provided in Code Section 29-9-18;

(14) Acquired by an agency for the purpose of establishing or implementing, or assisting in the establishment or implementation of, a carpooling or ridesharing program, to the extent such records would reveal the name, home address, employment address, home telephone number, employment telephone number, or hours of employment of any individual or would otherwise identify any individual who is participating in, or who has expressed an interest in participating in, any such program. As used in this paragraph, the term "carpooling or ridesharing program" means and includes, but is not limited to, the formation of carpools, vanpools, or buspools, the provision of transit routes, rideshare research, and the development of other demand management strategies such as variable working hours and telecommuting;

(15)(A) Records, the disclosure of which would compromise security against sabotage or criminal or terrorist acts and the nondisclosure of which is necessary for the protection of life, safety, or public property, which shall be limited to the following:

(i) Security plans and vulnerability assessments for any public utility, technology infrastructure, building, facility, function, or activity in effect at the time of the request for disclosure or pertaining to a plan or assessment in effect at such time;

(ii) Any plan for protection against terrorist or other attacks, which plan depends for its effectiveness in whole or in part upon a lack of general public knowledge of its details;

(iii) Any document relating to the existence, nature, location, or function of security devices designed to protect against terrorist or other attacks, which devices depend for their effectiveness in whole or in part upon a lack of general public knowledge; and

(iv) Any plan, blueprint, or other material which if made public could compromise security against sabotage, criminal, or terroristic acts.

(B) In the event of litigation challenging nondisclosure pursuant to this paragraph by an agency of a document covered by this paragraph, the court may review the documents in question in camera and may condition, in writing, any disclosure upon such measures as the court may find to be necessary to protect against endangerment of life, safety, or public property.

(C) As used in divisions (i) and (iv) of subparagraph (A) of this paragraph, the term "activity" means deployment or surveillance strategies, actions mandated by changes in the federal threat level, motorcades, contingency plans, proposed or alternative motorcade routes, executive and dignitary protection, planned responses to criminal or terrorist actions, after-action reports still in use, proposed or actual plans and responses to bioterrorism, and proposed or actual plans and responses to requesting and receiving the National Pharmacy Stockpile;

(16) Unless the request is made by the accused in a criminal case or by his or her attorney, public records of an emergency 9-1-1 system, as defined in paragraph (3) of Code Section 46-5-122, containing information which would reveal the name, address, or telephone number of a person placing a call to a public safety answering point, which information may be redacted from such records if

necessary to prevent the disclosure of the identity of a confidential source, to prevent disclosure of material which would endanger the life or physical safety of any person or persons, or to prevent the disclosure of the existence of a confidential surveillance or investigation;

(17) Records of athletic or recreational programs, available through the state or a political subdivision of the state, that include information identifying a child or children 12 years of age or under by name, address, telephone number, or emergency contact, unless such identifying information has been redacted;

(18) Records of the State Road and Tollway Authority which would reveal the financial accounts or travel history of any individual who is a motorist upon such toll project. Such financial records shall include but not be limited to social security number, home address, home telephone number, e-mail address, credit or debit card information, and bank account information but shall not include the user's name;

(19) Records maintained by public postsecondary educational institutions in this state and associated foundations of such institutions that contain personal information concerning donors or potential donors to such institutions or foundations; provided, however, that the name of any donor and the amount of donation made by such donor shall be subject to disclosure if such donor or any entity in which such donor has a substantial interest transacts business with the public postsecondary educational institution to which the donation is made within three years of the date of such donation. As used in this paragraph, the term "transact business" means to sell or lease any personal property, real property, or services on behalf of oneself or on behalf of any third party as an agent, broker, dealer, or representative in an amount in excess of $10,000.00 in the aggregate in a calendar year and the term "substantial interest" means the direct or indirect ownership of more than 25 percent of the assets or stock of an entity;

(20) Records of the Metropolitan Atlanta Rapid Transit Authority or of any other transit system that is connected to that system's TransCard or SmartCard system which would reveal the financial records or travel history of any individual who is a purchaser of a TransCard or SmartCard or similar fare medium. Such financial records shall include, but not be limited to, social security number, home address, home telephone number, e-mail address, credit or debit card information, and bank account information but shall not include the user's name;

(21) Building mapping information produced and maintained pursuant to Article 10 of Chapter 3 of Title 38; or

(22) Notwithstanding the provisions of paragraph (4) of this subsection, any physical evidence or investigatory materials that are evidence of an alleged violation of Part 2 of Article 3 of Chapter 12 of Title 16, which are in the possession, custody, or control of law enforcement, prosecution, or regulatory agencies.

(23) Records that are expressly exempt from public inspection pursuant to Code Sections 47-1-14 and 47-7-127.

(b) This article shall not be applicable to:

(1) Any trade secrets obtained from a person or business entity which are of a privileged or confidential nature and required by law to be submitted to a government agency or to data, records, or information of a proprietary nature, produced or collected by or for faculty or staff of state institutions of higher learning, or other governmental agencies, in the conduct of or as a result of, study or research on commercial, scientific, technical, or scholarly issues, whether sponsored by the institution alone or in conjunction with a governmental body or private concern, where such data, records, or information has not been publicly released, published, copyrighted, or patented;

(2) Any data, records, or information developed, collected, or received by or on behalf of faculty, staff, employees, or students of an institution of higher education or any public or private entity supporting or participating in the activities of an institution of higher education in the conduct of, or as a result of, study or research on medical, scientific, technical, scholarly, or artistic issues, whether

sponsored by the institution alone or in conjunction with a governmental body or private entity until such information is published, patented, otherwise publicly disseminated, or released to an agency whereupon the request must be made to the agency. This subsection applies to, but is not limited to, information provided by participants in research, research notes and data, discoveries, research projects, methodologies, protocols, and creative works; or

(3) Unless otherwise provided by law, contract, bid, or proposal, records consisting of questions, scoring keys, and other materials, constituting a test that derives value from being unknown to the test taker prior to administration, which is to be administered by the State Board of Education, the Office of Student Achievement, the Professional Standards Division, or a local school system, if reasonable measures are taken by the owner of the test to protect security and confidentiality; provided, however, that the State Board of Education may establish procedures whereby a person may view, but not copy, such records if viewing will not, in the judgment of the board, affect the result of administration of such test.

These limitations shall not be interpreted by any court of law to include or otherwise exempt from inspection the records of any athletic association or other nonprofit entity promoting intercollegiate athletics.

(c)(1) All public records of hospital authorities shall be subject to this article except for those otherwise excepted by this article or any other provision of law.

(2) All state officers and employees shall have a privilege to refuse to disclose the identity or personally identifiable information of any person participating in research on commercial, scientific, technical, medical, scholarly, or artistic issues conducted by the Department of Community Health, the Department of Behavioral Health and Developmental Disabilities, or a state institution of higher education whether sponsored by the institution alone or in conjunction with a governmental body or private entity. Personally identifiable information shall mean any information which if disclosed might reasonably reveal the identity of such person including but not limited to the person's name, address, and social security number. The identity of such informant shall not be admissible in evidence in any court of the state unless the court finds that the identity of the informant already has been disclosed otherwise.

(d) This article shall not be applicable to any application submitted to or any permanent records maintained by a judge of the probate court pursuant to Code Section 16-11-129, relating to weapons carry licenses, or pursuant to any other requirement for maintaining records relative to the possession of firearms. This subsection shall not preclude law enforcement agencies from obtaining records relating to licensing and possession of firearms as provided by law.

(e) This article shall not be construed to repeal:

(1) The attorney-client privilege recognized by state law to the extent that a record pertains to the requesting or giving of legal advice or the disclosure of facts concerning or pertaining to pending or potential litigation, settlement, claims, administrative proceedings, or other judicial actions brought or to be brought by or against the agency or any officer or employee; provided, however, attorney-client information may be obtained in a proceeding under Code Section 50-18-73 to prove justification or lack thereof in refusing disclosure of documents under this Code section provided the judge of the court in which said proceeding is pending shall first determine by an in camera examination that such disclosure would be relevant on that issue;

(2) The confidentiality of attorney work product; or

(3) State laws making certain tax matters confidential.

(f)(1) As used in this article, the term:

(A) "Computer program" means a set of instructions, statements, or related data that, in actual or modified form, is capable of causing a computer or computer system to perform specified functions.

(B) "Computer software" means one or more computer programs, existing in any form, or any associated operational procedures, manuals, or other documentation.

(2) This article shall not be applicable to any computer program or computer software used or maintained in the course of operation of a public office or agency.

(g) This Code section shall be interpreted narrowly so as to exclude from disclosure only that portion of a public record to which an exclusion is directly applicable. It shall be the duty of the agency having custody of a record to provide all other portions of a record for public inspection or copying.

(h) Within the three business days applicable to response to a request for access to records under this article, the public officer or agency having control of such record or records, if access to such record or records is denied in whole or in part, shall specify in writing the specific legal authority exempting such record or records from disclosure, by Code section, subsection, and paragraph. No addition to or amendment of such designation shall be permitted thereafter or in any proceeding to enforce the terms of this article; provided, however, that such designation may be amended or supplemented one time within five days of discovery of an error in such designation or within five days of the institution of an action to enforce this article, whichever is sooner; provided, further, that the right to amend or supplement based upon discovery of an error may be exercised on only one occasion. In the event that such designation includes provisions not relevant to the subject matter of the request, costs and reasonable attorney's fees may be awarded pursuant to Code Section 50-18-73.

Title 51.  Torts
Chapter 11.  Defenses to Tort Actions
Article 1.  General Provisions

## O.C.G.A. § 51-11-9.  Immunity from Liability of Person Who Used Justifiable Force in Defense of Habitat, Property, Self, or Others.

A person who is justified in threatening or using force against another under the provisions of Code Section 16-3-21, relating to the use of force in defense of self or others, Code Section 16-3-23, relating to the use of force in defense of a habitation, or Code Section 16-3-24, relating to the use of force in defense of property other than a habitation, has no duty to retreat from the use of such force and shall not be held liable to the person against whom the use of force was justified or to any person acting as an accomplice or assistant to such person in any civil action brought as a result of the threat or use of such force.

# Appendix Four

# United States Code
## Selected Sections

**18 U.S.C. § 921. Definitions.**

(a) As used in this chapter—

(1) The term "person" and the term "whoever" include any individual, corporation, company, association, firm, partnership, society, or joint stock company.

(2) The term "interstate or foreign commerce" includes commerce between any place in a State and any place outside of that State, or within any possession of the United States (not including the Canal Zone) or the District of Columbia, but such term does not include commerce between places within the same State but through any place outside of that State. The term "State" includes the District of Columbia, the Commonwealth of Puerto Rico, and the possessions of the United States (not including the Canal Zone).

(3) The term "firearm" means

(A) any weapon (including a starter gun) which will or is designed to or may readily be converted to expel a projectile by the action of an explosive;

(B) the frame or receiver of any such weapon;

(C) any firearm muffler or firearm silencer; or

(D) any destructive device. Such term does not include an antique firearm.

(4) The term "destructive device" means—

(A) any explosive, incendiary, or poison gas—

(i) bomb,

(ii) grenade,

(iii) rocket having a propellant charge of more than four ounces,

(iv) missile having an explosive or incendiary charge of more than one-quarter ounce,

(v) mine, or

(vi) device similar to any of the devices described in the preceding clauses;

(B) any type of weapon (other than a shotgun or a shotgun shell which the Attorney General finds is generally recognized as particularly suitable for sporting purposes) by whatever name known which will, or which may be readily converted to, expel a projectile by the action of an explosive or other propellant, and which has any barrel with a bore of more than one-half inch in diameter; and

(C) any combination of parts either designed or intended for use in converting any device into any destructive device described in subparagraph (A) or (B) and from which a destructive device may be readily assembled.

The term "destructive device" shall not include any device which is neither designed nor redesigned for use as a weapon; any device, although originally designed for use as a weapon, which is redesigned for use as a signaling, pyrotechnic, line throwing, safety, or similar device; surplus ordnance sold, loaned, or given by the Secretary of the Army pursuant to the provisions of section 4684 (2), 4685, or 4686 of title 10; or any other device which the Attorney General finds is not likely to be used as a weapon, is an antique, or is a rifle which the owner intends to use solely for sporting, recreational or cultural purposes.

(5) The term "shotgun" means a weapon designed or redesigned, made or remade, and intended to be fired from the shoulder and designed or redesigned and made or remade to use the energy of an explosive to fire through a smooth bore either a number of ball shot or a single projectile for each single pull of the trigger.

(6) The term "short-barreled shotgun" means a shotgun having one or more barrels less than eighteen inches in length and any weapon made from a shotgun (whether by alteration, modification or otherwise) if such a weapon as modified has an overall length of less than twenty-six inches.

(7) The term "rifle" means a weapon designed or redesigned, made or remade, and intended to be fired from the shoulder and designed or redesigned and made or remade to use the energy of an explosive to fire only a single projectile through a rifled bore for each single pull of the trigger.

(8) The term "short-barreled rifle" means a rifle having one or more barrels less than sixteen inches in length and any weapon made from a rifle (whether by alteration, modification, or otherwise) if such weapon, as modified, has an overall length of less than twenty-six inches.

(9) The term "importer" means any person engaged in the business of importing or bringing firearms or ammunition into the United States for purposes of sale or distribution; and the term "licensed importer" means any such person licensed under the provisions of this chapter.

(10) The term "manufacturer" means any person engaged in the business of manufacturing firearms or ammunition for purposes of sale or distribution; and the term "licensed manufacturer" means any such person licensed under the provisions of this chapter.

(11) The term "dealer" means

(A) any person engaged in the business of selling firearms at wholesale or retail,

(B) any person engaged in the business of repairing firearms or of making or fitting special barrels, stocks, or trigger mechanisms to firearms, or

(C) any person who is a pawnbroker. The term "licensed dealer" means any dealer who is licensed under the provisions of this chapter.

(12) The term "pawnbroker" means any person whose business or occupation includes the taking or receiving, by way of pledge or pawn, of any firearm as security for the payment or repayment of money.

(13) The term "collector" means any person who acquires, holds, or disposes of firearms as curios or relics, as the Attorney General shall by regulation define, and the term "licensed collector" means any such person licensed under the provisions of this chapter.

(14) The term "indictment" includes an indictment or information in any court under which a crime punishable by imprisonment for a term exceeding one year may be prosecuted.

(15) The term "fugitive from justice" means any person who has fled from any State to avoid prosecution for a crime or to avoid giving testimony in any criminal proceeding.

(16) The term "antique firearm" means—

(A) any firearm (including any firearm with a matchlock, flintlock, percussion cap, or similar type of ignition system) manufactured in or before 1898; or

(B) any replica of any firearm described in subparagraph (A) if such replica—

(i) is not designed or redesigned for using rimfire or conventional centerfire fixed ammunition, or

(ii) uses rimfire or conventional centerfire fixed ammunition which is no longer manufactured in the United States and which is not readily available in the ordinary channels of commercial trade; or

(C) any muzzle loading rifle, muzzle loading shotgun, or muzzle loading pistol, which is designed to use black powder, or a black powder substitute, and which cannot use fixed ammunition. For purposes of this subparagraph, the term "antique firearm" shall not include any weapon which incorporates a firearm frame or receiver, any firearm which is converted into a muzzle loading weapon, or any muzzle loading weapon which can be readily converted to fire fixed ammunition by replacing the barrel, bolt, breechblock, or any combination thereof.

(17)(A) The term "ammunition" means ammunition or cartridge cases, primers, bullets, or propellent powder designed for use in any firearm.

(B) The term "armor piercing ammunition" means—

(i) a projectile or projectile core which may be used in a handgun and which is constructed entirely (excluding the presence of traces of other substances) from one or a combination of tungsten alloys, steel, iron, brass, bronze, beryllium copper, or depleted uranium; or

(ii) a full jacketed projectile larger than .22 caliber designed and intended for use in a handgun and whose jacket has a weight of more than 25 percent of the total weight of the projectile.

(C) The term "armor piercing ammunition" does not include shotgun shot required by Federal or State environmental or game regulations for hunting purposes, a frangible projectile designed for target shooting, a projectile which the Attorney General finds is primarily intended to be used for sporting purposes, or any other projectile or projectile core which the Attorney General finds is intended to be used for industrial purposes, including a charge used in an oil and gas well perforating device.

(18) The term "Attorney General" means the Attorney General of the United States

(19) The term "published ordinance" means a published law of any political subdivision of a State which the Attorney General determines to be relevant to the enforcement of this chapter and which is contained on a list compiled by the Attorney General, which list shall be published in the Federal Register, revised annually, and furnished to each licensee under this chapter.

(20) The term "crime punishable by imprisonment for a term exceeding one year" does not include—

(A) any Federal or State offenses pertaining to antitrust violations, unfair trade practices, restraints of trade, or other similar offenses relating to the regulation of business practices, or

(B) any State offense classified by the laws of the State as a misdemeanor and punishable by a term of imprisonment of two years or less.

What constitutes a conviction of such a crime shall be determined in accordance with the law of the jurisdiction in which the proceedings were held. Any conviction which has been expunged, or set aside or for which a person has been pardoned or has had civil rights restored shall not be considered a conviction for purposes of this chapter, unless such pardon, expungement, or restoration of civil rights expressly provides that the person may not ship, transport, possess, or receive firearms.

(21) The term "engaged in the business" means—

(A) as applied to a manufacturer of firearms, a person who devotes time, attention, and labor to manufacturing firearms as a regular course of trade or business with the principal objective of livelihood and profit through the sale or distribution of the firearms manufactured;

(B) as applied to a manufacturer of ammunition, a person who devotes time, attention, and labor to manufacturing ammunition as a regular course of trade or business with the principal objective of livelihood and profit through the sale or distribution of the ammunition manufactured;

(C) as applied to a dealer in firearms, as defined in section 921 (a)(11)(A), a person who devotes time, attention, and labor to dealing in firearms as a regular course of trade or business with the principal objective of livelihood and profit through the repetitive purchase and resale of firearms, but such term shall not include a person who makes occasional sales, exchanges, or purchases of firearms for the enhancement of a personal collection or for a hobby, or who sells all or part of his personal collection of firearms;

(D) as applied to a dealer in firearms, as defined in section 921 (a)(11)(B), a person who devotes time, attention, and labor to engaging in such activity as a regular course of trade or business with the principal objective of livelihood and profit, but such term shall not include a person who makes occasional repairs of firearms, or who occasionally fits special barrels, stocks, or trigger mechanisms to firearms;

(E) as applied to an importer of firearms, a person who devotes time, attention, and labor to importing firearms as a regular course of trade or business with the principal objective of livelihood and profit through the sale or distribution of the firearms imported; and

(F) as applied to an importer of ammunition, a person who devotes time, attention, and labor to importing ammunition as a regular course of trade or business with the principal objective of livelihood and profit through the sale or distribution of the ammunition imported.

(22) The term "with the principal objective of livelihood and profit" means that the intent underlying the sale or disposition of firearms is predominantly one of obtaining livelihood and pecuniary gain, as opposed to other intents, such as improving or liquidating a personal firearms collection: Provided, That proof of profit shall not be required as to a person who engages in the regular and repetitive purchase and disposition of firearms for criminal purposes or terrorism. For purposes of this paragraph, the term "terrorism" means activity, directed against United States persons, which—

(A) is committed by an individual who is not a national or permanent resident alien of the United States;

(B) involves violent acts or acts dangerous to human life which would be a criminal violation if committed within the jurisdiction of the United States; and

(C) is intended—

(i) to intimidate or coerce a civilian population;

(ii) to influence the policy of a government by intimidation or coercion; or

(iii) to affect the conduct of a government by assassination or kidnapping.

(23) The term "machinegun" has the meaning given such term in section 5845(b) of the National Firearms Act (26 U.S.C. 5845 (b)).

(24) The terms "firearm silencer" and "firearm muffler" mean any device for silencing, muffling, or diminishing the report of a portable firearm, including any combination of parts, designed or redesigned, and intended for use in assembling or fabricating a firearm silencer or firearm muffler, and any part intended only for use in such assembly or fabrication.

(25) The term "school zone" means—

(A) in, or on the grounds of, a public, parochial or private school; or

(B) within a distance of 1,000 feet from the grounds of a public, parochial or private school.

(26) The term "school" means a school which provides elementary or secondary education, as determined under State law.

(27) The term "motor vehicle" has the meaning given such term in section 13102 of title 49, United States Code.

(28) The term "semiautomatic rifle" means any repeating rifle which utilizes a portion of the energy of a firing cartridge to extract the fired cartridge case and chamber the next round, and which requires a separate pull of the trigger to fire each cartridge.

(29) The term "handgun" means—

(A) a firearm which has a short stock and is designed to be held and fired by the use of a single hand; and

(B) any combination of parts from which a firearm described in subparagraph (A) can be assembled.

(30), (31) Repealed. Pub. L. 103–322, title XI, § 110105(2), Sept. 13, 1994, 108 Stat. 2000.

(32) The term "intimate partner" means, with respect to a person, the spouse of the person, a former spouse of the person, an individual who is a parent of a child of the person, and an individual who cohabitates or has cohabited with the person.

(33) (A) Except as provided in subparagraph (C), the term "misdemeanor crime of domestic violence" means an offense that—

(i) is a misdemeanor under Federal, State, or Tribal law; and

(ii) has, as an element, the use or attempted use of physical force, or the threatened use of a deadly weapon, committed by a current or former spouse, parent, or guardian of the victim, by a person with whom the victim shares a child in common, by a person who is cohabiting with or has cohabited with the victim as a spouse, parent, or guardian, or by a person similarly situated to a spouse, parent, or guardian of the victim.

(B) (i) A person shall not be considered to have been convicted of such an offense for purposes of this chapter, unless—

(I) the person was represented by counsel in the case, or knowingly and intelligently waived the right to counsel in the case; and

(II) in the case of a prosecution for an offense described in this paragraph for which a person was entitled to a jury trial in the jurisdiction in which the case was tried, either

(aa) the case was tried by a jury, or

(bb) the person knowingly and intelligently waived the right to have the case tried by a jury, by guilty plea or otherwise.

(ii) A person shall not be considered to have been convicted of such an offense for purposes of this chapter if the conviction has been expunged or set aside, or is an offense for which the person has been pardoned or has had civil rights restored (if the law of the applicable jurisdiction provides for the loss of civil rights under such an offense) unless the pardon, expungement, or restoration of civil rights expressly provides that the person may not ship, transport, possess, or receive firearms.

(34) The term "secure gun storage or safety device" means—

(A) a device that, when installed on a firearm, is designed to prevent the firearm from being operated without first deactivating the device;

(B) a device incorporated into the design of the firearm that is designed to prevent the operation of the firearm by anyone not having access to the device; or

(C) a safe, gun safe, gun case, lock box, or other device that is designed to be or can be used to store a firearm and that is designed to be unlocked only by means of a key, a combination, or other similar means.

(35) The term "body armor" means any product sold or offered for sale, in interstate or foreign commerce, as personal protective body covering intended to protect against gunfire, regardless of whether the product is to be worn alone or is sold as a complement to another product or garment.

(b) For the purposes of this chapter, a member of the Armed Forces on active duty is a resident of the State in which his permanent duty station is located.

## 18 U.S.C. § 922. Unlawful acts.

(a) It shall be unlawful—

(1) for any person—

(A) except a licensed importer, licensed manufacturer, or licensed dealer, to engage in the business of importing, manufacturing, or dealing in firearms, or in the course of such business to ship, transport, or receive any firearm in interstate or foreign commerce; or

(B) except a licensed importer or licensed manufacturer, to engage in the business of importing or manufacturing ammunition, or in the course of such business, to ship, transport, or receive any ammunition in interstate or foreign commerce;

(2) for any importer, manufacturer, dealer, or collector licensed under the provisions of this chapter to ship or transport in interstate or foreign commerce any firearm to any person other than a licensed importer, licensed manufacturer, licensed dealer, or licensed collector, except that—

(A) this paragraph and subsection (b)(3) shall not be held to preclude a licensed importer, licensed manufacturer, licensed dealer, or licensed collector from returning a firearm or replacement firearm of the same kind and type to a person from whom it was received; and this paragraph shall not be held to preclude an individual from mailing a firearm owned in compliance with Federal, State, and local law to a licensed importer, licensed manufacturer, licensed dealer, or licensed collector;

(B) this paragraph shall not be held to preclude a licensed importer, licensed manufacturer, or licensed dealer from depositing a firearm for conveyance in the mails to any officer, employee, agent, or watchman who, pursuant to the provisions of section 1715 of this title, is eligible to receive through the mails pistols, revolvers, and other firearms capable of being concealed on the person, for use in connection with his official duty; and

(C) nothing in this paragraph shall be construed as applying in any manner in the District of Columbia, the Commonwealth of Puerto Rico, or any possession of the United States differently than it would apply if the District of Columbia, the Commonwealth of Puerto Rico, or the possession were in fact a State of the United States;

(3) for any person, other than a licensed importer, licensed manufacturer, licensed dealer, or licensed collector to transport into or receive in the State where he resides (or if the person is a corporation or other business entity, the State where it maintains a place of business) any firearm purchased or otherwise obtained by such person outside that State, except that this paragraph (A) shall not preclude any person who lawfully acquires a firearm by bequest or intestate succession in a State other than his State of residence from transporting the firearm into or receiving it in that State, if it is lawful for such person to purchase or possess such firearm in that State, (B) shall not apply to the transportation or receipt of a firearm obtained in conformity with subsection (b)(3) of this section, and (C) shall not apply to the transportation of any firearm acquired in any State prior to the effective date of this chapter;

(4) for any person, other than a licensed importer, licensed manufacturer, licensed dealer, or licensed collector, to transport in interstate or foreign commerce any destructive device, machinegun (as defined in section 5845 of the Internal Revenue Code of 1986), short-barreled shotgun, or short-barreled rifle, except as specifically authorized by the Attorney General consistent with public safety and necessity;

(5) for any person (other than a licensed importer, licensed manufacturer, licensed dealer, or licensed collector) to transfer, sell, trade, give, transport, or deliver any firearm to any person (other than a licensed importer, licensed manufacturer, licensed dealer, or licensed collector) who the transferor knows or has reasonable cause to believe does not reside in (or if the person is a corporation or other business entity, does not maintain a place of business in) the State in which the transferor resides; except that this paragraph shall not apply to

(A) the transfer, transportation, or delivery of a firearm made to carry out a bequest of a firearm to, or an acquisition by intestate succession of a firearm by, a person who is permitted to acquire or possess a firearm under the laws of the State of his residence, and

(B) the loan or rental of a firearm to any person for temporary use for lawful sporting purposes;

(6) for any person in connection with the acquisition or attempted acquisition of any firearm or ammunition from a licensed importer, licensed manufacturer, licensed dealer, or licensed collector, knowingly to make any false or fictitious oral or written statement or to furnish or exhibit any false, fictitious, or misrepresented identification, intended or likely to deceive such importer, manufacturer, dealer, or collector with respect to any fact material to the lawfulness of the sale or other disposition of such firearm or ammunition under the provisions of this chapter;

(7) for any person to manufacture or import armor piercing ammunition, unless—

(A) the manufacture of such ammunition is for the use of the United States, any department or agency of the United States, any State, or any department, agency, or political subdivision of a State;

(B) the manufacture of such ammunition is for the purpose of exportation; or

(C) the manufacture or importation of such ammunition is for the purpose of testing or experimentation and has been authorized by the Attorney General;

(8) for any manufacturer or importer to sell or deliver armor piercing ammunition, unless such sale or delivery—

(A) is for the use of the United States, any department or agency of the United States, any State, or any department, agency, or political subdivision of a State;

(B) is for the purpose of exportation; or

(C) is for the purpose of testing or experimentation and has been authorized by the Attorney General;

(9) for any person, other than a licensed importer, licensed manufacturer, licensed dealer, or licensed collector, who does not reside in any State to receive any firearms unless such receipt is for lawful sporting purposes.

(b) It shall be unlawful for any licensed importer, licensed manufacturer, licensed dealer, or licensed collector to sell or deliver—

(1) any firearm or ammunition to any individual who the licensee knows or has reasonable cause to believe is less than eighteen years of age, and, if the firearm, or ammunition is other than a shotgun or rifle, or ammunition for a shotgun or rifle, to any individual who the licensee knows or has reasonable cause to believe is less than twenty-one years of age;

(2) any firearm to any person in any State where the purchase or possession by such person of such firearm would be in violation of any State law or any published ordinance applicable at the place of sale, delivery or other disposition, unless the licensee knows or has reasonable cause to believe that the purchase or possession would not be in violation of such State law or such published ordinance;

(3) any firearm to any person who the licensee knows or has reasonable cause to believe does not reside in (or if the person is a corporation or other business entity, does not maintain a place of business in) the State in which the licensee's place of business is located, except that this paragraph (A) shall not apply to the sale or delivery of any rifle or shotgun to a resident of a State other than a State in which the licensee's place of business is located if the transferee meets in person with the transferor to accomplish the transfer, and the sale, delivery, and receipt fully comply with the legal conditions of sale in both such States (and any licensed manufacturer, importer or dealer shall be presumed, for purposes of this subparagraph, in the absence of evidence to the contrary, to have had actual knowledge of the State laws and published ordinances of both States), and (B) shall not apply to the loan or rental of a firearm to any person for temporary use for lawful sporting purposes;

(4) to any person any destructive device, machinegun (as defined in section 5845 of the Internal Revenue Code of 1986), short-barreled shotgun, or short-barreled rifle, except as specifically authorized by the Attorney General consistent with public safety and necessity; and

(5) any firearm or armor-piercing ammunition to any person unless the licensee notes in his records, required to be kept pursuant to section 923 of this chapter, the name, age, and place of residence of such person if the person is an individual, or the identity and principal and local places of business of such person if the person is a corporation or other business entity.

Paragraphs (1), (2), (3), and (4) of this subsection shall not apply to transactions between licensed importers, licensed manufacturers, licensed dealers, and licensed collectors. Paragraph (4) of this subsection shall not apply to a sale or delivery to any research organization designated by the Attorney General.

(c) In any case not otherwise prohibited by this chapter, a licensed importer, licensed manufacturer, or licensed dealer may sell a firearm to a person who does not appear in person at the licensee's business premises (other than another licensed importer, manufacturer, or dealer) only if—

(1) the transferee submits to the transferor a sworn statement in the following form:

"Subject to penalties provided by law, I swear that, in the case of any firearm other than a shotgun or a rifle, I am twenty-one years or more of age, or that, in the case of a shotgun or a rifle, I am eighteen years or more of age; that I am not prohibited by the provisions of chapter 44 of title 18, United States Code, from receiving a firearm in interstate or foreign commerce; and that my receipt of this firearm will not be in violation of any statute of the State and published ordinance applicable to the locality in which I reside. Further, the true title, name, and address of the principal law enforcement officer of the locality to which the firearm will be delivered are _____

Signature _____ Date _____."

and containing blank spaces for the attachment of a true copy of any permit or other information required pursuant to such statute or published ordinance;

(2) the transferor has, prior to the shipment or delivery of the firearm, forwarded by

registered or certified mail (return receipt requested) a copy of the sworn statement, together with a description of the firearm, in a form prescribed by the Attorney General, to the chief law enforcement officer of the transferee's place of residence, and has received a return receipt evidencing delivery of the statement or has had the statement returned due to the refusal of the named addressee to accept such letter in accordance with United States Post Office Department regulations; and

(3) the transferor has delayed shipment or delivery for a period of at least seven days following receipt of the notification of the acceptance or refusal of delivery of the statement.
A copy of the sworn statement and a copy of the notification to the local law enforcement officer, together with evidence of receipt or rejection of that notification shall be retained by the licensee as a part of the records required to be kept under section 923 (g).

(d) It shall be unlawful for any person to sell or otherwise dispose of any firearm or ammunition to any person knowing or having reasonable cause to believe that such person—

(1) is under indictment for, or has been convicted in any court of, a crime punishable by imprisonment for a term exceeding one year;

(2) is a fugitive from justice;

(3) is an unlawful user of or addicted to any controlled substance (as defined in section 102 of the Controlled Substances Act (21 U.S.C. 802));

(4) has been adjudicated as a mental defective or has been committed to any mental institution;

(5) who, being an alien—

(A) is illegally or unlawfully in the United States; or

(B) except as provided in subsection (y)(2), has been admitted to the United States under a nonimmigrant visa (as that term is defined in section 101(a)(26) of the Immigration and Nationality Act (8 U.S.C. 1101 (a)(26)));

(6) who has been discharged from the Armed Forces under dishonorable conditions;

(7) who, having been a citizen of the United States, has renounced his citizenship;

(8) is subject to a court order that restrains such person from harassing, stalking, or threatening an intimate partner of such person or child of such intimate partner or person, or engaging in other conduct that would place an intimate partner in reasonable fear of bodily injury to the partner or child, except that this paragraph shall only apply to a court order that—
(A) was issued after a hearing of which such person received actual notice, and at which such person had the opportunity to participate; and

(B) (i) includes a finding that such person represents a credible threat to the physical safety of such intimate partner or child; or

(ii) by its terms explicitly prohibits the use, attempted use, or threatened use of physical force against such intimate partner or child that would reasonably be expected to cause bodily injury; or

(9) has been convicted in any court of a misdemeanor crime of domestic violence.
This subsection shall not apply with respect to the sale or disposition of a firearm or ammunition to a licensed importer, licensed manufacturer, licensed dealer, or licensed collector who pursuant to subsection (b) of section 925 of this chapter is not precluded from dealing in firearms or ammunition, or to a person who has been granted relief from disabilities pursuant to subsection (c) of section 925 of this chapter.

(e) It shall be unlawful for any person knowingly to deliver or cause to be delivered to any common or contract carrier for transportation or shipment in interstate or foreign commerce, to persons other than licensed importers, licensed manufacturers, licensed dealers, or licensed collectors, any package or other container in which there is any firearm or ammunition without written notice to the carrier that such firearm or ammunition is being transported or shipped; except that any passenger who owns or legally possesses a firearm or ammunition being transported aboard any common or contract carrier for movement with the passenger in interstate or foreign commerce may deliver said firearm or ammunition into the custody of the pilot, captain, conductor or operator of such common or contract carrier for the duration of the trip without violating any of the provisions of this chapter. No common or contract carrier shall require or cause any label, tag, or other written notice to be placed on the outside of any package, luggage, or other container that such package, luggage, or other container contains a firearm.

(f) (1) It shall be unlawful for any common or contract carrier to transport or deliver in interstate or foreign commerce any firearm or ammunition with knowledge or reasonable cause to believe that the shipment, transportation, or receipt thereof would be in violation of the provisions of this chapter.

(2) It shall be unlawful for any common or contract carrier to deliver in interstate or foreign commerce any firearm without obtaining written acknowledgment of receipt from the recipient of the package or other container in which there is a firearm.

(g) It shall be unlawful for any person—

(1) who has been convicted in any court of, a crime punishable by imprisonment for a term exceeding one year;

(2) who is a fugitive from justice;

(3) who is an unlawful user of or addicted to any controlled substance (as defined in section 102 of the Controlled Substances Act (21 U.S.C. 802));

(4) who has been adjudicated as a mental defective or who has been committed to a mental institution;

(5) who, being an alien—

(A) is illegally or unlawfully in the United States; or

(B) except as provided in subsection (y)(2), has been admitted to the United States under a nonimmigrant visa (as that term is defined in section 101(a)(26) of the Immigration and Nationality Act (8 U.S.C. 1101 (a)(26)));

(6) who has been discharged from the Armed Forces under dishonorable conditions;

(7) who, having been a citizen of the United States, has renounced his citizenship;

(8) who is subject to a court order that—

(A) was issued after a hearing of which such person received actual notice, and at which such person had an opportunity to participate;

(B) restrains such person from harassing, stalking, or threatening an intimate partner of such person or child of such intimate partner or person, or engaging in other conduct that would place an intimate partner in reasonable fear of bodily injury to the partner or child; and

(C) (i) includes a finding that such person represents a credible threat to the physical safety of such intimate partner or child; or

(ii) by its terms explicitly prohibits the use, attempted use, or threatened use of physical force against such intimate partner or child that would reasonably be expected to cause bodily injury; or

(9) who has been convicted in any court of a misdemeanor crime of domestic violence, to ship or transport in interstate or foreign commerce, or possess in or affecting commerce, any firearm or ammunition; or to receive any firearm or ammunition which has been shipped or transported in interstate or foreign commerce.

(h) It shall be unlawful for any individual, who to that individual's knowledge and while being employed for any person described in any paragraph of subsection (g) of this section, in the course of such employment—

(1) to receive, possess, or transport any firearm or ammunition in or affecting interstate or foreign commerce; or

(2) to receive any firearm or ammunition which has been shipped or transported in interstate

or foreign commerce.

(i) It shall be unlawful for any person to transport or ship in interstate or foreign commerce, any stolen firearm or stolen ammunition, knowing or having reasonable cause to believe that the firearm or ammunition was stolen.

(j) It shall be unlawful for any person to receive, possess, conceal, store, barter, sell, or dispose of any stolen firearm or stolen ammunition, or pledge or accept as security for a loan any stolen firearm or stolen ammunition, which is moving as, which is a part of, which constitutes, or which has been shipped or transported in, interstate or foreign commerce, either before or after it was stolen, knowing or having reasonable cause to believe that the firearm or ammunition was stolen.

(k) It shall be unlawful for any person knowingly to transport, ship, or receive, in interstate or foreign commerce, any firearm which has had the importer's or manufacturer's serial number removed, obliterated, or altered or to possess or receive any firearm which has had the importer's or manufacturer's serial number removed, obliterated, or altered and has, at any time, been shipped or transported in interstate or foreign commerce.

(l) Except as provided in section 925 (d) of this chapter, it shall be unlawful for any person knowingly to import or bring into the United States or any possession thereof any firearm or ammunition; and it shall be unlawful for any person knowingly to receive any firearm or ammunition which has been imported or brought into the United States or any possession thereof in violation of the provisions of this chapter.

(m) It shall be unlawful for any licensed importer, licensed manufacturer, licensed dealer, or licensed collector knowingly to make any false entry in, to fail to make appropriate entry in, or to fail to properly maintain, any record which he is required to keep pursuant to section 923 of this chapter or regulations promulgated thereunder.

(n) It shall be unlawful for any person who is under indictment for a crime punishable by imprisonment for a term exceeding one year to ship or transport in interstate or foreign commerce any firearm or ammunition or receive any firearm or ammunition which has been shipped or transported in interstate or foreign commerce.

(o) (1) Except as provided in paragraph (2), it shall be unlawful for any person to transfer or possess a machinegun.

(2) This subsection does not apply with respect to—

(A) a transfer to or by, or possession by or under the authority of, the United States or any department or agency thereof or a State, or a department, agency, or political subdivision thereof; or

(B) any lawful transfer or lawful possession of a machinegun that was lawfully possessed before the date this subsection takes effect.

(p) (1) It shall be unlawful for any person to manufacture, import, sell, ship, deliver, possess, transfer, or receive any firearm—

(A) that, after removal of grips, stocks, and magazines, is not as detectable as the Security Exemplar, by walk-through metal detectors calibrated and operated to detect the Security Exemplar; or

(B) any major component of which, when subjected to inspection by the types of x-ray machines commonly used at airports, does not generate an image that accurately depicts the shape of the component. Barium sulfate or other compounds may be used in the fabrication of the component.

(2) For purposes of this subsection—

(A) the term "firearm" does not include the frame or receiver of any such weapon;

(B) the term "major component" means, with respect to a firearm, the barrel, the slide or cylinder, or the frame or receiver of the firearm; and

(C) the term "Security Exemplar" means an object, to be fabricated at the direction of the Attorney General, that is—

(i) constructed of, during the 12-month period beginning on the date of the enactment of this subsection, 3.7 ounces of material type 17–4 PH stainless steel in a shape resembling a handgun; and

(ii) suitable for testing and calibrating metal detectors:

Provided, however, That at the close of such 12-month period, and at appropriate times thereafter the Attorney General shall promulgate regulations to permit the manufacture, importation, sale, shipment, delivery, possession, transfer, or receipt of firearms previously prohibited under this subparagraph that are as detectable as a "Security Exemplar" which contains 3.7 ounces of material type 17–4 PH stainless steel, in a shape resembling a handgun, or such lesser amount as is detectable in view of advances in state-of-the-art developments in weapons detection technology.

(3) Under such rules and regulations as the Attorney General shall prescribe, this subsection shall not apply to the manufacture, possession, transfer, receipt, shipment, or delivery of a firearm by a licensed manufacturer or any person acting pursuant to a contract with a licensed manufacturer, for the purpose of examining and testing such firearm to determine whether paragraph (1) applies to such firearm. The Attorney General shall ensure that rules and regulations adopted pursuant to this paragraph do not impair the manufacture of prototype firearms or the development of new technology.

(4) The Attorney General shall permit the conditional importation of a firearm by a licensed importer or licensed manufacturer, for examination and testing to determine whether or not the unconditional importation of such firearm would violate this subsection.

(5) This subsection shall not apply to any firearm which—

(A) has been certified by the Secretary of Defense or the Director of Central Intelligence, after consultation with the Attorney General and the Administrator of the Federal Aviation Administration, as necessary for military or intelligence applications; and

(B) is manufactured for and sold exclusively to military or intelligence agencies of the United States.

(6) This subsection shall not apply with respect to any firearm manufactured in, imported into, or possessed in the United States before the date of the enactment of the Undetectable Firearms Act of 1988.

(q) (1) The Congress finds and declares that—

(A) crime, particularly crime involving drugs and guns, is a pervasive, nationwide problem;

(B) crime at the local level is exacerbated by the interstate movement of drugs, guns, and criminal gangs;

(C) firearms and ammunition move easily in interstate commerce and have been found in increasing numbers in and around schools, as documented in numerous hearings in both the Committee on the Judiciary the House of Representatives and the Committee on the Judiciary of the Senate;

(D) in fact, even before the sale of a firearm, the gun, its component parts, ammunition, and the raw materials from which they are made have considerably moved in interstate commerce;

(E) while criminals freely move from State to State, ordinary citizens and foreign visitors may fear to travel to or through certain parts of the country due to concern about violent crime and gun violence, and parents may decline to send their children to school for the same reason;

(F) the occurrence of violent crime in school zones has resulted in a decline in the quality of education in our country;

(G) this decline in the quality of education has an adverse impact on interstate commerce and the foreign commerce of the United States;

(H) States, localities, and school systems find it almost impossible to handle gun-related crime by themselves—even States, localities, and school systems that have made strong efforts to prevent, detect, and punish gun-related crime find their efforts unavailing due in part to the failure or inability of other States or localities to take strong measures; and

(I) the Congress has the power, under the interstate commerce clause and other provisions of the Constitution, to enact measures to ensure the integrity and safety of the Nation's schools by enactment of this subsection.

(2) (A) It shall be unlawful for any individual knowingly to possess a firearm that has moved in or that otherwise affects interstate or foreign commerce at a place that the individual knows, or has reasonable cause to believe, is a school zone.

(B) Subparagraph (A) does not apply to the possession of a firearm—

(i) on private property not part of school grounds;

(ii) if the individual possessing the firearm is licensed to do so by the State in which the school zone is located or a political subdivision of the State, and the law of the State or political subdivision requires that, before an individual obtains such a license, the law enforcement authorities of the State or political subdivision verify that the individual is qualified under law to receive the license;

(iii) that is—

(I) not loaded; and

(II) in a locked container, or a locked firearms rack that is on a motor vehicle;

(iv) by an individual for use in a program approved by a school in the school zone;

(v) by an individual in accordance with a contract entered into between a school in the school zone and the individual or an employer of the individual;

(vi) by a law enforcement officer acting in his or her official capacity; or

(vii) that is unloaded and is possessed by an individual while traversing school premises for the purpose of gaining access to public or private lands open to hunting, if the entry on school premises is authorized by school authorities.

(3) (A) Except as provided in subparagraph (B), it shall be unlawful for any person, knowingly or with reckless disregard for the safety of another, to discharge or attempt to discharge a firearm that has moved in or that otherwise affects interstate or foreign commerce at a place that the person knows is a school zone.

(B) Subparagraph (A) does not apply to the discharge of a firearm—

(i) on private property not part of school grounds;

(ii) as part of a program approved by a school in the school zone, by an individual who is participating in the program;

(iii) by an individual in accordance with a contract entered into between a school in a school zone and the individual or an employer of the individual; or

(iv) by a law enforcement officer acting in his or her official capacity.

(4) Nothing in this subsection shall be construed as preempting or preventing a State or local government from enacting a statute establishing gun free school zones as provided in this subsection.

(r) It shall be unlawful for any person to assemble from imported parts any semiautomatic rifle or any shotgun which is identical to any rifle or shotgun prohibited from importation under section 925 (d)(3) of this chapter as not being particularly suitable for or readily adaptable to sporting purposes except that this subsection shall not apply to—

(1) the assembly of any such rifle or shotgun for sale or distribution by a licensed manufacturer to the United States or any department or agency thereof or to any State or any department, agency, or political subdivision thereof; or

(2) the assembly of any such rifle or shotgun for the purposes of testing or experimentation authorized by the Attorney General.

(s)(1) Beginning on the date that is 90 days after the date of enactment of this subsection and ending on the day before the date that is 60 months after such date of enactment, it shall be unlawful for any licensed importer, licensed manufacturer, or licensed dealer to sell, deliver, or transfer a handgun (other than the return of a handgun to the person from whom it was received) to an individual who is not licensed under section 923, unless—

(A) after the most recent proposal of such transfer by the transferee—

(i) the transferor has—

(I) received from the transferee a statement of the transferee containing the information described in paragraph (3);

(II) verified the identity of the transferee by examining the identification document presented;

(III) within I day after the transferee furnishes the statement, provided notice of the contents of the statement to the chief law enforcement officer of the place of residence of the transferee; and

(IV) within I day after the transferee furnishes the statement, transmitted a copy of the statement to the chief law enforcement officer of the place of residence of the transferee; and

(ii) (I) 5 business days (meaning days on which State offices are open) have elapsed from the date the transferor furnished notice of the contents of the statement to the chief law enforcement officer, during which period the transferor has not received information from the chief law enforcement officer that receipt or possession of the handgun by the transferee would be in violation of Federal, State, or local law; or

(II) the transferor has received notice from the chief law enforcement officer that the officer has no information indicating that receipt or possession of the handgun by the transferee would violate Federal, State, or local law;

(B) the transferee has presented to the transferor a written statement, issued by the chief law enforcement officer of the place of residence of the transferee during the 10-day period ending on the date of the most recent proposal of such transfer by the transferee, stating that the transferee requires access to a handgun because of a threat to the life of the transferee or of any member of the household of the transferee;

(C) (i) the transferee has presented to the transferor a permit that—

(I) allows the transferee to possess or acquire a handgun; and

(II) was issued not more than 5 years earlier by the State in which the transfer is to take place; and

(ii) the law of the State provides that such a permit is to be issued only after an authorized government official has verified that the information available to such official does not indicate that possession of a handgun by the transferee would be in violation of the law;

(D) the law of the State requires that, before any licensed importer, licensed manufacturer, or licensed dealer completes the transfer of a handgun to an individual who is not licensed under section 923, an authorized government official verify that the information available to such official does not indicate that possession of a handgun by the transferee would be in violation of law;

(E) the Attorney General has approved the transfer under section 5812 of the Internal Revenue Code of 1986; or

(F) on application of the transferor, the Attorney General has certified that compliance with subparagraph (A)(i)(III) is impracticable because—

(i) the ratio of the number of law enforcement officers of the State in which the transfer is to occur to the number of square miles of land area of the State does not exceed 0.0025;

(ii) the business premises of the transferor at which the transfer is to occur are extremely remote in relation to the chief law enforcement officer; and

(iii) there is an absence of telecommunications facilities in the geographical area in which the business premises are located.

(2) A chief law enforcement officer to whom a transferor has provided notice pursuant to paragraph (1)(A)(i)(III) shall make a reasonable effort to ascertain within 5 business days whether receipt or possession would be in violation of the law, including research in whatever State and local record keeping systems are available and in a national system designated by the Attorney General.

(3) The statement referred to in paragraph (1)(A)(i)(I) shall contain only—

(A) the name, address, and date of birth appearing on a valid identification document (as defined in section 1028 (d)(1)) of the transferee containing a photograph of the transferee and a description of the identification used;

(B) a statement that the transferee—

(i) is not under indictment for, and has not been convicted in any court of, a crime punishable by imprisonment for a term exceeding 1 year, and has not been convicted in any court of a misdemeanor crime of domestic violence;

(ii) is not a fugitive from justice;

(iii) is not an unlawful user of or addicted to any controlled substance (as defined in section 102 of the Controlled Substances Act);

(iv) has not been adjudicated as a mental defective or been committed to a mental institution;

(v) is not an alien who—

(I) is illegally or unlawfully in the United States; or

(II) subject to subsection (y)(2), has been admitted to the United States under a nonimmigrant visa (as that term is defined in section 101(a)(26) of the Immigration and Nationality Act (8 U.S.C. 1101 (a)(26)));

(vi) has not been discharged from the Armed Forces under dishonorable conditions; and

(vii) is not a person who, having been a citizen of the United States, has renounced such citizenship;

(C) the date the statement is made; and

(D) notice that the transferee intends to obtain a handgun from the transferor.

(4) Any transferor of a handgun who, after such transfer, receives a report from a chief law enforcement officer containing information that receipt or possession of the handgun by the transferee violates Federal, State, or local law shall, within 1 business day after receipt of such request, communicate any information related to the transfer that the transferor has about the transfer and the transferee to—

(A) the chief law enforcement officer of the place of business of the transferor; and

(B) the chief law enforcement officer of the place of residence of the transferee.

(5) Any transferor who receives information, not otherwise available to the public, in a report under this subsection shall not disclose such information except to the transferee, to law enforcement authorities, or pursuant to the direction of a court of law.

(6) (A) Any transferor who sells, delivers, or otherwise transfers a handgun to a transferee shall retain the copy of the statement of the transferee with respect to the handgun transaction, and shall retain evidence that the transferor has complied with subclauses (III) and (IV) of paragraph (1)(A)(i) with respect to the statement.

(B) Unless the chief law enforcement officer to whom a statement is transmitted under paragraph (1)(A)(i)(IV) determines that a transaction would violate Federal, State, or local law—

(i) the officer shall, within 20 business days after the date the transferee made the statement on the basis of which the notice was provided, destroy the statement, any record containing information derived from the statement, and any record created as a result of the notice required by paragraph (1)(A)(i)(III);

(ii) the information contained in the statement shall not be conveyed to any person except a person who has a need to know in order to carry out this subsection; and

(iii) the information contained in the statement shall not be used for any purpose other than to carry out this subsection.

(C) If a chief law enforcement officer determines that an individual is ineligible to receive a handgun and the individual requests the officer to provide the reason for such determination, the officer shall provide such reasons to the individual in writing within 20 business days after receipt of the request.

(7) A chief law enforcement officer or other person responsible for providing criminal history background information pursuant to this subsection shall not be liable in an action at law for damages—

(A) for failure to prevent the sale or transfer of a handgun to a person whose receipt or possession of the handgun is unlawful under this section; or

(B) for preventing such a sale or transfer to a person who may lawfully receive or possess a handgun.

(8) For purposes of this subsection, the term "chief law enforcement officer" means the chief of police, the sheriff, or an equivalent officer or the designee of any such individual.

(9) The Attorney General shall take necessary actions to ensure that the provisions of this subsection are published and disseminated to licensed dealers, law enforcement officials, and the public.

(t) (1) Beginning on the date that is 30 days after the Attorney General notifies licensees under section 103(d) of the Brady Handgun Violence Prevention Act that the national instant criminal background check system is established, a licensed importer, licensed manufacturer, or licensed dealer shall not transfer a firearm to any other person who is not licensed under this chapter, unless—

(A) before the completion of the transfer, the licensee contacts the national instant criminal background check system established under section 103 of that Act;

(B) (i) the system provides the licensee with a unique identification number; or

(ii) 3 business days (meaning a day on which State offices are open) have elapsed since the licensee contacted the system, and the system has not notified the licensee that the receipt of a firearm by such other person would violate subsection (g) or (n) of this section; and

(C) the transferor has verified the identity of the transferee by examining a valid identification document (as defined in section 1028 (d) of this title) of the transferee containing a photograph of the transferee.

(2) If receipt of a firearm would not violate subsection (g) or (n) or State law, the system shall—

(A) assign a unique identification number to the transfer;

(B) provide the licensee with the number; and

(C) destroy all records of the system with respect to the call (other than the identifying number and the date the number was assigned) and all records of the system relating to the person or the transfer.

(3) Paragraph (1) shall not apply to a firearm transfer between a licensee and another person if—

(A) (i) such other person has presented to the licensee a permit that—

(I) allows such other person to possess or acquire a firearm; and

(II) was issued not more than 5 years earlier by the State in which the transfer is to take place; and

(ii) the law of the State provides that such a permit is to be issued only after an authorized government official has verified that the information available to such official does not indicate that possession of a firearm by such other person would be in violation of law;

(B) the Attorney General has approved the transfer under section 5812 of the Internal Revenue Code of 1986; or

(C) on application of the transferor, the Attorney General has certified that compliance with paragraph (1)(A) is impracticable because—

(i) the ratio of the number of law enforcement officers of the State in which the transfer is to occur to the number of square miles of land area of the State does not exceed 0.0025;

(ii) the business premises of the licensee at which the transfer is to occur are extremely remote in relation to the chief law enforcement officer (as defined in subsection (s)(8)); and

(iii) there is an absence of telecommunications facilities in the geographical area in which the business premises are located.

(4) If the national instant criminal background check system notifies the licensee that the information available to the system does not demonstrate that the receipt of a firearm by such other

person would violate subsection (g) or (n) or State law, and the licensee transfers a firearm to such other person, the licensee shall include in the record of the transfer the unique identification number provided by the system with respect to the transfer.

(5) If the licensee knowingly transfers a firearm to such other person and knowingly fails to comply with paragraph (1) of this subsection with respect to the transfer and, at the time such other person most recently proposed the transfer, the national instant criminal background check system was operating and information was available to the system demonstrating that receipt of a firearm by such other person would violate subsection (g) or (n) of this section or State law, the Attorney General may, after notice and opportunity for a hearing, suspend for not more than 6 months or revoke any license issued to the licensee under section 923, and may impose on the licensee a civil fine of not more than $5,000.

(6) Neither a local government nor an employee of the Federal Government or of any State or local government, responsible for providing information to the national instant criminal background check system shall be liable in an action at law for damages—

(A) for failure to prevent the sale or transfer of a firearm to a person whose receipt or possession of the firearm is unlawful under this section; or

(B) for preventing such a sale or transfer to a person who may lawfully receive or possess a firearm.

(u) It shall be unlawful for a person to steal or unlawfully take or carry away from the person or the premises of a person who is licensed to engage in the business of importing, manufacturing, or dealing in firearms, any firearm in the licensee's business inventory that has been shipped or transported in interstate or foreign commerce.

(v) , (w) Repealed. Pub. L. 103–322, title XI, § 110105(2), Sept. 13, 1994, 108 Stat. 2000.

(x) (1) It shall be unlawful for a person to sell, deliver, or otherwise transfer to a person who the transferor knows or has reasonable cause to believe is a juvenile—

(A) a handgun; or

(B) ammunition that is suitable for use only in a handgun.

(2) It shall be unlawful for any person who is a juvenile to knowingly possess—

(A) a handgun; or

(B) ammunition that is suitable for use only in a handgun.

(3) This subsection does not apply to—

(A) a temporary transfer of a handgun or ammunition to a juvenile or to the possession or use of a handgun or ammunition by a juvenile if the handgun and ammunition are possessed and used by the juvenile—

(i) in the course of employment, in the course of ranching or farming related to activities at the residence of the juvenile (or on property used for ranching or farming at which the juvenile, with the permission of the property owner or lessee, is performing activities related to the operation of the farm or ranch), target practice, hunting, or a course of instruction in the safe and lawful use of a handgun;

(ii) with the prior written consent of the juvenile's parent or guardian who is not prohibited by Federal, State, or local law from possessing a firearm, except—

(I) during transportation by the juvenile of an unloaded handgun in a locked container directly from the place of transfer to a place at which an activity described in clause (i) is to take place and transportation by the juvenile of that handgun, unloaded and in a locked container, directly from the place at which such an activity took place to the transferor; or

(II) with respect to ranching or farming activities as described in clause (i), a juvenile may possess and use a handgun or ammunition with the prior written approval of the juvenile's parent or legal guardian and at the direction of an adult who is not prohibited by Federal, State or local law from possessing a firearm;

(iii) the juvenile has the prior written consent in the juvenile's possession at all times when a handgun is in the possession of the juvenile; and

(iv) in accordance with State and local law;

(B) a juvenile who is a member of the Armed Forces of the United States or the National Guard who possesses or is armed with a handgun in the line of duty;

(C) a transfer by inheritance of title (but not possession) of a handgun or ammunition to a juvenile; or

(D) the possession of a handgun or ammunition by a juvenile taken in defense of the juvenile or other persons against an intruder into the residence of the juvenile or a residence in which the juvenile is an invited guest.

(4) A handgun or ammunition, the possession of which is transferred to a juvenile in circumstances in which the transferor is not in violation of this subsection shall not be subject to permanent confiscation by the Government if its possession by the juvenile subsequently becomes unlawful because of the conduct of the juvenile, but shall be returned to the lawful owner when such handgun or ammunition is no longer required by the Government for the purposes of investigation or prosecution.

(5) For purposes of this subsection, the term "juvenile" means a person who is less than 18 years of age.

(6) (A) In a prosecution of a violation of this subsection, the court shall require the presence of a juvenile defendant's parent or legal guardian at all proceedings.

(B) The court may use the contempt power to enforce subparagraph (A).

(C) The court may excuse attendance of a parent or legal guardian of a juvenile defendant at a proceeding in a prosecution of a violation of this subsection for good cause shown.

(y) Provisions Relating to Aliens Admitted Under Nonimmigrant Visas.—

(1) Definitions.— In this subsection—

(A) the term "alien" has the same meaning as in section 101(a)(3) of the Immigration and Nationality Act (8 U.S.C. 1101 (a)(3)); and

(B) the term "nonimmigrant visa" has the same meaning as in section 101(a)(26) of the Immigration and Nationality Act (8 U.S.C. 1101 (a)(26)).

(2) Exceptions.— Subsections (d)(5)(B), (g)(5)(B), and (s)(3)(B)(v)(II) do not apply to any alien who has been lawfully admitted to the United States under a nonimmigrant visa, if that alien is—

(A) admitted to the United States for lawful hunting or sporting purposes or is in possession of a hunting license or permit lawfully issued in the United States;

(B) an official representative of a foreign government who is—

(i) accredited to the United States Government or the Government's mission to an international organization having its headquarters in the United States; or

(ii) en route to or from another country to which that alien is accredited;

(C) an official of a foreign government or a distinguished foreign visitor who has been so designated by the Department of State; or

(D) a foreign law enforcement officer of a friendly foreign government entering the United States on official law enforcement business.

(3) Waiver.—

(A) Conditions for waiver.— Any individual who has been admitted to the United States under a nonimmigrant visa may receive a waiver from the requirements of subsection (g)(5), if—

(i) the individual submits to the Attorney General a petition that meets the requirements of subparagraph (C); and

(ii) the Attorney General approves the petition.

(B) Petition.— Each petition under subparagraph (B) shall—

(i) demonstrate that the petitioner has resided in the United States for a continuous period of not less than 180 days before the date on which the petition is submitted under this paragraph; and

(ii) include a written statement from the embassy or consulate of the petitioner, authorizing the petitioner to acquire a firearm or ammunition and certifying that the alien would not, absent the application of subsection (g)(5)(B), otherwise be prohibited from such acquisition under subsection (g).

(C) Approval of petition.— The Attorney General shall approve a petition submitted in accordance with this paragraph, if the Attorney General determines that waiving the requirements of subsection (g)(5)(B) with respect to the petitioner—

(i) would be in the interests of justice; and

(ii) would not jeopardize the public safety.

(z) Secure Gun Storage or Safety Device.—

(1) In general.— Except as provided under paragraph (2), it shall be unlawful for any licensed importer, licensed manufacturer, or licensed dealer to sell, deliver, or transfer any handgun to any person other than any person licensed under this chapter, unless the transferee is provided with a secure gun storage or safety device (as defined in section 921 (a)(34)) for that handgun.

(2) Exceptions.— Paragraph (1) shall not apply to—

(A) (i) the manufacture for, transfer to, or possession by, the United States, a department or agency of the United States, a State, or a department, agency, or political subdivision of a State, of a handgun; or

(ii) the transfer to, or possession by, a law enforcement officer employed by an entity referred to in clause (i) of a handgun for law enforcement purposes (whether on or off duty); or

(B) the transfer to, or possession by, a rail police officer employed by a rail carrier and certified or commissioned as a police officer under the laws of a State of a handgun for purposes of law enforcement (whether on or off duty);

(C) the transfer to any person of a handgun listed as a curio or relic by the Secretary pursuant to section 921 (a)(13); or

(D) the transfer to any person of a handgun for which a secure gun storage or safety device is temporarily unavailable for the reasons described in the exceptions stated in section 923 (e), if the licensed manufacturer, licensed importer, or licensed dealer delivers to the transferee within 10 calendar days from the date of the delivery of the handgun to the transferee a secure gun storage or safety device for the handgun.

(3) Liability for use.—

(A) In general.— Notwithstanding any other provision of law, a person who has lawful possession and control of a handgun, and who uses a secure gun storage or safety device with the handgun, shall be entitled to immunity from a qualified civil liability action.

(B) Prospective actions.— A qualified civil liability action may not be brought in any Federal or State court.

(C) Defined term.— As used in this paragraph, the term "qualified civil liability action"—

(i) means a civil action brought by any person against a person described in subparagraph (A) for damages resulting from the criminal or unlawful misuse of the handgun by a third party, if—

(I) the handgun was accessed by another person who did not have the permission or authorization of the person having lawful possession and control of the handgun to have access to it; and

(II) at the time access was gained by the person not so authorized, the handgun had been made inoperable by use of a secure gun storage or safety device; and

(ii) shall not include an action brought against the person having lawful possession and control of the handgun for negligent entrustment or negligence per se.

## 18 U.S.C. § 924. Penalties.

(a) (1) Except as otherwise provided in this subsection, subsection (b), (c), (f), or (p) of this section, or in section 929, whoever—

(A) knowingly makes any false statement or representation with respect to the information required by this chapter to be kept in the records of a person licensed under this chapter or in applying for any license or exemption or relief from disability under the provisions of this chapter;

(B) knowingly violates subsection (a)(4), (f), (k), or (q) of section 922;

(C) knowingly imports or brings into the United States or any possession thereof any firearm or ammunition in violation of section 922 (l); or

(D) willfully violates any other provision of this chapter,

shall be fined under this title, imprisoned not more than five years, or both.

(2) Whoever knowingly violates subsection (a)(6), (d), (g), (h), (i), (j), or (o) of section 922 shall be fined as provided in this title, imprisoned not more than 10 years, or both.

(3) Any licensed dealer, licensed importer, licensed manufacturer, or licensed collector who knowingly—

(A) makes any false statement or representation with respect to the information required by the provisions of this chapter to be kept in the records of a person licensed under this chapter, or

(B) violates subsection (m) of section 922,

shall be fined under this title, imprisoned not more than one year, or both.

(4) Whoever violates section 922 (q) shall be fined under this title, imprisoned for not more than 5 years, or both. Notwithstanding any other provision of law, the term of imprisonment imposed under this paragraph shall not run concurrently with any other term of imprisonment imposed under any other provision of law. Except for the authorization of a term of imprisonment of not more than 5 years made in this paragraph, for the purpose of any other law a violation of section 922 (q) shall be deemed to be a misdemeanor.

(5) Whoever knowingly violates subsection (s) or (t) of section 922 shall be fined under this title, imprisoned for not more than 1 year, or both.

(6)(A)(i) A juvenile who violates section 922 (x) shall be fined under this title, imprisoned not more than 1 year, or both, except that a juvenile described in clause (ii) shall be sentenced to probation on appropriate conditions and shall not be incarcerated unless the juvenile fails to comply with a condition of probation.

(ii) A juvenile is described in this clause if—

(I) the offense of which the juvenile is charged is possession of a handgun or ammunition in violation of section 922 (x)(2); and

(II) the juvenile has not been convicted in any court of an offense (including an offense under section 922 (x) or a similar State law, but not including any other offense consisting of conduct that if engaged in by an adult would not constitute an offense) or adjudicated as a juvenile delinquent for conduct that if engaged in by an adult would constitute an offense.

(B) A person other than a juvenile who knowingly violates section 922 (x)—

(i) shall be fined under this title, imprisoned not more than 1 year, or both; and

(ii) if the person sold, delivered, or otherwise transferred a handgun or ammunition to a juvenile knowing or having reasonable cause to know that the juvenile intended to carry or otherwise possess or discharge or otherwise use the handgun or ammunition in the commission of a crime of violence, shall be fined under this title, imprisoned not more than 10 years, or both.

(7) Whoever knowingly violates section 931 shall be fined under this title, imprisoned not more than 3 years, or both.

(b) Whoever, with intent to commit therewith an offense punishable by imprisonment for a term exceeding one year, or with knowledge or reasonable cause to believe that an offense punishable by imprisonment for a term exceeding one year is to be committed therewith, ships, transports, or receives a firearm or any ammunition in interstate or foreign commerce shall be fined under this title, or imprisoned not more than ten years, or both.

(c) (1) (A) Except to the extent that a greater minimum sentence is otherwise provided by this subsection or by any other provision of law, any person who, during and in relation to any crime of violence or drug trafficking crime (including a crime of violence or drug trafficking crime that provides for an enhanced punishment if committed by the use of a deadly or dangerous weapon or device) for which the person may be prosecuted in a court of the United States, uses or carries a firearm, or who, in furtherance of any such crime, possesses a firearm, shall, in addition to the punishment provided for such crime of violence or drug trafficking crime—

(i) be sentenced to a term of imprisonment of not less than 5 years;

(ii) if the firearm is brandished, be sentenced to a term of imprisonment of not less than 7 years; and

(iii) if the firearm is discharged, be sentenced to a term of imprisonment of not less than 10 years.

(B) If the firearm possessed by a person convicted of a violation of this subsection—

(i) is a short-barreled rifle, short-barreled shotgun, or semiautomatic assault weapon, the person shall be sentenced to a term of imprisonment of not less than 10 years; or

(ii) is a machinegun or a destructive device, or is equipped with a firearm silencer or firearm muffler, the person shall be sentenced to a term of imprisonment of not less than 30 years.

(C) In the case of a second or subsequent conviction under this subsection, the person shall—

(i) be sentenced to a term of imprisonment of not less than 25 years; and

(ii) if the firearm involved is a machinegun or a destructive device, or is equipped with a firearm silencer or firearm muffler, be sentenced to imprisonment for life.

(D) Notwithstanding any other provision of law—

(i) a court shall not place on probation any person convicted of a violation of this subsection; and

(ii) no term of imprisonment imposed on a person under this subsection shall run concurrently with any other term of imprisonment imposed on the person, including any term of imprisonment imposed for the crime of violence or drug trafficking crime during which the firearm was used, carried, or possessed.

(2) For purposes of this subsection, the term "drug trafficking crime" means any felony punishable under the Controlled Substances Act (21 U.S.C. 801 et seq.), the Controlled Substances Import and Export Act (21 U.S.C. 951 et seq.), or chapter 705 of title 46.

(3) For purposes of this subsection the term "crime of violence" means an offense that is a felony and—

(A) has as an element the use, attempted use, or threatened use of physical force against the person or property of another, or

(B) that by its nature, involves a substantial risk that physical force against the person or property of another may be used in the course of committing the offense.

(4) For purposes of this subsection, the term "brandish" means, with respect to a firearm, to display all or part of the firearm, or otherwise make the presence of the firearm known to another person, in order to intimidate that person, regardless of whether the firearm is directly visible to that person.

(5) Except to the extent that a greater minimum sentence is otherwise provided under this subsection, or by any other provision of law, any person who, during and in relation to any crime of violence or drug trafficking crime (including a crime of violence or drug trafficking crime that provides for an enhanced punishment if committed by the use of a deadly or dangerous weapon or device) for which the person may be prosecuted in a court of the United States, uses or carries armor piercing ammunition, or who, in furtherance of any such crime, possesses armor piercing ammunition, shall, in addition to the punishment provided for such crime of violence or drug trafficking crime or conviction

under this section—

(A) be sentenced to a term of imprisonment of not less than 15 years; and

(B) if death results from the use of such ammunition—

(i) if the killing is murder (as defined in section 1111), be punished by death or sentenced to a term of imprisonment for any term of years or for life; and

(ii) if the killing is manslaughter (as defined in section 1112), be punished as provided in section 1112.

(d) (1) Any firearm or ammunition involved in or used in any knowing violation of subsection (a)(4), (a)(6), (f), (g), (h), (i), (j), or (k) of section 922, or knowing importation or bringing into the United States or any possession thereof any firearm or ammunition in violation of section 922 (l), or knowing violation of section 924, or willful violation of any other provision of this chapter or any rule or regulation promulgated thereunder, or any violation of any other criminal law of the United States, or any firearm or ammunition intended to be used in any offense referred to in paragraph (3) of this subsection, where such intent is demonstrated by clear and convincing evidence, shall be subject to seizure and forfeiture, and all provisions of the Internal Revenue Code of 1986 relating to the seizure, forfeiture, and disposition of firearms, as defined in section 5845(a) of that Code, shall, so far as applicable, extend to seizures and forfeitures under the provisions of this chapter: Provided, That upon acquittal of the owner or possessor, or dismissal of the charges against him other than upon motion of the Government prior to trial, or lapse of or court termination of the restraining order to which he is subject, the seized or relinquished firearms or ammunition shall be returned forthwith to the owner or possessor or to a person delegated by the owner or possessor unless the return of the firearms or ammunition would place the owner or possessor or his delegate in violation of law. Any action or proceeding for the forfeiture of firearms or ammunition shall be commenced within one hundred and twenty days of such seizure.

(2) (A) In any action or proceeding for the return of firearms or ammunition seized under the provisions of this chapter, the court shall allow the prevailing party, other than the United States, a reasonable attorney's fee, and the United States shall be liable therefor.

(B) In any other action or proceeding under the provisions of this chapter, the court, when it finds that such action was without foundation, or was initiated vexatiously, frivolously, or in bad faith, shall allow the prevailing party, other than the United States, a reasonable attorney's fee, and the United States shall be liable therefor.

(C) Only those firearms or quantities of ammunition particularly named and individually identified as involved in or used in any violation of the provisions of this chapter or any rule or regulation issued thereunder, or any other criminal law of the United States or as intended to be used in any offense referred to in paragraph (3) of this subsection, where such intent is demonstrated by clear and convincing evidence, shall be subject to seizure, forfeiture, and disposition.

(D) The United States shall be liable for attorneys' fees under this paragraph only to the extent provided in advance by appropriation Acts.

(3) The offenses referred to in paragraphs (1) and (2)(C) of this subsection are—

(A) any crime of violence, as that term is defined in section 924 (c)(3) of this title;

(B) any offense punishable under the Controlled Substances Act (21 U.S.C. 801 et seq.) or the Controlled Substances Import and Export Act (21 U.S.C. 951 et seq.);

(C) any offense described in section 922 (a)(1), 922 (a)(3), 922 (a)(5), or 922 (b)(3) of this title, where the firearm or ammunition intended to be used in any such offense is involved in a pattern of activities which includes a violation of any offense described in section 922 (a)(1), 922 (a)(3), 922 (a)(5), or 922 (b)(3) of this title;

(D) any offense described in section 922 (d) of this title where the firearm or ammunition is intended to be used in such offense by the transferor of such firearm or ammunition;

(E) any offense described in section 922 (i), 922 (j), 922 (l), 922 (n), or 924 (b) of this title;

and

(F) any offense which may be prosecuted in a court of the United States which involves the exportation of firearms or ammunition.

(e) (1) In the case of a person who violates section 922 (g) of this title and has three previous convictions by any court referred to in section 922 (g)(1) of this title for a violent felony or a serious drug offense, or both, committed on occasions different from one another, such person shall be fined under this title and imprisoned not less than fifteen years, and, notwithstanding any other provision of law, the court shall not suspend the sentence of, or grant a probationary sentence to, such person with respect to the conviction under section 922 (g).

(2) As used in this subsection—

(A) the term "serious drug offense" means—

(i) an offense under the Controlled Substances Act (21 U.S.C. 801 et seq.), the Controlled Substances Import and Export Act (21 U.S.C. 951 et seq.), or chapter 705 of title 46 for which a maximum term of imprisonment of ten years or more is prescribed by law; or

(ii) an offense under State law, involving manufacturing, distributing, or possessing with intent to manufacture or distribute, a controlled substance (as defined in section 102 of the Controlled Substances Act (21 U.S.C. 802)), for which a maximum term of imprisonment of ten years or more is prescribed by law;

(B) the term "violent felony" means any crime punishable by imprisonment for a term exceeding one year, or any act of juvenile delinquency involving the use or carrying of a firearm, knife, or destructive device that would be punishable by imprisonment for such term if committed by an adult, that—

(i) has as an element the use, attempted use, or threatened use of physical force against the person of another; or

(ii) is burglary, arson, or extortion, involves use of explosives, or otherwise involves conduct that presents a serious potential risk of physical injury to another; and

(C) the term "conviction" includes a finding that a person has committed an act of juvenile delinquency involving a violent felony.

(f) In the case of a person who knowingly violates section 922 (p), such person shall be fined under this title, or imprisoned not more than 5 years, or both.

(g) Whoever, with the intent to engage in conduct which—

(1) constitutes an offense listed in section 1961 (1),

(2) is punishable under the Controlled Substances Act (21 U.S.C. 801 et seq.), the Controlled Substances Import and Export Act (21 U.S.C. 951 et seq.), or chapter 705 of title 46,

(3) violates any State law relating to any controlled substance (as defined in section 102(6) of the Controlled Substances Act (21 U.S.C. 802 (6))), or

(4) constitutes a crime of violence (as defined in subsection (c)(3)),

travels from any State or foreign country into any other State and acquires, transfers, or attempts to acquire or transfer, a firearm in such other State in furtherance of such purpose, shall be imprisoned not more than 10 years, fined in accordance with this title, or both.

(h) Whoever knowingly transfers a firearm, knowing that such firearm will be used to commit a crime of violence (as defined in subsection (c)(3)) or drug trafficking crime (as defined in subsection (c)(2)) shall be imprisoned not more than 10 years, fined in accordance with this title, or both.

(i) (1) A person who knowingly violates section 922 (u) shall be fined under this title, imprisoned not more than 10 years, or both.

(2) Nothing contained in this subsection shall be construed as indicating an intent on the part of Congress to occupy the field in which provisions of this subsection operate to the exclusion of State laws on the same subject matter, nor shall any provision of this subsection be construed as invalidating

any provision of State law unless such provision is inconsistent with any of the purposes of this subsection.

(j) A person who, in the course of a violation of subsection (c), causes the death of a person through the use of a firearm, shall—

(1) if the killing is a murder (as defined in section 1111), be punished by death or by imprisonment for any term of years or for life; and

(2) if the killing is manslaughter (as defined in section 1112), be punished as provided in that section.

(k) A person who, with intent to engage in or to promote conduct that—

(1) is punishable under the Controlled Substances Act (21 U.S.C. 801 et seq.), the Controlled Substances Import and Export Act (21 U.S.C. 951 et seq.), or chapter 705 of title 46;

(2) violates any law of a State relating to any controlled substance (as defined in section 102 of the Controlled Substances Act, 21 U.S.C. 802); or

(3) constitutes a crime of violence (as defined in subsection (c)(3)),

smuggles or knowingly brings into the United States a firearm, or attempts to do so, shall be imprisoned not more than 10 years, fined under this title, or both.

(l) A person who steals any firearm which is moving as, or is a part of, or which has moved in, interstate or foreign commerce shall be imprisoned for not more than 10 years, fined under this title, or both.

(m) A person who steals any firearm from a licensed importer, licensed manufacturer, licensed dealer, or licensed collector shall be fined under this title, imprisoned not more than 10 years, or both.

(n) A person who, with the intent to engage in conduct that constitutes a violation of section 922 (a)(1)(A), travels from any State or foreign country into any other State and acquires, or attempts to acquire, a firearm in such other State in furtherance of such purpose shall be imprisoned for not more than 10 years.

(o) A person who conspires to commit an offense under subsection (c) shall be imprisoned for not more than 20 years, fined under this title, or both; and if the firearm is a machinegun or destructive device, or is equipped with a firearm silencer or muffler, shall be imprisoned for any term of years or life.

(p) Penalties Relating To Secure Gun Storage or Safety Device.—

(1) In general.—

(A) Suspension or revocation of license; civil penalties.— With respect to each violation of section 922 (z)(1) by a licensed manufacturer, licensed importer, or licensed dealer, the Secretary may, after notice and opportunity for hearing—

(i) suspend for not more than 6 months, or revoke, the license issued to the licensee under this chapter that was used to conduct the firearms transfer; or

(ii) subject the licensee to a civil penalty in an amount equal to not more than $2,500.

(B) Review.— An action of the Secretary under this paragraph may be reviewed only as provided under section 923 (f).

(2) Administrative remedies.— The suspension or revocation of a license or the imposition of a civil penalty under paragraph (1) shall not preclude any administrative remedy that is otherwise available to the Secretary.

## 18 U.S.C. § 925. Exceptions: Relief from disabilities.

(a)(1) The provisions of this chapter, except for sections 922 (d)(9) and 922 (g)(9) and provisions relating to firearms subject to the prohibitions of section 922 (p), shall not apply with respect to the transportation, shipment, receipt, possession, or importation of any firearm or ammunition imported for, sold or shipped to, or issued for the use of, the United States or any department or agency thereof or any State or any department, agency, or political subdivision thereof.

(2) The provisions of this chapter, except for provisions relating to firearms subject to the prohibitions of section 922 (p), shall not apply with respect to

(A) the shipment or receipt of firearms or ammunition when sold or issued by the Secretary of the Army pursuant to section 4308 of title 10 before the repeal of such section by section 1624(a) of the Corporation for the Promotion of Rifle Practice and Firearms Safety Act, and

(B) the transportation of any such firearm or ammunition carried out to enable a person, who lawfully received such firearm or ammunition from the Secretary of the Army, to engage in military training or in competitions.

(3) Unless otherwise prohibited by this chapter, except for provisions relating to firearms subject to the prohibitions of section 922 (p), or any other Federal law, a licensed importer, licensed manufacturer, or licensed dealer may ship to a member of the United States Armed Forces on active duty outside the United States or to clubs, recognized by the Department of Defense, whose entire membership is composed of such members, and such members or clubs may receive a firearm or ammunition determined by the Attorney General to be generally recognized as particularly suitable for sporting purposes and intended for the personal use of such member or club.

(4) When established to the satisfaction of the Attorney General to be consistent with the provisions of this chapter, except for provisions relating to firearms subject to the prohibitions of section 922 (p), and other applicable Federal and State laws and published ordinances, the Attorney General may authorize the transportation, shipment, receipt, or importation into the United States to the place of residence of any member of the United States Armed Forces who is on active duty outside the United States (or who has been on active duty outside the United States within the sixty day period immediately preceding the transportation, shipment, receipt, or importation), of any firearm or ammunition which is

(A) determined by the Attorney General to be generally recognized as particularly suitable for sporting purposes, or determined by the Department of Defense to be a type of firearm normally classified as a war souvenir, and

(B) intended for the personal use of such member.

(5) For the purpose of paragraph (3) of this subsection, the term "United States" means each of the several States and the District of Columbia.

(b) A licensed importer, licensed manufacturer, licensed dealer, or licensed collector who is indicted for a crime punishable by imprisonment for a term exceeding one year, may, notwithstanding any other provision of this chapter, continue operation pursuant to his existing license (if prior to the expiration of the term of the existing license timely application is made for a new license) during the term of such indictment and until any conviction pursuant to the indictment becomes final.

(c) A person who is prohibited from possessing, shipping, transporting, or receiving firearms or ammunition may make application to the Attorney General for relief from the disabilities imposed by Federal laws with respect to the acquisition, receipt, transfer, shipment, transportation, or possession of firearms, and the Attorney General may grant such relief if it is established to his satisfaction that the circumstances regarding the disability, and the applicant's record and reputation, are such that the applicant will not be likely to act in a manner dangerous to public safety and that the granting of the relief would not be contrary to the public interest. Any person whose application for relief from disabilities is denied by the Attorney General may file a petition with the United States district court for the district in which he resides for a judicial review of such denial. The court may in its discretion admit additional evidence where failure to do so would result in a miscarriage of justice. A licensed importer, licensed manufacturer, licensed dealer, or licensed collector conducting operations under this chapter, who makes application for relief from the disabilities incurred under this chapter, shall not be barred by such disability from further operations under his license pending final action on an application for relief filed pursuant to this section. Whenever the Attorney General grants relief to any person pursuant to this section he shall promptly publish in the Federal Register notice of such action, together with the reasons therefor.

(d) The Attorney General shall authorize a firearm or ammunition to be imported or brought into the United States or any possession thereof if the firearm or ammunition—

(1) is being imported or brought in for scientific or research purposes, or is for use in connection with competition or training pursuant to chapter 401 of title 10;

(2) is an unserviceable firearm, other than a machinegun as defined in section 5845(b) of the Internal Revenue Code of 1986 (not readily restorable to firing condition), imported or brought in as a curio or museum piece;

(3) is of a type that does not fall within the definition of a firearm as defined in section 5845(a) of the Internal Revenue Code of 1986 and is generally recognized as particularly suitable for or readily adaptable to sporting purposes, excluding surplus military firearms, except in any case where the Attorney General has not authorized the importation of the firearm pursuant to this paragraph, it shall be unlawful to import any frame, receiver, or barrel of such firearm which would be prohibited if assembled; or

(4) was previously taken out of the United States or a possession by the person who is bringing in the firearm or ammunition.

The Attorney General shall permit the conditional importation or bringing in of a firearm or ammunition for examination and testing in connection with the making of a determination as to whether the importation or bringing in of such firearm or ammunition will be allowed under this subsection.

(e) Notwithstanding any other provision of this title, the Attorney General shall authorize the importation of, by any licensed importer, the following:

(1) All rifles and shotguns listed as curios or relics by the Attorney General pursuant to section 921 (a)(13), and

(2) All handguns, listed as curios or relics by the Attorney General pursuant to section 921 (a)(13), provided that such handguns are generally recognized as particularly suitable for or readily adaptable to sporting purposes.

(f) The Attorney General shall not authorize, under subsection (d), the importation of any firearm the importation of which is prohibited by section 922 (p).

## 18 U.S.C. § 926A.  Interstate transportation of firearms

Notwithstanding any other provision of any law or any rule or regulation of a State or any political subdivision thereof, any person who is not otherwise prohibited by this chapter from transporting, shipping, or receiving a firearm shall be entitled to transport a firearm for any lawful purpose from any place where he may lawfully possess and carry such firearm to any other place where he may lawfully possess and carry such firearm if, during such transportation the firearm is unloaded, and neither the firearm nor any ammunition being transported is readily accessible or is directly accessible from the passenger compartment of such transporting vehicle: Provided, That in the case of a vehicle without a compartment separate from the driver's compartment the firearm or ammunition shall be contained in a locked container other than the glove compartment or console.

## 18 U.S.C. § 930.  Possession of firearms and dangerous weapons in Federal facilities

(a) Except as provided in subsection (d), whoever knowingly possesses or causes to be present a firearm or other dangerous weapon in a Federal facility (other than a Federal court facility), or attempts to do so, shall be fined under this title or imprisoned not more than 1 year, or both.

(b) Whoever, with intent that a firearm or other dangerous weapon be used in the commission of a crime, knowingly possesses or causes to be present such firearm or dangerous weapon in a Federal facility, or attempts to do so, shall be fined under this title or imprisoned not more than

5 years, or both.

(c) A person who kills any person in the course of a violation of subsection (a) or (b), or in the course of an attack on a Federal facility involving the use of a firearm or other dangerous weapon, or attempts or conspires to do such an act, shall be punished as provided in sections 1111, 1112, 1113, and 1117.

(d) Subsection (a) shall not apply to—

(1) the lawful performance of official duties by an officer, agent, or employee of the United States, a State, or a political subdivision thereof, who is authorized by law to engage in or supervise the prevention, detection, investigation, or prosecution of any violation of law;

(2) the possession of a firearm or other dangerous weapon by a Federal official or a member of the Armed Forces if such possession is authorized by law; or

(3) the lawful carrying of firearms or other dangerous weapons in a Federal facility incident to hunting or other lawful purposes.

(e) (1) Except as provided in paragraph (2), whoever knowingly possesses or causes to be present a firearm or other dangerous weapon in a Federal court facility, or attempts to do so, shall be fined under this title, imprisoned not more than 2 years, or both.

(2) Paragraph (1) shall not apply to conduct which is described in paragraph (1) or (2) of subsection (d).

(f) Nothing in this section limits the power of a court of the United States to punish for contempt or to promulgate rules or orders regulating, restricting, or prohibiting the possession of weapons within any building housing such court or any of its proceedings, or upon any grounds appurtenant to such building.

(g) As used in this section:

(1) The term "Federal facility" means a building or part thereof owned or leased by the Federal Government, where Federal employees are regularly present for the purpose of performing their official duties.

(2) The term "dangerous weapon" means a weapon, device, instrument, material, or substance, animate or inanimate, that is used for, or is readily capable of, causing death or serious bodily injury, except that such term does not include a pocket knife with a blade of less than 21/2 inches in length.

(3) The term "Federal court facility" means the courtroom, judges' chambers, witness rooms, jury deliberation rooms, attorney conference rooms, prisoner holding cells, offices of the court clerks, the United States attorney, and the United States marshal, probation and parole offices, and adjoining corridors of any court of the United States.

(h) Notice of the provisions of subsections (a) and (b) shall be posted conspicuously at each public entrance to each Federal facility, and notice of subsection (e) shall be posted conspicuously at each public entrance to each Federal court facility, and no person shall be convicted of an offense under subsection (a) or (e) with respect to a Federal facility if such notice is not so posted at such facility, unless such person had actual notice of subsection (a) or (e), as the case may be.

## 26 U.S.C. § 5845. Definitions.

For the purpose of this chapter—

(a) Firearm

The term "firearm" means

(1) a shotgun having a barrel or barrels of less than 18 inches in length;

(2) a weapon made from a shotgun if such weapon as modified has an overall length of less than 26 inches or a barrel or barrels of less than 18 inches in length;

(3) a rifle having a barrel or barrels of less than 16 inches in length;

(4) a weapon made from a rifle if such weapon as modified has an overall length of less than

314

26 inches or a barrel or barrels of less than 16 inches in length;

(5) any other weapon, as defined in subsection (e);

(6) a machinegun;

(7) any silencer (as defined in section 921 of title 18, United States Code); and

(8) a destructive device. The term "firearm" shall not include an antique firearm or any device (other than a machinegun or destructive device) which, although designed as a weapon, the Secretary finds by reason of the date of its manufacture, value, design, and other characteristics is primarily a collector's item and is not likely to be used as a weapon.

(b) Machinegun

The term "machinegun" means any weapon which shoots, is designed to shoot, or can be readily restored to shoot, automatically more than one shot, without manual reloading, by a single function of the trigger. The term shall also include the frame or receiver of any such weapon, any part designed and intended solely and exclusively, or combination of parts designed and intended, for use in converting a weapon into a machinegun, and any combination of parts from which a machinegun can be assembled if such parts are in the possession or under the control of a person.

(c) Rifle

The term "rifle" means a weapon designed or redesigned, made or remade, and intended to be fired from the shoulder and designed or redesigned and made or remade to use the energy of the explosive in a fixed cartridge to fire only a single projectile through a rifled bore for each single pull of the trigger, and shall include any such weapon which may be readily restored to fire a fixed cartridge.

(d) Shotgun

The term "shotgun" means a weapon designed or redesigned, made or remade, and intended to be fired from the shoulder and designed or redesigned and made or remade to use the energy of the explosive in a fixed shotgun shell to fire through a smooth bore either a number of projectiles (ball shot) or a single projectile for each pull of the trigger, and shall include any such weapon which may be readily restored to fire a fixed shotgun shell.

(e) Any other weapon

The term "any other weapon" means any weapon or device capable of being concealed on the person from which a shot can be discharged through the energy of an explosive, a pistol or revolver having a barrel with a smooth bore designed or redesigned to fire a fixed shotgun shell, weapons with combination shotgun and rifle barrels 12 inches or more, less than 18 inches in length, from which only a single discharge can be made from either barrel without manual reloading, and shall include any such weapon which may be readily restored to fire. Such term shall not include a pistol or a revolver having a rifled bore, or rifled bores, or weapons designed, made, or intended to be fired from the shoulder and not capable of firing fixed ammunition.

(f) Destructive device

The term "destructive device" means

(1) any explosive, incendiary, or poison gas

(A) bomb,

(B) grenade,

(C) rocket having a propellent charge of more than four ounces,

(D) missile having an explosive or incendiary charge of more than one-quarter ounce,

(E) mine, or

(F) similar device;

(2) any type of weapon by whatever name known which will, or which may be readily converted to, expel a projectile by the action of an explosive or other propellant, the barrel or barrels of which have a bore of more than one-half inch in diameter, except a shotgun or shotgun shell which the Secretary finds is generally recognized as particularly suitable for sporting purposes; and

(3) any combination of parts either designed or intended for use in converting any device into

a destructive device as defined in subparagraphs (1) and (2) and from which a destructive device may be readily assembled. The term "destructive device" shall not include any device which is neither designed nor redesigned for use as a weapon; any device, although originally designed for use as a weapon, which is redesigned for use as a signaling, pyrotechnic, line throwing, safety, or similar device; surplus ordnance sold, loaned, or given by the Secretary of the Army pursuant to the provisions of section 4684 (2), 4685, or 4686 of title 10 of the United States Code; or any other device which the Secretary finds is not likely to be used as a weapon, or is an antique or is a rifle which the owner intends to use solely for sporting purposes.

(g) Antique firearm

The term "antique firearm" means any firearm not designed or redesigned for using rim fire or conventional center fire ignition with fixed ammunition and manufactured in or before 1898 (including any matchlock, flintlock, percussion cap, or similar type of ignition system or replica thereof, whether actually manufactured before or after the year 1898) and also any firearm using fixed ammunition manufactured in or before 1898, for which ammunition is no longer manufactured in the United States and is not readily available in the ordinary channels of commercial trade.

(h) Unserviceable firearm

The term "unserviceable firearm" means a firearm which is incapable of discharging a shot by means of an explosive and incapable of being readily restored to a firing condition.

(i) Make

The term "make", and the various derivatives of such word, shall include manufacturing (other than by one qualified to engage in such business under this chapter), putting together, altering, any combination of these, or otherwise producing a firearm.

(j) Transfer

The term "transfer" and the various derivatives of such word, shall include selling, assigning, pledging, leasing, loaning, giving away, or otherwise disposing of.

(k) Dealer

The term "dealer" means any person, not a manufacturer or importer, engaged in the business of selling, renting, leasing, or loaning firearms and shall include pawnbrokers who accept firearms as collateral for loans.

(l) Importer

The term "importer" means any person who is engaged in the business of importing or bringing firearms into the United States.

(m) Manufacturer

The term "manufacturer" means any person who is engaged in the business of manufacturing firearms.

# Appendix Five

# Famous Gun Quotes

"A free people ought to be armed." - George Washington

"That rifle on the wall of the labourer's cottage or working class flat is the symbol of democracy. It is our job to see that it stays there." - George Orwell

"Our task of creating a Socialist America can only succeed when those who resist us are totally disarmed." - Sarah Brady

"Firearms are second only to the Constitution in importance; they are the peoples' liberty's teeth." - George Washington

"...the right to defend one's home and one's person when attacked has been guaranteed through the ages by common law." Martin Luther King

" A free people ought not only to be armed and disciplined, but they should have sufficient arms and ammunition to maintain a status of independence from any who might attempt to abuse them, which would include their own government." - George Washington

"If I could have banned them all - Mr. And Mrs. America turn in your guns - I would have!" - Diane Feinstein

"A woman who demands further gun control legislation is like a chicken who roots for Colonel Sanders." - Larry Elder

"Those who would give up essential liberty to purchase a little temporary safety, deserve neither liberty nor safety." - Benjamin Franklin

"But if someone has a gun and is trying to kill you...it would be reasonable to shoot back with your own gun." Dalai Lama

"The strongest reason for people to retain the right to keep and bear arms is, as a last resort, to protect themselves against tyranny in government." - Thomas Jefferson

"We would just go out and line up a bunch of cans and shoot with rifles, handguns, and at times, submachine guns...When I was a kid it was a controlled atmosphere, we weren't shooting at humans...we were shooting at cans and bottles mostly. I will certainly take my kids out for target practice." - Johnny Depp

"My view of guns is simple. I hate guns and I cannot imagine why anyone would want to own one. If I had my way, guns for sport would be registered, and all other guns would be banned." - Deborah Prothrow-Stith, Dean of Harvard School of Public Health

"No free man shall ever be debarred the use of arms." - Thomas Jefferson

"The laws that forbid the carrying of arms are laws of such a nature. They disarm only those who are neither inclined nor determined to commit crimes.... Such laws make things worse for the assaulted and better for the assailants; they serve rather to encourage than to prevent homicides, for an unarmed man may be attacked with greater confidence than an armed man." - Thomas Jefferson quoting Cesare Beccaria

"Among other evils which being unarmed brings you, it causes you to be despised." - Charlton Heston

"A strong body makes the mind strong. As to the species of exercises, I advise the gun. While this gives moderate exercise to the body, it gives boldness, enterprise and independence to the mind. Games played with the ball, and others of that nature, are too violent for the body and stamp no character on the mind. Let your gun therefore be your constant companion of your walks." - Thomas Jefferson

"There are no dangerous weapons. There are only dangerous men." - Robert A. Heinlein

The Constitution of most of our states (and of the United States) assert that all power is inherent in the people; that they may exercise it by themselves; that it is their right and duty to be at all times armed." - Thomas Jefferson

"Arms in the hands of citizens may be used at individual discretion in private self defense." - John Adams

"An armed society is a polite society." - Robert A. Heinlein

"All political power comes from the barrel of a gun. The communist party must command all the guns, that way, no guns may ever be used to command the party." - Mao Tse Tung

"To disarm the people is the most effectual way to enslave them." - George Mason

"A fear of weapons is a sign of retarded sexual and emotional maturity." - Sigmund Freud

"I ask sir, what is the militia? It is the whole people except for a few politicians." - George Mason

To my mind it is wholly irresponsible to go into the world incapable of preventing violence, injury, crime, and death. How feeble is the mind set to accept defenselessness. How unnatural. How cheap. How cowardly. How pathetic." - Ted Nugent

"All we ask for is registration, just like we do for cars." - Charles Schumer

"Before a standing army can rule, the people must be disarmed, as they are in almost every country in Europe." - Noah Webster

"There are hundreds of millions of gun owners in this country, and not one of them will have an accident today. The only misuse of guns comes in environments where there are drugs, alcohol, bad parents, and undisciplined children. Period." - Ted Nugent

"Good intentions will always be pleaded for every assumption of authority....The Constitution was made to guard against the dangers of good intentions. There are men in all ages who mean to govern well, but they mean to govern. They promise to be good masters, but they mean to be masters." - Noah Webster

"I have a love interest in every one of my films - a gun." - Arnold Schwarzenegger

"When we got organized as a country, [and] wrote a fairly radical Constitution, with a radical Bill of Rights, giving radical amounts of freedom to Americans, it was assumed that Americans who had that freedom would use it responsibly....When personal freedom is being abused, you have to move to limit it." - Bill Clinton

"The supreme power in America cannot enforce unjust laws by the sword; because the whole body of the people are armed, and constitute a force superior to any band of regular troops." - Noah Webster

"The most foolish mistake we could possibly make would be to allow the subject races to possess arms. History shows that all conquerors who have allowed their subject races to carry arms have prepared their own downfall by so doing. Indeed, I would go so far as to say that the supply of arms to the underdogs is a sine qua non for the overthrow of any sovereignty." - Adolf Hitler

"I have a very strict gun control policy: if there's a gun around, I want to be in control of it." - Clint Eastwood

"A government resting on the minority is an aristocracy, not a Republic, and could not be safe with a numerical and physical force against it, without a standing army, an enslaved press and a disarmed populace." - James Madison

"Waiting periods are only a step. Registration is only a step. The prohibition of private firearms is the goal." - Attorney General Janet Reno

"The world is filled with violence. Because criminals carry guns, we decent law-abiding citizens should also have guns. Otherwise, they will win and the decent people will lose." - James Earl Jones

"Americans have the right and advantage of being armed, unlike the peoples of other countries, whose leaders are afraid to trust them with arms." - James Madison

"The right of the people to keep and bear arms shall not be infringed. A well regulated militia, composed of the body of the people, trained to arms, is the best and most natural defense of a free country." - James Madison

"The measures adopted to restore public order are: First of all, the elimination of the so-called subversive elements....They were elements of disorder and subversion. On the morrow of each conflict I gave the categorical order to confiscate the largest possible number of weapons of every sort and kind. This confiscation, which continues with the utmost energy, has given satisfactory results." - Benito Mussolini

"The ultimate authority resides in the people alone." - James Madison

"Necessity is the plea for every infringement of human freedom. It is the argument of tyrants; it is the creed of slaves." - William Pitt

"To preserve liberty, it is essential that the whole body of the people always possess arms, and be taught alike, especially when young, how to use them." - Richard Henry Lee

"I don't care about crime; I just want to get the guns." - Senator Howard Metzenbaum

"The unarmed man is not just defenseless - he is also contemptible." - Machiavelli

"A militia, when properly formed, are in fact the people themselves....and include all men capable of bearing arms." - Richard Henry Lee

"Guard with jealous attention the public liberty. Suspect everyone who approaches that jewel. Unfortunately, nothing will preserve it but downright force, you are ruined....The great object is that every man be armed. Everyone who is able might have a gun." - Patrick Henry

"This may be considered as the true palladium of liberty....The right of self defense is the first law of nature: in most governments it has been the study of rulers to confine this right within the narrowest limits possible. Wherever standing armies are kept up, and the right of the people to keep and bear arms is, under any color or pretext whatsoever, prohibited, liberty, if not already annihilated, is on the brink of destruction." - St. George Tucker

"We are bending the law as far as we can to ban an entirely new class of guns." - Rahm Emmanuel

"The balance of power is the scale of peace. The same balance would be preserved were all the world not destitute of arms, for all would be alike; but since some will not, others dare not lay them aside. Horrible mischief would ensue were one half the world deprived the use of them...the weak will become prey to the strong.
- Thomas Paine

"I'm all in favor of keeping dangerous weapons out of the hands of fools. Let's start with typewriters." - Frank Lloyd Wright

"The Constitution shall never be construed to prevent the people of the United States who are peaceable citizens from keeping their own arms." - Samuel Adams

"The right of the citizens to keep and bear arms has been justly considered, as the palladium of the liberties of the republic; since it offers a strong moral check against the usurpation and arbitrary power of rulers; and will generally, even if these are successful in the first instance, enable the people to resist and triumph over them." - Joseph Story

""What, Sir, is the use of a militia? It is to prevent the establishment of a standing army, the bane of liberty....Whenever Governments mean to invade the rights and liberties of the people, they always attempt to destroy the militia, in order to raise an army upon their ruins." - Elbridge Gerry

"...for it is a truth, which the experience of all ages has attested, that the people are commonly most in danger when the means of insuring their rights are in the possession of those of whom they entertain the least suspicion." - Alexander Hamilton

"You cannot invade the mainland United States. There would be a rifle behind each blade of grass." Admiral Isoroku Yamamoto

"No free man shall ever be debarred the use of arms." - Thomas Jefferson

"We must get rid of all the guns." - Sarah Brady

"The beauty of the second amendment is that it will not be needed until they try to take it." - Thomas Jefferson

"Let us speak courteously, deal fairly, and keep ourselves armed and ready." - Theodore Roosevelt

"If the constitutional right to keep and bear arms is to mean anything, it must, as a general matter, permit a person to possess, carry and sometimes conceal arms to maintain the security of his private residence or privately operated business." David Prosser, Wisconsin Supreme Court Justice

"If the opposition disarms, well and good. If it refuses to disarm, we shall disarm it ourselves." - Joseph Stalin

"As a card-carrying member of the liberal media, producing this piece was an eye opening experience. I have to admit that I saw guns as inherently evil, violence begets violence, and so on. I have learned, however, that in trained hands, just the presence of a gun can be a real "man stopper." I am sorry that women have had to resort to this, but wishing it wasn't so won't make it any safer out there." - Jill Fieldstein, CBS Producer of Street Stories: Women and Guns

"Gun control? It's the best thing you can do for crooks and gangsters. I want you to have nothing. If I'm the bad guy, I'm always gonna have a gun. Safety locks? You can pull the trigger with the lock on, and I'll pull the trigger. We'll see who wins. - Sammy "The Bull" Gavano

If gun laws in fact worked, the sponsors of this type of legislation should have no difficulty drawing upon long lists of examples of crime rates reduced by such legislation. That they cannot do so after a century and a half of trying – that they must sweep under the rug the southern attempts at gun control of the 1870-1910 period, the northeastern attempts in the 1920-1939 period, the attempts at both Federal and State levels in 1965-1976 – establishes the repeated, complete, and inevitable failure of gun laws to control serious crime. - Senator Orrin Hatch

"Germans who wish to use firearms should join the SS or SA - ordinary citizens don't need guns, as their having guns doesn't serve the state." - Heinrich Himmler

"Gun bans don't disarm criminals, gun bans attract them." - Walter Mondale

"The rifle itself has no moral stature, since it has no will of its own. Naturally, it may be used by evil men for evil purposes, but there are more good men than evil, and while the latter cannot be persuaded to the path of righteousness by propaganda, they can certainly be corrected by good men with rifles." - Col. Jeff Cooper

# Pointed In!™ Press - Georgia Gun Law Blogs

www.GeorgiaGunLaw.com

www.GeorgiaGunLaws.com

# Pointed In!™ Press - California Gun Law Blogs

www.CAGunLaw.com

# Pointed In!™ Press - Colorado Law Blogs

www.ColoradoGunLaw.com

www.ColoradoGunLaws.com

# Pointed In!™ Press - Nevada Gun Law Blogs

www.NevadaGunLaw.com

www.NevadaGunLaws.com

Be sure to visit each Blog regularly for updated content, discussion, and links!

————————

# Current books offered by Pointed In!™ Press

California Firearm, Knife, and Weapon Law Compendium - Spring 2010

Nevada Firearm, Knife, and Weapon Law Compendium - Spring 2010

Colorado Firearm, Knife, and Weapon Law Compendium - Summer 2010

Georgia Firearm, Knife, and Weapon Law Compendium - Fall 2010

```
┌─────────────────────────────────────────┐
│ ┌─────────────────────────────────────┐ │
│ │                                     │ │
│ │     Ordering Copies of This Book    │ │
│ │   If you wish to purchase additional copies of │
│ │  this book, you may order it over the internet │
│ │  with a credit card at:             │ │
│ │                                     │ │
│ │                                     │ │
│ │        www.GeorgiaGunLaws.com       │ │
│ │                                     │ │
│ │                 or                  │ │
│ │                                     │ │
│ │          www.PointedIn.com          │ │
│ │                                     │ │
│ │   Substantial discounts may be had for dealers │
│ │  and instructors when ordering in quantities of │
│ │  fifteen books for more.  Please use the "Contact │
│ │  Us" form at the website listed above to inquire. │
│ │                                     │ │
│ └─────────────────────────────────────┘ │
└─────────────────────────────────────────┘
```

Consider joining or donating to these fine organizations, all dedicated to protecting your rights under the Second Amendment:[687]

Calguns Foundation
California Pistol and Rifle Association
GeorgiaCarry.org
GeorgiaPacking.org
Georgia Sports Shooting Association
Gun Owners of America
Gun Owners of California
Gun Owners of Nevada
Jews for the Preservation of Firearms Ownership
National Association for Gun Rights
National Rifle Association
Rocky Mountain Gun Owners
Second Amendment Foundation

---

[687]Mr. Bergin's recommended organizations are simply listed alphabetically, and not arranged in any certain order of importance or significance. Further, listing these organizations and suggesting that readers join and/or donate to these organizations is not to be construed as an endorsement by these organizations of this book.